SHAKES
SEC
MESSIAH

BY JOSEPH ATWILL

WITH AN INTRODUCTION BY JERRY RUSSELL, PH.D

MW00446140

Copyright © 2014 Joseph Atwill. All rights reserved under International and Pan American Copyright Conventions, including the right to reproduce this book or portions thereof in any form whatsoever, except by a reviewer in connection with a review.

Printed by CreateSpace, an Amazon.com company

ISBN: 978-1497579613

For more information please visit:

InsideOutAsylum.com
CaesarsMessiah.com

Book design by Ryan Gilmore
contact@urbanspaceman.net

I wish to thank the many people who helped with the creation of this manuscript, but three I most note directly; my wife for her good advice and forbearance, Ryan Gilmore for his courage and creativity and Jerry Russell for his edits, and original insights.

CONTENTS

INTRODUCTION: A REVIEW OF CAESAR'S MESSIAH

BY JERRY RUSSELL, PH.D

In *Caesar's Messiah*, Joseph Atwill showed that the Flavian Caesars, Vespasian and Titus, invented Christianity, that is the religion we know as Roman Catholicism. Remarkably, the emperors left behind a veiled confession (or boast) of their work, embedded in the Gospels and the works of Josephus. The religion was invented as wartime propaganda, primarily targeted at Hellenistic Jews of the Diaspora, and also at the Gentiles (who were being approached by Jewish evangelists.) This covert act of psychological warfare was successful beyond the Romans' wildest dreams: even today, the dominant view is that Christianity arose in humble circumstances, and grew to massive proportions while being driven by a variety of philosophical and religious trends, if not by God himself. However, as Atwill pointed out:

> ...as Christianity describes its origins, it was not only supernatural but also historically illogical. Christianity, a movement that encouraged pacifism and obedience to Rome, claims to have emerged from a nation engaged in a century-long struggle with Rome. An analogy to Christianity's purported origins might be a cult established by Polish Jews during World War II that set up its headquarters in Berlin and encouraged its members to pay taxes to the Third Reich (29).

Atwill's new finding is that the 'Shakespearean' literature was a deliberately veiled attack against the Flavian humor in the New Testament and the works of Josephus. In another words, Atwill has discovered another hidden genre of literature that connects 1st century Judea and Rome to 16th century Elizabethan England.

When Atwill published Caesar's Messiah, he was concerned that his work not be seen as anti-Christian, but rather that it would help Christians as well as others to see how Christianity was manipulated by its elite creators for their own benefits. With this new work, there is a concern that Atwill could be seen as anti-semitic as well, as his portrayal of 'Shakespeare' as Jewish revenge literature is hardly flattering to the Bard. However, Atwill would be horrified if his work is ever misused as a tool for those who would perpetuate the cycle of religious hate and revenge portrayed by the 'Shakespearean Project'. On the contrary, it is clear from his words that his hope is that humanity, by understanding the origins of these ancient wounds and ancient hatreds, can learn to overcome them, and that the people (regardless of their ethnic background or religious beliefs) can achieve the benefits of a more functional democracy that transcends the cycle of violence and genocide.

This volume also offers important new insights into the third Flavian emperor, Domitian, and his role in the Flavian conspiracy. Atwill argues that Domitian contributed to the single strand of typology shared by the Gospels and Shakespeare by inventing the Roman Catholic conception of the Trinity and a fictional character named 'Paul'. Ironically, it was Atwill's studies of Shakespeare that led him to this insight.

Shakespeare's muse, Christopher Marlowe, understood the real origins of Christianity as well, and spelled out his views in unmistakable terms. For example, Marlowe put the following words into the mouth of his character Barabas, a wealthy Jewish merchant in *The Jew of Malta*:

BARABAS

In spite of these swine-eating Christians,
(Unchosen nation, never circumcis'd,
Poor villains, such as were ne'er thought upon
Till Titus and Vespasian conquer'd us,)
Am I become as wealthy as I was   (II, 3)

With these words, Marlowe's character categorically denied the conventional wisdom that Christians were first "thought upon" as much as 40 years earlier, during the reign of Tiberius.

As to how Barabas arrived at this understanding, we can only speculate. Indeed, in terms of evidence for the Flavian Origins of Christianity theory, 'Shakespeare' and Marlowe obviously can only contribute as a very late secondary source, at the end of a long and problematic chain of custody of the information. Regardless, this book will show that 'Shakespeare' shared Atwill and Barabas's view that the Christians were "ne'er thought upon" until the Flavians invented them. Those who are inclined to dismiss Atwill as a "conspiracy theorist" will be surprised to learn that Shakespeare and Marlowe were also part of that club. And although it is not necessary to agree with Atwill's theory of the authorship of the New Testament, it is at least necessary to understand the literary basis for the theory, because 'Shakespeare' is built on that same basis. Thus, this introduction is a review of his earlier findings, to provide the necessary background for the reader to understand his new research.

Although Atwill's work is often (and rightly) seen as strikingly original, it should also be seen within the context of the theory of the Roman origins of the New Testament, which has much deeper roots. Bruno Bauer suggested as early as the 1840's that the New Testament is characteristically Hellenistic and Roman, rather than Judean.[1] Abelard Reuchlin[2] and Cliff Carrington[3] speculated that the Flavian emperors (Vespasian, Titus and Domitian) might have been specifically responsible.

---

[1] Bruno Bauer, *Christ and the Caesars: The Origin of Christianity from Romanized Greek Culture* (A. Davidonis, 1998).

[2] Abelard Reuchlin and Hevel V Reek, *The True Authorship of the New Testament* (Kent, WA: Abelard Reuchlin Foundation, 1979).

[3] 'Carringtons Classical & Christian Library' <http://carrington-arts.com/cliff/cccl.html> [accessed 26 February 2014].

Atwill's contribution to the Flavian Origins theory was his discovery of a carefully constructed literary subtext that links the New Testament and the works of Josephus into a comic typological and theological system. Within this system, the Biblical Jesus is seen as both prophesying and foreshadowing the true arrival of the messianic "Son of Man" in the military campaign of the Emperor Titus and his destruction of the Jewish Temple in Jerusalem. Atwill was baffled as to why this subtext had gone un-noticed for so long, even though, as he pointed out, "the works that reveal their satire—the New Testament and the histories of Josephus—are perhaps the most scrutinized books in literature" (10). His new discovery is that at least 'Shakespeare' also knew: a fact that he finds reassuring.

However, for the skeptical reader, the mystery is only compounded: if there is anything that can compete with the New Testament and Josephus as "the most scrutinized books in literature", it must surely be the works of 'Shakespeare'. Atwill is asking his readers to believe, not only that his occulted reading of the Gospels has been hidden in plain sight for two millennia, but that it also somehow became the hidden inspiration for the Bard's most famous plays — and then sunk back into the depths of obscurity again — only to be rediscovered now, when the truth can finally be spoken in straightforward language, without any typological veil, punning, or impenetrable sarcasm.

For many readers, this will be a tough pill to swallow. The claims put forward in *Caesar's Messiah* have generated a great deal of interest, but have also encountered great resistance. At a most basic level, the accusation leveled by Atwill's critics is that the entire system he proposes is nothing but a figment of his own imagination; a product of "parallelomania".

Furthermore, critics note, Atwill is a rather unlikely person to have made such a discovery. Although having studied Greek and Latin at a Jesuit school in Japan in his youth, he did not study any related subject in college, and his career was in the field of computer software. Only later in life did he return to his youthful preoccupation with New Testament studies.

Atwill reports that the Dead Sea Scrolls were crucial in re-calibrating his understanding of the historical milieu that gave rise to the New Testament. Many crucial aspects of the Scrolls were not unveiled to the public until 1991, at the instigation of Atwill's friend and colleague Robert Eisenman, who suggested that a 'Roman hand' was at work in the New Testament. Eisenman's work (for example, see *James the Brother of Jesus* and *The New Testament Code*) was an important influence to Atwill's discoveries.[4]

So perhaps Atwill is not such an unlikely pioneer after all: with a love of the field, the freedom to think radically and creatively without fear of repercussions to his career, and with connections going to the vanguard of New Testament scholarship at this exciting juncture, he is a formidable advocate for the Flavian Origins hypothesis.

JUDEA AND THE CYCLE OF REBELLION AGAINST ROMAN RULE

During the historical period surrounding the alleged life and times of the Biblical Jesus, Judea was (in reality) at the epicenter of an epic, violent conflict between the Roman Empire and the adherents of a virulently radical form of messianic Judaism. The roots of the conflict date back earlier, to the age when the zealous Maccabees (also known as Hasmoneans) rebelled against the Seleucids (the remnants of Alexander the Great's Hellenistic empire) and achieved an uneasy independence in 164 BCE. In 63 BCE, the Romans invaded Judea, and the Maccabees became Roman clients.

---

[4] Robert H Eisenman, *James, the Brother of Jesus: The Key to Unlocking the Secrets of Early Christianity and the Dead Sea Scrolls* (New York: Penguin Books, 1998); Robert H Eisenman, *The New Testament Code: The Cup of the Lord, the Damascus Covenant, and the Blood of Christ* (London; New York: Watkins Pub.; Distributed in the USA by Sterling Pub. Co., 2006).

A family of foreigners from Edom (in Arabia) eventually usurped the role of the Maccabees as the Romans' clients and tax farmers in Judea. The rise of this Herodian regime began when Antipater, born as an Edomite nobleman whose family had allegedly converted to Judaism, insinuated himself into Maccabean politics while simultaneously currying favor with the Romans. Antipater was appointed Roman Procurator of Judea under Julius Caesar (47 BCE), and his son Herod became the governor of Galilee, while the Hasmoneans continued to hold the office of high priest.

The Jewish people and their Hasmonean spiritual leaders were deeply hostile to Roman and Herodian rule, and in 40 BCE they revolted under the leadership of Antigonus II Mattathias, who forged an alliance with the Parthians. However, Herod put down the revolt with the help of Roman armies. The Roman senate awarded Herod the title of "King of the Jews", and Antigonus was sent to Mark Antony for execution in 37 BCE.

It is important to note that at this juncture, the Roman strategy of employing Hasmoneans under their control as high priests had ended in ignominious failure. From that point forward, Herod the Great and his successors appointed the high priests of Jerusalem from among their cronies. There was no way to hide the massive spiritual and nationalistic divide between the people of Palestine and the Herodians, who were hated Roman proxies. It was a problem that cried out for a solution.

CHRISTIANITY BEFORE THE FLAVIANS?

The true course of events in Palestine during the ~100 years between the Roman and Herodian takeover which was completed in 37 BCE, and the end of the Jewish war in ~73 CE, has always been a highly speculative topic, which scholarship is unlikely to resolve. In fact an essential aspect of Atwill's work is to show that the New Testament and the works of Josephus must both be regarded as Roman propaganda, and that treating these documents as factual reporting can only lead to serious analytical errors. Yet these same documents are viewed as far and away the most comprehensive and most primary sources that we have available for that entire historical epoch. Recovering the history of 1st century Judea is, therefore, a matter of judiciously paring away the layers of propaganda from Josephus and the New Testament, with the assistance of supplementary (sometimes complementary, sometimes contradictory) information provided by archaeology, source criticism, and other ancient sources.

In *Caesar's Messiah*, Atwill wrote: "This Imperial family, the Flavians, invented Christianity." By this he meant that the Flavians (and their court intellectuals) created the religion in the form that we know it, and wrote the Gospels as they have come down to us. However, this does not mean that they invented the religion as an entirely new creation, like Venus emerging from the sea-foam as a fully-grown woman. On the contrary, Flavian Christianity certainly had its precedents. Robert M. Price's review of *Caesar's Messiah* complained that "There is way, way, too much else in any and all of the gospel texts that cannot be dismissed (really, neglected) as mere padding, ballast, which is all it would be if Atwill is right." However, this was a misunderstanding of Atwill's position. He accepts the fact that the extant Gospels were written by several individuals in different times and places. And he would certainly agree that the Gospels were written with many earlier sources in mind.

At a philosophical and inspirational level, the sources of the Flavian gospels may have included Philo, Seneca, Pythagoras, other Stoics and Cynics, Homer, Gilgamesh, all the Hellenistic mystery cults of the Mediterranean region, and the astro-theological myths of the ancients. Sorting all of this out is a Herculean task that has consumed many scholarly lifetimes, and no doubt will consume many more. However, none of this analysis can account for the specific historical circumstances and events that caused the Christian religion to take the particular form that it did. Similarly, redaction criticism can identify the common source materials that were used by the four canonical evangelists, but they cannot tell us the entire contents of those sources, much less identify their ideological motivations or biases.

The search for the 'original sources' of the gospels, along with the search for the 'historical Jesus', is often a spiritually-driven quest: that is, once the seeker is convinced that Christianity has been 'corrupted' (whether by Paul, or by Flavian influences, or by the Papacy, or by modernity) the goal becomes to recover the purity of the message that was originally delivered by the revered prophet. In terms of its spiritual value, however, the enthusiasm for this quest may be misplaced, as there is no guarantee that the original message is recoverable, or that the prophet had any unique wisdom to impart in the first place. My interest is more from a historical point of view, to understand the dynamics of religious development, and the interplay of elite and populist forces in this process.

In his book *Did Jesus Exist*, Bart Ehrman gave the following summary of scholarly opinion about the 'historical Jesus':

> ...there are several points on which virtually all scholars of antiquity agree. Jesus was a Jewish man, known to be a preacher and teacher, who was crucified (a Roman form of execution) in Jerusalem during the reign of the Roman emperor Tiberius, when Pontius Pilate was the governor of Judea.[5]

If such a person did exist, he was certainly living within the historical milieu of that time, and interacting with the forces that were prevalent. To understand that environment, I recommend the works of Robert Eisenman, and also the highly readable summary and review of his work written by Andrew Gould, who wrote:

> By careful distillation, Eisenman is able to exhume the lost voice of the defeated rebellion, which, while it did leave some traces in the New Testament, now speaks directly and forcefully to us through the Dead Sea Scrolls. ...many scholars recognize that the ideological conflict between James and Paul is the engine that drives the entire New Testament. But Eisenman is able to show that this conflict is identical to the one between Jewish nationalists and the Roman-back Herodian state, which erupted

---

[5] Bart D Ehrman, *Did Jesus Exist?: The Historical Argument for Jesus of Nazareth* (New York: HarperOne, an imprint of HarperCollinsPublishers, 2013), p. 12.

into the conflagration of the Jewish War over exactly the same issues debated by James and Paul.[6]

Gould's review goes on to identify the driving issues behind this ideological conflict, which encompassed not only Judea, but also the entire Mediterranean region, wherever far-flung trading networks controlled by prosperous Jewish merchants and tradesmen of the diaspora competed with their Hellenistic counterparts. On the one side, the Zealots, Sicarii and radical Essenes of the rebellion, rooted in the nationalist tradition of the Maccabees, were concerned about circumcision; the purity of sacrifices and the presence or absence of foreign idols in the Temple; the Hellenistic elite's practices of niece marriage and sister marriage and intercourse during menstruation, all of which the Zealots viewed as fornication; the purity of dietary practices; the plight of the poor, pitted against the predations of the rich; and the doctrine of salvation by works as well as by faith. On the other side, the Herodians and their allies sought to develop tolerant, cosmopolitan attitudes, in order to facilitate the greatest possible integration with the broader Roman and Hellenistic world.

Eisenman recognized several episodes in the New Testament that appear to be parodies of historical incidents as they were described in Josephus and other sources. From this, he concludes that the Biblical characters of James and Simon Peter are also likely to be parodies of the real leaders of the Jewish rebellion. In *Caesar's Messiah*, Atwill reaches a similar conclusion, and also offers the view that another important rebel leader, and possibly a messiah figure to the rebels, was the character Eleazar.

The interpretation of the Dead Sea Scrolls is highly speculative because the scrolls were written as a sort of underground samizdat literature. All references to individuals were done using code words, and allegorical formulations were generally used for political commentary. However, based on a finely woven tapestry of comparisons to other sources, Eisenman argues that the Scrolls

---

[6] Andrew Gould, 'Robert Eisenman's "New Testament Code"' <http://roberteisenman.com/articles/ntc_review-gould.pdf> [accessed 14 March 2014].

are also referring to the events leading up to the Jewish War, and that the colorful depictions of the Righteous Teacher and the Spouter of Lying are referring to James and Paul, respectively.

In some aspects, we might recognize the religion of the Jewish rebels as a sort of embryonic Christianity. The representations of the earliest Christian 'koinonia' community in Jerusalem in the book of Acts may very well be a parody of James's church of rebels. Some of the wildly self-contradictory aspects of the New Testament may reflect the survival of the rebels' literature, which was too popular and well-known at the time to be denied or suppressed, but could be incorporated into the Flavian version of the Gospels alongside newer materials promoting the Roman viewpoint.

However, it would certainly be a mistake to view the Jewish rebel coalition as a purely populist, spiritually and economically progressive movement. Josephus pointed out that they received substantial leadership and economic and political support from the royalty of 'Adiabene', consisting of the family of King Monobazus, Queen Helena, and their son Izates. Eisenman noticed that the realms of 'Adiabene' and the land of the 'Edessenes' seem to be overlapping, and Ralph Ellis has argued that Monobazus, Helena and Izates should be identified as the royal family of the city of Edessa, who were covertly affiliated with the Parthians. According to Ellis, this Izates (who he identifies as the historical King Manu VI) saw himself not only as a messiah to the Jews, but also as a contender for the throne of Rome. If this is the case, then the Jewish rebels were pawns in a vast dynastic struggle being played out between the Parthians and the Romans; and Izates himself was another of (possibly several) rebel leaders parodied as Jesus in the New Testament.[7] Ellis argues that Izates was, quite simply, the 'historical Jesus'; but I would have to disagree, based simply on Ehrman's criterion that 'Jesus' was a Jewish man who was crucified under Pontius Pilate.

---

[7] R Ellis, *Jesus, King of Edessa* (Cheshire; Kempton, Ill.: Edfu Books ; Adventures Unlimited, 2012).

Both Ellis [8] and another self-taught Biblical scholar, Lena Einhorn,[9] have noticed extensive parallels between Josephus's narrative of events occurring between the years 44 and 56 CE, and a similar series of events and circumstances in the New Testament narrative covering the years 24 to 36 CE. A central figure in Josephus's account is the 'Egyptian prophet', whose story matches Biblical Jesus in many respects, except that his fate following his arrest at the Mount of Olives is not described by Josephus. Later on, according to Acts (21:38), the Apostle Paul was asked if he was the troublemaking 'Egyptian' who stirred up a revolt among the Zealots. Einhorn speculates that the New Testament authors told their story with a 20-year time shift, and that Jesus, Paul and 'The Egyptian prophet' may have all been the same individual;[10] or, I would add, perhaps 'The Egyptian' was indeed a rebel leader of the Zealots, and was the true (but, contrary to Ehrman, time-transposed) 'historical Jesus'; and that after his execution, Paul the Herodian stepped into his place and tried to lead his movement in a different direction.

Aside from all this speculation about the Jewish rebel movement, its leaders, and its relation to Christianity: it's also necessary to consider the possibility that there was an early Roman and Herodian-controlled form of Christianity which was invented well before the time of the Flavians, and which competed with the radical messianic Judaism of the rebels. This would explain the activities of 'Paul' in his conflicts with James, as a promoter of this early form of Christianity. As Gould wrote:

> Paul, in particular, was a political/intelligence operative for the Herodian kings, not only before his famous "conversion" on the road to Damascus, but after as well.

[8] R Ellis, *King Jesus: From Kam (Egypt) to Camelot* (Cheshire; Kempton, Ill.: Edfu Books ; Adventures Unlimited, 2008).

[9] Lena Einhorn, 'Jesus and the "Egyptian Prophet"', 2012 <http://lenaeinhorn.se/wp-content/uploads/2012/11/Jesus-and-the-Egyptian-Prophet-12.11.25.pdf> [accessed 15 March 2014].

[10] Lena Einhorn and Rodney Bradbury, *The Jesus Mystery: Astonishing Clues to the True Identities of Jesus and Paul* (Guilford, Conn.: Lyons Press, 2007).

In its most embryonic form, Paul's religion could have been developed as an abstraction of the cult of Julius Caesar, the founding deity of the Roman imperial cult of emperor worship.

During his lifetime, Julius Caesar had aligned himself with the far left wing of the Roman political spectrum; that is, he was one of the populares, a supporter of reforms such as land redistribution, wider access to citizenship, and better pay for soldiers and the lower class in general. In this position, Caesar was at odds with the majority of right-wing *optimates* on the senate, who were determined to maintain the same extreme level of social stratification that prevailed at the time.

In Caesar's sojourn in Egypt, he experienced the genuine adulation and reverence that the Egyptians felt for his paramour, Cleopatra VII of Egypt, who was not only admired for her statesmanship, but also was worshipped as a Goddess, an embodiment of Isis. Caesar was also a great admirer of Alexander the Great, who was similarly viewed as a sort of deity by the Greeks. As Pontifex Maximus, the head of the Roman priestly college, Caesar was already an honored religious leader of the Roman republic. And as a war hero and an advocate of the people's human dignity, Caesar was fabulously popular with the general public of Rome.[11]

In such circumstances, it seems perfectly natural that Caesar may have decided to orchestrate the process of his own deification. His image, carved in ivory, appeared among the assembly of gods at the Roman circus. A day in Caesar's honor was added to the calendar alongside the days of Jupiter. A temple was built in his honor in Rome.[12] Caesar was described as the savior of his nation, and was admired for his was willingness to extend forgiveness to his former enemies. He was revered as a liberator, a great giver of freedom to the Roman people. Reportedly, he was especially

---

[11] Michael Parenti, *The Assassination of Julius Caesar: A People's History of Ancient Rome* (New York: New Press, 2003).

[12] Stefan Weinstock, *Divus Julius* (Oxford; New York: Clarendon Press, 1971).

admired by the Jews, who regarded him as an ally in their struggle for religious freedom and self-determination.

Following Caesar's death in 44 BC, his apotheosis proceeded apace, driven not only by Caesar's enormous popularity amongst the rank-and-file people of Rome, but also by the industrious promotion by both of Caesar's designated successors, his adopted son Octavian and his chief priest Mark Anthony. The Roman senate officially consecrated Caesar's divinity in 42 BC, and thus Octavian obtained the title of Divi Filius, the Son of God, while Antony was confirmed as Flamine Divus Julius, the priest of the Divine Caesar. The memory of Caesar as a God served both of those men equally, so they both devoted the tremendous resources of the Roman state towards construction and promotion of temples of the Caesar cult, which were erected in Rome, Caesarea, Alexandria, Antioch, Corinth, Ephesus, Phillipi, Thessalonica and Smyrna. These were the same locations that were later named as the earliest centers of the Christian church.

In his book *Jesus was Caesar*,[13] Francesco Carotta postulated that a key ceremony of this Divus Julius cult might have been a re-enactment of Caesar's funeral and Mark Anthony's dramatic memorial oration. As it has come down to us in the histories of Suetonius and Appianus, a centerpiece of the memorial service was a *tropaeum*, which was a pole with horizontal arms that was used to display war trophies. In this case, the *tropaeum* was used to display an effigy or wax simulcram of Caesar's body cloaked in his blood-stained robe. In other words, it appeared as if Caesar was hung from a cross at his funeral.

Gary Courtney in *Et Tu Judas? Then Fall Jesus* also argued that the Biblical story of Jesus's trial and crucifixion contains many illogical aspects and contradictions, which can be plausibly explained with the realization that the Gospel stories of Jesus's trial, crucifixion and resurrection are dramatizations of the

---

[13] Francesco Carotta, *Jesus Was Caesar: On the Julian Origin of Christianity : An Investigative Report* (Soesterberg: Aspekt, 2005).

assassination of Julius Caesar, his funeral, and his apotheosis. Courtney wrote:

> This religious play...may have evolved to comprise the following essential elements:
>
> 1. A great and just man who astounds his age by instituting a comprehensive policy of forgiveness.
>
> 2. On the verge of becoming the king, he is betrayed and murdered by those he had saved — the treachery epitomized by his turncoat friend Brutus.
>
> 3. When his tribulation begins, his close friend and religious deputy, sworn to protect him, flees in fear and disguises himself.
>
> 4. The murdered man's ultimate triumph, being resurrected as a god.
>
> 5. His betrayer commits suicide.
>
> What better foundation 'myth' could a religion hope for? It would be difficult to create a fiction that could lend itself more readily to a theatrical presentation.... Is it not possible that the betrayal and murder of this ancient founder of the Roman Empire, *pontifex maximus* and common Savior of Mankind, whose name — Caesar, Kaiser, Czar — came to be synonymous with king throughout the Western world, and the shedding of whose blood "pierced the hearts of all mankind", influenced the development of the Christian religion? Is it merely a coincidence that the five points listed above constitute the heart and soul of the Passion of Christ?[14]

If the ceremonies of the hypothetical Julius Caesar cult eventually became the core of the Christians' Easter commemorations of Jesus Christ, this could have been the result of a gradual progression. The Roman imperial cult typically focused its public adulation on the current emperor and his father, the most recently deified Caesar. However, it is also believed that the imperial cult

---

[14] Gary Courtney, *ET TU, JUDAS? Then Fall Jesus!* (iUniverse, 2004), p. 61.

functioned as a Hellenistic mystery religion,[15] and my speculation is that Caesar's funeral may have continued to be secretly re-enacted as a rite of the cult for its more advanced members, while the association of the ritual with Julius Caesar (as a particular human being) was gradually de-emphasized and forgotten. Particularly among Hellenized Jews, a realization might have gradually dawned that Caesar was the messiah that the Jews had been waiting for.

Or it is also conceivable that the Herodians made a deliberate policy decision to adopt this re-enactment of Caesar's funeral as the core of their own new Hellenistic mystery cult, which would offer the abstracted Caesar to the Jews as the true incarnation of their Messiah. This could have begun at a very early date: Carotta has pointed out that according to tradition, *"The Gospel of Mark was written in Latin in Rome 12 years after the ascension of the Lord."*[16] If Julius Caesar was indeed the "Lord" being referred to, this would be just 5 years after the ignominious defeat of Antigonus, last of the Maccabees; and the 'Mark' who was attributed with responsibility for this first draft of the Roman Gospel would have been Mark Anthony, the Roman overseer of the Judean province at that time. However, although Caesar was undeniably a historical person, Carotta's claim that he was the 'historical Jesus' would obviously be rejected under Ehrman's criteria on the grounds that he lived at the wrong time and place.

In an ongoing process of religious innovation, the Romans and Herodians may have continued to develop this hybrid of Jewish and Roman spirituality during the 1st century of the common (that is, Christian) era. As I will relate later, I believe that the Gospels and other documents of the early Roman church were most likely maintained as secrets of the inner sanctuary of the cult, which was operated like other Hellenistic mystery religions of the time;

---

[15] Gary Forsythe, *Time in Roman Religion: One Thousand Years of Religious History* (Routledge, 2012), p. 98.

[16] Francesco Carotta, 'The Gospels as Diegetic Transposition', 2007 <http://carotta.de/subseite/texte/articula/Escorial_en.pdf> [accessed 16 March 2014].

which would explain why copies of these materials have not survived, and would also how the Romans were able to evolve the story over time, while redacting earlier versions.

Stephen Huller in *The Real Messiah*[17] proposed that the 'historical Jesus' was the leader of a rebellion of the Samaritans during the reign of Pontius Pilate. As Josephus told the story of this event, a certain rebel leader inspired "a multitude" of armed Samaritans to gather with the goal of climbing Mt. Gerizzim to see "sacred vessels" placed there by Moses; but Pilate's police routed the rebellion, and captured and executed the rebel leader (Josephus, Ant 18.4.85-87).

As a rebel "ordered to be slain" by Pontius Pilate in ~37 CE, this character seems to be an excellent candidate for 'historical Jesus' according to Ehrman's criteria: at least, he is a Jew (although presumably a Samaritan) who lives at the right time and place, and who was a popular preacher — although Josephus does not tell us exactly where or how he was executed.

Huller goes on to argue that this Jesus was portrayed by the Herodians as a forerunner to another Messiah who would come as the political savior of the Jews. In order to fulfill that prophecy, Huller argues, the young Marcus Julius Agrippa (that is, Herod Agrippa II, then age 8) went to Alexandria in 38 CE, where he was crowned as the Messiah and King of the Jews. This coronation was said to be engineered behind the scenes by Philo, Marcus's mother (or grandmother) Mary Salome, and the new Emperor Caligula.

The centerpiece of Huller's evidence for his theory is an artifact called the "Throne of St. Mark." Huller argues that this "Throne" could well date to the 1st century CE, as opposed to the dominant view that it is 5th century hagiographic relic. The throne has an inscription in Hebrew stating "Coronation of Marcus the Evangelist" and in Samaritan stating "Year 1". It is decorated with 50 stars, which Huller argues is another indication (along with

[17] Stephan Huller, *The Real Messiah: The Throne of St. Mark and the True Origins of Christianity*, Reprint edition (Watkins Publishing, 2012).

"year 1") that the throne dates to a Samaritan jubilee year, which fell in 38 CE. On the front, the throne has an image of a ram (or lamb?) standing under a bush, which Huller interprets as an image of the ram that was sacrificed by Abraham in place of his son Isaac, after God released Abraham from the obligation to sacrifice his first-born son. Huller thinks this reflects an early Christology, in which the political Messiah on the throne (that is, Marcus Agrippa) received the benefit of the spiritual Messiah's sacrifice as the Lamb or Ram of God; in other words, the sacrifice of the rebel leader who was executed by Pilate.

This Herodian form of Christianity would have been based on Philo's view of the amalgamation of Jewish and Platonic philosophy, and it might very well have incorporated an abstracted form of the cult of Julius Caesar's funeral re-enactment as well; and the 'Gospel of Mark Anthony' (if indeed it ever existed) evolved into the 'Gospel of Marcus Agrippa'. Aside from the "Throne of St. Mark", Huller offers a wide variety of tantalizingly suggestive evidence from other sources. However, sadly, the quality of his scholarship is (in my view) spotty at best, and one can only hope that his thesis will attract the attention of other scholars to either confirm or refute the hypothesis.

If indeed this primitive Herodian Christianity did exist, the Romans might well have been promoting it not only in Palestine but also throughout the Jewish Diaspora and indeed throughout the entire Hellenized portion of the planet. And if this is the case, there might well have been an "Apostle Paul" who was evangelizing around the Mediterranean and writing epistles to his churches, and if so, this "Paul" with his Roman and Herodian allegiances would have been seen by rebellious Messianic Jews in Jerusalem as a "Spouter of Lies", just as Eisenman says.

One of the most predominant criticisms of Caesar's Messiah is the evidence (however meager or controversial it might be) that Christianity existed much earlier than the time of Vespasian. And if any or all of this speculation is correct, then of course (literally speaking) the Flavians didn't exactly invent Christianity. But they certainly did re-invent it, while obliterating any conclusive evidence that there had been anything earlier.

The fact is that we don't have any of the source documents (such as "Q" or "proto-Luke" or the "Hebrew Gospel") that are postulated by redaction criticism; nor do we have the hypothetical original autographs of the (Julian) Gospel of Mark Anthony, nor the (Herodian) Gospel of Marcus Agrippa, nor the pre-Flavian Pauline epistles. If Atwill's hypothesis is correct, it certainly follows that any and all earlier sources have been heavily redacted if not completely re-written by the Flavians, and this fact needs to be the basis of any further analysis. While there may be some truth in what the redaction critics and the Julian Origins theorists and Huller are saying, Atwill is simply not interested in participating in this speculation: neither in *Caesar's Messiah* nor in this book.

THE FLAVIANS AND THE JEWISH REBELLION OF 66 CE

Regardless of whatever stratagems the Romans and Herodians might have devised during a hundred years of uneasy peace, they assuredly did not succeed in healing the deep wounds stemming from the Roman conquest. A movement organized by Jewish sects known as the Zealots and Sicarii was continually fomenting revolution, and in 66 CE the Jews rose up and drove the Romans and Herodians out of the country. Nero sent his general Vespasian, along with Vespasian's son Titus, to recover the lost territory.

Vespasian's family was intimately connected with the Herodians as well as another powerful Jewish family, the Alexanders of Egypt. When Nero was killed in suspicious circumstances, the support of the Alexanders and Herodians was crucial to Vespasian's effort to gain the throne. This group of families obviously had the means, the motive, and the opportunity to create a new religion for Judea, and indeed for the entire world. Atwill continues:

> ...it is odd that so many members of the Flavian family were recorded as having been among Christianity's first members. Why was a Judaic cult that advocated meekness and poverty so attractive to a family that practiced neither? The tradition connecting early Christianity and the Flavian family is based on solid evidence but has received little comment from scholars (38).

The rogue's gallery of possible Flavian Christians cited in *Caesar's Messiah* includes Titus's mistress Bernice (possibly the same person as St. Veronica), Titus Flavius Sabinus (consul in 82 CE, Vespasian's nephew), Sabinus's brother the theologian Titus Flavius Clemens, Sabinus's wife Flavia Domitilla, and the early Pope known as Clement. The patron Saint of France, St. Petronilla, was another member of what the Catholic Church refers to as the 'Christian Flavii'. Legend had it that Petronilla was the daughter of St. Peter, but sixteenth-century notices show that she was related to the Flavius Clemens mentioned above, whose great-grandfather was Titus Flavius Petronius. [18] The New Testament also records that the Flavians hosted leaders of the early church in their court. While in some cases the sources of this information are late and hagiographic, in other cases multiple and/or possibly primary sources attest to early Flavian involvement in Christianity. These circumstances are extraordinarily difficult to explain if the origins of Christianity are as they are usually depicted: a movement built of humble fishermen, merchants and slaves from Palestine. But, as Atwill noted:

> A Roman origin would also explain why so many members of a Roman imperial family, the Flavians, were recorded as being among the first Christians. The Flavians would have been among the first Christians because, having invented the religion, they were, in fact, the first Christians (33).

The great historian of that era, Josephus, soon became part of the Flavian milieu. As the story goes: initially a commander of the rebel forces in the Jewish War, Josephus (who claims to have been born as Josephus bar Matthias, a good Hasmonean name) was captured and delivered to the Romans. Given an audience with Vespasian, the historian predicted that the famous Star Prophecy of Isaiah would be fulfilled with Vespasian's rise to the throne of the Roman Empire. When the prophecy was fulfilled, the grateful Vespasian adopted 'Flavius' Josephus into the royal family, and

---

[18] 'CATHOLIC ENCYCLOPEDIA: Saint Petronilla' <http://www.newadvent.org/cathen/11781b.htm> [accessed 26 February 2014].

granted him the patronage necessary to write his extensive works. Therefore, Josephus's history of the Jewish War, which ended in a tremendous bloodbath and the defeat of the Jewish rebellion in 73 CE, must be read with the understanding that it is a perfect example of the proverb "history is written by the winners."

THE FLAVIAN ORIGINS THEORY IS STRAIGHT-TALKING COMMON SENSE

History tells us that Flavius Constantine the Great, inspired by a vision of a flaming cross of light at the Battle of Milvian Bridge in 312 CE, shifted the vast patronage of the Roman government and its tax revenues to Christianity. The Christian Church was endowed with lands and property, and the entire city of Constantinople was built from the ground up as a Christian city. The Council of Nicea was held to unify the tenets of the religion under Constantine's direction, and all the diverse sectarian forms of Christianity (aside from Roman Catholicism) became official heresies. Historians debate whether Constantine was truly a descendant of the Flavian dynasty of Vespasian, Titus and Domitian, or whether his genealogy was a fabrication, in which case his family name may have been chosen in homage to the Flavians and their creation of Christianity.

A brief pagan counter-revolution was attempted under Julian the Apostate (who reigned from 361-363 CE), but by 380 CE, the triumvirs Gratian, Valentinian II and Theodosius felt confident enough to issue the Edict of Thessalonica, which pronounced that all pagans and heretics in the entire Roman Empire *"will suffer in the first place the chastisement of the divine condemnation and in the second the punishment of our authority which in accordance with the will of Heaven we shall decide to inflict."*[19]

However, as the saying goes, "Rome was not built in a day." Constantine's experience in replacing the existing religions across the Roman Empire should be compared and contrasted with Akhenaten's experience in his attempt to uproot the old religion of

[19] Henry Scowcroft Bettenson, *Documents of the Christian Church* (Oxford University Press, H. Milford, 1943), p. 31.

Egypt. Within a single generation, Akhenaten's Atenite experiment was over, the old Gods and the old priesthood restored, and Akhenaten was all but erased from history (that is, unless he somehow lived on as a type of Moses in Canaan.) Religious beliefs are deeply and tenaciously held, and tend to be passed from generation to generation, so there is tremendous inertia and resistance to change. My view is that Constantine's success must have been a result of many generations of sustained effort.

Long before Constantine's time, Christianity (that is, Roman Catholicism) had manifested itself in a style that was clearly destined for Imperial greatness. As early as the epistle of Clement (~95 CE) the Church was already organized in a hierarchical, quasi-military fashion, taking orders from the Bishop of Rome, with a goal of evangelizing the world. Furthermore, as Atwill observed:

> When one looks at the form of early Christianity, one sees not Judea, but Rome. The church's structures of authority, its sacraments, its college of bishops, the title of the head of the religion — the supreme pontiff — were all based on Roman, not Judaic, traditions. Somehow, Judea left little trace on the form of a religion that purportedly originated inside of it (29).

Robert M. Price painted a vivid portrait of the absurdity of the conventional view of Christian origins:

> Picture a religious ethic of conspicuous compromise with the occupying authorities, a gospel that tells its believers not to resist any who confiscate their property, but to pay Roman taxes and to carry a legionary's field pack twice the distance stipulated by Roman law. Imagine a story that blames not just Jews but implicitly nationalistic, messianic Jews for the destruction of their temple. A story that has the messiah predict that the kingdom will be taken from Jews and given to a more worthy nation. Keep in mind how the preacher of this sect befriends Jews who collaborate with Rome and eulogizes a Roman centurion for having faith unparalleled among Jews. He is declared innocent by Roman authorities but nonetheless is done in by Jewish rulers. Then think of how the predictions of the fall of Jerusalem a single generation later correspond so closely to Josephus' account of the events, and furthermore, how Josephus even mentions Jesus as a righteous man and even as the messiah of prophetic prediction (though he

himself had proclaimed Vespasian the proper object of such prophecy). When someone suggests that Christianity may have been a "safe," denatured, Roman-domesticated, messianic Methadone to replace the real and dangerous messianic heroin of the Zealots, and that Josephus had something to do with it, it does not sound unreasonable on the face of it.

Price, unfortunately, went on to reject the implications of his own analysis, adding:

What about the Roman-tilting anti-Judaism (maybe anti-Semitism) of the gospels? Again, the old explanations are quite natural and adequate: we are reading the documents of Gentile Christianity which viewed itself as superseding Judaism and Jewish Christianity. Why do their authors seem to kiss the Roman posterior? For apologetical reasons, to avoid persecution. Brandon, Eisler, and others saw that long ago.[20]

Aside from begging the question of how and why these "Gentiles" would adopt a radical Jewish Messianic Christianity only to ultimately "supersede" it, or how any "Christian" sect that would kiss "the Roman posterior" could be considered anything other than a raw instrument of Roman government power: Price's argument here is also based on a failure to understand the nature and extent of the specific literary evidence for Flavian complicity, which I will explain below.

BUT WHAT ABOUT THE MARTYRS?

Doubters will scoff that the Romans couldn't have created and nurtured Christianity while they were simultaneously doing their best to stamp it out. A more extensive response to this question will be following in the third volume of this series, which will deal comprehensively with the supposed periods of persecution. Meanwhile I would like to make the following observations:

---

[20] 'Review - Atwill's Caesar's Messiah: The Roman Conspiracy to Invent Jesus by Robert M. Price'
<http://www.robertmprice.mindvendor.com/rev_atwill.htm> [accessed 26 February 2014].

1. Up until Constantine's edicts, all forms of Christianity were equally forbidden from a Roman legalistic perspective. However, in addition to the Roman Catholic form, there were many other nominally Christian sects, including Gnostic sects, as well as (quite possibly) genuinely Messianic Jewish sects. In many martyrdom narratives, it can be difficult or impossible to tell whether the victim was an orthodox Roman Catholic, or a follower of some more zealous sect.

2. Modern scholars have found that the scale of martyrdom has often been overestimated. For a discussion, see Candida Moss's *The Myth of Persecution*.[21]

3. Many of the 'Christian' martyrs were Jewish zealots. For example, Atwill shows in Caesar's Messiah that the martyrdom of Simon 'predicted' by Jesus in John 21 actually foresaw the execution of the zealot leader Simon in 73 CE. Rome had, in effect, used its martyrdom of the zealots as part of its pseudo-history of Roman Christianity.

LITERARY IMITATION, TYPOLOGY, AND ENIGMA

Regardless of any reader's intuition about the likelihood of a Roman conspiracy to invent Christianity, *Caesar's Messiah* is fundamentally evidence-based and grounded in literary analysis. The basic methodology is the assessment of literary imitation; that is, borrowing or mimesis. By borrowing literary elements from a predecessor, an author betrays his awareness of the precedent material, as well as revealing his viewpoint or analysis of it.

Literary imitation has been a common practice in all ages, and was highly revered among the authors of the Old Testament, who were especially fond of chiastic forms. Chiasm involves a series of literary elements that are placed in order and then referred to in reverse order, unwinding the chiasm: for example, ABCCBA. These structures can be brief, or very extensive: almost the entire

---

[21] Candida R Moss, *The Myth of Persecution: How Early Christians Invented a Story of Martyrdom* (New York, NY: HarperOne, 2013).

Torah from the middle of Exodus to the end of Leviticus is said to be a giant chiasm. New Testament scholars discovered that the Gospel characters and events are often foreshadowed in the Old Testament, in a relationship in which the Old Testament model is called the 'Type' and the New Testament embodiment is called the 'Antetype'. The theological study of 'Types' and 'Antetypes' is called Typology, and theological practitioners see New Testament events as evidence of Divine intervention in history. Modern secular literary critics, of course, see it as proof only that the New Testament authors studied the Old Testament and invoked its authority and wisdom in their writings.

In *Caesar's Messiah*, Atwill focused on a particular variety of typology that involves a series of parallels that are dense, sequential, distinctive, and interpretable.[22] When these criteria are met in abundance, they can be considered as sure evidence of literary dependency. 'Density' relates to the number of parallels that occur within a brief amount of text; 'sequence' relates to the extent that the parallel references occur in the same order; 'distinctiveness' relates to the degree that the parallels must relate to unusual and infrequent words, names or concepts; and 'interpretability' relates to the extent that we can understand the reasoning behind the choice to use a particular literary reference; the ways in which the reference has been transformed or slavishly copied, as the case may be; and the point that the author is trying to make.

The New Testament makes abundant use of dense, sequential, distinctive and interpretable mimesis of the Old Testament. A good example is Matthew's story of Jesus's empty tomb, which draws from the tale of Daniel in the lion's den.[23] The parallels are highlighted in **bold typeface**:

---

[22] Dennis R. MacDonald, *The Homeric Epics and the Gospel of Mark* (Yale University Press, 2000), pp. 8–9.

[23] Richard Carrier, *Proving History: Bayes's Theorem and the Quest for the Historical Jesus* (Amherst, N.Y.: Prometheus Books, 2012), p. 147.

DANIEL 6:17-28

Then **a stone was brought and laid on the mouth of the den**, and **the king sealed it**...Then the king arose **very early in the morning** and went in haste to the den of lions. And when he came to the den, he cried out...saying to Daniel, "Daniel, servant of the living God, has your God, whom you serve continually, been able to deliver you from the lions? Then Daniel said to the king, "**O king, live forever! My God sent His angel** and shut the lions' mouths, so that they have not hurt me...".....And the king gave the command, and **they brought those men who had accused Daniel, and they cast** *them* **into the den of lions**...**and the lions overpowered them, and broke all their bones in pieces**...Then King Darius wrote: **To all peoples, nations, and languages**...I make a decree that in every dominion of my kingdom *men must* tremble and fear before the God of Daniel. For He *is* the living God...**His dominion** *shall endure* **to the end**...And He works signs and wonders **in heaven and on earth**...

MATTHEW 27:59-28:20

When Joseph had taken the body...**he rolled a large stone against the door of the tomb**...[Pilate's guards] went and made the tomb secure, **sealing the stone** and setting the guard. Now after the Sabbath, **as the first** *day* **of the week began to dawn**, Mary Magdalene and the other Mary came to see the tomb. And behold, there was a great earthquake; for **an angel of the Lord descended from heaven**, and came and rolled back the stone...**And the guards**...**became like dead** *men*. But the angel answered and said to the women, "Do not be afraid, for I know that you seek Jesus who was crucified. He is not here; for **He is risen**... Then the eleven disciples went away into Galilee...And Jesus came and spoke to them, saying, "**All authority** has been given to Me **in heaven and on earth. Go therefore and make disciples of all the nations**...and lo, **I am with you always,** *even* **to the end of the age**."

Parallels include the stone; the seal; the time (early in the morning, or at dawn); the angel sent from God; the guards (accusers) "like dead men" (or, killed); Daniel's wish for the king to live forever, which foreshadows "Jesus is risen"; and the benediction to all nations in heaven and earth, under God's dominion (authority) to the end of the age. All these specific parallels occur in two short, dense passages; generally (but not exactly) in sequence; and of course the message is that Daniel is a 'Type', that is, a prefiguration of Jesus who is the 'Antetype'.

Similarly, the Old Testament Joseph (Genesis 45-50) is a type of the New Testament Joseph, and Moses (Exodus 1-32) is a type of Jesus (Matthew 2:13-4:10). As Atwill explains:

> Joseph is described as bringing Jesus, who represents the "new Israel," down to Egypt...a previous Joseph brought the "old Israel" down to Egypt...The New Testament Joseph is described, like his counterpart in the Hebrew Bible, as a dreamer of dreams and as having encounters with a star and wise men. Both stories regarding the journey of a Joseph to Egypt are immediately followed by a description of a massacre of innocents...each massacre of the innocents' story depicts young children being slaughtered by a fearful tyrant, but the future savior of Israel being saved. The authors of the New Testament then continue mirroring Exodus by having an angel tell Joseph, "They are dead which sought the young child's life" (Matt. 2:20). This statement is a clear parallel to the statement made to Moses, the first savior of Israel, in Exodus 4:19: "All the men are dead which sought thy life." The parallels then continue with Jesus receiving a baptism (Matt. 3:13), which mirrors the baptism of the Israelites (passing through water) described in Exodus 14. Next, Jesus spends 40 days in the desert, which parallels the 40 years the Israelites spend in the wilderness. Both sojourns in the desert involve three sets of temptations (16-17).

The first of these temptations involves bread; the second, tempting God; the third, worshiping and serving only God.

This typological mapping is widely acknowledged by scholars, even though the Old Testament half of the typology sprawls across acres and acres of Old Testament territory, and thus the entire argument could easily be criticized on the basis of Multiple Comparisons Fallacy (that is, each New Testament phrase is compared to many passages of the Old Testament, and thus you would expect a certain number of parallelisms to arise purely by random processes.) In other words, this example fails MacDonald's density criterion. In this case, we certainly agree with the scholarly consensus that each individual parallel is sufficiently powerful to overcome the Multiple Comparisons bias inherent in this typological example as a whole.

It is important to notice that the differences between the 'type' and the 'antetype' passages, cannot defeat the proof of literary dependence. On the contrary, it is the differences that allow the later author to convey his own unique message. This point may be illustrated graphically with the three images of the Mona Lisa above.[24] We know that the two images to the right are both inspired by the Mona Lisa (at the left) because of the shared theme and also because of the many shared details, even though the differences are also easy to spot, and each image has its own message to convey. Atwill's position is that common sense is a good guide in determining whether literary mimesis is involved in linking two passages in literature, just as it's a good guide in imagery.

Also, note that the use of literary mimesis does not (in itself) prove that the incident being described is fictional: a writer might easily decide to begin with a real but relatively mundane historical event, and dress it up with literary spices and delicacies. In our modern world, we would frown on a journalist or news reporter who was caught indulging in this sort of thing. However, no such code of ethics was even conceived of in ancient times; so the line between fact and fiction is not so easy to discern in ancient literature.

---

[24] 'Vridar » How Literary Imitation Works: Are Differences More Important than Similarities?' <http://vridar.org/2013/05/15/how-literary-imitation-works-are-differences-more-important-than-similarities/> [accessed 26 February 2014].

SENSE OF HUMOR REQUIRED

Another aspect of Atwill's view of Josephus and the Gospels is that they both represent a highly developed, wicked sense of humor. For most of us, who are trained in one way or another to respect the Christian religion as a source of at least symbolic or allegorical spiritual wisdom, this view of the Gospels can be difficult to accept. Similarly, there is a natural tendency to respect Josephus as one would respect any other historian, and to expect a journalistic perspective from him.

The problem is compounded because one of the essential aspects of humor is its trust and respect for the audience in their ability to grasp the humorist's perspective. That is, the comedian does not explain or expound upon the meaning of his joke — he just tells the joke, and then the audience laughs, which proves that they "got it." The magic is broken if the humorist needs to "spell it out" for the audience.

The problem with Josephan and Gospel humor is that, up until Atwill, the audience (for the most part) hasn't been laughing, because the ability to appreciate these subtle jokes has largely been lost. First of all, modern readers don't have the historical background, nor do they have the same command of the classical literature such as Homer and the Old Testament that was possessed by the well-educated elite of the ancients. Many jokes are based on a detailed knowledge of their context.

Another essential aspect of humor is that it is always at someone's expense; that is, the humorist is "making fun of" his target. Thus, I argue that humor can be a crucial clue in determining the directionality of literary dependence: humorous literature must always be written as a response to a prior source or event. That is, Sarah Palin's real-life political adventures came first, and Tina Fay's Saturday Night Live skits came afterwards, presumably to Palin's chagrin. Again, it's necessary to understand the historical context in order to see the arrow of time's ever-forward progression.

In the Flavian comic system, the attack on the targeted Jews is vicious, which presents another problem for modern readers. The era of the Flavians was an era when perhaps the majority of people were held as slaves, treated little better than cattle; an era when death in combat was "up close and personal"; and an era when gladiatorial blood and gore was considered entertainment. It was, overall, an age of great cruelty. The modern zeitgeist has changed: even if the material condition of billions of people is really little better, those of us in positions of some comfort are at least more circumspect about taking pleasure at their plight. Thus, the Flavian jokes tend to fall flat on modern ears because we feel that a more appropriate response would be "ugh" or "ick", rather than hearty laughter.

In spite of all these problems, my own experience in reading *Caesar's Messiah* is that the book is disturbingly amusing, because the Romans were ingenious humorists in their own way, and there is an emotional rush in suddenly seeing the hidden joke. I hope that other readers will have the same experience.

The other type of literary reference studied by Atwill is the enigma. As explained in the online Jewish Encyclopedia article on Philo Judaeus,[25] Philo taught that allegory or enigma is generally signaled by devices such as:

- the doubling of a phrase...
- an apparently superfluous expressing in the text...
- the repetition of statements previously made...
- a play upon words...
- any peculiarity in a phrase...
- noteworthy omissions...
- striking statements...
- [or] numerical symbolism.

In Josephus, enigmas are often signaled by the insertion of an obvious fable or fantasy within the flow of the historical narrative. Again, humor comes into play, as discovering the solution to an enigma often brings a smile, or perhaps a grimace.

Enigmas may be taken as a license to go searching across all preceding ancient literature, to find relevant information and clues that might explain the meaning of the enigma in its context. Readers who take issue with Atwill's solutions are, of course, invited to come up with their own, or search the literature for other solutions that have been offered in the past. The criteria for a good solution is that it fits all the information provided in the enigma

[25] 'Philo Judaeus', *Jewish Encyclopedia*, 1906
<http://www.jewishencyclopedia.com/articles/12116-philo-judaeus>
[accessed 16 March 2014].

(not just some of it) and that it makes a point consistent with the author's overtly expressed intentions.

THE GOSPELS' DEPENDENCY ON JOSEPHUS

The dependencies of the Gospels on Josephus's works are well known. While devout Christians might maintain that the striking parallels are a result of Jesus's supernatural ability to foresee the future, secular scholars agree that the Gospel authors drew several passages directly from Josephus. The parallels are detailed, specific, extensive, sequential, highly interpretable, and cannot be traced to any earlier common source. Therefore, I am satisfied that this dependency exists in the strongest possible form: the Gospel authors must have had access to a copy of Josephus's work and they intentionally chose to make use of it.

Atwill has gone beyond other scholars by discovering that the extent of subtle references to Josephus in the New Testament is much greater than has ever been recognized before. All of these parallels, both the well-known overt ones as well as the newly discovered ones, point to the interpretation that the Biblical Jesus foretells that his second coming as the Messiah will occur in 70 CE when the Son of Man comes to destroy the Temple in fulfillment of the prophecies of Daniel. In parallel passages in Josephus, we learn that these prophecies (from both Jesus and Daniel) were historically fulfilled in the person of Titus playing the role of the Son of Man, with his conquest of Jerusalem and the destruction of the Temple.

Of course this is not the Messianic outcome that the Jews expected — not only was Titus a Roman rather than a Jew, but he slaughtered the righteous Zealots and Sicarii and ordinary Jews by the hundreds of thousands, rather than concentrating his fury on the Romans and their Herodian collaborators. But the Biblical Jesus's prophecies were completely consistent with Josephus's viewpoint: if Vespasian were divine, then his son Titus would obviously share in that divine nature.

Also, the spiritual campaign of Jesus Christ as depicted in the book of Luke foreshadows the military campaign of Titus in

Judea, in a sequential series of parallels that Atwill calls "the Flavian Signature". This creates a Roman parody of a "typological mapping" between Jesus Christ and Titus Flavius, indicating that the Gospel authors must have wanted the sophisticated reader to understand that Titus Flavius, like Jesus Christ, is to be viewed as the fulfillment of the Messianic prophecies of Hebrew scripture.

When the Biblical Jesus is seen in this context as a typologically camouflaged Titus Flavius, suddenly a grimly humorous aspect of the narrative emerges. The reader realizes that the Gospels are filled with witty double entendres and punning satire, generally at the expense of the Jewish Zealots as well as Christian gentiles who take the Gospels at face value.

JOSEPHUS'S KNOWLEDGE OF CHRISTIANITY: THE DECIUS MUNDUS PUZZLE

While many scholars acknowledge that the Gospel authors were aware of Josephus, the topic of whether Josephus knew anything about Jesus Christ or Christianity is far more controversial, and has been an endless topic of debate.

What is widely acknowledged is that two brief, famous passages in Josephus's *Antiquities of the Jews* specifically mention the Biblical Jesus. In one of these, known as the "*Testimonium Flavianum*" (18, 3, 63-64), Josephus states that one Jesus (the Christ) was crucified under Pontius Pilate, but appeared alive "to those that loved him" after an interval of three days. This seems to be a clear enough statement of the basic tenets of the Christian faith, but the endless debate goes on over whether Josephus really said all these things. or whether the passage (or some part of it) was a late interpolation by pious scribes of the early Christian era.

In the other passage, Josephus briefly mentions "...the brother of Jesus, who was called Christ, whose name was James..." (20, 9, 200). Again, this seems to indicate that Josephus was well aware of the existence of Jesus Christ, although there is some debate about what Josephus meant by "Christ" or whether those few words might have been a late interpolation.

The vexing aspect of this, which is (or should be) so confounding to faithful believers, is that Josephus could have known this much about Christ and Christianity — and yet have said so little more about it. During the period between 30 AD and 70 AD, the years at the heart of Josephus's historical tale — were Christ's disciples not hard at work in Judea, growing their Church, doing great miracles, and generally promulgating their proud and excitingly novel religious faith? How could Josephus have been aware of this, and yet not dedicated at least a few chapters to giving his views of this 'good news'? Josephus was certainly never at a loss for words, in describing any other popular Jewish sect of the time.

Atwill argues that Josephus did indeed have an intimate knowledge of Christian narratives and theology, and that he referred to it often. However, instead of speaking plainly, Josephus wrote vicious satires of Christianity; and these satires were often placed within typological parallels to passages in the New Testament. Or in the case of the *Testimonium Flavianum*, Atwill argues that it can be recognized as genuine in its entirety, because it can be seen as part of a literary triptych, sandwiched alongside two enigmatic satires built on New Testament themes. Briefly stated: in the central satire, a rogue named Decius Mundus pretends to be the god Anubis, in order to trick a dignified lady named Paulina into having sex with her. The name 'Decius Mundus' is a pun on Decius Mus, the famous Roman war hero who gave himself as a sacrifice in battle to guarantee the Roman victory in war. 'Mundus' means 'World', so Decius Mundus is a 'Sacrifice for the World'. Paulina and her husband, Saturninus, laughably agree that making love to a God would be no sin against Paulina's chastity. So, Paulina and Mundus enjoy a night together, but then Mundus returns on the third day to boast that he is no God, much to Paulina's chagrin. In the other pedimental satire, a woman named Fulvia (whose husband's name, again, is Saturninus) is persuaded by three men to send her wealth to the Jewish temple; but in reality, the three men spend the money "for their own uses." In the first satire, Mundus is an 'antetype' of Jesus; in the second, the three men may represent the Roman Trinity. The two stories are, of course, typologically coupled to each other as well, as they both tell essentially the same tale of a dignified lady with a husband named Saturninus who is tricked by a religious swindle. The choice to use the name 'Paulina' in the story may be a hint that the Romans viewed the original St. Paul, the author of the epistles, as a feminized victim of the swindle as well.

Strangely enough, the fact that the *Testimonium Flavianum* tryptich was a satire of Christianity was apparently understood as early as the 4th century by the Christian author pseudo-Hegesippus, whose Latin paraphrase of Josephus elaborated on the satire by having Paulina and Mundus discuss the possibility of a pregnancy, thus making her into a parody of the Virgin Mary. This was pointed out by Albert A. Bell in his 1976 paper "*Josephus the Satirist?*",[26] who mentioned that a 1927 paper by C. Pharr had also fingered the Josephus passage about Paulina and Mundus as a parody of the Annunciation. Bell, however, withheld his own judgment on the matter, stating:

> [The view that Josephus was a satirist] has the decided disadvantage of being quite subjective. We must assume, on the basis of our own reactions, that the story of Paulina and Mundus appeared to Josephus as a parody of sorts of the Annunciation story and that he could depend on his readers to draw the same parallel. Lacking even a hint of literary evidence to support it, we are justifiably hesitant to accept this suggestion.

I can only hope that Bell was being ironic himself with this brief, dry spoof of hidebound academic caution and humorlessness — especially after having titled his paper with the bold assertion of Josephus's comedic aspect, hedged only with a question mark. However, I note with some discouragement that Bell's argument disappeared with hardly a ripple (three obscure mentions in the English language since 1976, in the Google Scholar citation index); this in spite of its obvious and even decisive relevance to the endless academic debate about the *Testimonium Flavianum*.

---

[26] Albert A. Bell, 'Josephus the Satirist? A Clue to the Original Form of the "Testimonium Flavianum"', *The Jewish Quarterly Review*, 67 (1976), 16 <http://dx.doi.org/10.2307/1454525>.

THE PROBLEM OF PLAUSIBLE DENIABILITY AND THE "SMOKING GUN FALLACY"

In *Caesar's Messiah*, Atwill argues that the Flavians were proud that they invented Christianity, and that they wanted to be remembered by posterity for their accomplishment. But on the other hand, he often mentions that a particularly complex and obscure typological device was invented because a simpler means of expression would have made Flavian complicity "too obvious". Is this a contradiction?

At first glance, this seems to be a serious problem with the Flavian Origins thesis. If, as Atwill claims, the Flavians created Christianity primarily for propaganda purposes, then they knew that their work needed to compete with all the other religious sects that were vying for the allegiance of Jews and Gentiles alike, anywhere in the Empire. For that reason, it was obviously essential that the texts be as appealing and as convincing as possible. It doesn't make sense that the authors would have included anything (such as a complex, self-incriminating typological framework with satirical overtones) that could divert from that goal.

In his review of *Caesar's Messiah*, Robert M. Price wrote: "only the most obtuse reader, the most tin-eared, can possibly fail to appreciate the sublime quality of so much of the New Testament", as if Atwill's theory does not recognize this; on the contrary, the Flavian Origins theory requires that the New Testament would be perceived as having just such a sublime quality, in order for it to succeed in its evangelical goals. Price continued: "As to Jesus' teachings, Atwill declares that 'those who see spiritual meaning in his words are being played for a fool'. Such a statement is only a damning self-condemnation, revealing the author's own absolute inability to appreciate what he is reading." This, again, is a mis-reading of Atwill's point. He is not saying that the surface-level spiritual meaning is missing from the text, but rather that it is being used as a sugar coating on a Trojan Horse full of Roman ideological foot-soldiers. I wonder if Price would deny that a multitude of impoverished and enslaved Christians have indeed been played for fools by their masters, the elite.

Furthermore, the Flavian intellectuals also needed to write material that would seem credible within the cultural milieu of the ancient Mediterranean region. That means they needed to write material that was consistent with the pre-existing source materials including both Zealot and Herodian documents, and consistent with the general level of historical understanding among the general public.

However, this latter constraint is not as tight as it would be in a modern environment. At the time that the Gospels were written, the period of its historical setting (that is, the time of Tiberius and Pontius Pilate) was receding into the distant past, and many readers would have only a very general (and highly colored) understanding of the period. Furthermore, literacy was fairly rare at the time, and most of the intended audience of the Gospels would be hearing about them second-hand from the clergy. Of course there was no printing press, so copies of any historical literature were rare and hard to come by. Thus, the Gospel authors could feel that they could indeed take some liberties with historical truth, without much risk of being caught by the general public.

Nevertheless, there certainly were some intellectuals who would have had a deep understanding of the historical literature, including many documents that have not survived to the present time. For those readers, the Gospels would have conveyed a powerful message that the Flavians were brazen enough to blatantly falsify and invert the factual record, in service of their own propaganda objectives.

In light of the mission-critical "Prime Directive" to avoid alerting 'hoi polloi' about the nature of this strange, alien Imperial religious conspiracy, it seems undeniable that the operational security of the project would have been enhanced if the Flavians had chosen to avoid inserting typological traces of their crime directly into the New Testament texts and the works of Josephus. We need an explanation of why they chose to do so, in spite of the fact that they might easily have been inconvenienced at times by the need to explain themselves to careful and suspicious readers, or even threatened with failure of the project if the truth became too widely known.

Contrary to Atwill's suggestions in *Caesar's Messiah*, I do not believe they ever intended for the crime to be discovered by the slaves and commoners ("hoi polloi") who made up the vast majority of Christian believers. However, considering the level of sophistication of the vast majority of people at the time, the Roman intellectuals simply weren't concerned that the public would recognize the fraud. All they needed to do, was avoid leaving any "smoking guns" that would overcome the level of plausible deniability in the Gospel texts, and make the deception obvious to even the most obtuse reader. Within that limitation, they apparently considered themselves free to consider a variety of objectives with their writing. (In fact, as a general rule, I believe that evidence of elite criminality and conspiracy is strewn about today by the same general standard: obvious to the sophisticated reader, but never so obvious as to represent a "smoking gun" that might alarm the general public.)

Based on the extensive monuments that the Caesars of the Imperial cult constructed for themselves, their vanity may have been so great that we can hardly imagine it today. While they may not have cared what the 'hoi polloi' knew, they might have been especially concerned to leave a message that future royals and their intellectuals would understand and view with respect and, presumably, admiration.

My view is that the typology may have also been used as a teaching tool in the Imperial secret service, which may have been embedded within the Roman Imperial cult. The early Roman Catholic (Christian) church may also have been operated at that time as a mystery cult.[27] Perhaps the temples dedicated to the worship of Jesus and/or the current Emperor were run like modern Masonic lodges, with the higher levels of membership (and the great secrets) reserved to loyal and long-term functionaries of the Imperial service, and that these higher levels were accompanied with appropriate accolades, prestige and financial rewards. And I'm imagining that, just as in the modern corporate and political

---

[27] Walter Burkert, *Ancient Mystery Cults* (Harvard University Press, 1987), p. 133.

system, exhibiting a certain level of sociopathy couldn't have done any harm to a young man's prospects. If this was the case, then Josephus was being ironical when wrote in his book *Against Apion*: "There have been indeed some bad men who have attempted to calumniate my history, and took it to be a kind of scholastic performance for the exercise of young men" (1, 53).

If this theory that the Gospels were primarily used as secret documents of the Roman imperial cult and the (closely related) embryonic Roman Catholic church, it would also help to explain the mystery of the Gospels' late appearance in the overt historical record. We argue that the Gospels must have been written under the Flavians, not only because they contain so much material that is pertinent to their agenda, but also because there is little if anything in the Gospels that would indicate any knowledge of events that transpired after the death of Domitian (96 CE). However, the first church father to write openly of the existence of four gospels was Irenaeus, in approximately 180 CE.[28] Because of this, there have been claims that the Gospels were first written at this time, falsifying Atwill's theory.[29]

But, Irenaeus clearly stated his own viewpoint that all four of the canonical gospels existed from the earliest days of Christianity, and possessed full apostolic authority:

> Matthew... issued a written Gospel among the Hebrews in their own dialect, while Peter and Paul were preaching at Rome, and laying the foundations of the Church. After their departure, Mark, the disciple and interpreter of Peter, did also hand down to us in writing what had been preached by Peter. Luke also, the companion of Paul, recorded in a book the Gospel preached by him. Afterwards, John, the disciple of the Lord, who also had leaned upon His breast, did himself publish a Gospel during his residence at Ephesus in Asia (Against Heresies, III, 1, 1).

[28] David Trobisch, *The First Edition of the New Testament* (Oxford University Press, 2000).

[29] 'A Conversation on the Caesar's Messiah Thesis', *Freethought Nation* <http://freethoughtnation.com/a-conversation-on-the-caesars-messiah-thesis/> [accessed 17 March 2014].

Those who claim that Irenaeus invented the four Gospels, or that they were first written during his time, have not explained how he could foist such a fiction on other members of the Catholic Church at such a late date, and hope to retain any credibility. It seems much more likely that there is some grain of truth in his claim that they had existed much earlier, and that his true purpose in writing about the Roman Gospels was to assert their claims of superiority over the many apocryphal "gospels" that were proliferating at the time. Some of these apocryphal gospels might have been earlier Roman drafts that had been superseded, and others might have been similar to modern "fan fiction". However, all of them needed to be stamped out, as the Roman hierarchy had determined that the time had come to bring Christianity into a single large tent. As Irenaeus explained:

> It is not possible that the Gospels can be either more or fewer in number than they are. For, since there are four zones of the world in which we live, and four principal winds, while the Church is scattered throughout all the world, and the "pillar and ground" of the Church is the Gospel and the spirit of life; it is fitting that she should have four pillars, breathing out immortality on every side, and vivifying men afresh (III, 11, 8).

Such arguments aside, the status of the four Gospels before Irenaeus remains a matter for speculation. However, considering the rapid spread of Christianity during the 1st and 2nd centuries,[30] the lack of any such documentary evidence is in itself quite surprising. From a Bayesian perspective, this increases the likelihood of the hypothesis that the Gospels were indeed maintained as secret documents of the early Roman Catholic Church.

Without further ado, let's look at this lesson plan that might have been taught at the thirty-second degree of the Imperial cult. The lessons are presented in the order that they appear in the Gospel of Luke.

---

[30] Susan Tyler Hitchcock and John L. Esposito, *Geography of Religion: Where God Lives, Where Pilgrims Walk* (National Geographic, 2004), p. 281.

FISHING FOR MEN

The parallels are highlighted in **bold typeface**.

LUKE 3:21

When all the people were being baptized, **Jesus** was baptized too. ...And a voice came from heaven: '**You are my Son, whom I love; with you I am well pleased.**' Now **Jesus...began his ministry...**" (Luke 5) "...**Jesus** was standing by the **Lake of Gennesaret**...all his companions were **astonished at the catch of fish they had taken**...Then Jesus said to Simon, '**Don't be afraid; from now on you will fish for people**.' So they...**followed him**."

MATT. 11:21

Jesus prophesied "**Woe to you, Chorazain**" .

JOSEPHUS (WARS 3.10)

"Vespasian pitched his camp...[at] the **Lake of Gennesareth**....**Jesu** and his party...made a sally upon them. Vespasian...thereupon **sent his son...**to disperse them." [Titus:] "**For you know very well that I shall go into the danger first, and make the first attack upon the enemy. Do not you therefore desert me, but persuade yourselves that God will be assisting to my onset...And now Titus made his own horse march first against the enemy, as did the others with a great noise after him....Jesus** fled over the country, while others of them ran down to the lake...and some were slain as they were getting up into the ships." The city was taken, but some rebels fled in ships. Vespasian went to the lake. [A long digression follows, describing the lake; the name **Gennesareth** is repeated **3x.**] "**Some have thought it to be a vein of the Nile, because it produces the Coracin fish as well as that lake does which is near to Alexandria**." [Vespasian's vessels destroyed the rebels' ships, leaving the rebels] "**drowning at sea**", [to be] "**killed by darts**," [or] "the Romans **cut off either their heads or their hands**."

As a typological sequential parallel, this is only moderately impressive. Critics will note that every military campaign has its onset; and the warrior's call for his troops to have courage, and his bravely leading them into battle, must be a commonplace across hundreds of ancient manuscripts. The somewhat distinctive shared elements between the New Testament and Josephus passages are: a son (of God, no less) sent into battle; the location (Genessereth); and the involvement of a character named Jesus (which was, however, apparently a very common Judean name at the time, judging from the sheer number of possibly distinct Jesus characters mentioned in Josephus's text.)

However, if we recognize that the Josephus passage contains an enigma, the situation becomes more interesting. He says: "**Some have thought it [the lake of Genessereth] to be a vein of the Nile, because it produces the Coracin fish as well as that lake does which is near to Alexandria**." It's obviously ridiculous that anyone would think that the Sea of Galilee (Genessereth) is a vein of the Nile: the ancients for millennia before Josephus knew their geography better than that. And, there is no lake anywhere near Alexandria: it's in the Nile delta, where any body of water would be more akin to a swamp. Such absurdities should surely be a clue that Josephus's warped sense of humor is coming into play.

The answer to the riddle is that the Jews are like fish, and that Hellenized Jews are found in great numbers in Alexandria, just as they are in the area of Palestine near the Sea of Galilee. The "Coracin Fish" seems to be a pun on the name of the town "Chorazain", which Jesus curses in the passage from Matthew. In Josephus's narrative, we find that Titus is slaughtering these "fish" by the thousands. To make the point clear, Josephus ends the story with his all too graphic description of the Romans killing men with darts, drowning them, or cutting their limbs off, in their rout of the Jewish rebels at sea.

This warrior's metaphor of "fishing for men" is a well-known literary trope; see for example:

> ...the mighty Laestrygonians came thronging from all sides...at once there rose throughout the ships a dreadful din, alike from men that were dying and from ships that were being crushed. And **spearing them like fishes** they bore them home, a loathly meal. (Odyssey 10:119-124; also see Odyssey 12:245-255, 22:381-389.)

Ancient readers of the New Testament, who learned their Homer in grammar school, might have been pleased to find that the Gospel authors appear to have inverted and ennobled this barbaric trope. However, in the final analysis, the joke is on the Christians, since Josephus's humorous point is that the "Coracin fish" in the lake are the Jewish rebels that are being "fished" by the Romans.

The New Testament passage is tightly coupled to the Josephus enigma by this distinctive concept of "Fishing for Men" as well as by the various less distinctive elements. Jesus's spiritual gathering of his followers and his call for them to be "fishing for men" grimly foreshadow Titus's actual slaughter of the Jews, occurring at the same location at Genessareth, allegedly forty years later.

THE DEMONS OF GADARA

In Josephus (Wars 4.7.389-437) we meet the rebel leader John, who was "beginning to **tyrannize**" in the countryside. He attracted a following among the rebels, who "thought they should be safer themselves, if the causes of their past **insolent actions** should now be **reduced** to **one head**, and not to a great many." Josephus explained that "**as it is in a human body, if the principal part be inflamed, all the members are subject to the same distemper; so, by means of the sedition and disorder that was in the metropolis … had the wicked men that were in the country opportunity to ravage the same.**" Men "joined in the conspiracy by **parties, too small for an army, and too many for a gang of thieves** … Nor was there now any part of Judea that was not in a miserable condition, as well as its most eminent city also." Getting word of the threat, Vespasian "marched against **Gadara**"...the Jews were quickly surrounded by the Roman forces "and, **like the wildest of wild beasts, rushed** upon the point of others' swords; so **some of them were destroyed**...and **others were dispersed**...But Placidus...slew all that he overtook, as far as Jordan; and **when he had driven the whole multitude to the riverside**...the number of those that were unwillingly **forced to leap into Jordan** was prodigious. There were besides **two thousand** and two hundred taken prisoners. **A mighty prey was**

taken also, consisting of **asses, and sheep, and camels, and oxen**…"

In other words, Josephus is expounding a theory which likens the spread of "sedition" to a disease, in which the "distemper" of "one head" infects the multitude, who seek to abandon their free will and responsibility to that one individual. The rebels then become like wild beasts, fit to be destroyed. Elsewhere, Josephus explains his view that "Demons … are no other than the spirits of the wicked" (Wars 7.6.185), so by that definition John and his followers may all be seen as demons.

In Mark 5:1-20 (also Luke 8:26-39) Jesus has come to the "**land of the Gadarenes**."   He met a man (the demoniac) who was possessed "with an **unclean spirit**" who was always "**crying, and cutting himself with stones**."   Jesus asked the demoniac, "What is thy name?" The demoniac replied, "**My name is Legion: for we are many**...Now there was there **nigh unto the mountains a great herd of swine feeding**...And **the unclean spirits went out, and entered into the swine**; and **the herd ran violently down a steep place into the sea (they were about two thousand**), and were choked in the sea."   The demoniac was healed, and "**began to publish in Decapolis** how great things Jesus had done for him." The version of the story in Matthew (8:28-33) has Jesus meet **two demon-possessed men**, who accuse Jesus of "**tormenting us before the time**".

There are several peculiar and enigmatic aspects to this pericope. Why should one man be possessed by a legion of demons? Why are swine being herded in such huge numbers, where pork is taboo? Why does Matthew mention two demoniacs, where Mark and Luke see only one?

The enigma is solved by recognizing that Josephus's John is an antetype to the demoniac: just as the Biblical Jesus meets a man who is possessed by demons, who are sent into wild beasts and destroyed, so also John is like a demon who infects a multitude of Jewish radicals, and they become like animals to be destroyed.

Within this conceptual framework, there are many specific verbal parallels: the location near Gadara (at least according to some early manuscripts); the size of the parties "too small for an army, and too large for a gang of thieves" (which is a good definition of the size of a legion); wild beasts rushing; Jewish rebels (like the swine) forced into the sea; and the number "about two thousand" (or in Josephus, to be exact, "two thousand two hundred") — although oddly, the two thousand Biblical swine are destroyed, while the 2200 rebels in Josephus are captured. In Josephus, the Romans also capture a "mighty prey" of livestock, but no swine, presumably because the swine have been drowned.

Atwill suggests that perhaps the 2nd demoniac in Matthew's version represents John's brother Simon (Peter), and that they are being tormented "before the time" because the time of their torment belongs later in the typological sequence. Later on, John and Simon are caught coming out of the tombs (like the demoniac), where they have been cut by stones in tight quarters (like the demoniac). Then John was sent to Rome, where he presumably published the gospel of John, just as the Biblical demon took the opportunity to publish in Decapolis.

DESTRUCTION OF JERUSALEM: PROPHECY AND FULFILLMENT

This set of parallels has been universally acclaimed since the early days of Christianity, so there should be no controversy that these are real parallels. Basically, the scheme is that Matthew's Jesus launches into a series of prophecies of the destruction of Jerusalem. The prophecies are fulfilled in Josephus's *Wars of the Jews* (6.5) and a few other scattered passages, as will be noted below.

The devoutly orthodox Catholic explanation for this, of course, is that Jesus's prophecies were fulfilled in history exactly as it unfolded, and as Josephus accurately reported. Unfortunately, the logic of this interpretation leads to the conclusion that Titus is the second coming of the Son of Man; an unpalatable conclusion which can be (rather awkwardly) finessed (but not really avoided) by viewing Titus as a passive instrument of God's wrath, and moving quickly on to the prophecies of Revelation, where the true coming of Jesus "in power and glory" might be (arguably) deferred to the infinite future. If there are any orthodox Catholics or other fundamentalists reading this, I can only ask them to consider whether Atwill's explanation makes more sense overall.

Liberal religious scholars prefer the explanation that the New Testament authors borrowed their quotes verbatim from Josephus.

It should be mentioned at this juncture, that Josephus in the Jewish Wars argued that all of the events that transpired, were in accordance with the arcane prophecies of the book of Daniel. As Josephus stated:

> ...And indeed it so came to pass, that our nation suffered these things under Antiochus Epiphanes, according to Daniel's vision, and what he wrote many years before they came to pass. In the very same manner Daniel also wrote concerning the Roman government, and that our country should be made desolate by them. All these things did this man leave in writing, as God had showed them to him ...(*Ant*. 10.11. 276-277).

And as Atwill explained, this led to some chronological claims by Josephus that seem suspect, to say the least:

> [Josephus's] recording of the perfect alignment of events in the time sequences Daniel predicted is either his witnessing of supernatural phenomena or a deliberate falsification. Currently there is contention among scholars regarding virtually all of the chronology Josephus gives in Wars of the Jews. For example, Josephus gives a later date than Suetonius and Dio for when Vespasian began to prepare for the civil war in Rome that led to his becoming emperor. It is probable that Josephus did this to provide support for the Flavian claim that Vespasian was not anxious to become Emperor. This "shaping" of time by Josephus to create Flavian propaganda is exactly the same technique he used to create the alignment between the Flavian campaign in Judea and the prophecies of Daniel (314).

Jesus, of course, endorses this same prophet Daniel; as well as, implicitly, the exact same jiggered interpretation of Daniel's ambiguous prophecy as Josephus devised:

> ...and then the End will come. **"When you have seen (to use the language of the Prophet Daniel) the 'Abomination of Desolation,' standing in the Holy Place**—let the reader observe those words—"then let those who are in Judea escape to the hills...(Matt. 24:14-16).

It is hard to escape the conclusion that Josephus and the New Testament authors conspired together to achieve this synchrony; or at least, that Josephus was working from some independent source of the Christian narrative, and that he labored to comply with its chronology and its interpretation of Daniel. If the New Testament authors copied their timeline from Josephus, there would have been no need for Josephus to tamper with real historical events.

Even more convincingly: to accept the conventional explanation that the New Testament copied Josephus, requires a severely impaired sense of humor, as I will explain.

Jesus begins his prophesying in Matthew with this curse:

> ...upon you may fall *the guilt of* all the righteous blood shed on earth, from the blood of righteous Abel to the blood of **Zechariah, the son of Berechiah, whom you murdered between the temple and the altar**. "Truly I say to you, all these things will come upon this generation (Matt 23:34-36).

The scenario Jesus foresees does indeed begin to unfold exactly one generation (40 years) later. Jesus invokes the memory of Abel and Zechariah son of Berechiah, who are both well-known Old Testament characters who were ignored or mistreated by their contemporaries. Somehow, Josephus doesn't seem to have gotten the memo that Jesus was talking about history, not prophecy; and in due course, we find that Zacharias amusingly meets his fate again in the temple, exactly as Jesus described. It comes as a humorous surprise to find history repeating itself as precisely as this.

...these zealots and Idumeans were quite weary of barely killing men, so they had the impudence of setting up fictitious tribunals and judicatures for that purpose; and... they intended to have **Zacharias the son of Baruch**, one of the most eminent of the citizens, slain... **Now the seventy judges brought in their verdict that the person accused was not guilty... hereupon there arose a great clamor of the zealots upon his acquittal... So two of the boldest of them fell upon Zacharias in the middle of the temple, and slew him** (*Wars* 4.5.338-344).

Surely Josephus knew his Old Testament well enough that we can be confident this joke was no accident.

After this, the prophecies and their fulfillment unfold smoothly enough (although the sequential order between Jesus and Josephus is not unbroken.)

JESUS

the disciples...said, "...**what will be the sign** of your Coming and of the Close of the Age?" "Take care that no one misleads you," answered Jesus..."Many **false prophets** will rise up and lead multitudes astray (Matt. 24:3-5);

JOSEPHUS

The great distress the jews were in upon the conflagration of the holy house. Concerning **a false prophet**, and **the signs that preceded this destruction** (*Wars*, Heading to Book 6, Chapter 5).

JESUS

"for then there will be **great tribulation**, such as has not been since the **beginning of the world** and assuredly never will be again (Matt. 24:21).

JOSEPHUS

...the **misfortunes of all men**, from **the beginning of the world**, if they be compared to these of the Jews, are not so considerable as they were (*Wars*, Preface, line 12).

JESUS

there will be **famines and earthquakes** in various places (Matt. 24:7);

JOSEPHUS

many...were worn away by the **famine**...Moreover...the priests... felt **a quaking**, and heard a great noise... (*Wars* 6.5.274, 299).

JESUS

"then let those who are in Judea **escape to the hills**; "let him who is on the roof **not go down to fetch what is in his house**; "nor let him who is outside the city stay to pick up his **outer garment (Matt. 24:16-18)**.

JOSEPHUS

the multitude also that was in the city joined in this outcry with those that were **upon the hill...And now the Romans,** judging that it was in vain to spare what was round about the holy house, **burnt all those places**... **They also burnt down** the treasury chambers, in which was an immense quantity of money, and **an immense number of garments**...(*Wars* 6.5.274, 281-282).

JESUS

"And **alas for the women** who at that time are **with child or have infants (Matt. 24:19)**!

JOSEPHUS

There was **a certain woman** that dwelt beyond Jordan, her name was Mary...snatching up her son, who was **a child sucking at her breast**, she said, "**O thou miserable infant!**..." As soon as she had said this, she slew her son, and then roasted him, and ate the one half of him...(*Wars* 6.3.201-208).

JESUS

...immediately after those times of distress **the sun will be darkened,** the moon will not shed her light, **the stars will fall from the firmament (Matt. 24:29),**

JOSEPHUS

Thus there was **a star resembling a sword**, which stood over the city, **and a comet**, that continued a whole year...(*Wars* 6.5.289).

JESUS

"Then will appear the Sign of the Son of Man in the sky; and then will all the nations of the earth lament, when they see the **Son of Man coming on the clouds of the sky** with great power and glory (Matt. 24:30).

JOSEPHUS

...a certain prodigious and incredible phenomenon appeared: I suppose the account of it would seem to be a fable, were it not related by those that saw it, and were not the events that followed it of so considerable a nature as to deserve such signals; for, **before sun-setting, chariots and troops of soldiers in their armor were seen running about among the clouds, and surrounding of cities** (*Wars* 6.5.297-299).

THE WOE-SAYING JESUS

Immediately after having described all of these amazing signs from the heavens, and great holocaust of conflagration and slaughter, Josephus gives us a signal that his sense of humor is undaunted by the disaster.

But, what is still more terrible, there was **one Jesus, the son of Ananus,** a plebeian and a husbandman...(*Wars* 6.5.300).

In what possible way could this "Jesus, the son of Ananus" be "still more terrible" than everything that has happened to this point in the destruction of Jerusalem? Josephus goes on to explain that this Jesus is nothing worse than a self-righteous big-mouth with a strange and repetitive message:

four years before the war began, and at a time when the city was in very great peace and prosperity, came to that feast whereon it is our custom for everyone to make tabernacles to God in the temple, began on a sudden to cry aloud, "**A voice from the east, a voice from the west, a voice from the four winds, a voice against Jerusalem and the holy house, a voice against the bridegrooms and the brides,** and a voice against this whole people!" This was his cry, as he went about by day and by night, in all the lanes of the city (*Wars* 6.5.300-301).

Hmm...why does this Jesus sound so much like Biblical Jesus?...

[arriving at Jerusalem at the time of the Passover feast]...His disciples came and called His attention to the **Temple buildings**. "You see all these?" He replied; "in solemn truth I tell you that there will not be left here one stone upon another that will not be pulled down" (Matt. 24:1-2).

"For just **as the lightning flashes in the east and is seen to the very west**, so will be the Coming of the Son of Man (Matt. 24:27).

the Kingdom of the Heavens be found to be like **ten bridesmaids who took their torches and went out to meet the bridegroom and the bride** (Matt. 25:1).

Josephus continues to regale us with the saga of Jesus ben Ananus thusly:

However, certain of the most eminent among the populace had **great indignation** at this dire cry of his, and took up the man, and gave him **a great number of severe stripes**; yet **did not he either say anything for himself**, or anything peculiar to those that chastised him, but still went on with the same words which he cried before. Hereupon our rulers, supposing, as the case proved to be, that this was a sort of divine fury in the man, **brought him to the Roman procurator**, where he was **whipped till his bones were laid bare;** yet he did not make any supplication for himself, nor shed any tears, but turning his voice to the most lamentable tone possible, at every stroke of the whip his answer was, "**Woe, woe to Jerusalem!**" (*Wars* 6.5.302-304).

Jesus ben Ananus's fate seems to be unfolding in a remarkably similar way to the Biblical Jesus of Nazareth: the indignation of the Jews, the beatings and chastisement, the trip to the Roman procurator, and the unresponsiveness to interrogation. Moreover, his repetitive curse "Woe, woe to Jerusalem" clearly echoes Luke 11:43-52, where Jesus calls down "woe to you, scribes and pharisees, hypocrites", repeating the curse five times, extending it to lawyers, and giving five different weighty justifications. In the synoptically parallel passage in Matthew (23:13-33), the curse "woe to you" is repeated eight times, again with eight different explanations.

However, unlike Biblical Jesus (who was, of course, crucified), this Jesus ben Ananus gets off with a warning (although, like Biblical Jesus, he is derisively referred to as a "madman"; see Mark 3:21 and John 7:20):

> And when Albinus (for he was then our procurator) asked him who he was, and whence he came, and why he uttered such words; **he made no manner of reply to what he said,** but still did not leave off his melancholy ditty, till **Albinus took him to be a madman**, and dismissed him (*Wars* 6.5.305).

Nevertheless, Jesus ben Ananus ultimately meets his demise during the Passover season, comically in the exact same moment as he prophesies his own doom.

> he continued this ditty for seven years and five months, without growing hoarse, or being tired therewith, until the very time that he saw his presage in earnest fulfilled in our siege, when it ceased; for as he was going round upon the wall, he cried out with his utmost force, **"Woe, woe to the city again, and to the people, and to the holy house!"** And just as he added at the last, **"Woe, woe to myself also!" there came a stone out of one of the engines, and smote him, and killed him immediately; and as he was uttering the very same presages he gave up the ghost** (*Wars* 6.5.308-309).

Biblical Jesus also mentioned the phenomenon of being crushed by stones:

> "Have you never read in the Scriptures," said Jesus, **"The Stone which the builders rejected has been made the Cornerstone:** this Cornerstone came from the Lord, and is wonderful in our eyes? That, I tell you, is the reason why **the Kingdom of God will be taken away from you, and given to a nation that will exhibit the power of it**. He who falls on this stone will be severely hurt; but **he on whom it falls will be utterly crushed"** (Matt. 21:42-44).

And also:

> And some of the Pharisees called to Him from the crowd, "Teacher, rebuke Your disciples." But He answered and said to

them, "I tell you that if these should keep silent, **the stones would immediately cry out"** (Luke 19:39-40).

But ironically, according to Josephus, when the stones came it was Jesus ben Ananus who was utterly crushed (thus making a mockery of Jesus's prophecy); and furthermore, when the Jews cried out the coming of the stones: it was not the stones themselves that they proclaimed, but rather they said "THE SON COMETH"; that is, the Son of Man; that is, Titus.

> …Now the stones that were cast were of the weight of a talent, and were carried two furlongs and further. The blow they gave was no way to be sustained….accordingly the watchmen that sat upon the towers gave them notice when the engine was let go, and **the stone came from it**, **and cried out aloud**, in their own country's language, **THE SON COMETH**…(*Wars* 5.6. 269-274; see 1915 Dent translation.)

It might be objected that perhaps Josephus is lampooning Jewish prophetic voices in general, or the rebels' messianic dreams and pretensions more particularly. But given all the detail in this portrayal of the woe-saying madman Jesus: in my opinion, Josephus could not possibly have made it any more clear that this Jesus ben Ananus is a parody of Biblical Jesus.

Moreover, time has proven that Josephus was exactly correct in his own prophecy that Jesus would become a more terrible calamity for the Jews than anything that happened in the war, by inspiring generations of anti-semitism. This is a clue that Josephus knew the Gospels were Imperial propaganda.

Although, as both Biblical Jesus and Josephus assure us, our individual fates are in our own hands:

JESUS

… those who stand firm to the End shall be saved (Matt. 24:13).

JOSEPHUS

Now if any one consider these things, he will find that God takes care of mankind, and by all ways possible foreshows to our race what is for their preservation; but that men perish by those miseries which they madly and voluntarily bring upon themselves… (*Wars* 6.5.310).

LAZARUS, THE HUMAN PASSOVER LAMB, AND THE LAST SUPPER

Josephus tells a story which becomes the causus belli for Titus's final assault on the Temple:

> …I am going to relate a matter of fact, the like to which no history relates, either among the Greeks or Barbarians? It is horrible to speak of it, and incredible when heard. I had indeed willingly omitted **this calamity of ours**, that I might not seem to deliver what is so portentous to posterity, but that **I have innumerable witnesses to it in my own age**…

> There was a certain woman that dwelt beyond Jordan, her name was **Mary**; her father was **Eleazar**, of the village Bethezob, which signifies the ***house of Hyssop***…and it was now become impossible for her any way to find any more food, while **the famine pierced through her very bowels and marrow**…She then attempted a most unnatural thing; and snatching up her son, who was **a child sucking at her breast**, she said, "O thou miserable infant! for whom shall I preserve thee in this war, this famine, and this sedition?…Come on; be thou my food, and **be thou a fury to these seditious varlets, and a by-word to the world**, which is all that is now wanting **to complete the calamities of us Jews**." As soon as she had said this, **she slew her son, and then roasted him,** and eat the one half of him, and kept the other half by her concealed. Upon this the seditious came in presently, and smelling the horrid scent of this food, they threatened her, that they would cut her throat immediately if she did not show them what food she had gotten ready. She replied that **she had saved a very fine portion** of it for them, and withal uncovered what was left of her son…she said to them, "This is mine own son, and what hath been done was mine own doing! **Come, eat of this food; for I have eaten of it myself!** Do not you pretend to be either more tender than a woman, or more compassionate than a mother; but if you be so scrupulous, and do abominate this my sacrifice, as I have eaten the one half, **let the rest be reserved for me also**" (*Wars* 6.3.199-211).

Josephus describes the incident as "so portentous to posterity, but that I have innumerable witnesses to it in my own age." Why would this event be "portentous to posterity" and how would Josephus have "innumerable witnesses"? With this introduction, Josephus seems to be signaling that this story represents an enigma to be solved. Although the event was reportedly discussed among many, there could be at most a few of the "seditious" who witnessed the Cannibal Mary's display of half her son's carcass, and no witnesses at all to Mary's first speech, or to the murder of the child.

The timing of this incident (at Passover), the reference to "the house of hyssop" (a plant used to mark Israelite houses at the time of passover), and the statement that the child is "roasted", lead to the conclusion that the child is a human passover sacrifice. Thus, Josephus's tale represents a grimly concrete actualization of the spiritualized ritual of the Christian eucharist.

The names of Mary and Eleazar also suggest a possible relationship to the New Testament. In Luke 2:34-35, Simeon gives Mary a prophecy that "a sword will pierce through your own soul": a prophecy apparently fulfilled by the famine, which "pierced through her very heart and marrow." Mary's admonition to the "varlets" to "Come, eat of this food" is reminiscent of Christ's words at the Last Supper, and the mention of "innumerable witnesses" seems to be an echo of the multitudes who reportedly witnessed Jesus' resurrection, which indeed was a myth "portentous to posterity".

Mary describes the event as a "myth for the world", and a "fury to the varlets" that would "complete the calamities of the Jews". Atwill further sees a pun on the words "mythos" (myth), "mysos" (an atrocity), and "misos" (inspiring bitter hatred, in this case the bitter hatred by the Romans against the Jews.) This again seems uncalibrated and inappropriate as a commentary on the plight of the starving Jews; but if it's talking about the anti-Semitic effects of the Christian myth against the Jews, it is tremendously perceptive, if not prescient.

Atwill noted another odd parallel between the Josephus passage and the New Testament. Luke 10:38-42 and John 12:2-3 both describe a dinner at which Mary and Jesus are present, and Martha is serving. If we assume that the two passages are both describing the same dinner, they may be taken together as follows:

> Six days before the Passover, Jesus came to Bethany, where Lazarus was, whom Jesus had raised from the dead. There **they made him a supper**; Martha served, and Lazarus was one of those at table with him. (John 12:2–3)... But Martha was distracted with much serving; and she went to him and said, "Lord, do you not care that my sister has left me to serve alone? Tell her then to help me." But the Lord answered her, "Martha, Martha, you are anxious and troubled about many things; one thing is needful. **Mary has chosen the good portion, which shall not be taken away from her**" (Luke 10:40–42).

In this pericope, Lazarus has just recently been raised from the dead. However, he's been dead for 4 days, which is one day later than his soul would have departed from his body, according to Jewish lore. So unless one is inclined to believe in very unlikely miracles (from either a Gentile or Jewish perspective), Lazarus is nothing but a dead body. We also meet Mary, who is served a meal of "the good portion, which shall not be taken away from her." This, of course, is exactly the same portion that Cannibal Mary has saved for herself of the child. And if Lazarus is dead, "they made him a supper" is an invitation to draw the conclusion that a macabre double entendre was intended.

Thus, to summarize: in Josephus, Mary is eating her child; in the NT pericope, Mary logically seems to be eating the body of Lazarus, who allegedly was resurrected but is obviously dead; and according to Christianity's spiritualized interpretation, the believers are eating the body of Christ the son of Mary, after his alleged resurrection on the third day. The passages from Josephus and the New Testament are tied together primarily by the central and distinctive themes of the Eucharist and its association to cannibalism, the Passover sacrifice of Jesus, and the Resurrection. But the grim joke is also pulled together by the very specific verbal motif of the "good portion... not taken away."

THE NEW ROOT AND BRANCH

Although "the New Root and Branch" is a many-tentacled and sprawling satire, it is relatively simple to understand. Atwill summarizes the system as follows:

> The purpose of this particular satire is to document that the "root" and "branch" of the Judaic messianic lineage has been destroyed and that a Roman lineage has been "grafted on" in its place (219).

A recurring aspect of the theme is that the character who is "pruned" is always named Eleazar. This, along with Eleazar's role in being "made [into] a supper" in the Cannibal Mary parallel, leads Atwill to conjecture that Eleazar is an antetype for the true leader of the Jewish rebellion, who was ignominiously pruned from history.

The reader is encouraged to refer to *Caesar's Messiah* for further information about this theme, which is repeatedly employed by 'Shakespeare', as Atwill demonstrates in this volume.

IS ATWILL GUILTY OF "PARALLELOMANIA"?

Perhaps the most common objection to Joseph Atwill's work in *Caesar's Messiah* is that his premises are based on what is called "parallelomania." Samuel Sandmel (*Journal of Biblical Literature* 81: 1-13, 1962) defined this error as follows:

> We might for our purposes define parallelomania as that extravagance among scholars which first overdoes the supposed similarity in passages and then proceeds to describe source and derivation as if implying literary connection flowing in an inevitable or predetermined direction...The key word in my essay is extravagance. I am not denying that literary parallels and literary influence, in the form of source and derivation, exist. I am not seeking to discourage the study of these parallels...Detailed study is the criterion, and the detailed study ought to respect the context and not be limited to juxtaposing mere excerpts.

In his writing in *Caesar's Messiah*, Atwill was not primarily concerned with mounting a scholarly defense against these concerns. Instead, he was simply writing down the parallels as he encountered them in the texts, and exploring the implications of his particular interpretation. The same is true of this volume: it is mostly expository, rather than analytical and comprehensive.

Nevertheless, his study is certainly detailed, the parallels are certainly extensive, and Atwill paints a compelling historical context.

In *Caesar's Messiah*, Atwill made an argument that the Gospels were all written together, based on his solution of a puzzle embedded in the various Gospel accounts of the apostles in the empty tomb, looking for Jesus. My view is that as a mathematical argument, this can be largely defeated based on the assumption that the author of the Gospel of John had access to the other three Gospels when he wrote his own version. Similarly, early editions of *Caesar's Messiah* included a statistical argument based on the sequential aspect of the parallels between Luke and Josephus; an argument that dismissed legitimate questions about the strength of the parallels, the possibility of common sources, the directionality of the parallels, and the effect of multiple comparisons.

Frustrated by criticisms, Atwill produced the Flavian Signature edition of *Caesar's Messiah* (2011), which provided many more parallels in the sequence relating Josephus's Jewish Wars to the gospel of Luke. However, this was arguably going in precisely the wrong direction to satisfy the critics, because the new parallels were, in general, not as convincing as the ones he had already identified. In the process of arguing from these new parallels, Atwill appeared to be violating Sandmel's caution against "overdoing the supposed similarity in passages."

Rather than relying on a simple combinatorial analysis of Atwill's parallels, I would suggest that a more viable approach is to start by considering those parallels which have already been widely recognized. Atwill's interpretive framework is far more powerful than any other framework in terms of explaining all aspects of these ancient literary devices, especially the ironic, enigmatic and humorous aspects. Once this is agreed to, the more obscure parallels in the Flavian Signature can only add to Atwill's case; especially considering that most of these parallels are highly interpretable within the Flavian Origins framework.

It is certainly possible, as Atwill suggests, that the Romans themselves were well aware that the creation of a long sequence of literary parallels represents an indisputable statistical and combinatorial signature that the parallels were intentionally planted. If modern mathematical and experimental approaches to textual analysis can overcome critical objections based on multiple-comparisons considerations and source criticism, then this combinatorial approach has the potential to provide an academically ironclad proof of the Caesar's Messiah thesis. The entire set of 46 parallels in the Flavian Signature is presented in Caesar's Messiah, which, of course, reader are encouraged to read and reach their own conclusions.

The critics have certainly not met the burden of proof of showing that there are any alternative source analyses or interpretations that could compete with Atwill's, or that the parallels are not compelling, or that his work fails to meet Sandmel's criteria of standing up to detailed analysis. However, fulfillment of any demand for a comprehensive, even Bayesian, analysis of the relative probabilities of the Flavian Origins hypothesis as compared to its competitors, will need to await the attention of a better (or at least, braver) mathematician. Meanwhile, it is my view that many of Atwill's critics are far more avid practitioners of the sins of "parallelomania", and that other authors generally attempt to support parallel source analyses that are far weaker; while *Caesar's Messiah* builds a mountain of evidence that can only be explained by the Flavian Origins thesis.

So let's move on to learn about Atwill's new discoveries!

SHAKESPEARE DECODED

In this chapter, I will explain the previously unrecognized symbolic system that stretches across all of the works of Shakespeare and provides them with their deepest level of meaning. I will argue that the entire Shakespearean corpus was written solely to provide a vehicle for this symbolic system. This understanding also reveals the true author of the 'Shakespearean' literature.

The purpose of this Shakespearean symbolic system was to reverse everything the Flavians had accomplished with the comic system of Josephus and the New Testament. Thus, whereas in the Gospels' hidden satire the Jewish royal family was ridiculed for having cannibalized themselves, in the Shakespearean system the Gentile royal family is ridiculed for having done so. And since the Gospels inserted a Roman into the Jew's royal lineage, in her literature Jews would be inserted into the Gentile's nobility. And, just as Titus had fooled the Jews into worshipping 'Jesus', so Shakespeare would fool the Gentiles into worshipping 'Shakespeare'. This interpretive framework provides an explanation for many heretofore-incomprehensible features of the plays.

THE REVERSAL

There is a whole category of passages in Shakespeare's plays that are classified as 'puzzles' by scholars because they have been unable to decode their meaning. A good example of this is the analysis of *Julius Caesar* by Steve Sohmer.[31] He has been able to

---

[31] Steve Sohmer, *Shakespeare's Mystery Play: The Opening of the Globe Theatre 1599* (Manchester, U.K.; New York; New York: Manchester University Press; Distributed in the USA by St. Martin's Press, 1999).

identify detailed uses of the New Testament in the characterization of Caesar, Anthony, and Cassius, as well as parodies of church services and hymns. But he could not provide an explanation as to why the playwright would embed these parodies of Christian imagery in a play about a Roman emperor. Another example is the work by Alice-Lyle Scoufos on Falstaff, showing that the character appears to be a satire of Jesus, but again she could not explain why the playwright had created such a representation.[32] Many critics have simply avoided commenting on passages for which they cannot offer an explanation. This is a poor methodology, and few scholars have been as honest as Sohmer and Scoufos in admitting that they are not able to understand much of the underlining symbolism of the plays.

The following passage from *Hamlet* is an example of a Shakespearean 'puzzle' that has not been decoded by critics. In the passage, Hamlet is said to have read a book that describes people with "weak hams" and, most strangely, having "eyes purging thick amber and plum-tree gum".

HAMLET [READING A BOOK]

Slanders, sir: for the satirical rogue says here
that old men have grey beards, that their faces are
wrinkled, their eyes purging thick amber and
plum-tree gum and that they have a plentiful lack of
wit, together with most weak hams: all which, sir,
though I most powerfully and potently believe, yet
I hold it not honesty to have it thus set down, for
yourself, sir, should be old as I am, if like a crab
you could go backward.

(II, 2, 214 — 222)

Remarkably, the passage has drawn little attention from critics even though it is Hamlet's reading of the unnamed book that precipitates his madness. Perhaps this lack of interest is because the passage contains so many questions that critics cannot answer. What was the book that Hamlet read, and who was the "satirical

---

[32] Alice-Lyle Scoufos, *Shakespeare's Typological Satire: A Study of the Falstaff-Oldcastle Problem* (Athens: Ohio University Press, 1979).

rogue" that wrote it? Who were the people described as having had "weak hams" and a lack of "wit", and why did the author characterize them like that? Why was it not honest to have "set it down thus" if Hamlet "potently believes" what was written was true? Moreover, why did Hamlet have such a profound reaction to the information he received from the book? The thesis presented in this work answers all of these questions concerning the passage. In fact it can explain virtually every passage in the Shakespearean literature because they were all created within the symbolic framework that the thesis identifies.

In some ways the findings of this work are related to preexisting scholarship. There is already a specialist literature on the over two thousand Biblical allusions in the works of Shakespeare. Writers like Steven Marx have attempted to explain the organizing principles that underlie the religious references in the plays.[33] There have also been a few scholars who have wondered if some interaction with a Jew might have influenced Shakespeare to write *The Merchant of Venice,* and identifying Christ parallels in the plays is certainly not new. In fact, as Richard Levin has observed, almost every play has had critics who have identified a possible Christ figure—sometimes several. [34]

G. Wilson Knight has argued that "the unique act of the Christ sacrifice" was central to all the tragedies.[35] He assumed that Shakespeare was writing to support the conventional Christology of the Church of England by providing a representation of the events in the Gospels. But he could not explain findings like those of Sohmer, who demonstrated that the Christian images in *Julius Caesar* are hostile satires of the Gospels, rather than straightforward allegory.

[33] Steven Marx, *Shakespeare and the Bible* ([Oxford]: Oxford University Press, 2000).

[34] Richard Levin, 'On Fluellen's Figures, Christ Figures, and James Figures', *PMLA*, 89 (1974), 302.

[35] G. Wilson Knight, *Principles of Shakespearean Production* (London: Faber & Faber, Ltd., 1936).

Virtually all critics have assumed that a Christian wrote the plays of Shakespeare, even though this premise has not led to any clear understanding of their underlining symbolic structures. This is the same situation that scholars faced when trying to understand the Gospels. The Gospels are generally seen as a sincere description of the ministry of a Jewish teacher written by his followers, but this approach leaves many mysteries unsolved. However, the enigmatic aspects are transparently resolved once the New Testament is recognized as the product of the intellectual circle that surrounded Titus Flavius. So it has been with the works of Shakespeare. Though scholars have tried at length to fathom the many seemingly incoherent passages within the literature, their time would have been better spent simply trying to learn more about the author. As soon as 'Shakespeare' is recognized as a Jew, the meaning of many of these passages becomes visible.

THE SYMBOLIC LEVEL IN SHAKESPEARE

The Preface to Shakespeare's First Folio states that the plays were written more to be studied than performed, thus acknowledging that (unlike most plays) their deeper meaning could only be understood by an alert reader. At the pace that the play's lines are spoken during a performance it is sometimes difficult to analyze their subtext, even if one understands the symbolic framework that they were created within.

The hidden level of Shakespeare is, in one sense, typical of the literary style of the era. Elizabethan playwrights had, as Pinciss wrote:

> …developed strategies of indirection and allusion, of ambiguity and suggestion, of hinting through seemingly trivial facts to accomplish what Martin Butler, called: "signaling according to cautious codes." By using such "signals," a playwright might hope to stay out of trouble, for these were the ways that he could imply meaning, enabling him to express himself on subjects that, though forbidden, were of intense concern." [36]

---

[36] G. M. Pinciss, 'Bartholomew Fair and Jonsonian Tolerance', *Studies in English Literature, 1500-1900*, 35 (1995), 345.

Since such literary codes were common at this time, it should be expected to find such a system in plays that are as clearly symbolic as Shakespeare's. Virtually all scholars agree that *King Lear* has multiple sub-texts, for example, though they cannot agree as to what they mean. One critic claimed that the play is a description of King James's plans for the British Union; others have seen it as a comment on Jesus' passion and death. As Anne Patterson complained thirty years ago, there has been no satisfactory resolution of the inquiry into the 'strategies of indirection' of Shakespeare's plays, whereby their symbolic meaning has been decoded to the satisfaction of the majority of scholars.[37]

Certainly the best example of the lack of agreement between scholars has been their interpretations of Christ figures. Richard Levin noted in his review of *Measure for Measure* that one critic proposed the Duke as a Christ figure, another Marina, another Isabella and yet another Angelo.[38] These contradictory findings were caused by the use of vague criteria, which Levin rightly criticized. If a character can be identified as a Christ figure because he moves from one station in life to another, resists evil or temptation, suffers or dies, loves, or forgives others, then such criteria is applicable to almost every character. Moreover if the case of parodies is included, where the critic identifies the same linkage except in reverse, then one can barely miss in an identification of a character as a depiction of 'Jesus'.

This work aims for a different standard. It seeks to demonstrate that the Shakespearean corpus was created as an allegorical counterattack of the satire in the New Testament, and that the

[37] Annabel M. Patterson, Censorship and Interpretation: The Conditions of Writing and Reading in Early Modern England (Univ of Wisconsin Press, 1984), p. 53; Roger Stritmatter, 'Shakespeare's Censored Personality', Shakespeare Oxford Fellowship
<http://www.shakespeareoxfordfellowship.org/shakespeares-censored-personality-by-roger-stritmatter/> [accessed 9 March 2014].

[38] Levin.

master-list of the components of the Flavian comic system below
is the basis for the entire symbolic level of Shakespeare.

THE FLAVIAN COMIC SYSTEM

- The cutting off of the Jewish Messiah's limbs
- The uprooting of the messianic 'root'
- The 'grafting' of a Roman onto the Jewish lineage
- The switching of Titus for the Jewish Messiah
- The cannibalism of itself by the Jewish 'royal family'
- The Decius Mundus puzzle: 'Paulina' seduced by 'Mundus', though he is no God
- The raping and muting of Judea
- The false chronology employed to prove Daniel's prophecies
- The comedy of errors in the 'empty tomb' puzzle

This list is the basis of my analysis that resolves so many
otherwise incoherent aspects of the Shakespearean plays. For
example, in *Romeo & Juliet* there is no obvious meaning to the
numerous characters who are described as flowers, or for the play
being set in the days leading up to the Christian feast day of
Lammastide; no obvious dramatic reason for Romeo's death to
correspond to the simultaneous uprooting of a mandrake plant; no
reason why Juliet should 'crosse' her parents; no reason why one
of the characters should be called 'Mercutio'; nor any reason for
the chronology given in the prophecy that predicts Juliet will 'fall
backwards'. Nor has any critic provided any real explanation for
the mass carnage at the play's end. But these diverse and
seemingly unrelated elements are all explicable by the
interpretative framework provided by the Flavian comic system.

'SHAKESPEARE': THE PERFECT GENTILE

The Elizabethan state referred to the basis for its authority as its
'divine right'. This combination of church and state was a
restrictive pall that made it theologically impossible to question
the state's right to rule or how it ruled. Despite being few in
number, the Jews were a special focus of Elizabethan Christianity.
Jews were seen as a threat to the state's authority because their
religion challenged the historical claims of Christianity, and
anyone caught practicing Judaism was executed.

During this era in Britain it was therefore necessary for Jews to pretend to have converted to Christianity and to perform Christian rituals, such as the taking of communion. To observe the sacraments of a religion someone saw as false would be difficult under any circumstances, but for a Jew who understood the real meaning of the ritual, receiving the Eucharist would have been an unimaginably macabre experience. And there may have been many such Jews. In this book, I argue that 'Shakespeare' must have been just such a crypto-Jew, who decided to fight back against the false religion that gave the Gentile nobility the 'divine right' to execute her people for practicing their faith. To attack the state overtly was suicide, so a more subtle method had to be found — this method was the works of 'Shakespeare'.

To understand the analysis in this work it is important for the reader to bear in mind that the author of the Shakespearean plays was not trying to directly communicate the truth about the Christian Gospels. There would have far easier ways for the playwright to have accomplished that than the complex satirical system embedded in the Shakespearean literature. On the contrary, it was crucially important for the author to maintain a level of "plausible deniability" to prevent government censorship or other repercussions, while also presenting an enormously entertaining and ingenious surface-level narration that would keep audiences entranced. I believe that the unmistakable presence of a profound and unsolved mystery also lends to the unique appeal of the Shakespearean literature, and the enduring loyalty of Shakespeare's many fans.

An ancient Latin proverb holds that "a word to the wise is sufficient", and the author can testify that the Flavian / Shakespearean comic system becomes much more transparent with familiarity. It is therefore likely that those in the author's inner circle would have come away from the theatre with a degree of understanding and delight that far surpassed their Gentile compatriots. However, 'Shakespeare' intended that her satires remained largely unappreciated until after the collapse of Christianity that she no doubt hoped would occur shortly. In this way, she could deliver the same blow to Gentiles that Titus intended for the Jews. Though often interpreted as an effort to elevate humanity, at their deepest level the works of Shakespeare were intended to inflict the same sense of humiliation on uncomprehending Gentiles that Titus intended for the Jews.

As was mentioned in the introduction: it is also important to note that it is not necessary to accept the analysis presented in *Caesar's Messiah* in order to agree with the thesis of this work. All that is required is to recognize that the author of the Shakespearean literature had come to the same conclusions regarding the Gospels given in that work, whether they are correct or not. Then having come to these conclusions, she created the literature as a counterattack to the satirical system she believed existed in the Gospels.

The starting point for her 'Shakespearean project' was a play satirizing Titus' invention of Christianity, entitled *Titus Andronicus*. She designed the play so that its satirical level would be invisible until Titus was understood to have been 'Jesus', at which point its real meaning would become clear. She did not, of course, give her name as the play's author, choosing instead to use a witty *nom de plume*. As a Jew and a woman claiming authorship would have been problematic in any case, but she had another reason for her pen name.

Though a Gentile actor may have been the inspiration for her *nom de plum*, the original spelling of his last name was not 'Shakespeare'. The actor's real name was more likely spelled the way it was recorded on his marriage license to Anne Hathwey: "William Shagspere." The playwright was clever with words, and saw that by modifying the spelling of "Shagspere" to "Shakespeare" she would create a declaration of Jewish defiance. With the name of her 'perfect Gentile' she notified posterity that the Jews had not been destroyed by Titus and his false Judaism but would keep on fighting: 'will shake speare'. This is why, in the first Folio, 'William Shakespeare' was abbreviated and hyphenated to 'Will Shake-Spear', so as to show posterity more clearly the name's satirical meaning.

To the actor 'Shagspere', the change in the spelling of his name would have been of little concern, because (like the vast majority of people from Stratford) he was completely illiterate. For his complicity in the plot, 'Shagspere' was apparently paid part of the plays' royalties, which enabled him to become a landowner in Stratford.

The other reason for her *nom de plume* was simply to create the impression the plays were the work of a Gentile. This was part of her plan to create a mirror image of the Gospels. The Gospels appeared to be written by Jews, but were actually written by Roman intellectuals ridiculing Jews. She therefore wished to create the impression that the plays were the words of a Gentile, although they were actually those of a Jewish intellectual, ridiculing Gentiles. In this way she applied the Hebrew dictum of an eye for an eye, or, in her words, 'measure for measure'.

THE SEARCH FOR 'SHAKESPEARE'

There are many problems with the claim that a Christian from Stratford wrote the plays published under the name William Shakespeare. The 'Will from Stratford' had parents who were illiterate, his few surviving signatures seem to be in different hands, he did not teach his daughter how to read or write, and he left no mention of owning any books or manuscripts in his will. Further, since the capacity to read and write was a prerequisite for admission to the school he would have attended, the fact that Shakespeare's parents were illiterate makes it unlikely that he ever attended school. The only contemporaneous literary figure that claimed to have known him was Ben Jonson, who referred to him as a plagiarist. Many of the documents that should have recorded the extent of his participation as an actor or playwright in the London theater scene during his era have either had the relevant sections removed, or do not mention Shakespeare at all. For example, the parts of his son in law Philip Henslowe's diary covering the period that the plays were written are mysteriously missing. The strange engravings of the Bard's face that were published in the early editions of the plays have the appearance of someone wearing a mask, and the Preface and Introduction to the First Folio of Shakespeare's works seem to ridicule, not praise, the 'swan of Avon'. Moreover, there is the seemingly insurmountable problem of Shakespeare's vocabulary of over 20,000 words and expressions. No other English writer used a vocabulary of even half this size. Milton, for example, used less than 8,000 words to produce all of his works. How did someone raised by illiterate parents come to possess this breadth of vocabulary? The answer that is always given is that Shakespeare was a genius and that this makes anything possible, but there are no other examples of this particular strain of genius in history. No other individual born into such circumstances is known to have developed a command of language that towered over his or her contemporaries.

In addition to the biographical problems is the unsatisfactory nature of the 'Will from Stratford' as an explanation for the many of the subjects of the plays. Why would a glover's son from Stratford have taken such an interest in the region around Venice or been so interested in Jews and Moors? Why would he have integrated so much Jewish musical material into the plays? If the 'Will from Stratford' wrote plays, why did he not write ones that more closely reflected his purported background?

For these reasons and others, there have been many searches for an alternative author for the literature published under the name of William Shakespeare. Books describing alternative authors now number in the thousands, and there are even a number of meta-reviews of the different theories that may be usefully consulted.[39] All of the alternative theories of authorship, however, proceed from evidence gleamed from only a small part of the total literature. These theories are only able to cite a possible anagram, a few unusual correspondences, or a similarity between one Shakespearean play with another by a different author. None of these efforts have been able to connect all of the plays that make up the Shakespearean corpus to another author. Since none of the candidates can explain more than a small percentage of the plays, and yet all seem minimally plausible (or at least, arguably more plausible than Shagspere of Stratford), "group theories" have become popular; yet the genius and the thematic unity of the

[39] Diana Price, *Shakespeare's Unorthodox Biography: New Evidence of an Authorship Problem* (Westport, Conn.: Greenwood Press, 2001); John Michell, *Who Wrote Shakespeare?* (New York, N.Y.: Thames and Hudson, 1996).

corpus bely the idea that the corpus was written by some committee process with no central driving force behind it. An adequate argument for an alternative author to the Shakespearean literature must explain more than a few isolated phrases or even a single play, it needs to link its candidate to all of the plays. Thus, any valid alternative authorship theory must be grounded in a global explanatory framework for the Shakespearean literature. Such a framework must fulfill the following criteria:

1. It must have *adequacy of scope.* It has to explain the literature as a unit, not as separate and unrelated bodies.

2. It must have *adequacy of depth.* It needs to be able to explain the entirety of the plays' symbolic structures, and not just their surface narration.

3. It must be supported by the historical and biographical evidence.

The thesis presented here attempts to meet these criteria. It maintains that the playwright used the same symbolic framework to convey the same meanings throughout all of the plays and that all of the plays reflect the mindset of a specific author. The symbolic framework of the Shakespearean literature is not difficult to understand, but it has not been recognized before simply because it was built upon another framework that critics were unaware of: the hidden satirical level of the Flavian typological system.

While the problematic aspects of the identification of 'Shagspere' as the author of Shakespeare have become fairly well known, the alternative research community is far from having reached any consensus about the true author. Because of the vast scope of the plays, the diversity of their style and topics, the huge vocabulary, and other reasons that I will develop in the course of this book, I believe that 'group authorship' theories are highly plausible, and yet also that the thematic unity and aggressive spirit of the plays suggests that a single mind was the inspiration of this Shakespearean project. The authorship candidates that have received the greatest attention are Edward de Vere (Earl of

Oxford), William Stanley (Earl of Derby), Mary Sidney, and Christopher Marlowe, with Oxford perhaps being the most common suggestions. While it is impossible to rule out the possibility that any of these authors were involved in the project, either as primary or secondary authors, I would argue that none of them meets the requirements for a fully adequate solution to the authorship problem, which must explain the nature of the Shakespearean literature as an inversion of the Flavian typology.

EDWARD DE VERE, EARL OF OXFORD

Efforts to connect the Earl usually involve taking isolated phrases from the Shakespearean plays and relating them to his life. For instance, in *Antony and Cleopatra* the word 'worm' is mentioned several times. This 'worm' can be translated into French as 'ver', a word that some critics have related to 'Vere', the family name of the Earls of Oxford.[40] The Earl of Oxford's Bible also has been found to have some of its verses underlined that were used by Shakespeare. This is not strong proof, however, as only 20% of the marked verses are alluded to by Shakespeare. Moreover, of the over 2000 Biblical allusions used by Shakespeare, Oxford's Bible marks only 10%.[41] For example, of the 39 different verses in the *Book of Ezekiel* that Shakespeare mentions,[42] the Earl's Bible underlines only one.[43]

Another investigation has focused on certain phrases that appear to be anagrams of the Earl's family motto. The title of the Preface

---

[40] Richard Whalen, 'The Queen's Worm', *Shakespeare Oxford Newsletter*, Summer 1998 <http://www.shakespeare-oxford.com/?p=59> [accessed 9 March 2014].

[41] David Kathman, 'Oxford's Bible' <http://shakespeareauthorship.com/ox5.html> [accessed 9 March 2014].

[42] Naseeb Shaheen, *Biblical References in Shakespeare's Plays* (University of Delaware, 2011).

[43] Mark Anderson, 'Shakespeare's Good Book', *Valley Advocate* (Massachusetts, 10 March 1994) <http://www.shakespeare-oxford.com/?p=2160> [accessed 9 March 2014].

to *Troilus and Cressida*, 'A N*ever* Writer to an *Ever* Reader', for example, is sometimes adduced as evidence that the author was de Vere because of the repetition of the letters 'EVER', which can be arranged as 'Vere'. The 1609 edition of '*Shake-speares Sonnettes*' are described on their title page as being by "OUR. EVER-LIVING POET", words that can be turned into the anagram '*nil vero veriug*', which nearly corresponds with Oxford's motto '*nil vero verius*' meaning 'nothing is more true than the truth'. Moreover, the second edition of the Sonnets in *The Poems of Will. Shakespeare, Gen*t. (1640) also includes a dedication to the Reader, which wishes glory to the 'deserved author': a curious phrase which can be formed into the anagram ED DE VERS.[44] Analysis from anagrams is open to multiple interpretations, of course, and the case for de Vere as Shakespeare is hardly conclusive.

WILLIAM STANLEY, EARL OF DERBY

George Fenner, allegedly a Jesuit spy, discovered in 1599 that the Earl of Derby had been secretly writing plays. These secret plays have never been identified, leading to a stream of speculation about possible connections to Shakespeare. However, the evidence that has emerged is largely circumstantial. William was undoubtedly part of the same social circle that produced the plays: his older brother was the founder of the "King's Men", and Derby was closely affiliated with the Earls of Pembroke and Montgomery, the dedicatees of the First Folio. Various similarities have been noted between the plays and episodes from Derby's life, and his first name and last initial are the same as the playwright 'William Shakespeare.' Derby knew French, which was put to use by 'Shakespeare' in *Henry V*. Derby's authorship was advocated by a stream of late 19th and early 20th century authors including James Greenstreet,[45] Robert Frazer,[46] Abel

---

[44] Michell, pp. 181–182.

[45] James Greenstreet, 'A Hitherto Unknown Noble Writer of Elizabethan Comedies', *The Genealogist*, 7 (1891); James Greenstreet, 'Testimonies against the Accepted Authorship of Shakespear's Plays', *The Genealogist*, 8 (1892).

Lefranc,[47] and Arthur W. Titherley.[48] Derby is also frequently mentioned in conjunction with "group theories" of Shakespearean authorship.

MARY SIDNEY HERBERT

Mary Sidney, also known as Mary Herbert following her marriage to Henry Herbert, Earl of Pembroke, has been nominated by Robin Williams as a likely author of the Shakespearean works,[49] as was discussed in a Newsweek article in 2004:

> In short, Mary Sidney had the motive, means and opportunity to write the plays. At her home in Wiltshire, she fostered a literary circle whose mission was to elevate English literature—a strong motive. Gary Waller, a Sidney scholar at Purchase College in New York, has called her salon "a seedbed of literary revolution" and Sidney herself "the first major female literary figure in England." With her vast library, education and command of foreign languages, Sidney also had the means to create the works. And with her extensive connections in the literary world, she had opportunity to smuggle the plays to theater companies. Perhaps it's just coincidence, but the first eight Shakespeare plays were published anonymously—"and three of them," says Williams, "provocatively note on the title page that they were produced by Pembroke's Men, the acting company that Mary Sidney and her husband sponsored."
>
> Sidney-as-Bard would solve a number of riddles, argues Williams. It would explain why Shakespeare wrote love sonnets to a younger man. (Sidney had a younger lover, Matthew Lister.) It could clarify why the first compilation of Shakespeare's plays, the

---

[46] Robert Frazer, *The Silent Shakespeare* (W. J. Campbell, 1915).

[47] Abel Lefranc, *Sous Le Masque de 'William Shakespeare'*, 2 vols. (Payot & cie, 1919).

[48] Arthur Walsh Titherley, *Shakespeare's Identity: William Stanley, 6th Earl of Derby* (Warren, 1952).

[49] Robin Williams, *Sweet Swan of Avon: Did a Woman Write Shakespeare?* (Santa Fe, NM: Wilton Circle Press, 2012).

First Folio of 1623, was dedicated to the earls of Pembroke and Montgomery (her sons). And it would explain Ben Jonson's First Folio eulogy to the "sweet swan of Avon." Sidney had an estate on the River Avon—and her personal symbol was the swan. "There are swans in the lace collar and cuffs of her last portrait," Williams notes.[50]

Considering Sidney's many literary connections, her vast library, and its many links to the Shakespearean literature, the conjecture that Sidney was involved in some way in what we are calling the 'Shakespearean Project' is quite plausible. However, I am not aware of any evidence that she would have been motivated to become the primary author of what I will show is a body of Jewish revenge literature.

MARLOWE AND THE BEGINNING OF THE COUNTERATTACK

I believe that Christopher Marlowe, on the other hand, was directly connected to the creation of the Shakespearean plays. Analysis presented in this work will show that he was certainly involved in the development of their hidden satirical system that attacked Christianity. As explained by 'The Marlowe Society':

Marlowe was a child of the English Renaissance and the Reformation, which was also that troubled period called by the great scholar Dame Frances Yates, "*the false dawn of the Enlightenment*", which was doomed to suppression and delay. He shared his birth year, 1564, with Galileo (and with Shakespeare, but that fact is never mentioned by the Shakespearean academic authors). It was a dangerous time in which to express an eager interest in the new scientific discoveries that were exciting the minds of intellectuals all over Europe.

In England Sir Walter Raleigh and the young (9th) Earl of Northumberland, Henry Percy (also born in 1564), led a group of intellectuals, a select band of advanced thinking noblemen,

---

[50] Anne Underwood, 'Was the Bard a Woman?', *Newsweek*, 2004 <http://www.newsweek.com/was-bard-woman-128759> [accessed 10 March 2014].

courtiers and educated commoners, including mathematicians, astronomers, voyagers who had explored the New World, geographers, philosophers and poets. They formed an esoteric club nicknamed "The School of Night" which met secretly to discuss this forbidden knowledge, always 'behind closed doors'. Marlowe became a member of this close circle, who were called Free-Thinkers and were all stigmatized as "Atheists" in order to blacken them in the eyes of the ignorant. [...]

A most important member of Sir Walter Raleigh's circle was the advanced thinker, brilliant mathematician and astronomer, Thomas Hariot. He was in the patronage of both Raleigh and the Earl of Northumberland, the latter nicknamed the "Wizard Earl" for his love of experimenting with chemistry for which he had laboratories built into all his houses.

Hariot, who has been called "the greatest scientific mind before Newton", was in secret correspondence with Johannes Kepler, who discovered that the orbits of the planets were not circular but elliptical. Hariot was Marlowe's friend in this circle, with whom he was often seen browsing at the bookstalls in St Paul's churchyard.

These Free Thinkers discussed a wide range of subjects and were avid in their pursuit of all knowledge. Such men, in the eyes of the church, were dangerous. The Earl of Northumberland had at an early age dedicated his life to the pursuit of knowledge. He was eventually imprisoned in the Tower of London by King James I for almost sixteen years on a false charge of involvement in the Gunpowder Plot, just as Sir Walter Raleigh was falsely charged, also by King James, with conspiring with the Spaniards. In fact, King James had a paranoid fear of these brilliant men because he suspected them of exercising magical powers, which the superstitious King held in terror. Both were accused of the "vile heresy" of Atheism. It was this that was also the cause of Marlowe's tragedy.

In 1593, Marlowe was apparently murdered under circumstances that have remained a matter of much speculation. While scholars have not conclusively linked Marlowe's murder specifically to his stance against Christianity, there is a clear path of circumstantial evidence leading to that conclusion. Shortly before Marlowe's death, the Court of the Star Chamber placed him under investigation. This was the dreaded institution that dealt with matters of heresy and was the English equivalent of the Holy Roman Inquisition. It was empowered to use torture to obtain confessions, and operated without a jury or written record.

A warrant was issued for Marlowe ordering that he be brought before the Council. The warrant indicated that Marlowe could be found at the house of Thomas Walsingham, brother of Francis Walsingham, the Queen's minister and a Star Chamber member. It is possible that Francis Walsingham had Marlowe under a form of house arrest at this point. At about the same time, Richard Baines, one of Walsingham's paid informants, wrote a letter indicating Marlowe's threat to Christianity, stating: "I think all men in Christianity ought to endeavor that the mouth of so dangerous a member may be stopped." His letter also made a number of absurd accusations against Marlowe — for example, that he believed that Jesus was a bastard and a homosexual and that his mother was a whore.

More interesting is the fact that Marlowe was accused of having some unmentioned *information* about Christianity that was dangerous to the religion. For example, Richard Cholmeley was said to have written: "... Marlowe is able to show more sound reasons for atheism than any divine in England is able to give to prove divinity". Cholmeley also allegedly claimed that Marlowe had read an Atheist lecture to Sir Walter Raleigh and other members of The School of the Night.[51]

As shown below by the analysis of the satire hidden within his play *The Jew of Malta,* Marlowe was indeed aware of the fact that the Flavians had invented Christianity. At some point, Marlowe decided to make a public declaration about the real origins of the religion and wrote a book to that effect—at least according to Simon Aldrich, who wrote a letter in which he stated: "Marlowe

---

[51] Peter Farey, 'Marlowe's Sudden and Fearful End', 2011
   <http://www2.prestel.co.uk/rey/sudden.htm> [accessed 11 March 2014].

was an atheist and had writ a book against scripture, how it was all one man's making."[52]

The government was successful in censoring Marlowe's 'book against scripture', however, and no copy of it has ever been found. Based upon the understanding of the Gospels' satirical system that Marlowe showed in his play *The Jew of Malta*, however, if a copy of his work ever comes to light I am certain it will contain essentially the same information as presented in *Caesar's Messiah*. The only sure difference is that his will have been well written.

The original Coroner's Inquisition into the death of Christopher Marlowe was discovered in 1925 by Leslie Hotson and was presented in his book *The Death of Christopher Marlowe*.[53] The document describes a fateful dinner shared by Christopher 'Morley' and 'Ingram' (that is, Ingram Frazier):

> ...& after supper the said Ingram & Christopher Morley...uttered one to the other divers malicious words for the reason that they could not be at one nor agree about the payment of the sum of pence, that is, le recknynge, ...Christopher Morley of a sudden & of his malice towards the said Ingram...maliciously drew the dagger of the said Ingram...& there maliciously gave the aforesaid Ingram two wounds on his head...whereupon the said Ingram...in defense of his life, with the dagger aforesaid...gave the said Christopher a mortal wound over his right eye of the depth of two inches & of the width of one inch; of which mortal wound the aforesaid Christopher Morley then & there instantly died;

Before this report surfaced, Marlowe was often portrayed as having been killed in a drunken pub fight with some ruffians. However, from the report, we learn that the building where the "pub fight" occurred was not a tavern, but a personal residence owned by a Mrs. Bull, a relative to Lord Burghley, the Treasurer of England. Historical records show that the man accused of

---

[52] Paul H. Kocher, *Christopher Marlowe* (New York: Russell and Russell, 1962), p. 30.

[53] Leslie Hotson, *The Death of Christopher Marlowe* (Nonesuch Press, 1925).

killing Marlowe, Ingram Frizer, was Thomas Walsingham's 'serving man'. The Queen pardoned Frizer within four weeks of the crime, an unusually short interval. Elizabeth also used the era's equivalent of the British Secrets Act to make any further investigation of the murder impossible, and she limited inquires into Frizer's crime to only those that were raised by her own Court. This legal maneuver assured that the case could not be reopened even if new evidence surfaced.

The discovery that Marlowe was allegedly killed over a dispute concerning *"le recknynge"*, the 'reckoning' or bill for the meal, enabled another scholar, O.W.F. Lodge, to see the connection between Marlowe's death and the following passage from *As You Like It* delivered by the clown Touchstone:[54]

> "When a man's verses cannot be understood, nor a man's good wit be seconded by the forward child, understanding, it strikes a man more dead than a great reckoning in a little room." (III, 3, 9-12)

Lodge noted the obvious conceptual parallels between the Shakespeare passage and Marlowe's death and pointed out that Marlowe was undoubtedly on the playwright's mind when he wrote *As You Like It,* as the Bard had also given Phebe a quotation from Marlowe's *Hero and Leander,* attributing it to a "dead Shepard". He also pointed out that in addition to 'reckoning' and 'struck dead', the passage had another odd parallel to Marlowe. In Marlowe's play *The Jew of Malta* there is a passage that also uses the expression "in a little room".

> And thus methinks should men of judgment frame
> Their means of traffic from the vulgar trade,
> And, as their wealth increaseth, so inclose
> Infinite riches in a little room.

> *(I, 1)*

---

[54] Oliver Lodge, 'Shakespeare and the Death of Marlowe', *Times Literary Supplement*, 1925.

Since Lodge's 1925 critique, many scholars have accepted this connection, though none has offered a good explanation as to why Shakespeare thought it was appropriate material for a clown. This is because the meaning of the three-way connection between the Coroner's Inquest into Marlowe's death and Shakespeare's and Marlowe's passages containing the phrase 'in a little room' can only understood by someone who was familiar with the hidden satire that lies within *The Jew of Malta.*

As noted earlier, Marlowe had somehow learned about the true meaning of the Gospels and *"had writ a book against scripture, how it was all one man's making."* But before Marlowe wrote his explicit denunciation of Christianity, he had written a number of plays and poems that attacked the religion satirically. One of these was *The Jew of Malta,* written around 1590.

Marlowe's plays are as interesting and as important as Shakespeare's in their depiction of the origin of Christianity and deserve an entire book explaining them, but within this work I shall only analyze *The Jew of Malta,* as it suffices to show how Marlowe's work was seminal to 'Shakespeare'

MARLOWE'S THE JEW OF MALTA

The *Jew of Malta* begins with a prologue spoken by 'Machevill', obviously a personification of 'Machiavelli', the Italian philosopher who (possibly satirically) advocated that rulers abandon morality in their use of authority. Machevill's speech takes on a religious connotation when he states that those who use his principles shall *"attain To Peter's chair"*, and lays out the basic moral framework of the play by stating that *"religion is but a childish toy, And I hold that there is no sin but ignorance."* He notes that kings who claim that they have some 'right' to the throne are naïve, and mentions that Caesar seized his empire through force and not any imagined 'right'. *"Many will talk of title to a crown. What right had Caesar to the empire?"* Obviously Marlowe is addressing a pressing issue of his day, the 'divine right' claimed by Christianity's rulers. The lead character of *The Jew of Malta,* Barabas, like the Popes and the Caesars, "favors" the nihilism of 'Machevil': *"I crave but this,—grace him as he deserves, And let him not be entertain'd the worse Because he favors me."*

Though the concepts in Machevill's soliloquy seem disjointed, they create a precise conceptual matrix that aligns to the Gospel's hidden satire. In other words, 'Machevill' is stating that Caesar saw religion as a toy to fool the ignorant and that this perspective was shared by those who "attained Peter's chair" and became Pope. The reason that the Caesar and the Pope shared the same philosophy was because a single group of men sharing a single mindset 'attained' both seats. And bear in mind that the Caesars held the title of Pontifex Maximus, the head of the Roman religion, which eventually became the title of the Roman Catholic Pope.

'Barabas' is a composite Hebrew word meaning 'son of the father' and was the name given to the individual who was tried alongside Jesus. As recorded by Origen, his full name was 'Jesus Barabas', and, as shown in *Caesar's Messiah,* this 'individual' was part of the comedy in the Gospels whereby a herd of 'Jesuses', who were all 'sons of the father', wandered about at the conclusions of the different Gospels. The many 'Jesus Barabases' created the confusion needed by Titus to switch himself for the Jew's Messiah and become the final 'Jesus' of the Gospels. Marlowe was aware of this comic theme and named his lead 'Barabas' to link to it.

In the play, Barabas positively relishes the murder of Christians. He poisons an entire nunnery including his own daughter, who has converted to Christianity. This portrayal has led to the understanding that Marlowe was anti-Semitic. However, this villainous portrayal may have been a necessary perspective for a playwright writing about Jews in England during the era. Marlowe left information hidden within the play to record Barabas's justification for his behavior. It is interesting to compare the typology in the Jew of Malta with that of Shakespeare's *Merchant of Venice* analyzed below. Marlowe's typology is cruder, and one can clearly see the development of the veiled Jewish literary response to the Gospels when comparing the two plays. While Marlowe's character Barabas's knowledge has rendered him an evil, murderous philosophical nihilist, we will see that Shakespeare's characters have a goal greater than themselves, as they are working for a general purpose of promoting Jewish interests.

When the play introduces Barabas, he is counting his enormous fortune, which he describes in loving detail. While describing his wealth, he makes the following comment, which is central to the satirical level of *The Jew of Malta*.

> And thus methinks should men of judgment frame
> Their means of traffic from the vulgar trade,
> And, as their wealth increaseth, so inclose
> Infinite riches in a little room.

(I, 1)

Marlowe is stating that the 'means of traffic', that is the method by which 'men of judgment' create their wealth, needs to be 'framed' or hidden from ordinary people — the 'vulgar trade'. Overtly, this 'means of traffic' seems to be referring to what we might call "white collar crimes" of high-level commerce. Moreover, I believe it can also be interpreted as a double entendre referring to Christianity, which was invented as a tool to create wealth for Caesar, and was still being used in Marlowe's lifetime for that purpose by those who profited from their 'divine right'. Only by such magic can "infinite riches" be created and maintained.

Three Jews arrive to inform Barabas that all Jews must go to the senate-house to meet the governor. Marlowe begins the description of Barabas as a person beyond the weakness of mercy by having him make a wry comment about his daughter, which foresees her fate later in the play.

> I have no charge, nor many children,
> But one sole daughter, whom I hold as dear
> As Agamemnon did his Iphigen;
> And all I have is hers.

(I, 1)

Since Agamemnon attempted to sacrifice Iphigen merely to have more favorable winds for his trip to Troy, Barabas's comment does not speak of fatherly love. Nor does Barabas care for his fellow Jews: as the following passage shows, he cares only for himself:

BARABAS

> Hum,—all the Jews in Malta must be there!
> Ay, like enough: why, then, let every man
> Provide him, and be there for fashion-sake.
> If any thing shall there concern our state,
> Assure yourselves I'll look—[aside] unto myself.

(I,1)

When Barabas arrives at the Senate, the government offers the Jews the following terms:

OFFICER

[reads] First, the tribute-money of the Turks shall all be levied amongst the Jews, and each of them to pay one half of his estate.

BARABAS

How! half his estate!—

[Aside]

I hope you mean not mine.

FERNEZE

Read on.

OFFICER

[reads] Secondly, he that denies to pay, shall straight-become a Christian.

BARABAS

How! A Christian! — Hum, — what's here to do?

OFFICER

[reads] Lastly, he that denies this, shall absolutely lose all he has.

(I, 2)

These are the same three choices that Shylock was offered in *Merchant of Venice*. The three choices are historically important, as they are the same ones that the Flavians offered to the messianic Jews. In other words, the Flavians attempted to tax the Jews, and when that failed they attempted to transform their religion into one (Christianity) that would cooperate with the empire, and finally those that refused the offer to become 'Christians' were destroyed.

It is at this point in the play — when the Turks demand their tax — that the broad satirical structure of *The Jew from Malta* begins to become visible. The play is building typologically upon the Romans' war with the Jews, which is why the demand for taxes leads to the siege. In the play, Malta represents Jerusalem, and the Turks take the place of the Romans who besiege the city. Eventually 'Barabas' joins them and lead them into the city and is made governor, which mirrors the Flavian conquest of Jerusalem. At the play's end 'Barabas' is even cannibalized like 'Jesus'.

Marlowe used the 'switching technique' to make the play's meaning difficult to see, but still apparent to the informed reader. When Marlowe wrote this play, playwrights were being executed in England for lampooning the state or its religion, and by switching the religion of the players and cities he made his satire invisible to censors. This reversal of the roles of the Romans in battle of Jerusalem also occurs in *Titus Andronicus* wherein the Romans were the besieged ones and the Goths where the invaders.

Barabas defies the governor, who confiscates his wealth and turns his house into a convent for nuns. Barabas tells his daughter that *"religion hides many mischiefs from suspicion"* and discloses where he has hidden his treasures: he has hidden them inside his house (that is, the convent), beneath the cross of Christianity.

BARABAS

> Nay, back, Abigail,
> And think upon the jewels and the gold;
> The board is marked thus that covers it.

[makes the sign of the cross]

[Aside to ABIGAIL in a whisper]

> Away, accursed, from thy father's sight!

FRIAR JACOMO

Barabas, although thou art in misbelief,
And wilt not see thine own afflictions,
Yet let thy daughter be no longer blind.

BARABAS

Blind friar, I reck not thy persuasions,
— The board is marked thus that covers it

[makes the sign of the cross]

(I,2)

By repeating the image of the 'sign of the cross', Marlowe is
indicating to the reader that something other than what is
suggested by the surface narration lies buried beneath it. As he has
just stated that *"religion hides many mischiefs from suspicion"*,
his meaning is not hard to understand. Marlowe is reiterating that
Christianity itself is the 'means of traffic' by which Barabas
creates his wealth, and that this is the 'treasure' that he has buried
beneath a cross. By linking this wealth to Christianity, Marlowe is
making a broad point. He is exposing the entire system of
European royal authority that was built upon a false religion
designed to keep the masses subservient and give to Caesar and
his heirs the 'divine right' to rob them of their wealth.

Abigail smuggles out her father's treasure at night. At this point,
governor Ferneze decides to break his alliance with the Turks in
return for Spanish protection, thus setting up a parallel to the siege
of Jerusalem, when the Jewish rebels turned to an alliance with the
Parthians for protection. A description of the coming siege
contains an allusion to the fate of the Jews that fought against the
Romans — that none survived to tell the truth to 'Christendom'.

MARTIN DEL BOSCO

So shall you imitate those you succeed;
For, when their hideous force environ'd Rhodes,
Small though the number was that kept the town,
They fought it out, and not a man surviv'd
To bring the hapless news to Christendom   (II, 2)

Barabas meets the son of the governor, Lodowick, who wishes to become a suitor to Barabas's daughter Abigail. In a plan to win revenge against the governor, Barabas promises Abigail to Lodowick even though he knows she is in love with Lodowick's friend Mathias. Barabas buys a slave whose name is Ithamore, a pun meaning 'I the Moor'. As I show below, this is the same Moor/Jew synonym used by Shakespeare. Ithamore is thus a Jew who hates Christians just as Barabas does. It is at this point that Barabas makes one of the clearest statements of the true origin of Christianity to be found in the literature of this period.

BARABAS

> In spite of these swine-eating Christians,
> (Unchosen nation, never circumcis'd,
> Poor villains, such as were ne'er thought upon
> Till Titus and Vespasian conquer'd us,)
> Am I become as wealthy as I was.

(II, 3)

Barabas's comment flatly indicates that 'Christians' were not 'thought upon' until after Titus and Vespasian had conquered Jerusalem. In other words, Marlowe is saying that there were no 'Christians' during the forty years between Jesus's purported death, and the destruction of Jerusalem. While the statement contradicts the traditional Christian perspective, it should be expected from Marlowe, the author of a book indicating that Christianity was all 'one man's doing'.

Returning to the play: 'Mathias' — Josephus's last name — and 'Lodowick' — a name that means 'war fame' — realize that they are both contending for Abigail's hand in marriage. As shown below, Mathias and Lodowick are typological characters representing Josephus and Titus. Marlowe is using his characters to produce a literary punishment for their treatment of Jews and their creation of the Josephus/Gospels typological satire. The connection between Matthias and Josephus bar Mathias is transparent. However, the connection between Titus and Lodowick is not merely through Lodowick's name, but also the fact that he is the son of the governor: echoing the fact that during the siege of Jerusalem, Titus was the son of Caesar.

The following passage is the most important in the play, and clarifies the author's symbolic level. 'Mathias' asks Barabas to borrow his books that he describes as 'comments upon the Maccabees'. Since Marlowe knew that Christians did not exist until Vespasian and Titus had conquered the Jews, he was aware that the Gospels were a 'comment' on the Maccabees. Therefore, the "book or two" Mathias wishes to borrow were the histories of Josephus and the New Testament. As he had with the indication that something mysterious was buried beneath a cross (above), Marlowe has Mathias repeat his request so as to underline its importance to the reader. However, this is the last time the books on the Maccabees are mentioned in the play. The reader must surmise what happened to them.

KATHARINE

Tell me, Mathias, is not that the Jew?

BARABAS

As for the comment on the Maccabees,
I have it, sir, and 'tis at your command.

MATHIAS

Yes, madam, and my talk with him was
About the borrowing of a book or two.

KATHARINE

Converse not with him; he is cast off from heaven.
—Thou hast thy crowns, fellow.—Come, let's away.

MATHIAS

Sirrah Jew, remember the book.

BARABAS

Marry, will I, sir.

(II, 3)

This 'missing' comment on the Maccabees begins a clever hidden satire. The first point the reader needs to grasp is that the books were part of the treasure buried beneath the cross. This must be deduced from the fact that Barabas had given up all of his possessions to the authorities, except for the treasure that had been buried beneath the cross. Though they are never mentioned again, these books dominate the rest of the play.

Barabas's slave 'Ithamore' is his alter ego: another Jew that has no moral concern over murdering Gentiles. The following famous passage describes the pair's hunting down of Christians and has been cited as an example of Marlowe's anti-Semitism. Notice that Barabas gets someone to 'hang' himself with a scroll, and that Ithamore 'prunes' those Christians that journeyed to Jerusalem. In other words, Barabas is reversing the fate the Flavian Emperors dealt out for the Jews and giving it to the Gentiles. It is difficult to say at this point whether Marlowe is cheering for Barabas as he lays these diabolical schemes, or whether he has discovered a Jewish plot against the Gentiles and is wryly going about exposing it. Perhaps he is simultaneously horrified at the discovery of the Flavians' historical deception, and also horrified at the crypto-Jewish response to it.

BARABAS

Now let me know thy name, and therewithal
Thy birth, condition, and profession.

ITHAMORE

Faith, sir, my birth is but mean; my name's
Ithamore; my profession what you please.

BARABAS

Hast thou no trade? then listen to my words,
And I will teach [thee] that shall stick by thee:
First, be thou void of these affections,
Compassion, love, vain hope, and heartless fear;
Be mov'd at nothing, see thou pity none,
But to thyself smile when the Christians moan.

ITHAMORE

O, brave, master! I worship your nose for this.

BARABAS

As for myself, I walk abroad o' nights,
And kill sick people groaning under walls:
Sometimes I go about and poison wells;
And now and then, to cherish Christian thieves,
I am content to lose some of my crowns,
That I may, walking in my gallery,
See 'em go pinion'd along by my door.
Being young, I studied physic, and began
To practice first upon the Italian;
There I enrich'd the priests with burials,
And always kept the sexton's arms in ure
With digging graves and ringing dead men's knells:
And, after that, was I an engineer,
And in the wars 'twixt France and Germany,
Under pretence of helping Charles the Fifth,
Slew friend and enemy with my stratagems:
Then, after that, was I an usurer,
And with extorting, cozening, forfeiting,
And tricks belonging unto brokery,
I fill'd the gaols with bankrupts in a year,
And with young orphans planted hospitals;
And every moon made some or other mad,
And now and then one hang himself for grief,
Pinning upon his breast a long great scroll
How I with interest tormented him.
But mark how I am blest for plaguing them;
—I have as much coin as will buy the town.
But tell me now, how hast thou spent thy time?

ITHAMORE

Faith, master,
In setting Christian villages on fire,
Chaining of eunuchs, binding galley-slaves.
One time I was an hostler in an inn,
And in the night-time secretly would I steal
To travellers' chambers, and there cut their throats:
Once at Jerusalem, where the pilgrims kneel'd,
I strewed powder on the marble stones,

And therewithal their knees would rankle so,
That I have laugh'd a-good to see the cripples
Go limping home to Christendom on stilts.

(II, 3)

The missing 'comments on the Maccabees' begin to make their presence felt as Barabas's plot to bring about the death of Mathias and Lodowick unfolds. This clever scenario, in which Jews conspire behind the scenes to mastermind the 'tragic' deaths of Gentiles, was developed into a subtler genre in the Shakespearean literature.

BARABAS

And mine you have; yet let me talk to her.
—This offspring of Cain, this Jebusite,
That never tasted of the Passover,
Nor e'er shall see the land of Canaan,
Nor our Messias that is yet to come;
This gentle maggot, Lodowick, I mean,
Must be deluded: let him have thy hand,
But keep thy heart till Don Mathias comes.

(II, 3)

As noted above, Barabas has assured Mathias that he will send him the "comment on the Maccabees", referring to the New Testament / Josephus satire. Ithamore then delivers a letter from Barabas to both Mathias and Lodowick, though its contents are not given. Ithamore asks Barabas if the letter is poisoned, and Barabas tells him it is not, but that "it might be done that way": suggesting that the content of the letters might act as poison.

However, when Lodowick confronts Mathias he refers to something — "base things" — that 'Mathias' has written, not Barabas. This seemingly incoherent plot point is critical in understanding the satire. Marlowe has created a puzzle or enigma: who wrote the letter, and what does it contain? Surely this can only be another typological reference to the 'letter' written by

Mathias's ancient 'type' Josephus, the 'comment on the Maccabbees' mentioned earlier. Barabas would understand the contents of such a letter, since he told us that there were no Christians until after Titus conquered the Jews; and Mathias, as a type of Josephus, would also be willing to take credit for the letter's message.

LODOWICK

[Looking at a letter.]

What, dares the villain write in such base terms?

MATHIAS

Thou villian, durst thou court my Abigail?

LODOWICK

I did it; and revenge it, if thou dar'st!

[They fight.]

[Enter BARABAS above.]

BARABAS

O, bravely fought! and yet they thrust not home.
Now, Lodovico! now, Mathias!—So;

[Both fall.]

So, now they have shew'd themselves to be tall fellows.

[CRIES WITHIN]

Part 'em, part 'em!

BARABAS

Ay, part 'em now they are dead. Farewell, farewell!

(III, 2)

Barabas's daughter joins the convent when she learns what her
father has done to Mathias and Lodowick. Barabas, being
thoroughly opposed to anything Christian, decides to poison her,
but before she dies, she writes down how her father arranged for
the Mathias and Lodowick to kill themselves. Once again, the
missing 'comments on the Maccabees' are lying just beneath the
surface narration. She gives the letter to a priest, but he cannot
utter what she has written aloud, as it was given to him during
confession. Over and over again, he begins to describe what
Abigail wrote, but then checks himself. This is a literary device to
inform the reader that he or she should try to understand what the
priest cannot say. What Abigail wrote, and the priests cannot say,
is simply the truth about the Gospels: as Marlowe wrote, "they
were all the work of a man".

[Enter ABIGAIL.]

FRIAR BARNARDINE

What, all dead, save only Abigail!

ABIGAIL

And I shall die too, for I feel death coming.
Where is the friar that convers'd with me?

FRIAR BARNARDINE

O, he is gone to see the other nuns.

ABIGAIL

I sent for him; but, seeing you are come,
Be you my ghostly father: and first know,
That in this house I liv'd religiously,
Chaste, and devout, much sorrowing for my sins;
But, ere I came—

FRIAR BARNARDINE

What then?

ABIGAIL

I did offend high heaven so grievously
As I am almost desperate for my sins;
And one offense torments me more than all.
You knew Mathias and Don Lodowick?

FRIAR BARNARDINE

Yes; what of them?

ABIGAIL

My father did contract me to 'em both;
First to Don Lodowick: him I never lov'd;
Mathias was the man that I held dear,
And for his sake did I become a nun.

FRIAR BARNARDINE

So: say how was their end?

ABIGAIL

Both, jealous of my love, envied each other;
And by my father's practice, which is there

[Gives writing.]

Set down at large, the gallants were both slain.

FRIAR BARNARDINE

O, monstrous villany!

ABIGAIL

To work my peace, this I confess to thee:
Reveal it not; for then my father dies.

FRIAR BARNARDINE

Know that confession must not be reveal'd;
The canon-law forbids it, and the priest
That makes it known, being degraded first,
Shall be condemn'd, and then sent to the fire.

ABIGAIL

So I have heard; pray, therefore, keep it close.
Death seizeth on my heart: ah, gentle friar,
Convert my father that he may be sav'd,
And witness that I die a Christian!

[Dies.]

FRIAR BARNARDINE

Ay, and a virgin too; that grieves me most.
But I must to the Jew, and exclaim on him,
And make him stand in fear of me.

[Re-enter FRIAR JACOMO.]

FRIAR JACOMO

O brother, all the nuns are dead! let's bury them.

FRIAR BARNARDINE

First help to bury this; then go with me,
And help me to exclaim against the Jew.

FRIAR JACOMO

Why, what has he done?

FRIAR BARNARDINE

A thing that makes me tremble to unfold.

FRIAR JACOMO

What, has he crucified a child?

FRIAR BARNARDINE

No, but a worse thing: 'twas told me in shrift;
Thou know'st 'tis death, an if it be reveal'd.
Come, let's away.

(III, 6).

[Enter FRIAR JACOMO and FRIAR BARNARDINE.]

ITHAMORE

Look, look, master. Here come two religious
caterpillars.

BARABAS

I smelt 'em ere they came.

ITHAMORE

God-a-mercy, nose! Come, let's begone.

FRIAR BARNARDINE

Stay, wicked Jew; repent, I say, and stay.

FRIAR JACOMO

Thou hast offended, therefore must be damn'd.

BARABAS

I fear they know we sent the poison'd broth.

ITHAMORE

And so do I, master; therefore speak 'em fair.

FRIAR BARNARDINE

Barabas, thou hast—

FRIAR JACOMO

Ay, that thou hast—

BARABAS

True, I have money; what though I have?

FRIAR BARNARDINE

Thou art a—

FRIAR JACOMO

Ay, that thou art, a—

BARABAS

What needs all this? I know I am a Jew.

FRIAR BARNARDINE

Thy daughter—

FRIAR JACOMO

Ay, thy daughter—

BARABAS

O, speak not of her! then I die with grief.

FRIAR BARNARDINE

Remember that—

FRIAR JACOMO

Ay, remember that—

BARABAS

I must needs say that I have been a great usurer.

FRIAR BARNARDINE

Thou hast committed—

BARABAS

Fornication: but that was in another country;
And besides, the wench is dead.

FRIAR BARNARDINE

Ay, but, Barabas, Remember Mathias and Don
Lodowick.

BARABAS

Why, what of them?

FRIAR BARNARDINE

I will not say that by a forged challenge they met.

(IV, 1)

Ithamore now meets the prostitute Bellamira and her pimp Pilia Borza, who attempt to blackmail Barabas, but he is enraged by their treachery, and poisons them. Before they pass away, Bellamira and Pilia-Borza confess Barabas's crimes to the governor. To avoid punishment, Barabas fakes his own death and is thrown over the city's wall. After his 'resurrection', he joins forces with the Turkish leader Calymath to besiege the city.

Barabas tells Calymath how best to storm the town. The method that Barabas reveals concretely identifies 'Malta' as a parallel to Jerusalem. The city of 'Malta' is conquered when Barabas shows the invaders that there is an underground waterway: "the rock is hollow and of purpose digged, To make a passage for the running streams" (V, 1, 85-6). This was the same method that David used to capture Jerusalem in the Old Testament. David instructed his men to climb the water shaft, now known as Warren's Shaft, to "attack the lame and the blind who David hates" (2 Sam 5:8). In that attack, David had said that whoever made the first attack would become "chief and commander" (I Chronicles 11.6). In the parallel version of the assault given in *Jew of Malta,* the person who plans the attack is Barabas, who is then made governor. The parallelism is extended even to Barabas's daughter 'Abigail', which was the name of David's sister. All of this is, at one level, a subterfuge to mislead pedantic academics into thinking that Marlowe is comparing Barabas to the Biblical King David. However, wiser readers will understand that although Marlowe is establishing that 'Malta' is a type for 'Jerusalem', Barabas and Ithamore should still be identified with the Flavian conquers of Jerusalem — Vespasian and Titus. Of course, the Biblical (that is, the fraudulent) Jesus was said to be from the house of David, so Marlowe's circular ironic connection of Barabas to "Jesus Barabbas" was completed.

The play concludes with the same comic theme that ends the Gospels and so many of the Shakespearean plays: that of the

cannibalistic feast on the body of 'Jesus'. Barabas invites the
Turks into the city, stating that he does not want them to leave
until he has 'feasted them' (V, 5). The fate he has in mind for the
Turks is the same one Titus gave to the Jews: that of unwitting
cannibalism. However, Barabas falls into the "cauldron" he
prepared for the Turks, obviously becoming the 'feast' himself.

Notice the witty question by Calymath, the leader of the Turks in
the following passage describing the 'feast': *"Tell me, you
Christians, what doth this portend?"* This comment is arch irony
from Marlowe, who on a portrait that is believed to be of him had
as his logo a comment on the Eucharist: "That which nourishes
me, destroys me."

KNIGHT

[Within] Sound a charge there!

[A charge sounded within: FERNEZE cuts the cord; the
floor of the gallery gives way, and BARABAS falls into
a caldron placed in a pit.]

[Enter KNIGHTS and MARTIN DEL BOSCO.]

CALYMATH

How now! what means this?

BARABAS

Help, help me, Christians, help!

FERNEZE

See, Calymath! this was devis'd for thee.

CALYMATH

Treason, treason! bassoes, fly!

FERNEZE

No, Selim, do not fly:
See his end first, and fly then if thou canst.

BARABAS

O, help me, Selim! help me, Christians!
Governor, why stand you all so pitiless?

FERNEZE

Should I in pity of thy plaints or thee,
Accursed Barabas, base Jew, relent?
No, thus I'll see thy treachery repaid,
But wish thou hadst behav'd thee otherwise.

BARABAS

You will not help me, then?

FERNEZE

No, villain, no.

BARABAS

And, villains, know you cannot help me now.
—Then, Barabas, breathe forth thy latest fate,
And in the fury of thy torments strive
To end thy life with resolution.
—Know, governor, 'twas I that slew thy son,
—I fram'd the challenge that did make them meet:
Know, Calymath, I aim'd thy overthrow:
And, had I but escap'd this stratagem,
I would have brought confusion on you all,
Damn'd Christian dogs, and Turkish infidels!
But now begins the extremity of heat
To pinch me with intolerable pangs:
Die, life! fly, soul! tongue, curse thy fill, and die!

[Dies.]

CALYMATH

Tell me, you Christians, what doth this portend?

FERNEZE

This train he laid to have entrapp'd thy life;
Now, Selim, note the unhallow'd deeds of Jews;

Thus he determin'd to have handled thee,
But I have rather chose to save thy life.

CALYMATH

Was this the banquet he prepar'd for us?
Let's hence, lest further mischief be pretended.

(V, 4)

It is interesting to note that Marlowe's Jewish protagonist, the antetype to Titus and the Roman Jesus, has ultimately met the same fate as the Jews themselves. That is, he has been boiled and figuratively cannibalized, while the Gentiles have escaped the grisly ending that Barabas devised for them. As we shall see, this is a very different outcome from the early works of 'Shakespeare' where the Jewish heroes are generally successful in achieving vengeance against the gentiles, while avoiding such shameful outcomes for themselves. However, the mockery of the Eucharist in the passage is consistent with the rest of the Shakespearean corpus, as I will show.

Marlowe's death, in May of 1593, ended his efforts to expose the truth about the origins of Christianity. The book he wrote about the religion's origins is gone from history. While some have argued that his death was staged and that he went into some secret refuge where he wrote the rest of the plays, I have no need for that hypothesis. In this book, I will make the case that another author stepped forward who shared Marlowe's understanding of the hidden meaning of the Gospels. She owed much to Marlowe for both the style and content of her writings. She wrote her plays in the blank verse style of prose that Marlowe had developed, and carried on the satire of the Gospels that he had begun with *The Jew of Malta.*

Her name was Emilia Bassano, and she wrote under the name 'Shakespeare'...

TITUS ANDRONICUS

Titus Andronicus was the earliest tragedy and the earliest Roman play attributed to Shakespeare. Given its title and the transparency of the relationship between its plot and the Gospels' satire, it is clear that it was created as an introduction to the symbolic meaning of Shakespeare. This was the play that alerted me to the relationship between Shakespeare's plays and the Gospels' satirical meaning, and it is interesting to consider that I followed a deliberately laid path. In other words, the author of *Titus Andronicus* believed that one day someone would recognize that Titus was 'Jesus' and therefore be drawn to a play that had both the names 'Titus' and, as I show below, 'Andronicus' as its title.

Though Harold Bloom called the play a 'parody' and a 'send up',[55] *Titus Andronicus* has generally been regarded as a 'puzzle play'— that is, one whose meaning has not been determined with any certainty. On its surface it appears to be an example of an Elizabethan genre called the revenge play, although, as F. T. Bowers once remarked, it is 'more like a pageant than a play'.[56] But, however one views the play, it is strangely gruesome spectacle with numerous severed hands, decapitations, a brutal rape and a cannibal supper. The sheer volume of carnage in the play is as much of a puzzle as its plot, until one understands the symbolism behind it. Only then does the meaning of the plot and the numerous mutilations become comprehensible. The plot of *Titus Andronicus* reverses the situation the Flavians encountered during their siege of Jerusalem that they used as the basis for their

---

[55] Harold Bloom, *Shakespeare: The Invention of the Human* (New York: Riverhead Books, 1998), pp. 77–78.

[56] Fredson Bowers, *Elizabethan Revenge Tragedy 1587-1642. [1940].* (Princeton University Press, 1971).

cannibal humor in the Gospels. In other words, in the play it is the Romans — not the Jews — who are in a besieged city, and 'Titus' in Shakespeare's story does not cause the Jews to unwittingly commit cannibalism, but the Gentile nobility.

The play's strange story begins as Saturninus and Bassianus, sons of a recently deceased emperor, are contending for the newly vacant throne. However, the tribune Marcus Andronicus announces that the people have elected his brother Titus, a returning war hero, to serve instead. Titus triumphantly enters the scene with his four sons, a coffin containing the remains of his other 21 sons that were killed in the war, and a group of captured Goths. Titus's son, Lucius, demands that Alarbus, the eldest son of the Goths' Queen Tamora, be turned over to him as a human sacrifice: he intends to *"hew his limbs till they be clean consumed"* (I, 1, 146). Queen Tamora's pleas for mercy go unheeded, and her remaining sons, Chiron and Demetrius, vow their revenge as Alarbus is slaughtered.

Titus turns the throne back over to Saturninus, and they agree that he will take Titus' daughter, Lavinia, as his empress. However, Saturninus strangely praises Tamora as "the hue that I would choose, were I to choose anew", and begins to court her. Bassianus seizes the slighted Lavinia, declaring that she is betrothed to him. Marcus approvingly remarks: *"this prince in justice seizeth but his own"* (I, 1, 284), and all of Titus's sons agree. Titus, however, is outraged at Bassianus's treacherous assault on his dynastic right to dispose of his daughter in marriage according to his will. As Bassianus flees with Lavinia and Marcus, Titus kills his son Mutius as he tries to block Titus's path.

Saturninus, offended by what he perceives as Titus's weakness and unfaithfulness, and Lavinia's duplicity and unavailability, chooses Tamora to be his empress. He seems rather more delighted than dismayed to be marrying Tamora rather than Lavinia.

At this point 'Aaron the Moor' becomes the play's central character. Standing in front of the imperial palace in Act II, scene

1, Aaron delights that Tamora is now the Queen of Rome, and boasts:

> Then, Aaron, arm thy heart, and fit thy thoughts,
> To mount aloft with thy imperial mistress,
> And mount her pitch, whom thou in triumph long
> Hast prisoner held, fetter'd in amorous chains
> And faster bound to Aaron's charming eyes
> Than is Prometheus tied to Caucasus.
> Away with slavish weeds and servile thoughts!
> I will be bright, and shine in pearl and gold,
> To wait upon this new-made empress.
> To wait, said I? to wanton with this queen,
> This goddess, this Semiramis, this nymph,
> This siren, that will charm Rome's Saturnine,
> And see his shipwreck and his commonweal's.

(II, 1, 12-24)

With this, the playwright has set up an identical subplot to the Decius Mundus puzzle in Josephus, with Saturninus in the role of the cuckold husband, Aaron as the divine pretender Decius Mundus, and Tamora as Paulina, the victim of his masquerade.

Aaron proceeds with his plan to destroy Saturninus and Titus and their households. Tamora's sons enter, lusting after Lavinia and planning to woo her. They draw their swords to contend over which of them will court her, but Aaron persuades them that if they rape her instead, they can both have her at the same time. Next, Aaron plots with Tamora: she is to argue with Bassanius, and then call upon her sons to avenge Bassanius's (imagined) insults. Bassanius is murdered, and Titus's sons Martius and Quintis are framed for the murder, falsely convicted, and executed. After raping Lavinia, Tamora's sons cut off her hands and tongue, rendering her mute.

Aaron informs Titus that the emperor has agreed that if Titus cuts off his hand he will spare his sons. Aaron 'prunes' Titus's hand and sends it to the emperor, but it returns with a bag containing the heads of Titus's sons.

Outside the city a Goth finds Aaron hiding. Aaron has had an affair with Tamora, who has had a child by him. Tamora's affair with Aaron has been foreseen by her name, which was invented by the playwright and is a condensation of the Italian words *T'amo mora*, meaning, 'I love you Moor'. His captors bring Aaron and his child to Lucius, who orders both Aaron and his child 'hung on a tree' or crucified. Aaron begs Lucius for the life of his 'royal child' and tells Lucius he will reveal all that he has done if he spares them. Lucius agrees, and Aaron is able to have the child removed from the cross. He then informs Lucius of the plots he and Tamora have carried out.

After Titus learns of his daughter's rape and mutilation, he seems to go insane. He attempts to communicate his misfortune to the gods by writing letters to them and then shooting these missives into the sky. A clown appears whom Titus thinks is bringing news from Heaven, and he sends the clown to the Emperor Saturninus with a private communication whose contents are not revealed to the readers of the play. The Emperor has the clown hung after he reads Titus's correspondence.

Tamora and her sons come to Titus presenting themselves as Revenge, Rapine and Murder, and offer him their assistance, but Titus recognizes them, sends Tamara away, and seizes her sons. A grand banquet is served. Titus asks Saturninus if a woman who has been raped, should be allowed to live on in her shame. Saturninus answers 'no', and Titus reveals that Lavinia has been raped, and he kills her. Identifying Tamora's sons as the rapists, he announces that they have already been baked into the pie that Tamora is eating. Then Titus kills Tamora, Saturninus kills Titus, and Lucius kills Saturninus, completing the cycle of revenge. Lucius is acclaimed as the new Emperor, and pronounces the sentence that Aaron is to be buried alive, but Aaron's child is allowed to live.

Several parallels between the play's seemingly incoherent plot and the Gospel's satire are apparent even on its surface. The central satirical element of the Gospels concerns the Jewish Messiah 'Eleazar', who Titus Flavius 'pruned' like an olive tree and was cannibalized by his followers. The amputation of limbs and cannibalism are also themes in *Titus Andronicus*, where three hands are amputated, two characters are 'delimbed', and Titus himself has his hand 'pruned'. Moreover, at the play's conclusion Titus repeats his namesake's 'achievement' by causing characters to eat human flesh without their knowing it.

Titus Andronicus was so entitled to indicate some connection between the play and Titus Flavius. The character's surname 'Andronicus' was also chosen to create a link to the Flavian emperor. Andronicus was the individual named in 2 Maccabees who was a conqueror of Jerusalem and received treasure stolen from its Temple (2 Macc. 4; 30-38). As Andronicus and Titus Flavius are among a handful of individuals to have sacked Jerusalem and taken artifacts taken from its Temple, the linkage of their names was a deliberate clue. In other words, the author intended the reference to 'Andronicus' — the sacker of Jerusalem's temple — to help the reader recognize the play's symbolic linkage to the 'Titus' who was history's most famous sacker of Jerusalem's temple — Titus Flavius. The clue created by combining the two names had its intended result, and was the reason I was curious regarding the play in the first place and began to study it.

The premise that the author linked his 'Titus' to the Flavian Titus is confirmed by the passage given below. One of the puzzles of *Titus Andronicus* is the exchange between Titus and his brother 'Marcus', who killed a fly with a knife. The odd passage is tangential to the storyline but for some reason the author felt required to spend 30 lines on the subject (III, 2, 52-80). Notice that the playwright 'underlined' the fact that the 'fly killer' was a 'brother of Titus'.

TITUS ANDRONICUS

What dost thou strike at, Marcus, with thy knife?

MARCUS

At that that I have kill'd, my lord; a fly.

TITUS ANDRONICUS

Out on thee, murderer! thou kill'st my heart;
Mine eyes are cloy'd with view of tyranny:
A deed of death done on the innocent
Becomes not Titus' brother:
get thee gone: I see thou art not for my company.

MARCUS

Alas, my lord, I have but kill'd a fly. (III, 2, 52-59)

A classically educated reader will recognize that the 'brother of Titus' who stabbed flies in Shakespeare's play is an obvious spoof of Titus Flavius's brother Domitian. Domitian also made a habit of stabbing flies, and was the only patrician known for this strange proclivity. Suetonius wrote:

> At the beginning of his reign he (Domitian) used to spend hours in seclusion every day, doing nothing but catch flies and stab them with a keenly-sharpened stylus. Consequently, when someone once asked whether anyone was in there with Caesar, Vibius Crispus made the witty reply: "Not even a fly." (Suetonius, Domitian, 3)

Further, the character called 'Lucius' was named 'Vespasian' in the surviving 1619 German text, showing that some early editor of the play clearly recognized that the play was a comment upon the Flavian Emperors.

The playwright provided a more subtle way of understanding that the play is a comment on the Flavians by the fact that the plot *reverses* the situation they encountered during their siege of Jerusalem and parodied in the Gospels. The most obvious reversals of circumstance are that the Romans — not the Jews — are the ones in a besieged city and that the 'Titus' in this story causes the Roman nobility to commit cannibalism, rather than the Jews.

But if the author of *Titus Andronicus* deliberately linked the play to the Flavian Emperors, what was the purpose?

The key to understanding the play's symbolic level is Aaron, who is described as a 'Moor'. Though Shakespeare's use of the term 'Moor' has often been seen as describing someone of African (Negro) descent, in Elizabethan England the word could be applied to any dark-skinned person. In the Shakespearean literature, the term is used as a euphemism for Jews. For example, Othello, Shakespeare's most famous 'Moor', indicated in his death soliloquy that he was a Jew by referring to himself as a 'base Judean' and a 'circumcised dog'. Further, Emilia Bassano's family were swarthy Moroccan Jews who were referred to as 'black' by Gentiles. They called themselves 'Moors' and took the mulberry tree (morus) as their family's symbol.

In the case of the character Aaron, the playwright makes his Jewishness obvious by giving him the Biblical name of the grandson of the founder of the priestly Levite tribe. This was the ancestral tribe of the Maccabees, the Jewish messianic family that Titus inserted himself into.

To understand Aaron's role in the play's symbolic level one must first recognize that the playwright used Josephus as a 'type' for the character. The character's very name begins the linkage, as Josephus claimed to have been a member of the tribe of Aaron. Aaron is also described as *"Chief architect and plotter of these woes"* (V, 3, 122), which could be only a slight exaggeration of Josephus's importance in the Roman conspiracy to create Christianity. Aaron is also like Josephus in that he became an advisor to the besiegers of a city after they had captured him.

The authors of the Gospels created a typological connection between 'Joseph of Arimathea' and Josephus bar Mathias by having each of the 'Josephs' take down from a cross someone crucified in a group of three men who miraculously survived. Moreover, 'Joseph of Arimathea' is a pun on 'Joseph bar Mathias'. The *Gospel of Barnabas,* a non-canonical Gospel from the middle ages, does not even bother with the wordplay and states that the name of the individual who took Jesus down from the cross was Joseph of 'Barimathea'. Joseph of Arimathea is also referred to as a 'counselor', which was the same as Josephus' role with Titus and Aaron's role in *Titus Andronicus.*

The following passage from Josephus' autobiography describes how Josephus bar Matthias took the 'Messiah' down from the cross.

> Moreover, when the city Jerusalem was taken by force, I was sent by Titus Caesar, to a certain village called Thecoa, in order to know whether it were a place fit for a camp. As I came back, I saw many captives crucified, and remembered three of them as my former acquaintance. I was very sorry at this in my mind, and went with tears in my eyes to Titus, and told him of them. So he immediately commanded them to be taken down, and to have the greatest care taken of them, in order to their recovery; yet two of them died under the physician's hands, while the third recovered. (Josephus, Vita, 26)

Knowing that the Joseph of Arimathea's actions in the Gospels 'foresaw' Josephus bar Matthias bringing a 'royal child' down from the cross clarifies the meaning of the following amazing passage from *Titus Andronicus*. This is the passage that alerted me to the hidden satire in the Shakespearean literature. Aaron continues the typology begun by 'Joseph of Arimathea' by bringing yet *another* 'royal child' down from a cross. Notice that Shakespeare makes the point that the child is to be crucified with the exact words that Paul used in describing Jesus' crucifixion — "hanged on a tree" (Acts 5:30).

The passage begins with Aaron and his 'royal child' being captured and brought for judgment to Lucius, Titus's son who has been made leader of the Goths.

[Enter a Goth, leading AARON with his Child in his arms]

SECOND GOTH

Renowned Lucius, from our troops I stray'd
To gaze upon a ruinous monastery;
And, as I earnestly did fix mine eye
Upon the wasted building, suddenly
I heard a child cry underneath a wall.
I made unto the noise; when soon I heard
The crying babe controll'd with this discourse:

'Peace, tawny slave, half me and half thy dam!
Did not thy hue bewray whose brat thou art,
Had nature lent thee but thy mother's look,
Villain, thou mightst have been an emperor:
But where the bull and cow are both milk-white,
They never do beget a coal-black calf.
Peace, villain, peace!'—even thus he rates the
babe,—
'For I must bear thee to a trusty Goth;
Who, when he knows thou art the empress' babe,
Will hold thee dearly for thy mother's sake.'
With this, my weapon drawn, I rush'd upon him,
Surprised him suddenly, and brought him hither,
To use as you think needful of the man.

LUCIUS

O worthy Goth, this is the incarnate devil
That robb'd Andronicus of his good hand;
This is the pearl that pleased your empress' eye,
And here's the base fruit of his burning lust.
Say, wall-eyed slave, whither wouldst thou convey
This growing image of thy fiend-like face?
Why dost not speak? what, deaf? not a word?
A halter, soldiers! **Hang him on this tree.**
And by his side his fruit of bastardy.

AARON

Touch not the boy; he is of royal blood.

LUCIUS

Too like the sire for ever being good.
First hang the child, that he may see it sprawl;
A sight to vex the father's soul withal.
Get me a ladder.

[A ladder is brought, which **Aaron is made to ascend**]

AARON

Lucius, save the child,
And bear it from me to the empress.
If thou do this, I'll show thee wondrous things,
That highly may advantage thee to hear:

If thou wilt not, befall what may befall,
I'll speak no more but 'Vengeance rot you all!'

[...]

AARON

First know thou, I begot him on the empress.

LUCIUS

O most insatiate and luxurious woman!

In the following lines the author repeats the concept of 'trimming'
human limbs creating an enigma the reader must decode. In other
words, the reader must recognize that the author is typologically
linking to Josephus' version of a crucifixion which also described
a 'trimming' or 'pruning'.

AARON

Tut, Lucius, this was but a deed of charity
To that which thou shalt hear of me anon.
'Twas her two sons that murder'd Bassianus;
They cut thy sister's tongue and ravish'd her
And cut her hands and trimm'd her as thou saw'st.

LUCIUS

O detestable villain! call'st thou that trimming?

AARON

Why, she was wash'd and cut and trimm'd, and 'twas
Trim sport for them that had the doing of it.

LUCIUS

O barbarous, beastly villains, like thyself!

AARON

Indeed, I was their tutor to instruct them:
...I play'd the cheater for thy father's hand,
And, when I had it, drew myself apart

And almost broke my heart with extreme laughter:
I pry'd me through the crevice of a wall
When, for his hand, he had his two sons' heads;
Beheld his tears, and laugh'd so heartily,
That both mine eyes were rainy like to his...

[...]

LUCIUS

Bring down the devil; for he must not die
So sweet a death as hanging presently.

AARON

If there be devils, would I were a devil,
To live and burn in everlasting fire,
So I might have your company in hell,
But to torment you with my bitter tongue!

(V, 1, 20-150)

Throughout the play 'Aaron' inflicts one torture after another on
Titus to satirically punish Titus Flavius for his crimes against the
Jews. He causes his sons to be beheaded and his daughter to be
raped and mutilated. Aaron even tricks Titus into letting him
'prune' off one of his hands by claiming that by doing so he will
win the release of his sons. In the following passage Titus watches
helplessly as his sons are led off to be beheaded, a plight that Titus
Flavius handed to many Jews.

[Enter Judges, Senators and Tribunes, with MARTIUS
and QUINTUS, bound, passing on to the place of
execution; TITUS going before, pleading]

TITUS ANDRONICUS

Hear me, grave fathers! noble tribunes, stay!
For pity of mine age, whose youth was spent
In dangerous wars, whilst you securely slept;
For all my blood in Rome's great quarrel shed;
For all the frosty nights that I have watch'd;
And for these bitter tears, which now you see
Filling the aged wrinkles in my cheeks;

Be pitiful to my condemned sons,
Whose souls are not corrupted as 'tis thought.
For two and twenty sons I never wept,
Because they died in honour's lofty bed.

[Lieth down; the Judges, & c., pass by him, and Exeunt]

O reverend tribunes! O gentle, aged men!
Unbind my sons, reverse the doom of death;
And let me say, that never wept before,
My tears are now prevailing orators.

(III, 1, 1-26)

Titus then finds out that, just as his namesake did to the Jewish
Messiah, his daughter has been 'pruned', that is her arms and
tongue have been cut off.

[Enter MARCUS and LAVINIA]

MARCUS ANDRONICUS

Titus, prepare thy aged eyes to weep;
Or, if not so, thy noble heart to break:
I bring consuming sorrow to thine age.

TITUS ANDRONICUS

Will it consume me? let me see it, then.

MARCUS ANDRONICUS

This was thy daughter.

TITUS ANDRONICUS

Why, Marcus, so she is.

LUCIUS

Ay me, this object kills me!

TITUS ANDRONICUS

Faint-hearted boy, arise, and look upon her.
Speak, Lavinia, what accursed hand
Hath made thee handless in thy father's sight?
What fool hath added water to the sea,
Or brought a faggot to bright-burning Troy?
My grief was at the height before thou camest,
And now like Nilus, it disdaineth bounds.
Give me a sword, I'll chop off my hands too;
For they have fought for Rome, and all in vain;
And they have nursed this woe, in feeding life;
In bootless prayer have they been held up,
And they have served me to effectless use:
Now all the service I require of them
Is that the one will help to cut the other.
'Tis well, Lavinia, that thou hast no hands;
For hands, to do Rome service, are but vain.

LUCIUS

Speak, gentle sister, who hath martyr'd thee?

MARCUS ANDRONICUS

O, that delightful engine of her thoughts
That blabb'd them with such pleasing eloquence,
Is torn from forth that pretty hollow cage,
Where, like a sweet melodious bird, it sung
Sweet varied notes, enchanting every ear!

LUCIUS

O, say thou for her, who hath done this deed?

MARCUS ANDRONICUS

O, thus I found her, straying in the park,
Seeking to hide herself, as doth the deer
That hath received some unrecuring wound.

TITUS ANDRONICUS

It was my deer; and he that wounded her
Hath hurt me more than had he killed me dead:
For now I stand as one upon a rock
Environed with a wilderness of sea,

Who marks the waxing tide grow wave by wave,
Expecting ever when some envious surge
Will in his brinish bowels swallow him.
This way to death my wretched sons are gone;
Here stands my other son, a banished man,
And here my brother, weeping at my woes.
But that which gives my soul the greatest spurn,
Is dear Lavinia, dearer than my soul.
Had I but seen thy picture in this plight,
It would have madded me: what shall I do
Now I behold thy lively body so?
Thou hast no hands, to wipe away thy tears:
Nor tongue, to tell me who hath martyr'd thee:
Thy husband he is dead: and for his death
Thy brothers are condemn'd, and dead by this.
Look, Marcus! ah, son Lucius, look on her!
When I did name her brothers, then fresh tears
Stood on her cheeks, as doth the honey-dew
Upon a gather'd lily almost wither'd.

MARCUS ANDRONICUS

Perchance she weeps because they kill'd her
husband;
Perchance because she knows them innocent.

(III, 1, 59-115)

The above passage, like many in Shakespeare's works, uses Ovid's story of Philomel as a metaphor for the fact that Titus Flavius 'raped' the Jews and took away their 'tongue', that is their ability to tell posterity what the Romans had done to them and their religion. In Ovid's story, Philomel was raped and then had her tongue cut out by her attacker so she could not identify him. She therefore wove a tapestry that told the story of her rape and revealed her attacker.

Since Philomel gained her revenge by cooking the child born out of his assault and then serving him to her rapist, Ovid's story works perfectly for someone wishing to reverse the cannibalism satire of the Gospels. Thus, after having her tongue and hands cut off by her rapists, Lavinia (like Philomel) uses her mouth and feet to control a stick and write her attackers' names in the sand. The playwright makes the reference to Philomel obvious by having Lavinia turn the pages of Ovid with her stumps until she reaches the correct story. The playwright is explicitly inviting the reader to make a typological parallel between Lavinia and Philomel, and goes on to mention the need to look at movements in "sequence" "Pattern'd by that the poet here describes". The playwright's reference to 'patterns' refers to the parallel sequences of events between Jesus and Titus's 'ministries', which she knew would be comprehensible to the reader once the satire in the Gospels was made known. Imagery linked to Ovid's character 'Philomel' is used throughout the works of Shakespeare and *Salve Deus* to symbolize the truth as Emilia saw it. Her religion had been 'raped' and 'muted' and could not speak this truth plainly. She therefore created her work as a 'tapestry' that revealed through art what could not be stated plainly, and that portrayed her enemies cannibalizing themselves.

The following statement by 'Titus', made after he has discovered that his daughter has been 'trimmed', is a direct communication from the playwright to the 'informed' reader.

> What shall we do? let us, that have our tongues,
> Plot some device of further misery,
> To make us wonder'd at in time to come.

> *(III, 1, 134-6)*

This is an important statement from 'Titus' that clearly shows that Emilia Bassano understood Titus Flavius's reason for creating the Gospels. Titus had a 'tongue' — the ability to write history — and "plotted' some "further misery" — the humiliation of the Jews he believed would happen after its satirical level was understood — for the express purpose of making posterity "wonder" at him. The context that the statement is made — Titus's misery after learning that his daughter has suffered the fate of the Jewish Messiah — shows Emilia's desire to prevent Titus from obtaining the posthumous glory he sought.

Following Titus's discovery of what has happened to his daughter, Aaron appears and tells Titus that the emperor will pardon his sons if Titus cuts off his hand and sends it to him. Aaron is lying, of course, and no such deal has been struck. The playwright then arranges for Aaron to be the one to deliver the blow that cuts off Titus's hand, thus creating a perfect reversal of the Gospel's satire wherein Titus 'pruned' the Messiah of the family of Aaron. In this version of the story, 'Aaron' is not the one who is pruned, but instead he takes an 'eye for an eye' as instructed by the Hebrew Bible.

[Enter AARON]

AARON

Titus Andronicus, my lord the emperor
Sends thee this word,—that, if thou love thy sons,
Let Marcus, Lucius, or thyself, old Titus,
Or any one of you, chop off your hand,
And send it to the king: he for the same
Will send thee hither both thy sons alive;
And that shall be the ransom for their fault.

TITUS ANDRONICUS

O gracious emperor! O gentle Aaron!
Did ever raven sing so like a lark,
That gives sweet tidings of the sun's uprise?
With all my heart, I'll send the emperor My hand:
Good Aaron, wilt thou help to chop it off?

LUCIUS

Stay, father! for that noble hand of thine,
That hath thrown down so many enemies,
Shall not be sent: my hand will serve the turn:
My youth can better spare my blood than you;
And therefore mine shall save my brothers' lives.

MARCUS ANDRONICUS

Which of your hands hath not defended Rome,
And rear'd aloft the bloody battle-axe,
Writing destruction on the enemy's castle?
O, none of both but are of high desert:
My hand hath been but idle; let it serve
To ransom my two nephews from their death;
Then have I kept it to a worthy end.

AARON

Nay, come, agree whose hand shall go along,
For fear they die before their pardon come.

MARCUS ANDRONICUS

My hand shall go.

LUCIUS

By heaven, it shall not go!

TITUS ANDRONICUS

Sirs, strive no more: such wither'd herbs as these
Are meet for plucking up, and therefore mine.

LUCIUS

Sweet father, if I shall be thought thy son,
Let me redeem my brothers both from death.

MARCUS ANDRONICUS

And, for our father's sake and mother's care,
Now let me show a brother's love to thee.

TITUS ANDRONICUS

Agree between you; I will spare my hand.

LUCIUS

Then I'll go fetch an axe.

MARCUS ANDRONICUS

But I will use the axe.

[Exeunt LUCIUS and MARCUS]

TITUS ANDRONICUS

Come hither, Aaron; I'll deceive them both:
Lend me thy hand, and I will give thee mine.

AARON

[Aside] If that be call'd deceit, I will be honest,
And never, whilst I live, deceive men so:
But I'll deceive you in another sort,
And that you'll say, ere half an hour pass.

[Cuts off TITUS's hand]

[Re-enter LUCIUS and MARCUS]

TITUS ANDRONICUS

Now stay your strife: what shall be is dispatch'd.
Good Aaron, give his majesty my hand:
Tell him it was a hand that warded him
From thousand dangers; bid him bury it
More hath it merited; that let it have.
As for my sons, say I account of them
As jewels purchased at an easy price;
And yet dear too, because I bought mine own.

AARON

I go, Andronicus: and for thy hand
Look by and by to have thy sons with thee.

[Aside]

Their heads, I mean. O, how this villany
Doth fat me with the very thoughts of it!
Let fools do good, and fair men call for grace.
Aaron will have his soul black like his face.

[Exit]

TITUS ANDRONICUS

O, here I lift this one hand up to heaven,
And bow this feeble ruin to the earth:
If any power pities wretched tears, To that I call!

(III, 1, 150-208)

The following passage has been seen as one of Shakespeare's 'puzzles', but is simply a spoof in which the fool mistakes 'Titus' for Titus Flavius, which is the exact understanding that the playwright is trying to get the reader to come to. As the clown believes he is speaking with Titus Flavius, he must also believe that 'Titus' is referring to the Gospels. He refers to Titus as a 'gibbet maker' because Titus Flavius was a 'gibbet maker' or cross-maker: Titus indeed crucified thousands of Jews, including his literary creation 'Jesus'. Another incoherent aspect of the passage that is now sensible is the clown's statement that *'the gibbet-maker says that he hath taken them down again because the man must not be hanged till the next week'*. The clown is simply continuing his 'confusion' by comically 'mistaking' the 'royal child' who will be 'hung on a tree' later in *Titus Andronicus* with those already 'taken down from the cross' in the other stories (the Gospels and *Wars of the Jews*). Titus, for his part, is convinced that the fool is carrying a message from Jupiter (that is, God himself) while the Fool thinks his mission has something to do with a brawl involving his uncle.

Notice the explanatory power of the thesis. This seemingly incoherent dialogue is rendered comprehensible by the understanding it is playing off of Titus' invention of Christianity.

TITUS ANDRONICUS

> We will solicit heaven and move the gods
> To send down Justice for to wreak our wrongs.
> Come, to this gear. You are a good archer, Marcus;
> (He gives them the arrows)
> 'Ad Jovem,' that's for you: here, 'Ad Apollinem:'
> 'Ad Martem,' that's for myself:
> Here, boy, to Pallas: here, to Mercury:
> To Saturn, Caius, not to Saturnine;
> You were as good to shoot against the wind.
> To it, boy! Marcus, loose when I bid.
> Of my word, I have written to effect;
> There's not a god left unsolicited.

MARCUS

Kinsmen, shoot all your shafts into the court:
We will afflict the emperor in his pride.

TITUS ANDRONICUS

Now, masters, draw. (They shoot)
O, well said, Lucius!
Good boy, in Virgo's lap; give it Pallas.

MARCUS

My lord, I aim a mile beyond the moon;
Your letter is with Jupiter by this...

(IV, 3, 51-67)

[Enter a Clown, with a basket, and two pigeons in it]

TITUS ANDRONICUS

News, news from heaven!
Marcus, the post is come.
Sirrah, what tidings? have you any letters?
Shall I have justice? what says Jupiter?

CLOWN

Ho, the gibbet-maker! he says that he hath taken
them down again, for the man must not be hanged till
the next week.

TITUS ANDRONICUS

But what says Jupiter, I ask thee?

CLOWN

Alas, sir, I know not Jubiter; I never drank with him
in all my life.

(IV,3,77-86)

Titus's instruction (below) to the clown to deliver a 'supplication'
is also consistent with this comic theme. In ancient Rome, a
supplication was a religious document notifying of a military

success. It was a synonym for 'Gospel', meaning 'the good news of a military victory.' The fool is, thus, bringing Titus's 'Gospels' to the emperor. Notice above that Titus says he will be 'at hand' when the clown delivers the supplication. Within the play's symbolic framework, he will be 'at hand' because he is the character 'Jesus' in the Gospels, which will be contained 'within' the clown's hand.

TITUS ANDRONICUS

Why, villain, art not thou the carrier?

CLOWN

Ay, of my pigeons, sir; nothing else.

TITUS ANDRONICUS

Why, didst thou not come from heaven?

CLOWN

From heaven! alas, sir, I never came there God
forbid I should be so bold to press to heaven in my
young days. Why, I am going with my pigeons to the
tribunal plebs, to take up a matter of brawl
betwixt my uncle and one of the emperial's men.

MARCUS

Why, sir, that is as fit as can be to serve for
your oration; and let him deliver the pigeons to
the emperor from you.

TITUS ANDRONICUS

Tell me, can you deliver an oration to the emperor
with a grace?

CLOWN

Nay, truly, sir, I could never say grace in all my life.

TITUS ANDRONICUS

Sirrah, come hither: make no more ado,
But give your pigeons to the emperor:

By me thou shalt have justice at his hands.
Hold, hold; meanwhile here's money for thy charges.
Give me pen and ink. Sirrah, can you with a grace
deliver a supplication?

CLOWN

Ay, sir.

TITUS ANDRONICUS

Then here is a supplication for you. And when you
come to him, at the first approach you must kneel,
then kiss his foot, then deliver up your pigeons, and
then look for your reward. I'll be at hand, sir; see
you do it bravely.

(IV, 3, 87-113)

The playwright continues the parody of the Flavian invention of
Christianity by having the clown bring two pigeons to the
emperor. The clown tells Saturninus that God (that is, Titus) and
Saint Stephen say hello. The clown brings the two pigeons to
indicate that the Messiah — Aaron's child — has been born, since
the Gospels (Luke 2:24) state that when the Messiah was born, the
law required that two pigeons be sacrificed.

TAMORA

...How now, good fellow! wouldst thou speak with us?

CLOWN

Yea, forsooth, an your mistership be emperial.

TAMORA

Empress I am, but yonder sits the emperor.

CLOWN

'Tis he. God and Saint Stephen give you good den
(good day): I have brought you a letter and a couple
of pigeons here.

[Saturninus reads the letter]

SATURNINUS

Go, take him away, and hang him presently.

CLOWN

How much money must I have?

TAMORA

Come, sirrah, you must be hanged.

CLOWN

Hanged! by'r lady, then I have brought up a neck to
a fair end.

(IV, 4, 39-50)

The clown gives a salutation in the passage above from "God"
because the fool believes that Titus is Jesus. The fool is executed
because the emperor, understandably, is displeased to receive a
'Gospel' in which Titus claims to be God.

The play concludes with its most obvious reversal of the Gospels'
satire: the scene in which Titus fools, not the Jewish royal family,
but the Gentile nobility into eating human flesh. This passage
completes Aaron's triumph over all the Gentiles, including not
only Titus and the Roman royals, but also Tamora the Goth and
her two sons. Aaron has already humiliated Saturninus by
seducing and impregnating Tamora, in a re-enactment of
Josephus's parody of the Annunciation. Aaron (as a type of Joseph
of Arimathea) confirmed that this child was a 'Messiah' by
bringing the child down from the cross. Now, at this 'feast', some
Gentiles are served as pie, while others are hacked to pieces.
However, one individual surprisingly survives the carnage: the son
of Aaron, the new 'Moorish' — that is Jewish — introduction into
the Roman royal family. The 'royal child' has been inserted into
the Gentile's royal linage to complete the reversal of the Roman
satire in the Gospels whereby Caesar inserted himself into the
Jews' messianic lineage. We can only conjecture whether this
depiction of a Jew inserted into the royal family of the Gentiles
represents a wishful fantasy by Emilia Bassano, or whether she

was depicting a real organization that tried to gain control over the Gentiles by secretly planting crypto Jews in positions of authority.

However, it is interesting to note both the similarities and the differences between Marlowe and 'Shakespeare' in their treatment of their Jewish protagonists. In both cases, the surface presentation is of unremitting and unrepentant evil on the part of the 'Moor', giving an impression that both authors are anti-Semitic, and thus compliant to the political pressures of their times. But while Marlowe's 'Barabas' is boiled and metaphorically cannibalized in the end, 'Aaron' is merely to be buried alive (but with no cannibalistic references) and the survival of his child represents the ultimate success of Aaron's dramatic reversal of the Flavian comic system.

[Enter LUCIUS, MARCUS, and Goths, with AARON prisoner]

LUCIUS

Uncle Marcus, since it is my father's mind
That I repair to Rome, I am content.

FIRST GOTH

And ours with thine, befall what fortune will.

LUCIUS

Good uncle, take you in this barbarous Moor,
This ravenous tiger, this accursed devil;
Let him receive no sustenance, fetter him
Till he be brought unto the empress' face,
For testimony of her foul proceedings:
And see the ambush of our friends be strong;
I fear the emperor means no good to us.

AARON

Some devil whisper curses in mine ear,
And prompt me, that my tongue may utter forth
The venomous malice of my swelling heart!

LUCIUS

Away, inhuman dog! unhallow'd slave!
Sirs, help our uncle to convey him in.

[Exeunt Goths, with AARON. Flourish within]

The trumpets show the emperor is at hand.

[Enter SATURNINUS and TAMORA, with
AEMILIUS, Tribunes, Senators, and others]

SATURNINUS

What, hath the firmament more suns than one?

LUCIUS

What boots it thee to call thyself a sun?

MARCUS ANDRONICUS

Rome's emperor, and nephew, break the parle;
These quarrels must be quietly debated.
The feast is ready, which the careful Titus
Hath ordain'd to an honourable end,
For peace, for love, for league, and good to Rome:
Please you, therefore, draw nigh, and take your
places.

SATURNINUS

Marcus, we will.

[Hautboys sound. The Company sit down at table]

[Enter TITUS dressed like a Cook, LAVINIA veiled,
Young LUCIUS, and others. TITUS places the dishes
on the table]

TITUS ANDRONICUS

Welcome, my gracious lord; welcome, dread queen;
Welcome, ye warlike Goths; welcome, Lucius;
And welcome, all: although the cheer be poor,
'Twill fill your stomachs; please you eat of it.

SATURNINUS

Why art thou thus attired, Andronicus?

TITUS ANDRONICUS

Because I would be sure to have all well,
To entertain your highness and your empress.

TAMORA

We are beholding to you, good Andronicus.

TITUS ANDRONICUS

An if your highness knew my heart, you were.
My lord the emperor, resolve me this:
Was it well done of rash Virginius
To slay his daughter with his own right hand,
Because she was enforced, stain'd, and deflower'd?

SATURNINUS

It was, Andronicus.

TITUS ANDRONICUS

Your reason, mighty lord?

SATURNINUS

Because the girl should not survive her shame,
And by her presence still renew his sorrows.

TITUS ANDRONICUS

A reason mighty, strong, and effectual;
A pattern, precedent, and lively warrant,
For me, most wretched, to perform the like.
Die, die, Lavinia, and thy shame with thee;

[Kills LAVINIA]

And, with thy shame, thy father's sorrow die!

SATURNINUS

What hast thou done, unnatural and unkind?

TITUS ANDRONICUS

Kill'd her, for whom my tears have made me blind.
I am as woful as Virginius was,
And have a thousand times more cause than he
To do this outrage: and it now is done.

SATURNINUS

What, was she ravish'd? tell who did the deed.

TITUS ANDRONICUS

Will't please you eat? will't please your highness
feed?

TAMORA

Why hast thou slain thine only daughter thus?

TITUS ANDRONICUS

Not I; 'twas Chiron and Demetrius:
They ravish'd her, and cut away her tongue;
And they, 'twas they, that did her all this wrong.

SATURNINUS

Go fetch them hither to us presently.

TITUS ANDRONICUS

Why, there they are both, baked in that pie;
Whereof their mother daintily hath fed,
Eating the flesh that she herself hath bred.
'Tis true, 'tis true; witness my knife's sharp point.

[Kills TAMORA]

SATURNINUS

Die, frantic wretch, for this accursed deed!

[Kills TITUS]

LUCIUS

Can the son's eye behold his father bleed?
There's meed for meed, death for a deadly deed!

[Kills SATURNINUS. A great tumult. LUCIUS,
MARCUS, and others go up into the balcony]

MARCUS ANDRONICUS

You sad-faced men, people and sons of Rome,
By uproar sever'd, like a flight of fowl
Scatter'd by winds and high tempestuous gusts,
O, let me teach you how to knit again
This scatter'd corn into one mutual sheaf,
These broken limbs again into one body;
Lest Rome herself be bane unto herself,
And she whom mighty kingdoms court'sy to,
Like a forlorn and desperate castaway,
Do shameful execution on herself.
But if my frosty signs and chaps of age,
Grave witnesses of true experience,
Cannot induce you to attend my words,

[To LUCIUS]

Speak, Rome's dear friend, as erst our ancestor,
When with his solemn tongue he did discourse
To love-sick Dido's sad attending ear
The story of that baleful burning night
When subtle Greeks surprised King Priam's Troy,
Tell us what Sinon hath bewitch'd our ears,
Or who hath brought the fatal engine in
That gives our Troy, our Rome, the civil wound.
My heart is not compact of flint nor steel;
Nor can I utter all our bitter grief,
But floods of tears will drown my oratory,
And break my utterance, even in the time
When it should move you to attend me most,
Lending your kind commiseration.
Here is a captain, let him tell the tale;
Your hearts will throb and weep to hear him speak.

LUCIUS

Then, noble auditory, be it known to you,
That cursed Chiron and Demetrius
Were they that murdered our emperor's brother;
And they it were that ravished our sister:
For their fell faults our brothers were beheaded;
Our father's tears despised, and basely cozen'd
Of that true hand that fought Rome's quarrel out,
And sent her enemies unto the grave.
Lastly, myself unkindly banished,
The gates shut on me, and turn'd weeping out,
To beg relief among Rome's enemies:
Who drown'd their enmity in my true tears.
And oped their arms to embrace me as a friend.
I am the turned forth, be it known to you,
That have preserved her welfare in my blood;
And from her bosom took the enemy's point,
Sheathing the steel in my adventurous body.
Alas, you know I am no vaunter, I;
My scars can witness, dumb although they are,
That my report is just and full of truth.
But, soft! methinks I do digress too much,
Citing my worthless praise: O, pardon me;
For when no friends are by, men praise themselves.

(V, 3, 1-117)

At this point the child of 'Aaron' — which must be remembered is the name of the Jews' Maccabean messianic lineage recorded in the Dead Sea Scrolls — is introduced. His appearance is subtle and its meaning can only be understood in the context of the play being a reversal of the Gospels' typology. The Jewish child is now inside the Gentile's royal lineage just as Caesar had done to the Jews' in the Gospels. The point is that child will eventually rise to the throne.

MARCUS ANDRONICUS

Now is my turn to speak. Behold this child:

[Pointing to the Child in the arms of an Attendant]

Of this was Tamora delivered;
The issue of an irreligious Moor,
Chief architect and plotter of these woes:
The villain is alive in Titus' house,
And as he is, to witness this is true.
Now judge what cause had Titus to revenge
These wrongs, unspeakable, past patience,
Or more than any living man could bear.
Now you have heard the truth, what say you,
Romans?
Have we done aught amiss,—show us wherein,
And, from the place where you behold us now,
The poor remainder of Andronici
Will, hand in hand, all headlong cast us down.
And on the ragged stones beat forth our brains,
And make a mutual closure of our house.
Speak, Romans, speak; and if you say we shall,
Lo, hand in hand, Lucius and I will fall.

AEMILIUS

Come, come, thou reverend man of Rome,
And bring our emperor gently in thy hand,
Lucius our emperor; for well I know
The common voice do cry it shall be so.

ALL

Lucius, all hail, Rome's royal emperor!

MARCUS ANDRONICUS

Go, go into old Titus' sorrowful house,

[To Attendants]

And hither hale that misbelieving Moor,
To be adjudged some direful slaughtering death,
As punishment for his most wicked life.

[Exeunt Attendants]

[LUCIUS, MARCUS, and the others descend]

ALL

Lucius, all hail, Rome's gracious governor!

LUCIUS

Thanks, gentle Romans: may I govern so,
To heal Rome's harms, and wipe away her woe!
But, gentle people, give me aim awhile,
For nature puts me to a heavy task:
Stand all aloof: but, uncle, draw you near,
To shed obsequious tears upon this trunk.
O, take this warm kiss on thy pale cold lips,

[Kissing TITUS]

These sorrowful drops upon thy blood-stain'd face,
The last true duties of thy noble son!

MARCUS ANDRONICUS

Tear for tear, and loving kiss for kiss,
Thy brother Marcus tenders on thy lips:
O were the sum of these that I should pay
Countless and infinite, yet would I pay them!

LUCIUS

Come hither, boy; come, come, and learn of us
To melt in showers: thy grandsire loved thee
well: Many a time he danced thee on his knee,
Sung thee asleep, his loving breast thy pillow:
Many a matter hath he told to thee,
Meet and agreeing with thine infancy;
In that respect, then, like a loving child,
Shed yet some small drops from thy tender
spring, Because kind nature doth require it so:
Friends should associate friends in grief and woe:
Bid him farewell; commit him to the grave;
Do him that kindness, and take leave of him.

YOUNG LUCIUS

O grandsire, grandsire! even with all my heart
Would I were dead, so you did live again!

O Lord, I cannot speak to him for weeping;
My tears will choke me, if I ope my mouth.

[Re-enter Attendants with AARON]

AEMILIUS

You sad Andronici, have done with woes:
Give sentence on this execrable wretch,
That hath been breeder of these dire events.

LUCIUS

Set him breast-deep in earth, and famish him;
There let him stand, and rave, and cry for food;
If any one relieves or pities him,
For the offence he dies. This is our doom:
Some stay to see him fasten'd in the earth.

AARON

O, why should wrath be mute, and fury dumb?
I am no baby, I, that with base prayers
I should repent the evils I have done:
Ten thousand worse than ever yet I did
Would I perform, if I might have my will;
If one good deed in all my life I did,
I do repent it from my very soul.

LUCIUS

Some loving friends convey the emperor hence,
And give him burial in his father's grave:
My father and Lavinia shall forthwith
Be closed in our household's monument.
As for that heinous tiger, Tamora,
No funeral rite, nor man m mourning weeds,
No mournful bell shall ring her burial;
But throw her forth to beasts and birds of prey:
Her life was beast-like, and devoid of pity;
And, being so, shall have like want of pity.
See justice done on Aaron, that damn'd Moor,

By whom our heavy haps had their beginning:
Then, afterwards, to order well the state,
That like events may ne'er it ruinate.

[Exeunt]

(V, 3, 118-199)

Emilia Bassano's understanding of the Flavian typology was
evidentially passed on to certain Jewish groups. Julie Taymor, the
Jewish director of the 1994 film adaptation of *Titus Andronicus*,
choose to conclude the play with a scene of the blonde haired
Lucius carrying the dark skinned child of Aaron into a bright
future. Such a departure from the play's script could only have
been selected by someone who understood the play's symbolic
level.

EMILIA BASSANO

Though Emilia Bassano has escaped the scrutiny of scholars looking for the author of the Shakespearean literature, simply describing her life shows that she is a logical candidate. She was a poet active during the period in which the plays were written, and was the mistress of Lord Hunsdon, who was the sponsor of the Lord Chamberlain's Men, the theatrical company that Shakespeare purportedly owned a share of and that put on many of the plays. Her family was multilingual and came from the area of Italy that was the setting for many of Shakespeare's plays. She had attended the royal court and was thus familiar with the aristocratic mind and language. She had also been exposed to the arcane jargons used in the sport of hawking and the British military that found their way into the plays. And as a woman from a family of Jewish heritage, she would have shared an interest in Judaism with the author of the Shakespearean plays, not a common thing in England during this era. Emilia was the first woman to have ever registered an original poem in England, and is believed by many scholars to have been the 'dark lady' described in Shakespeare's sonnets. In addition to her many surface qualifications, however, she also possessed the true key to creating the Shakespearean literature: an understanding of the satirical system within the Gospels.

To digress, some confusion has arisen over who actually made the discovery that Emilia Bassano was the author of the Shakespearian plays and that they are typological reversals of the Flavians' comic perspective in the NT. To clarify, I would note that after I had made these discoveries I showed them to a colleague, John Hudson, who then went on to produce plays based upon this framework. Hudson has subsequently published a book on this topic, and we discussed these matters in an interview taped by 'Rodeph Emet' on 6/20/2008. John has assured me that he will assert that these are the facts; that I discovered both that Emilia was the author and that the plays were reversals of the Flavians' typology.

THE BASSANO FAMILY

Emilia Bassano came from a family of Sephardic Jews of Moroccan ancestry that had moved to London from Venice in the middle of the sixteenth century after being hired by Henry the eighth as court musicians. The family purchased three contiguous houses in Shoreditch, the area of London where William Shakespeare purportedly lived. They were part of a small Jewish immigration to England brought about by Henry VIII. Henry imported a group of Jewish Bible scholars to help him with his theological struggle with the Papacy concerning divorce. He also imported Italian musicians to improve the quality of his court music and some of these, like the Bassanos, were Jews. [57]

When Henry permitted the immigration of certain Jews, he reversed a long-standing policy. In 1290 over two thousand Jews had been expelled from England, and those who remained were forced to convert to Christianity, though some of them are known to have secretly continued to practice Judaism.[58] In Spain, under similar oppression, the secret Jews became known as Marranos. However, the use of this terminology is no longer acceptable because of its anti-Semitic connotations: the word means "filthy pig" in Spanish.

Henry continued to require that Jews who wished to immigrate be baptized and desist from practicing any Jewish rituals. The consequences for violating this dictum were severe. The Lupos, another family of Jewish musicians who had emigrated from Italy on an invitation from Henry VIII, experienced the full weight of the Christian State's attitude towards Jews who retained their religion. Members within her family's circle were charged with

[57] Roger Prior, 'Jewish Musicians at the Tudor Court', *The Musical Quarterly*, 69 (1983), 253–265.

[58] James Shapiro, *Shakespeare and the Jews* (Columbia University Press, 1996).

secretly practicing Judaism, and a number of them were imprisoned. Two of these — Anthony Moses and Ambrose de Almaliach — died after being racked. This episode would have been well known to Emilia Bassano, as Anthony's son Joseph Lupo married her cousin Laura.

The Bassanos are believed to have taken their name from Bassano, a city in the province of Venice; or, conversely, the city may have taken its name from the family. As the online Jewish Encyclopedia explains:

> City in the province of Venice, Italy. Here, as in all the surrounding places, Jews were living at a very early period, engaged in commerce and industry, and especially in money-lending, as is shown by contemporary documents dating back to 1264. In the first half of the fifteenth century, they formed a large and prosperous community. Subsequently they were persecuted; and, in 1468, a decree of perpetual banishment was issued against them. Nevertheless they returned, only to be again banished by the city council in 1481.
>
> No documents are extant to show the existence of a Jewish congregation, recognized and regulated by law. The Jews were obliged to live huddled together in one little street, still called "Callesella dei Zudii"; but, as their numbers increased, more spacious quarters were assigned to them, which popular tradition still calls "Il Ghetto."
>
> While some of the Jewish families, Bassan, Bassano, Bassani, may have been called from this city, the name is more probably of Hebrew origin. Some slight notices of the Jews of Bassano may be found in the rare pamphlet of Brenteri, "Fondazione del Monte di Pietà," 1882. There are no longer any Jews at Bassano, nor are there any traces of a synagogue or a cemetery.[59]

Bassani or Bassano was the last name of many well-known Rabbis from the region around Venice. It is notable that a number of them were authors and poets and hailed from the exact towns that would

---

[59] 'Bassano', *Jewish Encyclopedia*, 1906 <http://www.jewishencyclopedia.com/articles/2642-bassano> [accessed 14 March 2014].

later be referenced in Shakespeare's Italian plays. One of these was the famous rabbi and poet Samuel Bassani who lived in Verona at the end of the sixteenth century.

In 1548 Baptista Bassano and his four brothers established a contract with Henry VIII to become recorder consorts (musicians) for his court and immigrated to England. Appearing to comply with Henry's wishes, they publicly converted to Christianity and faithfully observed the rituals of the English Protestant church. They may very well have secretly retained their Jewish religious practices and beliefs, but if so, they were successful in concealing any convincing evidence of that fact from the authorities, and from history.

Emilia Bassano was born in London to Margaret Johnson, and Baptista was generally acknowledged as Johnson's domestic partner, and the father of the child. In his will, Baptista referred to Margaret as "my reputed wife", a hedged statement that might conceivably have been related to religious differences; however, Margaret's will clearly identified Baptista as her husband. Margaret Johnson apparently had close relationships with members of the radical Protestant movement, which might have complimented the (possibly radical) Jewish viewpoint coming out of the Bassano side of the family.[60] Emilia was christened at St. Botolph, Bishopsgate, the London neighborhood where foreign musicians and theatre folk lived, on January 27, 1569.[61]

There is a court document given below showing that Emilia's uncles had a confrontation with the authorities in which they were described as being 'black' in skin color and of talking back sharply to the sheriff.

---

[60] Susanne Woods, *Lanyer: A Renaissance Woman Poet* (New York; Oxford: Oxford University Press, 1999), pp. 5–7.

[61] Kari Boyd McBride, 'Biography of Aemilia Lanyer' <http://nzr.mvnu.edu/faculty/trearick/english/rearick/readings/authors/specifi c/lanyer.htm> [accessed 11 March 2014].

"On 22 September 1584, John Spencer, a former Sheriff of London, asked by the Crown to account for his behavior towards Arthur, Edward I and Jeronimo II Bassano, 'which were committed to ward [prison] for their misdemeanor', twice went out of his way to point out that neither he nor any of his fellow law officers knew the identity of the men they were arresting." The occasion was a street skirmish caused by the blocking up of a street by the authorities, which angered the residents who began dismantling the blockage. "At this point the Bassanos came near to the site and stayed talking and looking at the work until they too were ordered to leave. 'They eft soons very obstinately refused,' saying to Spencer, "This is the Queen's ground and we will stand here.' When told that if they would not depart 'by fair means' they would be sent to ward, 'one of them a little black man who was booted answered in a very despiteful manner, saying ,"Send us to ward? Thou were as good (be the words with reverence named) kiss our etc", and another of them being a tall black man said, "Sheriff Spencer, we have as good friends in the court as thou hast and better too."[62]

While the document may seem innocuous, it is absolutely critical to understanding the Shakespearean literature. The passage shows that though the Bassanos, swarthy Sephardic Jews, were routinely called 'black' by the English even though they were not of African (Negro) descent. Emilia was actually called 'the Moor' by her family. This might mean that she had especially dark skin and been a bright target for racial insults; or perhaps she and her family may have been especially conscious of the darkness of her skin in contrast to her English mother. The many 'Moors' or 'Eithiopes' of the plays, and the 'black mistress' of the sonnets, may be readily explained as Emilia Bassano's response to English discrimination against blacks such as herself.[63]

[62] David Lasocki and Roger Prior, *The Bassanos: Venetian Musicians and Instrument Makers in England, 1531-1665* (Aldershot, England; Brookfield, Vt., USA: Scolar Press ; Ashgate Pub. Co., 1995), p. 78.

[63] Considering these facts, it seems improbable that Hilliard's miniature of a pale skinned blue eyed woman 'Mrs Holland' (at the Victoria & Albert Museum) is Emilia, as claimed by Tony Haygarth in 2003.

The passage also sheds light on another important point; the relationship between the Bassanos and the nobility. Being both 'black' and constantly under threat of execution as secret practitioners of Judaism (whether or not such an accusation was even true), the Bassanos played a high stakes game in Elizabethan England. In order to survive in such a hostile environment they needed the protection of 'friends in the court'. But how could such 'friends' be obtained? To survive anywhere in Christendom, Jews needed skills that would make them valuable to those in power. This is perhaps why the Bassano family developed their instrument-making and music-playing talents. These were skills that they could exchange with the nobility for money and a protected status. This intellectually driven, but conspiratorial world was the environment from which 'Shakespeare' sprang.

The British attitude towards dark skinned people during this era is also made clear in the following commission from the Queen to a merchant named Caspar Van Zeuden, which calls on him to arrange for the deportation from the country of the "negroes and blackamoors" that had "crept into the realm".[64]

ORDERS TO EXPEL BLACKAMOORS & NEGROES 1601

—Whereas the Queen's Majesty is discontented at the great numbers of negars and blackamoores which are crept into the realm since the troubles between her Highness and the King of Spain, and are fostered here to the annoyance of her own people...In order to discharge them out of the country, her Majesty hath appointed Caspar Van Zeuden, merchant of Lubeck, for their transportation...This is to require you to assist him to collecty such negroes and blackamoors for this purpose.

Emilia's father died when she was seven, and her family somehow arranged for her to be raised by Susan Wingfield, Countess of Kent, and Margaret, Countess of Cumberland. Emilia wrote about their estate of Cookham Dean in her poem *The Description of Cooke-ham*. She was presumably educated along with the other

---

[64] Eldred D. Jones and Fourah Bay College, *Othello's Countrymen: The African in English Renaissance Drama* (Published on behalf of Fourah Bay College, the University College of Sierra Leone [by] Oxford University Press, 1965).

girls of these noble households, as she later became a tutor to the children of the nobility.

It is difficult to speculate as to how Emilia was able to maintain her Jewish identity under such circumstances. However, if the other evidence of Emilia's authorship of 'Shakespeare' that I have presented is deemed acceptable by the reader, then the Jewish agenda of the Shakespearean literature becomes very powerful evidence that Emilia indeed was able to retain her Jewish faith and identity. On the other hand, no other candidate for the authorship of the plays (and certainly not 'Shagspere') can explain this extensive Jewish content. And considering her family's Jewish heritage, it is entirely credible that their "conversion" to Christianity was only a matter of conformance with the royal imperative of the time.

At any rate, it is clear from the plays that 'Shakespeare' learned to speak a number of languages. Emilia was a native English speaker, but might have been taught Italian and Hebrew by her father and family, and certainly would have studied Latin and French during her aristocratic upbringing. It is entirely possible that Emilia had the early training in a number of languages needed to become one of the most productive wordsmiths in history.

As a young woman, Emilia attended the court of Elizabeth I, and shortly became the mistress to the Queen's first cousin Henry Carey, Lord Hunsdon, who was forty-five years her senior. Hunsdon links Emilia to the world of Shakespeare's plays because his acting troop performed many of them. She became pregnant at the age of twenty-three and then, as was routine with the pregnant mistresses of Lords in this era, was given a farewell and a stipend by Hunsdon. In October 1592 she married her cousin, Captain Alphonso Lanier, a Queen's musician and volunteer navy man. Following the Queen's death he moved into the service of James I. Emilia's relationship with Nicholas would have been the source of Emilia's knowledge of the arcane jargons of the British military and navy that found its way into the plays.

Emilia consulted Dr. Simon Forman, a physician and astrologer, in May 1597, hoping to learn if her husband would receive any preferment so that she might discover 'whether she should be a lady or no'. She was then living in the fashionable area of Longditch, Westminster, next to Canon Row. Forman kept a diary describing his interactions with his clients. He found her 'high minded', which meant either that he saw her as intelligent or that she was interested in the affairs of the aristocracy. And, mysteriously, he wrote that she "hath some thing in mind that she would have done for her. She can hardly keep secret." He also noted her difficult life, stating: "it seemth she had ill fortune in her youth". Emilia again consulted Forman in June of the same year. She complained that her husband had "dealt hardly with her" and "spent and consumed her goods", presumably both the money she had inherited from her father as well as what she had saved from her allowance from Lord Hunsdon. She lied when Foreman asked her age, claiming to be 24 when she was actually 28.

In 1613 her husband died, the same year that the last Shakespearean play *The Two Noble Kinsmen* was written. Emilia now had to earn her own living since she no longer had the income from her husband's Court musician's appointment and only a portion of the income he had derived from a monopoly on the weighing of hay and straw. She attempted to support herself as a tutor for the children of "persons of worth and understanding". In 1617 she leased a new house for that purpose on St. Giles in the Fields, an aristocratic London suburb. She immediately became engaged in a series of lawsuits and countersuits relating to the building, and a dispute with a relative over the income from the hay monopoly. Having lost most of her pupils, she left the St. Giles residence in 1619 without paying her midsummer rent, whereupon she was arrested.

She appears again in the London legal records in 1635 at the age of 66, claiming that she was obliged to provide for two grandchildren, and was in misery because she was being cheated out of her full entitlement to the income from the hay royalties. The lawsuits continued for three years. She died in April 1645 at age seventy-six, a 'pensioner', meaning that she was possessed of some regular income. She had at least two children. The first, presumably the son of Lord Hunsdon, was named Henry and had been born early in 1593. She also had a daughter who died in infancy.

THE BASSANOS AND THE MUSIC OF THE PLAYS

The Shakespearean plays are intensely musical, and the focus on music in the plays suggests that their author came from an environment that included some study of it. Most of the plays refer to music in their text, and there are in total more than 300 musical stage directions. The plays incorporate about a hundred ballads, popular songs and other secular music. In the early history plays, the musical references tend to be limited to flourishes of trumpets, drums, and alarms such as in *Troilus and Cressida*. However, by the middle period, the plays began to incorporate more sophisticated music, such as the consort of mixed instruments in *Midsummer Night's Dream* and the use of hautboys in *Anthony and Cleopatra*. This increasing sophistication leads to the integrated use of ballads in *The Winter's Tale*. As Ross Duffin has pointed out, the playwright also uses song titles as literary puzzles, for instance, the character 'Rogero' in *The Winter's Tale* is intended to remind the audience of a ballad by that name and thereby bring up the imagery of a jealous husband who killed his wife.[65]

Many of the songs used in the Shakespearean plays can be seen as autobiographical to Emilia Bassano. The heroine of the song *Oyster Pie* (mentioned in *Taming of the Shrew* IV, 2) goes to church not for devotion's sake, but to spy out the one who will be her true love. The female subject of *Heigh Ho for a Husband* (mentioned in *Much Ado About Nothing* (III, 4 & II, 1) ends up like Emilia, with a much older man groaning at her side.

The plays include a number of songs about Jews, but there is virtually no Christian music. For example, *Hamlet* (II, 2) used *Jephata Judge of Israel* as a portent for the fate of Ophelia. It is a song that describes how Jephata kept his vow to God to sacrifice the first thing that he met on his return home, which turned out to

---

[65] Ross W. Duffin, *Shakespeare's Songbook* (W. W. Norton & Company, 2004).

be his daughter. A song praising Solomon simply entitled, *King Solomon,* was referenced twice in *Love's Labours' Lost* (I, 2 & IV, 3). Another Jewish song, one that can be seen as autobiographical to Emilia, was *The Ballad of the godly constant wife Susanna.* This song, used in *Twelfth Night* (II, 3), *The Merry Wives of Windsor* (III, 1) and *Merchant of Venice* (IV, 1), tells the story of a virtuous Jewish wife who resisted evil. It is easy to see how Emilia Bassano might have seen a connection between the song's lyrics, given below, and her own life. On the other hand, it is difficult to explain why such a Jewish song would have made so strong an impression on the 'Will from Stratford' as to have caused him to use it in three of his plays.

> There dwelt a man in Babylon
> Of reputation great by fame
> He took to wife Susanna
> A woman of fair name
> Brought up on Moses' Law.
>
> But resting in the orchard by
> Two Elders had a lust and
> Tried her chastity, and when
> She resisted, brought her to trial
> So that she would die
>
> Then the Lord raised up Daniel
> To deal with these wicked men
> (Who falsely lied that they had seen her
> With a young man under a tree)
> And have them put to death
> Under Moses Law

A possible member of Emilia's family is known to have worked on the musical performances in Shakespeare's plays. The flutist Robert Johnson, who wrote the music for songs in several plays including *'Full Fathom Five'* and *'Where the Bee Sucks'* from *The Tempest,* and songs for *Cymbeline* and *A Winter's Tale,*[66] may have been her maternal cousin. Robert also worked with Ben Jonson to produce the music for his plays, as did Emilia's second

---

[66] George Grove, *Grove's Dictionary of Music and Musicians* (T. Presser Col, 1918), p. 539.

cousin Thomas Lupo, the son of her uncle Alvise's daughter Laura Bassano.

THE PLAYS AND EMILIA'S IDENTITY

It is known that some of the sources used by the author of the Shakespearean corpus existed at the time only in Italian, such as *Il Pecorone,* so the playwright was able to read in that language. While some scholars dispute this, the playwright does seem to have been knowledgeable in the area of Italian-English translation. The character 'Holofernes' in *Love's Labor's Lost,* for example, was created as a caricature of Florio, the compiler of the Italian-English dictionary used in England in this era.

Having come from Italy, the generation of Bassanos prior to Emilia's could, of course, speak Italian, as attested by a letter of their correspondence with the Queen in that language. Understanding different languages was a valuable skill, and knowledge of Italian would probably have been passed along to Emilia from her father and family. More than a third of Shakespeare's plays reveal a detailed knowledge of the Bassano's home near Venice. Shakespeare knew the length of the 'Lombardy mile', was familiar with the canal system linking Verona, Milan and Padua, understood the unique Venetian calendar, the *More Veneto,*[67] and used proverbs unique to Italy such as 'sound as a fish'.[68] It can therefore be inferred that the playwright had a degree of knowledge of both Italy and its language that was unusual for an Englishman. Moreover, as shown below, the playwright needed to have at least some understanding of Hebrew in order to create the various puns in the play that used that language.[69] This combination of areas of knowledge was unusual

---

[67] Steve Sohmer, 'Another Time: The Venetian Calendar in Shakespeare's Plays', *Shakespeare Yearbook*, X (1999), 141–161.

[68] Ernesto Grillo, *Shakespeare and Italy* (The University Press, 1949).

[69] Gary Goldstein, 'Shakespeare's Little Hebrew', *Elizabethan Review*, 7 (1999), 70–77.

in England during this era, restricting the pool of possible authors for the plays.

Many names of Bassano family members appear in the plays, especially in the ones set in Italy.[70] In *Merchant of Venice*, for instance, a character is actually called Bassanio — the spelling of the familial name that is recorded in the London church where many of the family are buried.[71] An 'Emelia' appears in Venice in *Othello* as the wife of Iago, as does a 'Lodovicio', the name of one of her first cousins. In *Taming of the Shrew* there is a girl who needed to find a good husband and who had, like Emilia, a father named 'Baptista'. Another Emilia appears in *Comedy of Errors*, another in *Two Noble Kinsmen*, yet another in *A Winter's Tale*.

In *Hamlet* there is a clue that the author of the verse is a woman who must speak her mind or the play will not get written — "the lady shall say her mind freely, or the blank verse shall halt for't" (II, 2, 324). There is also a hint that a group of theatrical players might be Jews, as they don't have the "accent" or the "walk of Christians" (III, 2, 30-35).

Another clue suggesting that Emilia Bassano wrote the Shakespearean literature was the famous mulberry tree purportedly planted by Shakespeare in his garden at Stratford. It would have been appropriate for Emilia to plant such a tree, since the coat of arms granted to her family featured a mulberry tree. The mulberry tree is called *morus* in Latin, which is translated as 'moor' in English. As Emilia Bassano was nicknamed the 'Moor', and her family used the mulberry tree as its symbol, the tradition concerning the 'Stratford mulberry tree' suggests a link between the Bassanos and Shakespeare. The planting of the 'moor' tree in Stratford was likely both a clue left to indicate Shakespeare's identity, as well as a clever reversal of the humor regarding 'trees' in the Gospels. Emilia Bassano planted her 'tree' — Shakespeare

---

[70] Stephanie Hughes, 'New Light on the Dark Lady', *Shakespeare Oxford Newsletter*, 36 (2000), 1, 8–15.

[71] Barbara E. Harrison, *The Bassanos: Italian Musicians at the English Court, 1531-1664*, 1991.

— in the middle of Christendom just as the Romans had 'grafted' their 'branch' — Caesar — onto the messianic 'root' of Judaism.

The Bassano coat of arms bore three silkworms over a mulberry tree that was no doubt related to the fact that the Bassanos came from the region of Italy that produced silk. Jewish traders originally brought silkworms to Italy, and it is likely that at some point the Bassano family had a connection to the silk producing business. However, symbolism within a coat of arms was typical in this era, and the mulberry tree was almost certainly chosen as a deliberate representation of the family, who had originally come from Morocco, as 'Moors'. Elizabethans took heraldry seriously, and a family's coat of arms was more than a decoration but a symbolic identification of the family that bore it. For example, Queen Elizabeth addressed her friend Lady Norris as 'Myne owne Crowe'; since the crow was the Norris family's crest. Heraldry often used puns on the family it depicted. The Luce family had *luces* or pikes blazoned on their shields.

Many of Shakespeare's works contain references from a strange poem by Thomas Moffet entitled *The Silkworms, and their Flies*. It was used a source for several of the sonnets, *A Midsummer's Night Dream, Romeo and Juliet* and a number of other plays. Indeed, Shakespeare's works are embedded with references to silkworms and Moors to such an extent that one scholar, after identifying Emilia as the 'dark lady' of the sonnets, wrote that Shakespeare must have been "obsessed about Emilia Bassano and everything about her". Of course another explanation would be that the many unusual intersections between Shakespeare's works and Emilia's life came about because the literature was, as literature always is, to some extent, autobiographical.

THE SHAKESPEAREAN PROJECT

The missing pages from Shakespeare's son in law's diary and Ben Johnson's complicity in the plot (as shown below in the analysis of his descriptions of Shakespeare) suggest that a number of people helped Emilia Bassano with the 'Shakespearean project'. This group was likely made up of other hidden Jews and, at least at its beginning, one sympathetic Gentile secularist — Christopher

Marlowe. Certainly the most audacious act perpetrated by this group was to implant the name of their 'Gentile Jesus' — Shakespeare — directly into the King James Bible. They did this to mirror Titus's 'miraculous' linkage of his Gospels to Hebraic literature.

During the creation of the King James Bible, a number of Hebrew scholars were consulted to help with the translation. One of them apparently was also working with Emilia on her 'Shakespeare project' and changed the translation of the 46th Psalm to 'miraculously' record the name 'Shakespeare' within the Christian canon. This strange phenomenon is well known to scholars who heretofore have had no explanation for it. In the King James Bible the word 'shake' appears 46 words from the beginning of the 46th Psalm and the word 'speare' 46 words from the end. This was a different translation than had previously been given for the Psalm, which is not surprising as the words 'shake' and 'speare' do not exist in the original Hebrew. Adding to the 'arithmetical humor' was the fact that the King James Bible was published in 1610, the year Shakespeare turned 46. The 46th Psalm was chosen for the 'miracle' as it is a declaration that "the God of Jacob" will be a refuge for Jews no matter where "earthly kingdoms were moved" or how hard the "heathen raged". This prayer would have resonated with Jews like Emilia Bassano living inside English Christendom.

[1] God is our refuge and strength, a very present help in trouble.

[2] Therefore will not we fear, though the earth be removed, and though the mountains be carried into the midst of the sea;

[3] Though the waters thereof roar and be troubled, though the mountains **shake** with the swelling thereof.

[4] There is a river, the streams whereof shall make glad the city of God, the holy place of the tabernacles of the most High.

[5] God is in the midst of her; she shall not be moved: God shall help her, and that right early.

⁶ The heathen raged, the kingdoms were moved: he uttered his voice, the earth melted.

⁷ The LORD of hosts is with us; the God of Jacob is our refuge.

⁸ Come, behold the works of the LORD, what desolations he hath made in the earth.

⁹ He maketh wars to cease unto the end of the earth; he breaketh the bow, and cutteth the **spear** in sunder; he burneth the chariot in the fire.

¹⁰ Be still, and know that I am God: I will be exalted among the heathen, I will be exalted in the earth.

¹¹ The LORD of hosts is with us; the God of Jacob is our refuge.

It is also likely that the dates of Shakespeare's birth and death were forged as part of the project. The records of Stratford's Holy Trinity Church state that Shakespeare was baptized on April 26. Since it was customary to baptize infants three days after their birth, this indicates that he was born on April 23, which is St. George's day, the patron saint of England. Shakespeare is also recorded as having died exactly 52 years later on April 23. This 'miraculous' occurrence was likely brought about by Emilia and her allies working to propel their 'perfect Gentile' into English history. They simply forged the documents that placed his birthday and death on the feast day of England's patron Saint. They did so to make him more seem more perfectly 'English' and to mirror the 'miraculous' chronology that the Roman's created for Jesus's life.

The records regarding Shakespeare's son were also very likely forgeries because his son's name of 'Hamnet' certainly seems to be part of the humor regarding 'Ham' that runs throughout the Shakespearean literature. For example, just as 'Hamlet' means maker of ham, 'Hamnet' would comically suggest a collector of ham. Falsifying historical documents was, evidently, not a difficult thing to do during this era. The Jews who created these forgeries would have been inspired by Titus, who once claimed that he could have "under other circumstances" become the greatest forger in history, and who presented bald-faced lies as historical facts to certify the historicity of Jesus.

Another example showing the scope to the Shakespearean 'project', or at least Ben Jonson's awareness of it, was his parody of Shakespeare's coat of arms, which had as its logo "not without right". Jonson created a well-known spoof of Shakespeare in his play entitled *Every Man out of His Humor,* wherein a country bumpkin who states that he *"can write himself a gentleman now"* applies for a coat of arms which would feature a hog's cheek between two puddings -'pudding' being a meat pie or sausage. The bumpkin's coats of arms had the logo "Not without mustard".

Though at this point a reader may find Jonson's humor hard to understand, it will become obvious in light of the analysis of Shakespeare plays given below. The 'swine flesh' between the puddings on the fool's coat of arms was a comic reversal of the cannibalism humor in the Gospels that described the eating of the 'bread' of Jewish flesh with the eating of the 'swine flesh' of Gentiles'. The coat of arms' reference to 'mustard' also played on the comic theme concerning cannibalism — the comic point being that the Gentiles would need mustard to go with their 'ham'. Jonson, whose portrait suggests someone of Semitic background, may have been a crypto-Jew. In any event, he was certainly one of those that assisted Emilia with her project.

Though Emilia 'spearheaded' the project, she kept her identity as the authors of the plays secret for a number of reasons, one, of course, being that she was a woman. At this time, women did not even attend the theater in Elizabethan England unless they were whores or adulterous.[72] Though this began to change after 1600, women still were not encouraged to write works of original literature — which is why intellectual women like Mary Sidney confined most of their writing to translations, and Emilia's poetry was so unusual.

---

[72] Andrew Gurr, *Playgoing in Shakespeare's London* (Cambridge: Cambridge University Press, 1987).

EMILIA AS THE DARK LADY

A. L. Rowse popularized the view that Emilia was the 'dark lady' of the Sonnets during the 1970's, though his arguments have subsequently received various criticisms. [73] Research by Peter Goodwin has shown that her family called Emilia 'the Moor',[74] suggesting that she had a 'black' or swarthy skin tone and was indeed a 'dark lady'.

The author of the Shakespearean plays had a keen interest in young women with dark skin. They are a constant feature of the Italian plays and are responsible for the fair/foul imagery in many others. This imagery focuses on the question of whether or not black can be 'fair' — a theme that modern critics interested in race and gender issues also tend to dwell upon. There are multiple characters referred to as 'Moors' in the plays and multiple indirect references to Moors such as being 'sick as a Moor' (sycamore), and the name of the Empress 'Tamora' — who has a child by the 'moor' Aaron — in *Titus Andronicus.* 'Tamora' is an Italian abbreviation of "I love you Moor' (*t'amo mora*).

---

[73] Aemilia Lanyer and A. L Rowse, *The Poems of Shakespeare's Dark Lady = Salve Deus Rex Judaeorum* (New York: C.N. Potter : Distributed by Crown Publishers, 1979); D Bevington, 'A.L. Rowse's Dark Lady', in *Aemilia Lanyer: Gender, Genre, and the Canon,* by Marshall Grossman (University Press of Kentucky, 1998).

[74] Lasocki and Prior; Roger Prior, 'More (Moor? Moro?) Light on the Dark Lady', *Financial Times (London),* 10 October 1987, p. 17.

SALVE DEUS, REX JUDAEORUM

Following her father's death, her family arranged for the seven-year-old Emilia to live with purportedly Gentile nobles, perhaps as a way to improve the family's social status. As a dark skinned Jewess growing up in a Christian world, however, where 'fair' was beauty and one's lineage was the avenue to status, her life would have likely been filled with disappointments. Every social event held the possibility of humiliation for a dark skinned 'Moor', and perhaps many occurred. If this was the case, Emilia certainly had her revenge. *Salve Deus, Rex Judaeorum* (Hail God, King of the Jews) is an invitation to the noble ladies of England to the 'feast' hidden within the works of Shakespeare, in which the Gentile nobility cannibalize themselves. As Emilia actually knew many of her dedicatees, it is likely she was taking a personal as well as a historical vengeance with her dedications.

Emilia published *Salve Deus* under her own name in 1611, when she was forty-two years old.[75] The publisher, Valentine Simmes, had previously printed several of the Shakespearean quartos. *Salve Deus* was 'registered' by Emilia, the equivalent of a book being copyrighted today. It was the first book written by a woman to acquire this legal designation in England.

With her creation of the theme of a literary 'Paschal lamb' to be eaten by the Gentile nobility, as well as a punning system based on the word 'Will', I contend that Emilia Bassano created a unified literary system encompassing *Salve Deus* and the Sonnets of 'Shakespeare', satirically inviting the Gentile readers to 'feast' on the 'remains' of the playwright. With this comic system, she also identified herself as the author of the Shakespearean 'canon'.

---

[75] Aemilia Lanyer, *The Poems of Aemilia Lanyer: Salve Deus Rex Judaeorum*, ed. by Susanne Woods (Oxford University Press, 1993).

Her inspiration for this inter-textual design was the satirical system that exists between New Testament and the works of Josephus, which was also based on the eating of a symbolic 'Paschal Lamb'.

The work's title — *Hail God, King of the Jews* — is an overt clue as to real meaning of her literature because with her Shakespearean 'canon' Emilia was attempting to reclaim the Messianic title that Titus stole from the Jews. In the post-Christian world Emilia envisioned, God would be once more the 'King of the Jews', not the King of the Gentiles.

Salve Deus has a number of distinct components. Two of the prefatory pieces and an afterword are in prose. All of the poems are in iambic pentameter, although the verse forms vary. The volume consists of the following:

- A short poem *The Description of Cooke-ham,* which was the first country-house poem to be published in English;

- A set of prefatory letters to various noble ladies;

- The 1840-line epic poem boldly titled *Salve Deus Rex Judaeorum (Hail, God, King of the Jews)*;

- A final prose address 'To the doubtful reader'

On its surface *Salve Deus* appears to be an especially free adaptation of the Gospels, primarily describing Christ's Passion. Emilia claimed that the title of her work appeared to her in a dream, though she did not state what specifically brought her to write such bizarre poetry.

Feminist scholars have focused on 'proto-feminist' aspects of the poem, such as Emilia's argument that men (not women) were responsible for the crucifixion of Christ.[76] Emilia also argued in a section entitled *'Eve's Apologia in Defense of Women'* that Eve

---

[76] Marshall Grossman, ed., *Aemilia Lanyer: Gender, Genre, and the Canon* (University Press of Kentucky, 1998).

was less culpable than Adam for the original sin. Emilia compares
Eve's sinfulness to men's in the context of their crucifixion of the
'King of the Jews' apparently to argue for women's social
equality. Both the prefatory poems and the epic poem seem to
argue for women's religious and social equality, and one of the
prefatory poems criticizes class privilege. However, while
Emilia's 'proto-feminism' may have been real, it was not the
primary reason she produced *Salve Deus.*

As shown below, Emilia Bassano somehow learned about the
satirical system that Titus had placed into the Gospels, either from
her father Baptista — who would have brought this information
with him from Italy — or from Christopher Marlowe. In either
case, the revelation shaped her entire life. She dedicated herself to
creating a literary counterattack to the satire that the Romans had
placed into the New Testament as a way of humiliating Jews.
Salve Deus was a key component of this effort.

On its surface, the work is an earnest — albeit macabre —
exposition of Christian faith dedicated to a group of English
noblewoman from an overwrought believer in 'Jesus'. In the
poem, Jesus is represented as a beautiful 'fair' Gentile with his
skin described as 'snow', lips of 'coral' with 'spices' and
'flowers' in his cheeks. Emilia built upon the 'bridegroom'
analogy of the Gospels and referred to Jesus as a 'lover'
throughout her work. The noblewomen were even advised to
"Take this faire Bridegroom in your soules pure bed."

Shakespeare's works and Emilia's share a similar vocabulary and
classical sources, and *Salve Deus* contains a number of
metaphorical devices that are clearly 'Shakespearean'. For
example, the following passage from *Salve Deus* uses the analogy
of the extremes so common in the works of Shakespeare.

> I doe but set a candle in the sunne,
> And adde one drop of water to the sea,
> Virtue and Beautie both together run,
> When you were borne, within your breast to stay;

(1739-42)

The following passage from the dedication to Lady Anne repeats perhaps the best known of all of Shakespeare's metaphors, which, it should be noted, is also found in a number of other authors' works.

> For well you knowe, this world is but a Stage
> Where all doe play their parts, and must be gone;

Emilia's poetry shares other stylistic devices in with the Shakespearean literature. For example, she uses phrases such as 'aromatic gum' and the 'unjointing of joints' found in the Shakespearean plays, both of which are also found in the Roman satirical system in the Gospels. Many of her country references are similar to those in the plays, and she makes puns on 'grace' like in *Love's Labors Lost*.

On its surface, *The Description of Cook ham* is a simple poem, which begins with a description of a pleasant rural scene in which the nightingale Philomela is singing. However, Philomela is a character from Ovid's *Metamorphoses* who was raped and had her tongue cut out. As I will show, 'Shakespeare' used this character in *Titus Andronicus* as a metaphor for the rape of Judea by the Romans. As Philomela continues to sing in *The Description of Cook ham,* Christ and the Apostles suddenly appear and his "Writ" is placed in a fair tree, at which point Emilia claims to have had an 'inkling', though she does not say what this insight was. But thereafter the 'clean fair brooks' become 'christal' and everything suddenly is in 'dismay', "their dying bodied half alive half dead" and the nightingale now sings a "mournful Ditty", unable to chirp or sing.

The poem would appear to indicate that the arrival of the New Testament did not help Cook-Ham remain a rural Garden of Eden, which would have been the reaction of a Jew who learned about the satirical system in the Gospels. This reaction is reflected in the very unkosher title of the poem 'Cook — ham', which slyly implies that Emilia is leaving a Gentile place that eats swine flesh.

The most important connection between *Salve Deus Rex Judaeorum* and the works of Shakespeare, however, can only be

seen in the light of the Gospels' satire of its 'Paschal lamb' —
Jesus, who was cannibalized by his followers, most of whom were
members of the Jew's royal family, the Maccabees. As shown
below, *Salve Deus* is like the Gospels in that it symbolically
presented the body of Jesus to the noble ladies of England as a
Paschal 'feast'.

Emilia extended numerous invitations to her "wholesome feast".
In fact, as Schnell observed, such imagery is "ubiquitous" in
Emilia's poetry. [77] Such language is a total departure from
traditional Christian imagery and theology: no other author has
ever had the impudence to claim to be being able to 'serve' Jesus.
This begs the question: Why did Emilia wish to feed a 'literary
Paschal lamb' to the English nobility? The answer to this question
lies in the works of 'Shakespeare'.

Salve Deus's first dedication is to the Queen herself, who Emilia
refers to, somewhat brazenly, as an 'empress'. She asks the
Queen: *"to view that which is seldome seene, A Womans writing of
divinest things."* Emilia begins to speak directly to Elizabeth, and
invites her to a singularly odd 'feast'. In the passage, she equates
her book as 'preparing' Jesus the 'Paschal lamb'.

> That you faire Queene, of all the world admired,
> May take the more delight to looke upon her:
> For she must entertaine you to this Feast,
> To which your Highnesse is the welcom'st guest.
>
> For here I haue prepar'd my Paschal Lambe,
> The figure of the liuing Sacrifice;
> Who dying, all th'Infernall powres orecame,
> That we with him t'Eternitie might rise:
> This pretious Passeouer feed upon, O Queene,
> Let your faire Virtues in my Glasse be seene.

> *(80-90)*

---

[77] Lisa Jane Schnell, 'Breaking "the Rule of Cortezia: Aemilia Lanyer's
Dedications to Salve Deus Rex Judaeorum', *Journal of Medieval and Early
Modern Studies*, 27 (1997), 77–101.

Even on its surface level the language is startling. *Salve Deus* is
perhaps the only passage in Christian literature wherein the author
presumes to be able 'create' a 'Paschal lamb'. I believe she is
referring to her writings, that she sees as a literary 'body' of Jesus
— that will somehow be 'eaten' at a 'feast'. Though the
strangeness of the language is tempered perhaps by the
fundamentally odd nature of the communion sacrament it plays
upon, the boldness of the statement is nevertheless striking.

Emilia then repeats the bizarre 'invitation' to her 'feast' in her
subsequent dedications to other noble women. To the Queen's
sister she wrote:

> …you faire Princess next our famous Queen,
> I doe invite unto this wholesome feast…
> Though your faire eyes farre better
>   Bookes have seene;
> Yet being the first fruits of a womans wit,
> Vouchsafe you[r] favour in accepting it.

Emilia builds upon the theme of her Paschal 'feast' in subsequent
dedications and actually describes how 'sweet' Jesus will taste
when he is eaten.

> To taste his sweetnesse, whom they so adored:
> Sweetnesse that makes our flesh a burthen to us,
> Knowing it serves but onely to undoe us.

> *(1742-45)*

To the Lady Susan, Countesses Dowager of Kent, with whom she
purportedly lived with during her youth, she wrote:

> Come you that were the Mistris of my youth,
> The noble guide of my vngouern'd days;
> Come you that haue delighted in Gods truth,
> Help now your handmaid to sound foorth his praise:
> You that are pleas'd in his pure excellencie,
> Vouchsafe to grace this holy feast, and me.

She also wrote that Lady Susan would be able to 'taste' Jesus at
the feast.

> When with Christ Iesus she did meane to goe,
> From sweet delights to taste part of his woe.

She repeats her theme in a dedication entitled 'The Authors Dream to the Lady Marie." In the poem Emilia again describes her literature as a religious 'feast' to which Marie was invited. She wrote:

> For to this Lady now I will repaire,
> Presenting her the fruits of idle houres;
> Thogh many Books she writes that are more rare,
> Yet there is hony in the meanest flowres:
>
> Which is both wholesome, and delights the taste:
> Though sugar be more finer, higher priz'd,
> Yet is the painefull Bee no whit disgrac'd,
> Nor her faire wax, or hony more despiz'd.
>
> And though that learned damsell and the rest,
> Haue in the higher style her Trophie fram'd;
> Yet these vnlearned lines beeing my best,
> Of her great wisedom can no whit be blam'd.
>
> And therefore, first I here presend my Dreame,
> And next, inuite her Honour to my feast;

To Lady Katherine, Countess of Suffolk, Emilia asked that her 'food' be passed on to subsequent generations of Gentile noblewomen, she wrote:

> And let your noble daughters likewise reade
> This little Books that I present to you;
> On heavenly food let them vouchsafe to feede;

To the Lady Anne, Countess of Dorset, Emilia composed a dedication that again invited a noblewoman to the 'Paschal feast' of her literature, and made use of a pun found in Shakespeare's Sonnets: that is, exchanging the meaning of the word 'will' (one's intention) with the name of the individual, i.e. 'Will' Shakespeare.

> Then in this Mirrour let your faire eyes looke,
> To view your virtues in this blessed Booke.
> Blest by our Sauiours merits, not my skil,

> Which I acknowledge to be very small;
> Yet if the least part of his blessed **Will**
> I haue perform'd, I count I haue done all:
> One sparke of grace sufficient is to fill
> Our Lampes with oyle, ready when he doth call
> To enter with the Bridegroome to the feast,
> Where he that is the greatest may be least.

This pun on 'Will' found in the line — *Yet if the least part of his blessed Will I haue perform'd, I count I haue done all* — within the context I am indicating suggests that Emilia was claiming sole authorship of the Shakespearean literature. Notice also that the word 'Will' is 'correctly' capitalized because it is the name of a person, not the intent of God. This method of differentiating the person "Will" from someone's 'will' is a key to understanding the meaning of the Sonnets.

In order to fully expose the typological link between Bassano's work in *Salve Deus* and her work as 'Shakespeare', it is necessary to digress at this point and review the Sonnets. The poems develop the theme that whoever has "her wish" — that is to say whoever reads the literature of Shakespeare — has "thy Will", that is, the Paschal lamb sacrifice.

The punning system begins in Sonnets 133 and 134, and continues thru 135 and 136:

> ...And yest thou wilt; fir I being pent in thee,
> Perforce am thine, and all that is in me.

> *(Sonnet 133)*

> ...So, now I have confessed that he is thine,
> And I myself am mortgaged to thy will.

> *(Sonnet 134)*

> And 'Will' to boot, and 'Will' in overplus;
> More than enough am I that vex thee still,
> To thy sweet will making addition thus.
> Wilt thou, whose will is large and spacious,
> Not once vouchsafe to hide my will in thine?

Shall will in others seem right gracious,
And in my will no fair acceptance shine?
The sea all water, yet receives rain still
And in abundance addeth to his store;
So thou, being rich in 'Will,' add to thy 'Will'
One will of mine, to make thy large 'Will' more.
Let no unkind, no fair beseechers kill;
Think all but one, and me in that one 'Will.

(Sonnet 135)

If thy soul cheque thee that I come so near,
Swear to thy blind soul that I was thy 'Will,'
And will, thy soul knows, is admitted there;
Thus far for love my love-suit, sweet, fulfil.
'Will' will fulfil the treasure of thy love,
Ay, fill it full with wills, and my will one.
In things of great receipt with ease we prove
Among a number one is reckon'd none:
Then in the number let me pass untold,
Though in thy stores' account I one must be;
For nothing hold me, so it please thee hold
That nothing me, a something sweet to thee:
Make but my name thy love, and love that still,
And then thou lovest me, for my name is 'Will.'

(Sonnet 136)

The play on Shakespeare's first name was a mirror of Titus's comedy in the Gospels concerning the name of 'Jesus'. In the Gospels a number of different individuals were called 'Jesus', which created a number of misunderstandings that enabled Titus to assume the name of 'Jesus' and switch himself for the Jewish Messiah. Therefore, Emilia created a parallel brand of humor concerning the name of her Gentile replacement for the cannibalized Jewish Messiah. She used Titus's name switching comedy to introduce 'Will" — as a person, rather than as someone's intent — into her paraphrasing of the New Testament in *Salve Deus*. This 'Will' is the same 'Will' described above in the Sonnets.

How can we be sure that Emilia Bassano's punning on 'Will' in *Salve Deus* is part of the same system found in the Sonnets? I expect that all but the most skeptical readers will be convinced simply by Emilia's repetitious quotes of this device from Shakespeare's sonnets in this context, where the double entendre on the word 'will' appears to be quite intentional. However, as shown in *Caesar's Messiah,* the sequence in which events occur is very important to the typology found in the Gospels, and provides further evidence that the typology is intentional. Emilia used this same technique, and switched her 'Will' with Titus in *Salve Deus* at the exact point in her narrative on Jesus' passion where Titus inserted himself in the Gospels. This was the clever proof that she left for us to show that the 'Will' in *Salve Deus,* like the 'Will' described in the sonnets, is to be seen as Titus's replacement. Emilia borrowed this intertextual technique from the authors of the Gospels and *Wars of the Jews* whose comic system spanned a number of books.

To notify the 'informed reader' of *Salve Deus* that she was creating a subtext, Emilia introduced two deliberate errors into her narration. In the passage from *Salve Deus* below, an Angel appears to comfort Jesus in line 403, exactly as was the case in the Gospels — Luke 22:43. To this point in her depiction of Christ's Passion, Emilia was very careful to mirror the exact events and sequence of the Gospels. However, in line 431 she gives a description of another angel. This 'second angel' does not appear in the Gospels. But what is recognizable — to those familiar with the satire in the Gospels — is that it is at this point that Titus is first described as the "naked young man" of Mark 14:51. Emilia's second 'error' is the omission of the naked young man. Thus, in Emilia's 'correction' of Jesus's Passion, Titus does not have a place: only 'thy Will' is in the garden with Jesus.

Within the punning system Emilia has set up, this second Angel, described as 'thy Will' — the "Will' of God, not the false Messiah of the Romans — has been 'introduced' in line 409 where she describes Titus as 'his Will'. The entire critical passage from *Salve Deus,* with comments, follows. Notice that the word 'Will' is capitalized in the line — *If 'twere his Will that Cup might passe away.*

Bidding them tarry, thou didst further goe,
To meet affliction in such gracefull sort,
395 As might moove pitie both in friend and foe,

Thy sorowes such, as none could them comport,
Such great Indurements who did ever know,
When to th' Almighty thou didst make resort?
And falling on thy face didst humbly pray,
400 If 'twere his Will that Cup might passe away.

Saying, Not my will, but thy will Lord be done.
When as thou prayedst an Angel did appeare
From Heaven, to comfort thee Gods onely Sonne,
That thou thy Suffrings might'st the better beare,
405 Beeing in an agony, thy glasse neere run,

Thou prayedst more earnestly, in so great feare,
That pretious sweat came trickling to the ground,
Like drops of blood thy sences to confound.

The following line is the point where Emilia introduces the two 'Wills'- His 'Will' is the 'will' of Titus and 'thy Will' is Shakespeare, who she saw as representing the 'will' of God. Notice that she again capitalizes the two 'Wills', which would be the correct grammar if the 'Wills' she were referring to were persons.

The statement means that Titus was able to insert his "will" — in other words, it was at this point in the Gospels that Titus began the process to kill the Jewish Christ and take on the identity of 'Jesus'. But, in her version, Emilia builds atop Titus's literature just as he had built atop Hebraic literature. Thus, just as Titus had done, she inserts a second character in this point in the story of Christ's passion. 'Will'— "thy Will", the 'Will' of the sonnets, who was truly — in her opinion — the 'Will' of the Lord, because he was the 'Will' of Yahweh.

Loe here his Will, not thy Will, Lord was done,
410 And thou content to undergoe all paines,

Sweet Lambe of God, his deare beloved Sonne,
By this great purchase, what to thee remaines?

Of Heaven and Earth thou hast a Kingdom wonne,
Thy Glory beeing equall with thy Gaines,
415 In ratifying Gods promise on the Earth,
Made many hundred yeares before thy birth.

But now returning to thy sleeping Friends,
That could not watch one houre for love of thee,
Even those three Friends, which on thy Grace depends,
420 Yet shut those Eies that should their Maker see;
What colour, what excuse, or what amends,
From thy Displeasure now can set them free?
Yet thy pure Pietie bids them Watch and Pray,
Lest in Temptation they be led away.

425 Although the Spirit was willing to obay,
Yet what great weakenesse in the Flesh was found!
They slept in Ease, whilst thou in Paine didst pray;
Loe, they in Sleepe, and thou in Sorow drown'd:
Yet Gods right Hand was unto thee a stay,
430 When horror, griefe, and sorow did abound:

The following lines describe the 'second angel', the one that is not found in the Gospels. Emilia then goes on to detail the great sin that has been done. She exits the Gospels' narration of Jesus's passion to point out that David and Solomon had Kingdoms taken from them because of their sins. In the context she is operating in — the Romans arrest of Jesus — she is suggesting that Roman kingdom will be taken away from them by God for their wickedness. Notice that she is not referring to Judas's sin but to the sin of someone who loses a 'Kingdom'. From this point forward she takes a completely different stance concerning the Romans than found in the Gospels, which is that they were the ones guilty of killing the Christ. Her point has a larger historical meaning: Emilia believed that a Jewish empire would replace the Christian one, once the truth of Christianity was revealed.

His Angel did appeare from Heaven to thee,
To yeeld thee comfort in Extremitie.

But what could comfort then thy troubled Minde,
When Heaven and Earth were both against thee bent?
435 And thou no hope, no ease, no rest could'st finde,

But must restore that Life, which was but lent;
Was ever Creature in the World so kinde,
But he that from Eternitie was sent?
To satisfie for many Worlds of Sinne,
440 Whose matchlesse Torments did but then begin.

If one Mans sinne doth challendge Death and Hell,
With all the Torments that belong thereto:
If for one sinne such Plagues on David fell,
As grieved him, and did his Seed undoe:
445 If Salomon, for that he did not well,
Falling from Grace, did loose his Kingdome too:
Ten Tribes beeing taken from his wilfull Sonne
And Sinne the Cause that they were all undone.

What could thy Innocency now expect,
450 When all the Sinnes that ever were committed,
Were laid to thee, whom no man could detect?
Yet farre thou wert of Man from beeing pittied,
The Judge so just could yeeld thee no respect,
Nor would one jot of penance be remitted;
455 But greater horror to thy Soule must rise,
Than Heart can thinke, or any Wit devise.

There are a number of passages within *Salve Deus* that have struck critics as anti-Semitic. For example, she describes 'Jewish wolves' that 'bit' the Savior. However, in my view these passages simply reflect the history that Emilia was disclosing, wherein a number of Jews had assisted Titus in his destruction of the Jewish Messiah. Such passages also hid the poem's real meaning from the censors, who if they had uncovered it would have had Emilia executed. One of these 'Jewish wolves', Josephus, appears again and again as a 'type' throughout the Shakespearean plays, usually experiencing some horrible fate as a symbolic punishment for helping Titus.

A 'TRIFLING' STRAND FROM PLINY TO SHAKESPEARE

This chapter presents two discoveries, both of which are related to the symbolic level in the Shakespearean literature. The first is that Pliny's dedication to Titus in his *History of Nature* contains sarcastic references to the satirical system that the Romans placed in the Gospels. The second is that the author of the dedication to Shakespeare in the 1623 Folio, which presented the first collection of the plays, understood Pliny's sarcasm and created the entire dedication to Shakespeare as an extension of Pliny's black humor.

The first part of this analysis concerns translations of Latin that laymen will perhaps find difficult to understand and, as is always the case with translations, other specialists can contest. If the reader bears with this, however, he or she will be rewarded at the conclusion of this chapter with simple and clear evidence that Pliny and the author of the dedication to Shakespeare in the 1623 Folio were operating from the same comic theme concerning Christianity.

Pliny's dedication to Titus begins with a strange paragraph, which was translated in 1601 by Philemon Holland as follows:

> …I purpose by this Epistle of mine to present and consecrate unto you, most sweet and gentle Prince [for this title accorded fittest unto you, seeing that the name of Most mighty sort well with the age of that Emperor your father:] which haply might seem bold and presumption in me, but that **I know how at other times you were wont to have some good opinion of my toies and fooleries. Where, by the way, you must give me leave to mollify a little the verses which I borrow of my countryman Catullus. (See also how I light upon a word used among soldiers, which you are acquainted with, since time we served both together in the camp)**

Pliny's dedication is among a very small collection of extant writing wherein a member of Titus' intellectual circle directly addressed him. I believe that Pliny references Christianity a number of times in his Preface, the first occurring in the above paragraph in the portion marked in **bold typeface**. The sarcastic meaning of Pliny's words is invisible in the English translation. To get the joke, it is first necessary to recognize that the Latin verse that Pliny "borrowed" was from Catullus' poem *Carmina* verse 1.3 ("*Dedication to Cornelius*"), wherein he wrote:[78] "*For you used to deem my triflings of account.*"

Pliny, however, permuted the order of the words in Catullus's original Latin, creating an awkward and ungrammatical sentence.[79] In a footnote, Holland wrote that Pliny's version *"indeed was but a hard composition and couching of the words."* I believe that this grammatical violation signals a puzzle or double entendre, and that Pliny intended for the reader to realize that the Latin word "putare", translated above as "to deem", has an alternative meaning which is to *trim, prune*, or *lop*. (This meaning is the root of the English word "amputate".) This is, in my opinion, the word that Pliny states that he "lights upon" in order to "mollify a little" the meaning.

Holland translated the phrase as "**at other times you were wont to have some good opinion of my toies and fooleries**", producing an interpretation consistent with Catullus's original poem, and ignoring Pliny's grammatical faux pas. Note that Holland's word "toies" means 'mockeries', which is not

[78] In Latin, "namque tu solebas meas esse aliquid putare nugas". The manner that Catullus uses "tu…esse aliquid putare" in conjunction with 'nugas' - which means '*jests*',' *idle speeches*', or '*trifles*' - produces the meaning. "Esse" and "putare" are both present infinitive verbs, while the compound phrase "esse… putare" forms the perfect passive tense of "putare", "having deemed worthy".

[79] Pliny wrote *"namque tu solebas nugas esse aliquid meas putare".* Holland, in his footnote, changed the order of the words again: *Tu putare namque, Nugas esse aliquid meas solebas.* Thus, Pliny pulled the word *putare* out of the phase "esse aliquid putare nugas", moving it to the end of the sentence; while Holland in his version moved it to the beginning. These versions are strangely ungrammatical. The words "esse aliquid" are stranded, and the verb "putare" is forced back into the infinitive tense.

necessarily an exact implication of the Latin. However, flipping to the alternate interpretation of the double entendre, Pliny's phrase might also be translated as *For indeed you have been using my mockeries for pruning.*

In *Caesar's Messiah* the word 'prune' is shown to be a key word in the comic system that runs between the Gospels and *Wars of the Jews.* Titus "pruned" the Jewish Messiah he captured on the Mount of Olives and — using the language of the Gospels — "grafted in" a new Roman messianic lineage onto the "root and branch" of Judaism. Pliny helps the informed reader understand his sarcasm by noting that the word he "lights upon" was one that Titus was "acquainted with, since time we served both together in the camp." This is an important detail because the place where the Jewish Messiah was "pruned" was Thecoa, which Josephus mentioned was a 'camp' where Titus was stationed.

Pliny's sarcasm in the rest of the dedication will be transparent to those familiar with the Gospels' satire. He goes on to state that he hopes that Titus enjoys this present work — which he presents as a religious document and consecrates to Titus — as much as he did his previous one, which he referred to above as his 'mockery'. He then goes on to compare his 'offering' to those of "poor country peasants".

> In which regard, exceeding care above all things would be had, that whatsoever is said or dedicated unto you, may beseem your person, & be worth acceptation. **And yet the gods reject not the humble prayers of poor country peasants**, yea, and of many nations, who offer nothing but milk unto them: and such as have no Incense, find grace and favor many times with the oblation of **a plain cake made only of meal and salt;** and never was any man blamed yet for his devotion to the gods, so he offered according to his ability, were the thing never so simple.

"Plain cake made only of meal and salt" is, of course, unleavened bread, a requirement for Jews at the Passover meal. While it is possible in this phase that Pliny is referring only to Judaism, this seems unlikely in view of his patron Titus's conquest of the Jews, and his distaste for that religion. The satirical system in the Gospels (as revealed by Josephus) revolves around a black comic

theme of cannibalism whereby the Romans satirically transformed the 'unleavened bread' served at the Passover meal into the flesh of their Messiah. Moreover, note that this reference to Jews supports the contention that Pliny was referring above to 'camps' during Titus's Judean campaign, as that was Titus's most significant military campaign.

If Pliny is operating in the context of the Gospels' comedy, his statement about the offerings of "poor country peasants" (Jews) to gods (Titus and his father Vespasian) is certainly a witticism related upon its black comic theme. In other words, Pliny is building upon the Gospels' satirical level whereby 'poor country' Jews were fooled into symbolically eating the flesh of their Messiah as the Passover meal. Notice Pliny's comment — "were the thing never so simple". What could be complex about the offerings of poor country peasants? Given the fact that Pliny is addressing the creator of Christianity, the most obvious answer is simply that Pliny was joking on the fact that the 'new Judaism' fooled its followers into symbolic cannibalism.

Another statement in the dedication comments on how easy it is to fool "poor countrymen" with religion. Pliny wrote: *many things there that seem right and dear and be holden for precious, only because they are consecrated to some sacred things.* If this statement is referring to the Gospels, it is brutally cynical, which is just what one would expect from one of the authors of the Gospels.

While all of this suggests the possibility that Pliny is commenting upon Titus's new religion, the next passage provides even greater support for the premise. The passage begins with Pliny expressing concern that critics in the future will criticize his writings. He then switches gears and focuses, not on the general critics of his work, but upon a single woman. In the Holland translation, the woman's name is 'Mary':

> But this troubled me never a whit, for I am not ignorant that a silly woman, even a harlot and no better, durst encounter Theophrastus and write a book against him, notwithstanding he was a man of so incomparable eloquence that thereupon he came by his divine

name Theophrastus: from whence arose this proverb and by-word, Mary then go choose a tree to hang thy self.

In *Caesar's Messiah,* the famous early botanist Theophrastus was noted as the scientific predecessor of Pedanius Dioscorides, the physician and botanist who accompanied Titus to Judea. Pedanius is satirically described in *Wars of the Jews* as capturing the Jewish Messiah and then metaphorically "pruning" him and grafting a Roman Messiah onto the Jewish 'root'. In his writings, Theophrastus used the same key Greek word — 'kolasai' — to describe the pruning of trees that Josephus used to describe Titus' instruction as to what to do with the captured Jewish Messiah, thereby beginning the comic 'root, branch and pruning' theme found in the Gospels. Further, Josephus describes Mary's son 'Jesus' (in the Cannibal Mary parallel) as a "by-word" who will "complete the calamity of the Jews." Therefore, Pliny's creating the absurd phrase "*Mary then go choose a tree to hang thy self*" and then calling it a "*by-word*" is a reference to the system of satire in the Gospels and *Wars of the Jews*. This phrase was not a proverb or "by-word" — it is not in any other extant Roman literature — and Pliny calling it such simply highlights the comic theme he is creating.

If one reads any modern translation of Pliny's dedication to Titus it will not contain the word 'Mary' that is found in Holland's. For example, in the current Loeb edition of Pliny's work the passage is translated: "*Theophrastus, a mortal whose eminence as an orator won him the title of 'the divine' actually had a book written against him by a woman — which was the origin of the proverb about choosing your tree to hang from.*"

This means that either someone removed the word 'Mary' from the extant copies of Pliny — which is doubtful considering that there are a number of such editions — or Holland simply decided to add 'Mary' to the sentence.

The following footnote given by Holland to his translation of the critical 'Mary' sentence seemingly builds upon this connection to being 'hung on a tree'. (Pliny actually used the word 'thisera', which specifically means 'crucifixion'.) The footnote speaks about women who 'controll men's writing'. Emilia's sister's husband's last name was also Holland, which permits the conjecture that the translator, Philemon Holland, may have been an in-law. With all this information, it is hard not to speculate that Emilia Bassano had a hand in Holland's translation, or that Holland was aware that 'Shakespeare' was a man whose writing was 'controlled' by a woman, or both.

> If women may be allowd to controll men's writings, wee may be wearie of our lives and goe hang our selves well enough.

The concepts 'Mary' and 'crucifixion' are so associated with Christianity as to be self-evident. Holland's 1602 translation that claimed that a 'Mary' wrote a book against a specialist in 'pruning' that became a "by-word"- and bear in mind that no such book is known to exist — could not be circumstantial in a dedication to the inventor of Christianity. To have added 'Mary' to Pliny's collection of concepts related to Christianity — 'pruning', 'crucifixion', and 'by-word' — suggests that Holland was aware that Pliny's dedication to Titus was sarcastically referring to the Christian Gospels.

Before showing how Pliny's dedication is linked to the Shakespearean literature it is important to provide yet another passage from Pliny's *History of Nature* that relates to the creation of Christianity. The sarcasm in this passage should be comprehensible to readers familiar with the system of comedy presented in *Caesar's Messiah*.

Pliny's description below of the Balsam plant relates to the 'root and branch' comedy within the Gospels. To see the linkage it only needs to be understood that the oil from the Balsam plant was used by the Jews to anoint their Messiah. Therefore, it was natural for Pliny to have used the plant as a symbol of 'Jesus' and thereby create a witticism depicting the Romans capturing this specific 'root' from the Jews.

> But to all other odours that of balsamum is considered preferable, **a plant that has been only bestowed by Nature upon the land of Judæa.** In former times it was cultivated in two gardens only, both of which belonged to the kings of that country: one of them

was no more than twenty jugera in extent, and the other somewhat smaller. **The emperors Vespasianus and Titus had this shrub exhibited at Rome; indeed, it is worthy of signal remark, that since the time of Pompeius Magnus, we have been in the habit of carrying trees even in our triumphal processions.** At the present day this tree pays us homage and tribute along with its native land, but it has been found to be of altogether a different nature to that which our own as well as foreign writers had attributed to it: for, in fact, it bears a much stronger resemblance to the vine than to the myrtle. This recent acquisition by conquest has learned, like the vine, to be reproduced by mallet-shoots, and it covers declivities just like the vine, which supports its own weight without the aid of stays. When it puts forth branches it is pruned in a similar manner, and it thrives by being well raked at the roots, growing with remarkable rapidity, and bearing fruit at the end of three years. **The leaf bears a very considerable resemblance to that of rue, and it is an evergreen. The Jews vented their rage upon this shrub just as they were in the habit of doing against their own lives and persons, while, on the other hand, the Romans protected it; indeed, combats have taken place before now in defense of a shrub** (Pliny, *Natural History*, 12.54).

Pliny's choice to quote from a poem of 'Catullus' is also notable. In *Caesar's Messiah*, I showed that the identity of the authors of the New Testament was revealed by the solution of a puzzle at the end of Josephus's *Wars of the Jews* (7.11.437-453). In this puzzle, Jonathan (a Jewish rebel, a type of Jesus) accused Alexander and his wife Bernice of having "put him upon what he did" — that is, putting up Jonathan as their front man for the purpose of fomenting rebellion among the Jews in Cyrene. This accusation was presented to "Catullus, the governor of the Libyan Pentapolis", who acted upon it and had Bernice and Alexander put to death, along with three thousand other wealthy Jews. Jonathan and Catullus then accused Josephus and other Jews of Alexandria and Rome as well, at which point Vespasian stepped in to clear Josephus's name. Catullus fell ill and "his very entrails were so corroded, that they fell out of his body, and in that condition he died", which is the same unique fate that befell Judas Iscariot: "And falling headlong, he burst asunder in the midst, and all his bowels gushed out" (Acts 1:18).

Of course, the historical Bernice and Alexander were never actually put to death for any crime whatsoever, nor could 'Catullus' have died in the way the story claims, thus demonstrating that the entire passage must be treated as an enigma, rather than as literal history. In the enigma, Catullus is typologically linked to Judas, but the relation is a mirror image: whereas Judas falsely accused Jesus of being King of the Jews, Catullus's accusation seems to be the truth: by writing the Gospels, Bernice, Alexander and Josephus did indeed "put [Jesus] upon what he did". Pliny's choice to pay homage to 'Catullus' in his dedication to Titus was intended to link himself to the 'Catullus' in the Josephus passage that identified the authors of the Gospels, as a record of his role in the creation of Christianity.

Recognizing that Pliny was sarcastically commenting upon Christianity leads directly to the next discovery. The fact that the dedication in the 1623 Folio of the works of Shakespeare was based upon Pliny's dedication to Titus is well known to scholars. What has not been understood heretofore is that the author of the 1623 Folio dedication to Shakespeare understood that Pliny was playing off of the Gospels' satirical level, and linked his dedication to the same comic theme.

The dedication is quoted below. Most scholars believe that Ben Jonson, a member of Emilia Bassano's inner circle who apparently shared her knowledge of the Gospel's satirical code, was the author. The dedication is to William (Earle of Pembroke) and Philip (Earle of Montgomery), both of the "Noble Order of the Garter", and continues:

Right Honorable,

Whilst we study to be thankful in our particular, for the many favors we have received from your L.L (Lords) we are fallen upon the ill fortune, to mingle two the most diverse things that can bee, fear, and rashness; rashness in the enterprise, and fear of the success. **For, when we value the places your H.H. sustain, we cannot but know their dignity greater, then to descend to the reading of these trifles: and, while we name them trifles, we have depriu'd our selves of the defense of our Dedication. But since your L.L. have been pleased to think these trifles**

something, heretofore; and have prosecuted both them, and their Author living, with so much favor: we hope, that (they out- living him, and he not having the fate, common with some, to be executor to his own writings) you will use the like indulgence toward them, you have done onto their parent. There is a great difference, whether any Book choose his Patrons, or find them: This hath done both. For, so much were your LL. likings of the several parts, when they were acted, as before they were published, the Volume asked to be yours. We have but collected them, and done an office to the dead, to procure his Orphans, Guardians; without ambition either of self- profit, or fame: only to keep the memory of so worthy a Friend, & Fellow alive, as was our SHAKESPEARE, by humble offer of his plays, to your most noble patronage. **Wherein, as we have justly observed, no man to come near your L.L. but witha kind of religious addressed;** it hath bin the height of our care, who are the Presenters, to make the present worthy of your H.H. by the perfection. But, there we must also crave our abilities to be considered, my Lords. We cannot go beyond our own powers. **Country hands reach forth milk, cream, fruits, or what they have: and many Nations (we have heard) that had not gummes & incense, obtained their requests with a leavened Cake.** It was no fault to approach their Gods, by what mean they could: And the most, though meanest, of things are made more precious, when they are dedicated to Temples. In that name therefore, **we most humbly consecrate to your H.H. these remains of your servants Shakespeare**; that what delight is in them, may be ever your L.L. the reputation his, & the faults ours, if any be committed, by a prayer so careful to show their gratitude both to the living, and the dead, as is Your Lordshippes most bounden, John Heminge.

Henry Condell

The author links his dedication to Pliny's sarcasm concerning the Gospels in a number of ways. The first is by the use of the word "trifles", which he repeats three times at the beginning of his statement, the same point that Pliny uses the word in his dedication. Though 'trifle' is normally thought of today as something trivial or insignificant, its original meaning is actually "mockery" as the word stemmed from 'truffe', which means to mock or gibe. This may have also been Pliny's meaning when he used the equivalent Latin word in reference to the Gospels. The author of the folio's dedication is thereby repeating the wordplay concerning 'mockery' that Pliny created using the key Latin word "putare" above. The author is reversing Pliny's sarcasm, however. It is not the Jews who are being 'mocked' but the Gentile believers in 'Shakespeare'.

The folio's dedication also reveres Pliny's sarcasm by paraphrasing two of his two passages that wryly commented upon the Gospels:

> Country hands reach forth milk, cream, fruits, or what they have: and many Nations (we have heard) that had not gummes & incense, obtained their requests with a leavened Cake. It was no fault to approach their Gods, by what mean they could: And the most, though meanest, of things are made more precious, when they are dedicated to Temples.

These statements are clearly reiterations of the two statements in Pliny's dedication that are sarcastic comments upon Christianity.

> ...poor country peasants, yea, and of many nations, who offer nothing but milk unto them: and such as have no Incense, find grace and favor many times with the oblation of a plain cake made only of meal and salt; and never was any man blamed yet for his devotion to the gods, so he offered according to his ability...

> many things there that seem right and dear and be made precious, only because they are consecrated to some sacred things.

Notice, however, that the author of Shakespeare's dedication — though clearly basing his text upon Pliny's — has carefully changed a "plain cake made of meal and salt " to a "leavened Cake", thereby satirically indicating that Shakespeare was not Jewish but was Gentile 'bread'. The author of the dedication in Shakespeare's folio ends his spoof of Pliny's dedication to Titus by referring to Shakespeare's literature as "these remains of your servants Shakespeare", which clearly can be seen as relating to the 'corpse' of Shakespeare. Further, by connecting Shakespeare's "remains" to the Passover meal, the author repeats the extraordinary theme that runs throughout Emilia Bassano's poem "*Salve Deus Rex Judaeorum*" — the creation of a 'literary Paschal lamb' or 'Passover lamb'. In this instance, however, it is not a Jew but the 'perfect' Gentile Shakespeare who is the 'supper', and the author is not suggesting that he will be 'eaten' by Jews but (as in *Salve Deus*) by Christians.

Following its dedication, the Folio has a number of comments regarding Shakespeare that can be seen as relating to the Gospels' comic theme regarding 'pruning'. Shakespeare's plays in the folio are said to be 'perfect of limb', while those copies of the plays found in other sources are said to be 'maimed'. A number of statements contain references that can also be seen as witticisms ridiculing Shakespeare's wit, which is said to be no more able to be "hid than it could be lost". Shakespeare is said to have "small Latin, less Greek", and his face was writ in 'Brasse', which had the same connotation then as it does today — a bold fraud.

The 1640 edition of the Sonnets quotes Jonson's poem to Shakespeare but makes a travesty of it by the insertion of question marks. The comments appear directly below an engraving of Shakespeare that appears to be that of someone wearing a mask.

> This shadow is renowned Shakespeare's? Soul of the age. The applause? Delight? The wonder of the stage.

Ben Jonson wrote about Shakespeare in his work '*Timber*' where he continued the theme of humor concerning Shakespeare having not written his plays. He wrote:

> De Shakspeare nostrat. — Augustus in Hat. — I remember the players have often mentioned it as an honour to Shakspeare, that in his writing (whatsoever he penned) he never blotted out a line. My answer hath been, "Would he had blotted a thousand," which they thought a malevolent speech. I had not told posterity this but for their ignorance who chose that circumstance to commend their friend by wherein he most faulted; and to justify mine own candour, for I loved the man, and do honour his memory on this side idolatry as much as any. He was, indeed, honest, and of an open and free nature, had an excellent phantasy, brave notions, and gentle expressions, wherein he flowed with that facility that sometimes it was necessary he should be stopped. "Sufflaminandus erat," as Augustus said of Haterius. His wit was in his own power; would the rule of it had

been so, too. Many times he fell into those things, could not escape laughter, as when he said in the person of Cæsar, one speaking to him, " Cæsar, thou dost me wrong." He replied, "Cæsar did never wrong but with just cause;" and such like, which were ridiculous. But he redeemed his vices with his virtues. There was ever more in him to be praised than to be pardoned. (Ben Jonson, *Timber*, ed. Schelling, 1892, p. 23)

The sarcasm is not difficult to understand: he stated that Shakespeare "*never blotted a line*" — because he never wrote one — and the rule of his wit was "*not in his own power*" — as it was in someone else's power. Jonson stated that he loved him '*this side idolatry*' — because he was an idol and not a real author.

Jonson wrote that Shakespeare had to be "repressed" from time to time — "'*Sufflaminadus erat,*' *as Augustus said of Haterius*." Haterius was the Roman architect who constructed the Arch of Titus, the most famous monument to his divinity. Jonson recited an anecdote wherein Shakespeare stated: "*Caesar never did wrong but with just cause*", a statement that Jonson wrote was "ridiculous". Jonson was wryly commenting upon the real nature of Shakespeare's plays, which was to show that Caesar had, in fact, 'done wrong without cause'.

ROMEO AND JULIET

Having established with *Titus Andronicus* the symbolic framework of her work as an extension and counterattack to Titus and his Gospels, Emilia then 'branched' out. Though she often used Titus as a type for her characters, she never again made such an obvious attack against him. Instead, she often employed subtle subtexts and wordplay to make her characters into 'antetypes' of the Flavian villains. She wished to make the point that the Gentiles, who had ruled through 'Divine Right' throughout Christendom's history, shared Titus's guilt in the use of a false religion to maintain their power. This nobility had not only waged a general persecution of her race and religion since Titus, but had murdered Christopher Marlowe, as I show below perhaps her lover and certainly her mentor and friend. Typically, the Gentile royalty depicted in the Shakespearean plays are cursed with the same unwitting cannibalism that was inflicted in *Titus Andronicus.* With her typology, Emilia reversed Titus's cannibalistic curse on the Jews

Romeo and Juliet is an excellent example of this cannibalistic reversal. As with virtually all of the Shakespearean plays, the plot of *Romeo and Juliet* was derived from prior works. The primary source was Arthur Brooke's *Romeus and Juliet*, which used essentially the same plot. Brooke's poem was first published in 1562 and reprinted in 1587, eight years before the first performance of *Romeo and Juliet*. One of the major changes in the version of the story attributed to Shakespeare was the compression of the story's timeline. In Brooke's version, the events unfold over several months, whereas in the Shakespearean version the events take place in just over four days.

Shakespeare's *Romeo and Juliet* is one of the most beloved plays in the English language and is seen as beautiful but tragic story of an ill-fated love affair. However, its real meaning is a satire that reverses the Gospel's humor regarding the Jew's cannibalism of the Messiah on their Passover. At the conclusion of the play, the gentile nobility are turned into'bread'. And this occurs, not on the Passover, but near the Christian feast day of the 'consecrated bread'.

Romeo and Juliet is one of the Shakespearean plays that take place in the region of Italy from which Emilia Bassano's family emigrated. Shakespeare's focus upon this region has been a mystery, but now can now be explained. The Bassanos had lived in the area around Venice for generations, and Emilia would have either traveled to the region or learned enough about it from her family to be able to write about it in such detail. In fact the volume of plays set in the area were, like the numbers of 'Moors' in the plays, a clue left by the author as to her identity. By leaving such clues, Emilia was 'mirroring' the clues left by Titus in the Gospels.

As with so many of the plays, *Romeo and Juliet* harbors enigmas that have resisted all attempts at literary analysis. On the surface, the play seems to represent a senseless tragedy, as hasty but well-intentioned plans are continually going horribly awry. Perhaps because the original poem by Brooke mentioned 'Fortune' over forty times it has been suggested that the mass slaughter in *Romeo and Juliet* may be due simply to the stars or 'Fortune'. As one critic remarked, since there are no obviously evil characters in the play, the end result would consequentially seem to be simply an "unfortunate" accident. However, such a conclusion is unsatisfying, inadequate and ultimately incorrect.

In fact, one character in the play, the 'gardener' Friar Lawrence, can rightly be seen as a villain, at least from the perspective of the Gentile nobility. When the play is read in the light of the typology used in Titus Andronicus, a veiled subtext becomes clear in which Friar Lawrence deliberately manipulates the characters in order to create the bloody outcome. This subtext uses many of the same core metaphors as the Gospels: for example, a 'Messiah' who is portrayed as a mandrake root and is uprooted.

The Friar is named 'Lawrence' because the word derives from 'Laurentum', or one who wears the laurel wreath of victory. His name is appropriate in that Friar Lawrence is certainly the 'victor' at the end of the play. When we first encounter Friar Laurence he has just returned from a stint of gardening and delivers a monologue concerning the nature of plants. In his speech he states that plants have two natures, one evil and one good: *"baleful weeds and precious-juiced flowers"* (II, 3, 8).

On its surface level, the Friar's odd speech about the two moral essences of plants seems to be yet another incomprehensible Shakespearean 'puzzle'. He is certainly not commenting upon any moral differences between the two central families, the Capulets and the Montagues, as the playwright goes out of his way to make certain that the reader understands that the families are morally equivalent. For example, the play begins with the ironic statement *"Two households both alike in dignity"* (Prologue, 1). Later in the play the dying Mercutio builds upon this theme by proclaiming *"A plague o' both your houses"* (III, 1, 91).

Understanding that the play was written in the genre of Titus Andronicus (in other words, as a reversal of the satirical system in the Gospels) reveals the soliloquy's real meaning. It is a comment upon the two messianic lineages or 'branches' described in the Gospels: the 'vile' one created by the Romans and the real one that the Jews believed would produce their Messiah. The Friar is stating that the plant whose nature is evil, obviously the Christian 'branch', will be destroyed by its own wickedness — will be "eaten" by the "canker" of its hatred.

The word 'cankered' also refers to both the Capulets and the Montagues: *"Cankered with peace, to part your cankered hate"* (I, 1, 97). The Friar's use of the words "eaten" and "eats up" foreshadow the fate that awaits the two families who are "alike in dignity": that they will be eaten.

FRIAR LAURENCE

The grey-eyed morn smiles on the frowning night,
Chequering the eastern clouds with streaks of light,
And flecked darkness like a drunkard reels
From forth day's path and Titan's fiery wheels:
Now, ere the sun advance his burning eye,
The day to cheer and night's dank dew to dry,
I must up-fill this osier cage of ours
With baleful weeds and precious-juiced flowers.
The earth that's nature's mother is her tomb;

What is her burying grave that is her womb,
And from her womb children of divers kind
We sucking on her natural bosom find,
Many for many virtues excellent,
None but for some and yet all different.
O, mickle is the powerful grace that lies
In herbs, plants, stones, and their true qualities:
For nought so vile that on the earth doth live
But to the earth some special good doth give,
Nor aught so good but strain'd from that fair use
Revolts from true birth, stumbling on abuse:
Virtue itself turns vice, being misapplied;
And vice sometimes by action dignified.

[Enter Romeo]

Within the infant rind of this small flower
Poison hath residence and medicine power:
For this, being smelt, with that part cheers each part;
Being tasted, slays all senses with the heart.
Two such opposed kings encamp them still
In man as well as herbs, grace and rude will;
And where the worser is predominant,
Full soon the canker death eats up that plant.

(II, 3, 1-30)

The fact that the Friar believes that Christians are a 'cankerous' messianic root is a key link in the logic of Romeo and Juliet's satirical level. Friar Laurence's understanding that the Montagues and the Capulets are wicked 'branches' provides the motivation for his orchestrating their destruction. As was the case with 'Aaron' in *Titus Andronicus* above, the author used the Jewish turncoat priest, Josephus, as the 'type' for Friar Lawrence. Just as Josephus was a Jewish priest who worked for the Romans to help them cause the Jews to cannibalize one another, Friar Laurence (judging from his statements and actions) is a crypto-Jew who has become a Christian priest to cause the Christians to cannibalize themselves.

In the above passage, the timing of Romeo's entrance is critical as the point in the speech that he enters designates him as the 'branch' of the wicked Christian 'root'. The author is playing off of the 'root and branch' comedy in the Gospels. Romeo is the "infant rind" with the "canker that eats up the plant" that the Friar is referring to at his entrance.

This establishing of Romeo as a 'plant' is important because it links the character to the symbolism used later in the play regarding the Mandrake root. Readers of *Caesar's Messiah* will recall that Josephus used the Mandrake root as a metaphor for the messianic 'root' of the Jews that was 'uprooted' by the Romans. In *Romeo and Juliet* the playwright uses the same metaphor but in reverse to show that the false messianic 'Mandrake' root of the Gentiles — Romeo — had been 'uprooted' or killed.

Whereas the character 'Romeus' in Brooke's original poem was an ordinary man, the symbolism in *Romeo and Juliet* suggests that the lead has been transformed into a religious personage. In fact, Romeo represents the false Roman messiah — Jesus Christ. Juliet calls Romeo a "damned saint" (III, ii, 72-9), who appears with the name and disguise of a Pilgrim, so that Juliet quickly views him as "the god of my idolatry" (II, ii, 112-115). She also refers to him — using a phrase from the Gospels — as a "wolf in lamb's clothing."

The following seemingly contradictory descriptions of Romeo by Juliet are part of the representation of Romeo as the false 'Jesus' or 'root' of Christianity.

> O serpent heart, hid with a flowering face!
> Did ever dragon keep so fair a cave?
> Beautiful tyrant! fiend angelical!
> Dove-feather'd raven! wolvish-ravening lamb!
> Despised substance of divinest show!
> Just opposite to what thou justly seem'st,
> A damned saint, an honourable villain!
> O nature, what hadst thou to do in hell,
> When thou didst bower the spirit of a fiend
> In moral paradise of such sweet flesh?
> Was ever book containing such vile matter
> So fairly bound? O that deceit should dwell
> In such a gorgeous palace!

(III, 2, 73-85)

Traditional Christian interpretation cannot explain Juliet's contradictory descriptions of Romeo — as a saint that could be "damned"; as "angelical" but also a "fiend"; or as a "divine show" that concealed something "despicable"; or as the most "fairly bound book" (in Elizabethan England, this must certainly be the Bible) containing "vile matter" or a "god of idolatry". But these images are explicable if the playwright is comparing Romeo to the false Jesus, Titus, something that could not be imagined within the classic understanding of the Messiah of Christianity. The playwright knew, however, that once the secret satire in the Gospels was discovered such a characterization of Jesus would be comprehensible, and the meaning of the seemingly contradictory 'Jesus metaphors' in *Romeo and Juliet* would then be understood.

Titus tried to fool the Jews by creating a "divine show" that featured a 'Jesus' who seemingly rose from the dead, but was really the Emperor himself. Once it is understood that the playwright is playing off of Titus's deception then it is becomes clear what Romeo is referring to when he appears to come back from the dead and says: "I dreamt...That I revived and was an emperor" (V, 1, 6-9). The author is typologically linking Romeo to 'Titus/Jesus' who seemed to have died but was 'revived'.

To completely clarify Romeo's — whose name plays on this theme — linkages to the Caesars, he is described as the heir of 'Tiberio', obviously indicating Tiberius.

NURSE

He is the son and heir of old Tiberio.

(I, 5,129)

The name of Romeo's servant, 'Balthasar', was the name ascribed in the Middle Ages to one of the three wise men who brought gifts to the new born Messiah in the Gospels, thus contributing to the theme connecting Romeo with 'Jesus'. It was also the name given to the prophet Daniel by Gentiles. This helps with the understanding of the character's hidden Jewish identity and begins to establish the play's relationship to the prophecies of Daniel.

Juliet's birthday is also part of the play's broad reversal of the Gospels' satirical system. Juliet was born on July 31 — Lammas Eve, the day before Lammastide, the Christian 'feast' day that is the most similar to Passover. It was held every August first and, like Passover, was a feast that featured the eating of consecrated bread. The term 'Lammas' derives from the words 'loaf' and 'mass' and refers to the consecration of the bread made from the first fruits of the harvest. *Romeo and Juliet* builds towards its dramatic cannibalistic conclusion during the Lammastide season as a Jewish parody of the Gospels' building to their cannibalistic conclusion at Passover.

The following passage reverses the usage of Daniel's prophecies in the New Testament. In *Romeo and Juliet,* Daniel's prophecies envision the Gentile's destruction at the play's end, rather than the Jews. Notice in the passage that Juliet's birthday is mentioned three times. The highlighting by repetition of concepts particularly important to the satirical level was a technique the author borrowed from the Gospels: for example, the key word "soudarion" is repeated thrice in the description of Jesus's tomb. The numbers fourteen and eleven (which are associated with Daniel's prophecies) are also repeated, and that the nurse's deceased husband makes a 'prophesy' regarding Juliet — that she would "fall backwards" when she has "more wit"; i.e. when she reached her fourteenth birthday.

NURSE

Faith, I can tell her age unto an hour.

LADY CAPULET

She's not fourteen.

NURSE

I'll lay fourteen of my teeth,—
And yet, to my teeth be it spoken, I have but four—
She is not fourteen. How long is it now
To Lammas-tide?

LADY CAPULET

A fortnight and odd days.

NURSE

Even or odd, of all days in the year,
Come Lammas-eve at night shall she be fourteen.

Susan and she—God rest all Christian souls!—
Were of an age: well, Susan is with God;
She was too good for me: but, as I said,
On Lammas-eve at night shall she be fourteen;
That shall she, marry; I remember it well.
'Tis since the earthquake now eleven years;
And she was wean'd,—I never shall forget it,—
Of all the days of the year, upon that day:
For I had then laid wormwood to my dug,
Sitting in the sun under the dove-house wall;
My lord and you were then at Mantua:—
Nay, I do bear a brain:—but, as I said,
When it did taste the wormwood on the nipple
Of my dug and felt it bitter, pretty fool,
To see it tetchy and fall out with the dug!
Shake quoth the dove-house: 'twas no need, I trow,
To bid me trudge:
And since that time it is eleven years;
For then she could stand alone; nay, by the rood,
She could have run and waddled all about;
For even the day before, she broke her brow:
And then my husband—God be with his soul!
A' was a merry man—took up the child:
'Yea,' quoth he, 'dost thou fall upon thy face?
Thou wilt fall backward when thou hast more wit;
Wilt thou not, Jule?' and, by my holidame,
The pretty wretch left crying and said 'Ay.'
To see, now, how a jest shall come about!
I warrant, an I should live a thousand years,
I never should forget it: 'Wilt thou not, Jule?' quoth he;
And, pretty fool, it stinted and said 'Ay.'

(I. 3. 11-48)

Josephus falsified the prophecies of Daniel to show *hoi polloi* that
the Roman's destruction of the Jews had been ordained by God.
The above passage cleverly reverses this and is a spoof of the
Gospels' and *Wars of the Jews'* improbable linkage of Daniel's
prophecies to the Jewish feast day of the Passover. The spoof is
created by linking the time spans of fourteen and eleven years to a
prophecy regarding the Christian holy day of Lammastide. In the
Bible, Daniel's prophecies were presented in time spans of
"weeks", which are periods of seven years. The fact that Juliet will
be exactly fourteen years old on the upcoming feast of

Lammastide indicates that this will be the closing of the second week — the second period of seven years.

The authors of the Gospels and *Wars of the Jews* brazenly falsified history to create the impression that Daniel's prophecy (echoed by Jesus) concerning the 'abomination of desolation' had 'come to pass' exactly as the prophets had predicted, three and a half years from the beginning of the war between the Romans and the Jews. Josephus continued this fiction by recording that the war then ended precisely three and a half years later with the self-destruction by the last of the Jewish rebels at Masada.

To reverse the falsification of Daniel's prophesies, the nurse in the above passage indicates that at the mid point of the previous 'week', in other words eleven years ago, a disaster had occurred — the earthquake that led to Juliet's breaking "her brow". On that 'portentous' day, the nurse's deceased husband had made a prediction concerning Juliet — that she would "fall backwards" — indicating she will die — once she has "some wit". As this 'comes to pass' at the play's end, this 'fulfilled prophecy' satirically reverses the fictitious 'Daniel prophecies' described by Josephus and the Gospels so that in *Romeo and Juliet* Daniel is 'envisioning' the destruction of the Gentiles not the Jews. The "dove house" was shaken as a spoof of the use of doves in the Gospels to designate the Messiah as in Matthew 3:16. The passage's absurd nature is deliberate. It parodies the ludicrous application of the prophecies of Daniel in the Gospels and *Wars of the Jews* and those foolish enough to believe them.

Scholars have previously noticed *Romeo and Juliet*'s numerous citations of New Testament passages related to the apostle Peter, and also the speeches of the 'Peter' who is a servant to the Capulets. These allusions begin with a quote from 1 Peter (3:7) suggesting that women are "weaker vessels" (I, 1, 15). Next is a passage in which Peter rashly draws his sword (II, 4,154-157), bringing to mind the event in the Garden of Gethsemane where Peter drew his sword to cut off a priest's servant's ear (John 18:10). Mr. Goodwill tells the men to put away their swords since they "know not what you do" (I, I, 65), blending Jesus' instruction to Peter to put his sword away (John 18:11) with his words from the cross "forgive them; for they know not what they do" (Luke 23:34). Finally, the wedding of Paris and Juliet was to be celebrated at Saint Peter's Church. In my view, these 'Saint Peter' references are included in the play simply to help the reader understand that it is a reworking of Gospel's story concerning the

Passover and Christ's Passion, in which Peter played a central role.

Knowing that the character 'Peter' is related to the Apostle Peter explains the mysterious and irreverent exchange between Peter and a group of musicians (IV, 5,100-140) following Juliet's feigned death. Peter asks the musicians to play "some merry dump", an oxymoron meaning a song that is both merry and sad. The musicians ask what reward they will be given. Peter refuses to give them money and offers them a minstrel or vagabond instead, but the musicians say that they only play for silver. The passage is notable in that Emilia Bassano came from a family of Jewish musicians (recorders) — who would have also known the truth of the Gospels' satire — and may represent actual witticisms exchanged between Emilia and her musician cousins and uncles while they played at Christian events.

Their comedy is black. The 'dump', a sad song, is now "merry" because the death of a Gentile it commemorates is a merry event to this particular group of recorders. They are paid in silver because the scene takes place just before the 'Last Supper' and that was the currency paid to Judas at the same point in the version of the story given in the Gospels.

Peter says "on my faith" that he will give the musicians the 'gleek', meaning jest or riddle, in exchange for their playing. A musician responds saying that if Peter gives them the solution that they will give him the "serving creature". In other words, the joke is that the Christ was the 'serving creature': that is, he was cannibalized.

Being crypto-Jews, the recorders have false names. All Jews had to adopt Christian names in England during the period. They decide to avoid dinner, unlike the unknowing Gentiles who are about to participate in an unsavory 'feast'. Note that the song Peter describes relates to the end of the play, in that the destruction of the Gentile nobility is the "redress" for their execution of the Jew's Messiah.

PETER

Musicians, O, musicians, 'Heart's ease,
Heart's ease:' O, an you will have me live, play
'Heart's ease.'

FIRST MUSICIAN

Why 'Heart's ease?'

PETER

O, musicians, because my heart itself plays
'My heart is full of woe:' O, play me some
merry dump, to comfort me.

FIRST MUSICIAN

Not a dump we; 'tis no time to play now.

PETER

You will not, then?

FIRST MUSICIAN

No.

PETER

I will then give it you soundly.

FIRST MUSICIAN

What will you give us?

PETER

No money, on my faith, but the gleek;
I will give you the minstrel.

FIRST MUSICIAN

Then I will give you the serving-creature.

PETER

Then will I lay the serving-creature's dagger on
your pate. I will carry no crotchets: I'll re you,
I'll fa you; do you note me?

FIRST MUSICIAN

An you re us and fa us, you note us

SECOND MUSICIAN

Pray you, put up your dagger, and put out your wit.

PETER

Then have at you with my wit! I will dry-beat you with an iron wit, and put up my iron dagger. Answer me like men:
'When griping grief the heart doth wound,
And doleful dumps the mind oppress,
Then music with her silver sound'—
why 'silver sound'? why 'music with her silver sound'? What say you, Simon Catling?

MUSICIAN

Marry, sir, because silver hath a sweet sound.

PETER

Pretty! What say you, Hugh Rebeck?

SECOND MUSICIAN

I say 'silver sound,' because musicians sound for silver.

PETER

Pretty too! What say you, James Soundpost?

THIRD MUSICIAN

Faith, I know not what to say.

PETER

O, I cry you mercy; you are the singer: I will say for you. It is 'music with her silver sound,' because musicians have no gold for sounding:
'Then music with her silver sound
With speedy help doth lend redress.'

[Exit]

FIRST MUSICIAN

What a pestilent knave is this same!

SECOND MUSICIAN

Hang him, Jack! Come, we'll in here; tarry for the
mourners, and stay dinner.

(IV, 5, 148)

This scene also sets up a playful typological (sequential) parallel
to the passion story in the Gospels. The sequence begins with the
nurse's sevenfold repetition of the word 'woe' as she discovers
Juliet has (apparently) died, echoing Jesus's repetitious curse
"woe to you, scribes and Pharisees" of Matt. 23.

NURSE

O woe! O woeful, woeful, woeful day!
Most lamentable day, most woeful day
That ever, ever, I did yet behold!
O day, O day, O day, O hateful day!
Never was seen so black a day as this.
O woeful day, O woeful day!

(IV, 5, 55)

The narration then moves on to the scene with Peter and the
musician, which includes textual elements invoking Jesus's
capture, the thirty pieces of silver, trial and beating, and concludes
with the statement "hang him, Jack" describing the crucifixion.
Notice how the scene's incoherency fades away once the play is
read with the correct interpretive framework.

Friar Lawrence's hidden plot to destroy the Gentiles begins when
Romeo tells Friar Lawrence that he has fallen in love with Juliet,
and asks him to preside over their wedding. The Friar agrees, and
'foresees' the future:

But come, young waverer, come, go with me.
In one respect I'll thy assistant be,

> For this alliance may so happy prove
> To turn your household' rancor to pure love.

> *(II, 3, 95)*

On the surface this appears to be a blessing, however unlikely the Friar's reasoning might be, as it is difficult to believe that the Friar expects that such a secret elopement will be endearing to the youths' parents. But I believe this is also a double entendre: the Friar is referring to the pile of dead Gentiles at the play's end as 'pure love'. In other words, his goal is to orchestrate the eating of the cankerous weeds he described in his previous soliloquy. From this point forward, he causes every action or decision central to the storyline. It must be remembered when evaluating Friar Lawrence's behavior that he believes the Gentile nobility is a false 'root' that will be destroyed by the 'canker' of its own hatred.

As the Friar commences the wedding of the ill-fated couple, he repeats the ominous request to "Come with me".

> Come, come with me, and we will make short work,

> *(II, 6, 35)*

In a moment of passion, Romeo kills Tybalt and is banished from Verona. Friar Lawrence meets with him and Juliet's nurse. The Friar is in complete control of the characters that are 'coming' with him to their destruction. He instructs the nurse to *"Commend me to your lady"* (III, 3, 165), which begins the set-up for Juliet's agreement to take a potion that will cause the appearance of death. Friar Lawrence then instructs Romeo:

> Sojourn in Mantua. I'll find out your man.
> And he shall signify from time to time
> Every good hap to you that chances here.

> *(III, 3, 169-172)*

By telling Romeo that he will "find out" his man (Balthasar) and have him bring "every good hap" (news), Friar Lawrence sets his plot in motion and leaves a clue for the alert reader whose meaning will become clear later in the play.

Once Juliet learns that her parents are going to force her to marry Count Paris, she meets privately with the Friar to seek his advice.

Father Lawrence tells her that does "spy a kind of hope" (IV, 1, 68) and instructs her to take his death-simulating potion. He tells her that once she is buried in her family's crypt, she will be revived, and Romeo will come and take her to his place of exile. Of course he could simply tell her to flee with Romeo to Mantua, but that would not create the situation the Friar is trying to create. The Friar tells Juliet that the drug will make her appear lifeless for exactly *"forty and two hours"* (IV, 1, 107). The author is creating a symbolic 'numerical landscape' that mirrors the Passover story in the Gospels in which Daniel's prophecies also formed the backdrop. In this case, the number 42 is 'miraculously' related to Daniel by his prediction that there would be 1290 days (that is, 42 months, or three and a half years) between the end of the daily sacrifice and the abomination of desolation (Daniel 12:11- 12).

Scholars have been puzzled by the length of time Juliet is drugged. Though the first three acts have specific time references, the overall timeline of the play becomes strangely ambiguous at its end. We know that the play begins on Sunday morning; that Romeo and Juliet are married on Monday afternoon; and that plans for Juliet's wedding to Paris are settled on Tuesday evening. However, from that point forward, the play avoids making specific statements about the weekday of each scene's occurrence.

If the events precede according Capulet's proclaimed plans, then the wedding guests should be arriving Wednesday morning only to find that a 'funeral' is taking place instead. Balthasar watches Juliet placed in the crypt, and then *"presently"* brings the news to Romeo (V, 1, 21). Thus, traveling on a swift horse he would be meeting with Romeo on Wednesday afternoon, which places Romeo at Juliet's grave Wednesday evening. This timeline encompasses three and a half days from its beginning Sunday morning to the bloodbath of Wednesday night, in order to comically reverse the Gentile's use of Daniel in the Gospels. In other words, the play's three and a half day timespan links to Daniel's prophecy that the end of the sacrifice would come at the midpoint of the week (Daniel 9:27).

However, this timeline seemingly contradicts Friar Lawrence's statement that Juliet would be drugged for 42 hours, as well as the night watchman's statement that Juliet has been in the grave for two days (V, 3, 176). To resolve the contradictions, scholars have suggested that Shakespeare was sloppy and simply forgot to insert an extra day before Balthasar's meeting with Romeo, thereby delaying the discovery of the drugged Juliet (and all subsequent events) until Thursday. In fact, the author wants an alert reader to recognize that Friar Lawrence's 'prophecy' about the 42 hours as an enigma.

To solve Shakespeare's enigma, a reader must first recognize that the "borrowed likeness of shrunk death" Friar Laurence referred to was the false religion of the Gentiles — Christianity — which uses the "borrowed likeness" of the dead Jewish Messiah as its symbol.

> And in this borrowed likeness of shrunk death
> Thou shall continue two and forty hour

> *(4,1, 106-107)*

Friar Lawrence's statement is a double entendre whose subtle meaning comically mirrors the absurd use of Daniel in the Gospels. In other words, his apparent error was a 'divinely inspired' prediction that the sacrifice of the false Christian messiah would occur at the mid point of a week, the moment when Romeo would, in Daniel's terms, be "cut off".

The prophetic burlesque works like clockwork, and Juliet not only wakes up early enough to hear the Mandrake scream, but also late enough to bring about the cutting off of the Gentile's false messiah. Scholars who don't get the joke are forced to conjecture about the timeline in order to make it coherent. But the playwright did not blunder, and was simply mocking Josephus's jiggering the course of events in the Jewish War to make it appear that Daniel's prophecies were coming to pass.

In Act V, scene 2, Friar Lawrence did not send Balthasar with the crucial message to Romeo, but rather the scatterbrained Friar John, who managed to get himself caught up in a quarantine. Meanwhile, by failing to inform Balthasar that Juliet was really still alive, the Friar (knowing Balthasar's loyalty to Romeo) insured that Romeo would be swiftly and wrongly notified of Juliet's death.

After Friar Lawrence learns that Friar John had not delivered the
letter, he is alone and mentions that he intends to write again to
Romeo in Mantua and that he intends to keep Juliet in his cell (V,
2, 29). This begs the question, of course, why he did not do these
obvious things instead of faking Juliet's death. The solution to this
enigma is revealed by the Friar's final prophecy:

"Poor living corse, closed in a dead man's tomb"

(V, 2, 30)

The statement is 'prophetic' in that Juliet will soon be in a tomb
with the dead Romeo. It is also a pun, as Juliet will be a 'course'
in the subsequent meal. The Friar can see the future because he is
bringing it about. One can see the explanatory power of the
interpretation that the play reverses the Flavians' typology in the
Gospels. This interpretation resolves all of the play's
contradictions and incoherencies.

For example, the fatal events Friar Lawrence orchestrated at the
Capulets' tomb occur in a perfect order. The Friar himself arrives
at the tomb at just the right moment to be able to inform Juliet that
Romeo has killed himself because he thought that she was dead.
Instead of helping Juliet with her grief, however, Friar Lawrence
abandons Juliet because "a noise did scare me from the tomb" (V,
3, 268).

The noise that 'frightened' Friar Lawrence (overtly, the sound of
the night watch arriving) also represents the mandrake root
screaming with the death of Romeo. This is the reason why Juliet
was afraid that she would hear a mandrake scream if she awoke
"early" (IV, 3, 47). Her 'prophecy' was correct, and she awoke as
Romeo was dying (his lips were still warm — V, 3, 167) and
figuratively she heard the 'mandrake' scream as it was 'torn from
the earth'. All of the seemingly irrelevant details of the play come
together within the correct interpretation, and create a logical
subtext.

Within the satirical level of *Romeo and Juliet*, the 'bread' the
Gentile celebrants of the festival of Lammastide ate following the
mass slaughter of Gentiles at the tomb was the same 'bread' that
the Jews ate at Passover described in the Gospels, namely human
flesh. The author builds this subtext by the chronic use of imagery
that describes humans as food, or by the tearing off of human

joints. The sheer preponderance of this theme is telling, and some of the related passages are given below.

At the beginning of the play someone called 'Sampson' is told that he is not 'fish'. This is because someone with the name 'Sampson' would be a Jew, and in this play Jews are not fish. In this satire, the Christians are the 'fish' — "poorJohn" being a simple meal of fish.

GREGORY

'Tis well thou art not fish; if thou hadst,
thou hadst been poor John.

(I, 1, 30)

Mercutio, when he understood that he was about to die, announced that he was "peppered". Friar Lawrence tossed rosemary unto Juliet's lifeless body before she was placed into the crypt. When Juliet foresaw their death, Romeo replied: "dry sorrow drinks our blood" (III, 5, 58). Juliet's last name 'Capulet' is also part of this theme, as it is a pun on 'capulin', a fish from the North Sea common to English diets, better known as 'capers'. Another example of the theme occurs when Romeo enters Juliet's tomb and senses a "feasting presence."

ROMEO

I'll bury thee in a triumphant grave; A grave?
O no! a lantern, slaughter'd youth,
For here lies Juliet, and her beauty makes
This vault a feasting presence full of light.
Death, lie thou there, by a dead man interr'd.

(V, 3, 84)

The clearest representation of the coming cannibalism on Lammastide occurs in another of Romeo's statements as he enters the tomb.

ROMEO

Thou detestable maw, thou womb of death,
Gorged with the dearest morsel of the earth,
Thus I enforce thy rotten jaws to open,
And, in despite, I'll cram thee with more food!

(V, 3, 45)

Perhaps the wittiest example, if the term can be applied here, of the wordplay concerning cannibalism is a theme that runs throughout the play regarding 'joints'. The author begins her punning on the word 'joint' in the following passage in which Juliet's father instructs her to take her 'joints' to church, and then refers to her as 'carrion'.

CAPULET

How now, how now, chop-logic! What is this?
'Proud,' and 'I thank you,' and 'I thank you not;'
And yet 'not proud,' mistress minion, you,
Thank me no thankings, nor, proud me no prouds,
But fettle your fine joints 'gainst Thursday next,
To go with Paris to Saint Peter's Church,
Or I will drag thee on a hurdle thither.
Out, you green-sickness carrion! out, you baggage!
You tallow-face!

(III, 5, 149-157)

The author then builds upon the theme in the following passage in which Juliet envisions playing madly with 'joints' at her family tomb.

JULIET

So early waking, what with loathsome smells,
And shrieks like mandrakes' torn out of the earth,
That living mortals, hearing them, run mad:—
O, if I wake, shall I not be distraught,
Environed with all these hideous fears?
And madly play with my forefather's joints?
And pluck the mangled Tybalt from his shroud?
And, in this rage, with some great kinsman's bone,
As with a club, dash out my desperate brains?
O, look! methinks I see my cousin's ghost
Seeking out Romeo, that did spit his body
Upon a rapier's point.

(IV, 3, 46-57)

The theme becomes completely clarified in the following passage in which Romeo foresees the strewing of joints and limbs throughout a hungry churchyard. It must be remembered that the Flavian satirical system indicated that the Jewish Messiah was 'pruned' — that is, his limbs were taken off — and eaten by his followers. In Romeo and Juliet this grim joke was reversed back upon the Gentile's royal family.

ROMEO

> In what I further shall intend to do,
> By heaven, I will tear thee joint by joint
> And strew this hungry churchyard with thy limbs.

(V, 3, 36)

Having established the punning theme on 'joint', the author delivers the punch line at the conclusion of the play. In the following passage, Juliet's father asks for Montague's 'hand', calling it his daughter's 'jointure' (dowry).

CAPULET

> O brother Montague, give me your hand.
> This is my daughter's jointure,
> for no more can I demand.

(V, 3, 296-298)

The satire of cannibalism in the Shakespearean literature is taken to perhaps the highest metaphorical pitch in *Romeo and Juliet*. The 'first fruits' in *Romeo & Juliet* are a punning substance, the 'flower' — that is the 'flour' — of youth. Juliet and Romeo are 'incorporated' — made into "One Body and Flesh" — in the marriage service. They "shall not stay alone, Til Holy Church incorporate two into one" (II, 6, 37). This metaphorical logic continues with Juliet's father who is opposed to the marriage stating: "God's bread! It makes me mad" (III, 5, 18).

The list of 'flours' for the Lammastide 'bread' includes; the handsome but weak "flower' of Romeo; the "sweetest flower"(IV, 5, 28); Juliet, now 'deflowered' (IV, 5, 37) although she was not really "ripe"; Paris who is "a flower, in very faith a flower" (I, 3, 78) ; Mercutio who is the flower known as a 'pink' (II, 4, 60) and has already been "peppered"; and Juliet's relative Tybalt, who may belong to a floral family, but is "green in earth" (IV, 3, 42).

From the tomb, the various bodies will provide the 'flour' for the feast of Lammastide. The playwright is simply reversing the 'joint' and 'bread' humor of the Gospels that concluded on the Passover, with a Gentile version of the story that concludes on their feast day of the consecrated bread.

HAMLET

Hamlet is the most researched play in the world, with a bibliography that reached over 12,000 listings in 2004. Despite this effort, much of the play is still a 'puzzle' to many modern critics. Analyzing the play in the light of the Flavian typology, however, renders it completely coherent.

Hamlet was based upon a tale in Saxo's *Historiae Danicae.* In that story, Fengo bloodily butchers his brother, Ameltath, at a banquet and then marries his wife Gerutha. Ameltath's son, the young prince Ameltath, pretends to go mad with anguish, and is sent to England to recuperate. A year later, he returns—analogous to the return of Ulysses— and gets Fengo and his nobles drunk at a feast and kills them all by setting fire to the hall.

Shakespeare's version has far more carnage than its source. A critic noted that the script is so stocked with limbs, organs, and body fluids that "the play looks like a dissecting room"[80]. Eyes, tongues, hands, arms, faces and brains are mentioned "incessantly". In total, 60 different body parts are depicted. Hamlet, discussing a prospective swordfight with Laertes, suggests to "divide him inventorially" (V, 2, 114). There are references to pieces (I, 1, 19) and carving up (I, 3,30). Hamlet goes to "draw apart the body he hath kill'd" (IV, 1, 24). Such carving is also emphasized by one of the players of the play within the play:

---

[80] John Hunt, 'A Thing of Nothing: The Catastrophic Body in Hamlet', *Shakespeare Quarterly*, 39 (1988), 27.

When she saw Pyrrhus make malicious sport
In mincing with his sword her husband's limbs.

(II, 2, 513-14)

The play also incorporates a vast amount of cannibalistic imagery, as has been noted before,[81] and although it has been suggested that this imagery is related to the play's general preoccupation with death and the fate of the human body,[82] this does not seem to be a completely satisfactory explanation. The problem is particularly vexing because the theme does not occur at all in Saxo's *Historiae Danicae* (the source for *Hamlet*), and some critics have complained that this constitutes a structural problem in understanding the play's meaning. Critics have wondered: if the playwright is implying that cannibalism is occurring, who is eating whom, and why? For example, what is the meaning of the statement that indicates that Hamlet's father was eaten: *"most holy and religious fear it is to keep those many bodies safe that live and feed upon your majesty"* (III, 3, 8-10).

The sheer volume of cannibalistic imagery in Hamlet suggests that this question must be answered before the play can be understood. My solution, of course, is that 'Shakespeare' constructed a reversal of the cannibal theme of the Flavian comic system. The key character in this reversal is 'Fortinbras', whose name means 'Strong Arm': so named by the playwright because he was one of the few characters at the play's conclusion with his limbs intact.

Hamlet encounters his father's ghost, who informs him that he has been murdered by his brother, Hamlet's uncle, the new king. The character Fortinbras is introduced at this point and is established

---

[81] Lalita Pandit, 'Language and the Textual Unconscious: Shakespeare, Ovid and Saxo Grammaticus', in *Criticism and Lacan: essays and dialogue on language, structure, and the unconscious*, ed. by Patrick Colm Hogan and Lalita Pandit (Athens: University of Georgia Press, 1990), p. 264.

[82] Yasuhiro Ogawa, 'Grinning Death's-Head: Hamlet and the Vision of the Grotesque', *eNotes* <http://www.enotes.com/topics/hamlet/critical-essays/grinning-deaths-head-hamlet-and-vision-grotesque> [accessed 13 March 2014].

as a mirror image of Hamlet. Like Hamlet, Fortinbras was named for his father, who was King but has been recently killed by Hamlet's father, who was also named Hamlet. And like Prince Hamlet, Fortinbras's uncle seized the throne after his father's death. However, Fortinbras and his family are unstained by the violence of brother on brother, while the bad karma of both regicides falls upon Prince Hamlet. Thus, it seems fitting that a better fate awaits Fortinbras than for Hamlet.

With these devices, the author is using concepts from the Flavian comical system to construct a hidden storyline, which is submerged beneath the surface narration. Like Titus Andronicus above, the storyline reverses the Gospels' typology that mocks the Jews' cannibalism during the siege of Jerusalem. To achieve this literary reversal of fate, the play sets up two generations with parallel names. In the first generation, Hamlet defeated Fortinbras and seized his land, but in the second generation this will be reversed, and Fortinbras will reclaim his territory.

Fortinbras's name is one of an unusual number of references in the play to 'arms', which foreshadow the limbs that will be pruned and cannibalized at the conclusion of the play. At one point in the play, a gardener who has trouble digging because he is an amputee (V, 1, 30) is contrasted with Fortinbras and his strong arms. The humor is accentuated with the understanding that the author is intentionally juxtaposing his play to the "pruning' of the Jewish Messiah satirically depicted in the Gospels. The following examples of the 'hand and arm' humor are just those found in Act I, scene 2:

HORATIO

In the dead vast and middle of the night,
Been thus encounter'd. A figure like your father,
Armed at point exactly, cap-a-pe,
Appears before them, and with solemn march...
The apparition comes: I knew your father;
These hands are not more like.

[...]

HAMLET

Arm'd, say you?

MARCELLUS BERNARDO

Arm'd, my lord.

HAMLET

From top to toe?

MARCELLUS BERNARDO

My lord, from head to foot.

[...]

HAMLET

My father's spirit in arms! all is not well;

(I, 2, 198-254)

The name of the character 'Polonius' is also related to the cannibal theme. His name is a play upon 'polony', a word that meant 'sausage' in medieval English. Polonius's body parts are referred to as "offal" (II, 2, 580) and "guts" (III, 4, 212) that have to be carried off stage. Guts, of course, are used for sausage making. After Hamlet kills Polonius, pointing to his dead body in a tirade against his mother Gertrude, Hamlet makes it crystal clear that this 'sausage' will be eaten: *Could you on this fair mountain leave to feed and batten (glut yourself) on this moor* (III, 4, 66-67). Polonius's name and fate occur because he is another of Shakespeare's characters representing a 'type' of Josephus — the Jewish or 'moor' turncoat who helped the Romans write the Gospels. Notice that Polonius is identified as a 'Moor' above. 'Shakespeare' typically brings her Josephus figures to a justly ignoble fate. In this case, Polonius has become food for worms; but in due time, as Hamlet explains, fish will eat the worms, and men will eat the fish, thus completing the cannibalistic cycle.

The passage below may also be an ironic reference to the Imperial Diet of Worms, where Martin Luther was declared an outlaw in 1521. If so, the playwright's not-so-subtle comic point was that the Catholic hierarchy was consuming Luther for supper.

KING CLAUDIUS

Now, Hamlet, where's Polonius?

HAMLET

At supper.

KING CLAUDIUS

At supper! where?

HAMLET

Not where he eats, but where he is eaten: a certain convocation of politic worms are e'en at him. Your worm is your only emperor for diet: we fat all creatures else to fat us, and we fat ourselves for maggots: your fat king and your lean beggar is but variable service, two dishes, but to one table: that's the end.

KING CLAUDIUS

Alas, alas!

HAMLET

A man may fish with the worm that hath eat of a king, and cat of the fish that hath fed of that worm.

KING CLAUDIUS

What dost you mean by this?

HAMLET

Nothing but to show you how a king may go a progress through the guts of a beggar.

(IV, 3, 16-31)

Within the context of the Flavian's comic system, Hamlet's comment above *"Not where he eats, but where he is eaten"* is a reference to the double entendre regarding Lazarus being 'made a supper' at John 12:2. Due to its macabre nature, the Gospel's joke regarding someone being "made a supper" is certainly among the very few times in literature that this genre of humor has ever been used. It is unlikely that the author of *Hamlet* also used this precise format by accident; but rather, its use in this context is evidence that 'Shakespeare' was aware of the Flavian cannibalistic theme.

The passage in *Hamlet* is also clever irony in that it was Josephus (that is, Joseph of Arimathea) who, after he took Jesus's body down from the cross, placed the body in the sepulcher where the stone could be used to hide it. Polonius's fate is a reversal of Josephus's action: while Josephus was hiding a body, it is Polonius's own body that is being hidden before it is 'eaten'. Further, as shown below, the author helps the reader understand that the play is taking place within a 'Lazarus context' by playing on the word 'lazar'.

Other references to cannibalism in *Hamlet* draw on Seneca's *Thyestes,* the story of a King named Atreus who killed his nephews and served them as a dinner to their father. These subtle references may have been apparent to erudite Elizabethans, since Jasper Heywood's translation of Seneca's works had been published by 1566. Nashe commented that *"Seneca read by candle light 'yeeldes manie good sentences…and if you intreate him faire in a frostie morning, he will affoord you whole Hamlets'"* (Nashe, Preface to Greene's Menathon).

Hamlet's desire to drink "hot blood" echoes the desire of Atreus to pour "hot blood" down his brother's throat in *Thyestes* (1060). Less obvious is the playwright's use of Seneca's description that one of the nephew's head 'fell thrice' and sighed as it fell off its body. *"The royal diadem fell twice, yea thrice. With a whispered sound the head rolled downward"* (*Thyestes*, 705-6).

Ophelia's description of Hamlet's madness uses Seneca's imagery of the three head motions and the sighing. The playwright is, thus, using Thyestes' nephew as a 'type' for Hamlet to indicate that the same fate awaits the Dane: in other words, he will be eaten.

> At last, a little shaking of mine arm
> And thrice his head thus waving up and down,
> He raised a sigh so piteous and profound
> As it did seem to shatter all his bulk
> And end his being: that done, he lets me go.

(II, 1, 89-93)

The following comment about how quickly Hamlet's mother married after his father's death is an example of the clever wordplay the author created that becomes visible once the play is understood as a reversal of the cannibalism humor in the Gospels.

> The funeral baked meats.
> Did coldly furnish forth the marriage tables.

(I, 2, 180-181)

What were these 'funeral baked meats'? The author makes this known with the statement: *"many bodies,,, feed upon your majesty"* (III, 3, 9-10). Thus, the 'meat' at King Hamlet's funeral was his flesh.

The author set up the cannibalism of Hamlet's father in another way. The author used Lazarus as a 'type' for Hamlet's father to communicate that he also underwent Lazarus's grim cannibalized fate. This was established by describing the effect of the poison that killed the King as making him 'Lazar like.' The word 'lazar' stems from 'Lazarus', who was described in the Gospels as a beggar with skin ulcers licked by dogs as well as being cannibalized.

> The leperous distilment;
> whose effect Holds such an enmity with blood of man
> That swift as quicksilver it courses through
> The natural gates and alleys of the body,
> And with a sudden vigour doth posset
> And curd, like eager droppings into milk,

The thin and wholesome blood: so did it mine;
And a most instant tetter bark'd about,
Most lazar-like, with vile and loathsome crust,
All my smooth body.

(I, 5, 64-73)

The storyline of the satirical level of Hamlet begins in Act 1,
scene 5 when Hamlet, after he has spoken with his father's ghost,
states that he is going to pray. When we next hear of Hamlet,
Ophelia describes him as a changed man who has gone mad.

OPHELIA

My lord, as I was sewing in my closet,
Lord Hamlet, with his doublet all unbraced;
No hat upon his head; his stockings foul'd,
Ungarter'd, and down-gyved to his ancle;
Pale as his shirt; his knees knocking each other;
And with a look so piteous in purport
As if he had been loosed out of hell
To speak of horrors,—he comes before me.

LORD POLONIUS

Mad for thy love?

OPHELIA

My lord, I do not know;
But truly, I do fear it.

(II, 1, 74-83)

Soon we learn that Hamlet has not been driven mad by love, but
rather by his reading of a book:

[Enter HAMLET, reading a book...]

POLONIUS

O, give me leave:
How does my good Lord Hamlet?

HAMLET

Well, God-a-mercy.

LORD POLONIUS

Do you know me, my lord?

HAMLET

Excellent well; you are a fishmonger.

LORD POLONIUS

Not I, my lord.

HAMLET

Then I would you were so honest a man.

LORD POLONIUS

Honest, my lord!

HAMLET

Ay, sir; to be honest, as this world goes, is to be
one man picked out of ten thousand.

LORD POLONIUS

That's very true, my lord.

HAMLET

For if the sun breed maggots in a dead dog, being a
god kissing carrion,—Have you a daughter?

LORD POLONIUS

I have, my lord.

HAMLET

Let her not walk i' the sun: conception is a
blessing: but not as your daughter may conceive.
Friend, look to 't.

LORD POLONIUS

[Aside]

How say you by that? Still harping on my
daughter: yet he knew me not at first; he said I
was a fishmonger: he is far gone, far gone: and
truly in my youth I suffered much extremity for
love; very near this. I'll speak to him again.
What do you read, my lord?

HAMLET

Words, words, words.

LORD POLONIUS

What is the matter, my lord?

HAMLET

Between who?

LORD POLONIUS

I mean, the matter that you read, my lord.

HAMLET

Slanders, sir: for the satirical rogue says here that old
men have grey beards, that their faces are wrinkled,
their eyes purging thick amber and plum-tree gum
and that they have a plentiful lack of wit, together
with most weak hams: all which, sir, though I most
powerfully and potently believe, yet I hold it not
honesty to have it thus set down, for yourself, sir,
should be old as I am, if like a crab you could go
backward.

LORD POLONIUS

[Aside]

Though this be madness, yet there is method in 't.
Will you walk out of the air, my lord?

(II, 2, 168-206)

Tantalizingly, the playwright does not state the name of the book, which can only be inferred by the reader. There have been attempts to identify the book as Juvenal's *Satires* or as Erasmus' *The Praise of Folly*, though neither of these works relates to the description of its content that Hamlet gives. Hamlet tells us that the author of the book was a "satirical rogue" and that it was "not honesty to have it thus set down". Apparently, Hamlet found the book while praying, since that was where he was going when we last saw him (I, 5, 138-195).

All of this, of course, is consistent with my view that the book was the histories of Josephus, which were sometimes bound with the New Testament. What drove Hamlet mad was that he recognized the Flavian conspiracy. Notice that Hamlet replies: *"Well, God-a-mercy"* when Polonius asks "How does my good Lord Hamlet" while he reads the unnamed book. The playwright depicts Hamlet as struggling with the implications that the New Testament is a Roman forgery. It is easy to understand how in Elizabethan England such knowledge could be seen as having the power to drive a man mad. Even today the fact is difficult to comprehend, as it requires a re-orientation of many of our basic assumptions. Notice that the use of a 'hidden letter' or book to stand in for the Flavian texts is a device we have seen elsewhere: the "comments on the Maccabees" in Marlowe's Jew of Malta, and Titus's "supplication" carried to the Emperor by the clown, who was immediately hung for his innocent role as a messenger.

Hamlet calls Polonius a 'fishmonger' (II, 2,174) because he recognizes that Polonius is a parallel of Josephus—who flattered and ministered to the Flavian Emperors, just as Polonius does for the Danish royalty. In the Flavian typology, 'fish' represent the flesh of the Jews. An example of this typology is the Roman battle at the lake of Galilee, in which the Jews were pulled out of the water like fish. This battle was satirized in the Gospels when Jesus stated, at the same place, that his disciples would become "fishers of men". Thus, Hamlet refers to Polonius as a 'fishmonger' because as a minister to the Danish nobility, he peddles wickedly in Jewish flesh.

There is, as Polonius states, a 'method' to Hamlet's madness. His statements are not gibberish, but rather they are references to the 'method' that linked the war between the Romans and Jews to the Gospels. For example, Hamlet relates a description in the book he is reading of a people who were physically ravaged and who had weak 'hams', suggesting the starving Jews during the siege of Jerusalem — notice the use of the word 'ham' for a human body part. Hamlet also states that he believes most 'potently' that the events the book describes occurred but "hold it not honesty to have it thus set down." This would certainly have been the position of the playwright, who must have known that famine did occur, but also knew that the depiction of the consequences of the famine in the Gospels and *Wars of the Jews* was Roman propaganda.

Along with the reference to "weak hams", the above-mentioned "amber" also relates to the siege of Jerusalem. Amber, of course, is the gummy extrusion from the wounds of trees. But amber is produced only from coniferous trees, the trees that surrounded Jerusalem, the sanctuary of the Lord — "the fir tree, the pine tree, together…beautify the place of my sanctuary" (Isaiah 60:13). In other words, Hamlet is describing the amber that flowed from the trees when the Romans "cut down all the trees on the mountains" during their siege of Jerusalem to make crucifixes.

Far from being random, the 'method' to Hamlet's madness throughout the rest of the play is entirely related to Hamlet's understanding of the Flavian satirical system. For example, Hamlet's remark above, about the 'son' breeding maggots in a dog, refers to Luke 16:20 and Matthew 15:26-28 which describes Lazarus, full of sores ('lazar like' above) being food for dogs. Another example of his 'method' is the passage below in which

Hamlet states the "news" that Flavian actors had taken the role of the 'Christ' and therefore rode an ass as Jesus did in the Gospels.

POLONIUS

My lord, I have news to tell you.

HAMLET

My lord, I have news to tell you.
When Roscius was an actor in Rome,—

LORD POLONIUS

The actors are come hither, my lord.

HAMLET

Buz, buz!

LORD POLONIUS

Upon mine honour,—

HAMLET

Then came each actor on his ass,— (II, 2, 389-395)

In order to 'catch the King' — his murderous uncle Claudius — Hamlet arranges for a group of actors to put on a play that will represent the attack upon his father so closely that it will force his uncle to reveal his guilt. To test the troop on their acting ability, Hamlet has them first perform a separate play for him. They choose the story of Troy, which had a special significance to the author of the Shakespearean literature. The Greek conquest of Troy was a parallel to Rome's conquest of Jerusalem: notice that Troy was defeated by the wily Odysseus's treacherous gift of a religious idol, just as Jerusalem was defeated by Titus who brought the false religion of Christianity. The players' recital of the story of the city's fall creates a nesting effect, like a Russian matryoshka doll set. In other words, the play-within-a-play about Troy is really about the establishment of Christianity, and it reveals the truth about Hamlet's situation, just as the larger play does. Both are symbolic comments upon the Romans' creation of a false religion.

King Claudius is a 'type' for Caesar Claudius, who was murdered by poison in October of 54 CE. Thus, the play's 'mass poisoning' can be understood as a play on Claudius's death. Moreover, as noted below, Claudius was the third angel in Revelation who was associated with the poison 'wormwood'. The author of Hamlet understood Revelation's typology, and linked to it in the following exchange.

PLAYER QUEEN

O, confound the rest!
Such love must needs be treason in my breast:
In second husband let me be accurst!
None wed the second but who kill'd the first

HAMLET

[Aside]

Wormwood, wormwood.

(III, 2 , 177-181)

The fate of Ophelia, which has mystified scholars to date, is clear within this interpretation. Hamlet told Polonius that Ophelia is a "daughter of Jephthah", the Biblical character who sacrificed herself rather than violate her father's oath to God. The reason that Hamlet tells her to 'get to a nunnery' is to prevent her from breeding more bourgeois 'fishmongers' like Polonius and herself. Her ensuing madness and suicide is because, like Hamlet, she learns that Jesus — Titus — is a false god who did not rise from the dead.

OPHELIA

How should I your true love know
From another one?
By his cockle hat and staff,
And his sandal shoon.

[...]

He is dead and gone lady
He is dead and gone
At his head is a patch of green grass,
And at his feet there is a tomb stone.

(IV, 5, 23-32)

Hamlet's famous soliloquy, "to be or not to be", is in this same comic genre.   The playwright is reversing the conclusion of Josephus's *Jewish Wars*, wherein Eleazar purportedly told his Jewish followers that suicide was a good idea, while Hamlet is asking himself whether it is a good idea to commit suicide. The typological humor may seem in good fun, but it is quite possible that the playwright mirrored the Romans' hatred, and had a murderous intent with such satires.

Hamlet journeys to England, but when he unexpectedly returns, his arrival sets off a group slaughter of the remaining principle characters. The slaughter echoes the carnage at the denouements of *Titus Andronicus* and *Romeo & Juliet*. In the subtle conclusion, Fortinbras arrives and takes note of the 'feast'; in other words, of the Gentiles' cannibalism.

FORTINBRAS

This quarry cries on havoc. O proud Death,
What feast is toward in thy eternal cell
That thou hast so many princes at a shot
So bloodily has struck?

(V, 2, 364-365)

This conclusion also shows why Fortinbras was set up as a mirror of Hamlet.   Now that Denmark's royalty has self-destructed, he will inherit both the kingdoms of Norway and Denmark, and thus reclaim the land that was taken from his father.   Of course since one generation was a 'type' for another it is easy to see that the real point was linked to generations long gone. Thus the violence of the struggle between the Romans and Jews lives on within our literature.

It is interesting to note, however, that Norway (like Denmark) is a Gentile kingdom, and there is no direct indication in the play that Fortinbras was Jewish, which is a conjecture based upon the fact that the play is reversing the typology in the Gospels. In other words, in Hamlet the victorious king 'Strong Arm' was not 'delimbed' and thus can be seen as a 'type' that reversed the fate given to the Jewish King captured on the Mount of Olives and was ordered 'pruned' by Titus (Josephus, *Wars* 6, 2, 167). It seems reasonable to suspect that Fortinbras (like Friar Lawrence in *Romeo & Juliet*) is a crypto-Jew who hides his faith and pretends to be Christian.

The blackness of the comedy makes it highly unlikely that the play was constructed as a memorial to Shakespeare's son purportedly named 'Hamnet', as many scholars have claimed, and many others have just as adamantly disputed. The name 'Hamlet' was a pun upon the name of the lead character in the source — 'Ameltath'. In my view, it may also have been a witticism describing the behavior of the character responsible for creating the 'Ham' — that is, the human flesh that was available in such abundance at the conclusion of the play — 'ham' 'let' meaning to make ham. The same witticism is found in the title of Emilia Bassano's poem 'Cook — Ham', which told the story of a Jewess isolated in a world of Gentiles, in a place where 'ham' was 'cooked'. In this case the joke is created by combining 'Ham' with 'let', which meant to cause or bring about, a wry description of 'Hamlet's' real accomplishment. If this is correct, it begs the question of whether 'Hamnet' existed at all.

A number of details within the play support the premise that Emilia Bassano was the true author. She gave the Queen her father's name of Baptista, and in some versions of the text name the murdered Duke/King's name was Hudson—-recalling the name of her former patron/lover Lord Hunsdon.

Further, the presence of recorder players (III, 2l, 285-375), including a discussion of recorder fingering, brings to mind the Bassano recorder ensemble. The numerous scenes in Shakespeare where a recorder group plays may have been simply Emilia's effort to create additional employment for her family's musicians.

Two other passages also provide interesting autobiographical insights. There is a suggestion that some of this company of players that don't have the accent or the walk of Christians (III, 2, 30-35). A possible conjecture from statement is that those players were crypto-Jews. Moreover, there is also a passage that seems to state that the writer of the verse is a woman—and one who is insistent that she is able to speak her mind or the blank verse shall cease.

HAMLET

'the lady shall say her mind freely, or the blank verse shall halt for't.'

(II, 2, 324)

While on the surface Hamlet appears to be talking about the upcoming arrival of an actors' troupe, it is easy to imagine that the comment also suggests that "a lady" was the author of the 'blank verse' that is *Hamlet* itself. It was quite in keeping with Emilia's sense of wit to have signed her name to the work in this manner.

THE MERCHANT OF VENICE

Norman Rabkin uses *The Merchant of Venice* as his first example of "the problem of meaning" in Shakespeare, complaining that *"...for all of its virtues much of the best criticism leaves us with the sense that it has somehow failed to come to grips with or has even in some way denied the existence of essential qualities of the play."* [83] While Rabkin also cautions against *"self-aggrandizing"* critics who believe *"they must possess the key that everyone else has missed, the secret hidden from all previous critics and scholars"*,[84] I hope the reader will recognize that the Flavian comic system represents exactly the hidden key that is needed.

To begin to make sense of the play, one must start by trying to understand how the author is representing Jews. As shown above, Marlowe in *The Jew of Malta,* one of the plays that *The Merchant of Venice* was loosely based upon, placed Jews into three categories; those who refused conversion, those who truly converted to Christianity, and those who pretended to have converted to Christianity. In *The Merchant of Venice,* the playwright repeats Marlowe and makes the same three distinctions.

---

[83] Norman Rabkin, *Shakespeare and the Problem of Meaning* (University of Chicago Press, 1981), pp. 4–5.

[84] Rabkin, p. 2.

Antonio is an ex-Jew who has made a heartfelt conversion to Christianity.[85] His conversion is the source of Shylock's deep grudge against him, because he has abandoned their religion, which his daughter Jessica will also do. This is the reason why Shylock refers to Antonio as a 'prodigal': because he has left the religion of Israel for the luxuries and non-kosher food of the Gentiles. Shylock also highlights Antonio's turncoat nature by calling him a "fawning publican" or tax gatherer, linking Antonio to those Jews who served the Romans as tax gatherers, like the apostle Matthew.

The character 'Bassanio' is a 'kinsman' to Antonio (I, 1, 57), and thus also of Jewish ethnicity. However, he never says or does anything that would indicate that his adoption of Christianity is anything other than a sham for public consumption. His name indicates that he is from the Bassano family; that is, Emelia's Jewish family that immigrated to England from the exact area near Venice where the play is set. The register of births and deaths for the church in which many of them were buried has the spelling of their name as Bassanio. They were presumably crypto-Jews who were baptized as Christians but practiced Judaism in secret. Thus, this would be the type of Jew the character 'Bassanio' represents. In the play, Bassanio is referred to as a "scholar and a soldier" (I, 2, 113), which would appear to be a self-designation by Emilia Bassano of herself and her family. She saw her family as warriors of Judaism, still carrying on the fight against the Gentiles — 'Will Shake Speare'.

Shylock is a traditional Hebrew, who will talk and walk and engage in commerce with Christians, but will not eat, drink or pray with anyone except religious Jews for fear of breaking the laws of *kashrus*. He keeps a "sober house" (II, 5, 36) that frippery does not enter. In Pauline theology, he represents the 'old man' who Paul wanted the Jews to cast-off. In Venice (unlike in England at the time) it is still legal, albeit dangerous, to be openly

---

[85] S. M. Finn, 'Antonio: The Other Jew in The Merchant of Venice', *Literator*, 10 (1989) <http://www.literator.org.za/index.php/literator/article/view/819/0> [accessed 28 February 2014].

Jewish. He lends money to Christians, usury being legal in Elizabethan England since 1571. But he is treated badly by the Jew who converted to Christianity. Antonio, who spits at him, calls him 'misbeliever' and dog. Antonio even rejects his humanity, stating that he has no sense, passions or affections. Shylock is not even called by his name but is referred to only as the 'Jew'. As a covert Jew himself, Bassanio treats Shylock with a quiet respect that seems kind by comparison, but Bassanio's companion Gratiano tells Shylock:

> O, be thou damn'd, inexecrable dog!
> And for thy life let justice be accused.
> Thou almost makest me waver in my faith
> To hold opinion with Pythagoras,
> That souls of animals infuse themselves
> Into the trunks of men: thy currish spirit
> Govern'd a wolf, who, hang'd for human slaughter,
> Even from the gallows did his fell soul fleet,
> And, whilst thou lay'st in thy unhallow'd dam,
> Infused itself in thee; for thy desires
> Are wolvish, bloody, starved and ravenous.

(IV, 1, 138-148)

This passage is often taken as a reference to Roderigo Lopez, a Portuguese physician and affiliate of Don Antonio (a pretender to the Portuguese throne), who was widely believed to be a crypto-Jew and who had risen to become Queen Elizabeth's personal physician. He was accused of conspiring with the Spanish to poison the Queen, and was hung in 1594. Emilia may well have been inspired to write *Merchant of Venice* as a timely response to these events, and the reference to a wolf's spirit above may have been a pun on Lopez's name (Latin: Lupus).[86] However, as I hope will be clear to the reader, there is far more going on in the play than a simple allegory of the Lopez incident.

---

[86] William Meyers, '« Shakespeare, Shylock, and the Jews Commentary Magazine', *Commentary*, April 1996 <http://www.commentarymagazine.com/article/shakespeare-shylock-and-the-jews/> [accessed 25 February 2014].

As Steven Marx noted, the play contains more Biblical allusions than any other of Shakespeare's plays, and in some ways is parallel to Paul's *Letter to the Romans*, which also dealt with the same issue of Christian-Jewish relationships.[87] In that letter, Paul (continuing the satire in the Gospels) sought to turn Jews into Christians who would take Communion and eat the body and blood of Christ. The author of *Merchant of Venice* was aware of the Roman literary satire, and the play was written — like all of the Shakespearean plays — to *reverse* the satire.

Titus, who had become the final 'Jesus' depicted in the Gospels, is satirized in *Merchant of Venice* with the character of the clown, Launcelot Gobbo, a servant to Shylock. The name 'Gobbo' is a play on 'gobbet', meaning a mouthful of flesh, and Shylock refers to him as a 'huge feeder' (II, 5, 46). The character that plays Launcelot's father (a satire of Vespasian) suffers the fate he intended for the Jews: he cannot recognize his royal son and is even unsure that they dwell together. Launcelot has to explain to his father that he is "your boy that was, your son that is, and your child that shall be" (II, 2, 84-86). This is a parody on the Hebrew Bible's passage that provides the name of God and which was the basis of the description of Jesus as "the same yesterday, and today and for ever" (Hebrews 13:8).

The fact that Launcelot is a parody of Titus/Jesus explains his desire to "serve" the Jew, as he says: "the short and the long is, I serve the Jew" (II, 2, 127). The nature of Gobbo's 'service' to the Jews is not difficult to grasp: someone whose name is 'Gobbo' and who is a "huge feeder", must be a send-up of Titus's desire to 'serve himself' to those Jews who convert to the false Judaism and eat the communion 'bread'.

In the passage below, Gobbo seeks directions from his son. As a clown, Launcelot always misunderstands what is said to him, and he hears not "which is the way to Master Jew's" but rather "which is the way to master Jews?" But, of course (since the character 'Launcelot' depicts Titus Flavius) this mistake was quite natural.

---

[87] Marx.

'Mastering Jews' was Titus's obsession. The answer Launcelot gives is not a comic misdirection, therefore, but rather an instruction on how to arrange one's hands to pray. In other words, the best way to master the Jews is by turning them into worshipping Christians. Note also, in the following dialogue, that Gobbo has become the 'true-begotten' father, just as Jesus was called the only-begotten son.

GOBBO

Master young man, you, I pray you, which is the way to master Jew's?

LAUNCELOT

[Aside]

O heavens, this is my true-begotten father! who, being more than sand-blind, high-gravel blind, knows me not: I will try confusions with him.

GOBBO

Master young gentleman, I pray you, which is the way to master Jew's?

LAUNCELOT

Turn up on your right hand at the next turning, but, at the next turning of all, on your left; marry, at the very next turning, turn of no hand, but turn down indirectly to the Jew's house.

GOBBO

By God's sonties, 'twill be a hard way to hit.

(II, 2, 33-45)

By mutual agreement, Launcelot has given up on his 'service' to Shylock, who dismisses Launcelot as a lazy patch. For his part, recognizing that all attempts to 'serve' Flavian Christianity to Rabbinical Jews have become utterly hopeless, Launcelot laughably goes to peddle his wares to Bassanio the crypto-Jew instead. Father Gobbo brings along a "dish of doves that I would bestow on your worship" (II, 2, 135-136). However, this renewed effort to sell Jesus's flesh is obviously a futile burlesque, although Launcelot does make an effort to ingratiate himself with Jessica, his most likely customer.

Antonio describes himself as a "blemished lamb", which indicates he is also a type for the Gentile Messiah. As the play opens, Antonio is filled with sadness, apparently because his beloved Bassanio is leaving him to court the beautiful Queen Portia of Belmont. In the 2005 film version of the *Merchant of Venice*, produced by Barry Navidi, this love of Bassanio and Antonio is portrayed as discreetly homosexual.[88] Because of his love for Bassanio, Antonio is willing to pledge his 'pound of flesh' as security for a loan to fund Bassanio's courtship of Portia. Shylock is delighted to lend funds for this purpose, not only because of the opportunity for revenge against Anotonio, but also because if Bassanio succeeds in marrying Portia, he will 'graft' his Jewish lineage into the Gentile royalty.

Queen Portia has much in common with Queen Elizabeth.[89] Like Elizabeth, Portia is a beautiful young blonde who is besieged by suitors from royal families all over the world, but she cannot freely make her choice among them because of her dead father's will. Portia is highly educated (knowing many languages) and skilled in the arts of rhetoric, but to practice her skills in Venice she must disguise herself as a man. Elizabeth also often boasted of her masculine aspect, most notably in her Tilbury speech, where she proclaimed *"I have the heart and stomach of a king, and of a king of England too,... "*.[90]

---

[88] Alan Stone, 'Redeeming Shylock', *Boston Review*, May 2005
<http://new.bostonreview.net/BR30.2/stone.php> [accessed 28 February 2014].

[89] Deborah Van Pelt, '"I Stand for Sovereignty": Reading Portia in Shakespeare's The Merchant of Venice', 2009
<http://scholarcommons.usf.edu/etd/65>.

[90] Van Pelt, p. 12.

However, unlike Elizabeth who never married, Portia is smitten with love for the gallant Bassanio, who nevertheless must run the gauntlet set up by Portia's father, just like all the other suitors. Portia's likeness has been hidden in one of three caskets (one gold, one silver and one lead) and Bassanio must guess which one. Portia overtly acquiesces to her father's prohibition on giving Bassanio any clues, but her speech is laced with "L" sounds, and her court musicians sing a song whose lines rhyme with "lead", and whose surface narrative complains of the brevity of love based on appearances. Bassanio gets the hint, and correctly chooses the lead casket. Thus, Portia is a willing, indeed eager, accomplice in the crypto-Jewish conspiracy to invert the Flavian 'root and branch' theme.

Time passes quickly, and word comes from Venice that Antonio's ships have foundered, and Shylock wants to collect his pound of flesh. The validity of the bond is to be tried before the Duke, in a crucial scene that parallels Jesus's trial in the Gospels. Bassanio and his entourage travel from Belmont to advocate for their friend Anthony, and Portia also secretly travels to the trial after sending a message to her cousin Dr. Bellario, a legal expert.

To emphasize that the play is operating within the context of the New Testament, Launcelot warns Jessica: "the sins of the father are to be laid upon the children" (III, 5, 1). He is restating the request of the Jewish mob that called for the death of Jesus in Matthew 27:25: "His blood be on us, and on our children". At the trial, Shylock reinforces this, saying "my deeds upon my head" (IV, 1, 206). However, in this case the people clamoring for violence are not Jews but Gentiles, and Shylock ironically does not accept responsibility for the deeds of his ancestors, but only his own. Very subtly, the playwright is suggesting that the curse on the Jews that was cast in Jesus's trial is being reversed from the Jews to the Gentiles.

Portia has obtained a message from Dr. Bellario, authorizing her (in the guise of 'Balthazar', a young man) to give a legal opinion for the Duke in Shylock's case. She determines that the bond is valid and that Shylock may rightfully take his pound of flesh from Anthony's breast. Shylock praises 'Balthazar' as another Daniel

('Balthazar' is, as mentioned above, another name for Daniel) and delights in the prospect of collecting his revenge.

As Shylock's knife is poised over Anthony's heart, Bassanio dramatically proclaims his great love for Anthony, and that he would gladly sacrifice not only his own life, but that of his new wife as well, if only he could save Anthony from the devil (that is, the Jew); Portia (as 'Balthazar') humorously notices that "your wife would give you little thanks for that, if she were by, to hear you make that offer" (IV, 1, 288-289).

Nevertheless, Portia (perhaps moved by her husband's wish, or perhaps in accordance with a carefully laid plan) warns Shylock that he is entitled to his pound of flesh, but not to any blood; and that if he sheds a drop of Christian blood, all his goods are forfeit to the Venetian state. Shylock asks: "Is that the law?" and Portia tells him that it is so.

This is a crucial moment for the entire 'Shakespearean' campaign of vengeance by 'pruning' (that is, murder and mayhem) and cannibalization of the Gentiles. One can easily imagine that the Aaron of *Titus Andronicus* would have seized the moment's opportunity to extract Anthony's heart, bake it into a pie, and serve it at Jessica's wedding, while laughing heartily all the way to the gallows.

However, Shylock stops abruptly and relinquishes his claim, because he suddenly comes to his senses and realizes that Portia is correct: murder (even for vengeance) is against the Ten Commandments, which apply to Jews as much as Gentiles.

My conjecture is that perhaps the conviction of Dr. Lopez on charges of conspiring to murder the Queen had similarly been a defining moment for Emilia Bassano. Indeed, if there had ever been any real-life conspiracy of revenge against Gentile royalty (and the evidence presented at trial including Lopez's testimony, albeit extracted under torture, suggested that there was) then the entire crypto-Jewish community would likely have been aware of the plot. If this was the case then the insertion of the child into the

Gentile's royal lineage described in Titus Andronicus described above was not metaphorical but a description of a real plan.

However these facts may be, unlike Queen Elizabeth in Lopez's case, Portia insists on inflicting the maximum punishment on Shylock, even though his murderous intent has been thwarted and indeed abandoned. For his crime, all of Shylock's possessions are forfeited and he is to be hanged. However, Anthony and the Duke agree that if Shylock signs a "deed of gift" and becomes a Christian, he will receive immunity from hanging (a 'halter gratis'), and half of his possessions—instead of going to the state—can be passed on to his daughter Jessica and son-in-law Lorenzo. Portia assigns her clerk to draw up this 'deed' and Shylock agrees that he will sign it.

At this point Shylock exits (IV, 1, 359) and is not seen again but at the end of the play he sends a "special deed of gift" that gives "all he dies possessed of" to his daughter and her Gentile husband (V, 1, 293). The playwright leaves it to the audience to make the determination as to what Shylock has done offstage, and what exactly he has left to his heirs. Since this play uses the word 'choice', or its derivatives, over forty times, it is appropriate that the audience is presented with a choice as to how to Shylock responded.

The surface narration suggests that Shylock decided that he loved his daughter, so he has converted to Christianity and signed the "deed of gift" that allowed her to inherit his wealth. This interpretation is 'unsatisfying' because it has no relation to several of the major themes of the play, particularly the treatment of Shylock by his daughter. Shylock has promised to sign the "deed" but he has not made any promise to convert to Christianity, which is a necessity to give any effect to his signature.

What Shylock actually did can be determined by the facts presented in the play. We know that Shylock was strongly committed to Judaism and that he did not like "Christian fools" (II, 5, 33). We also know that "the role of Jessica is a troubled and troubling one".

Jessica stole her father's ducats and used them for a spending spree. She has even stolen his turquoise wedding ring and traded it for a monkey. She was ashamed to be his daughter, married a Gentile and has changed her religion to Christianity. We know that Shylock thinks that his daughter is "damned" (III, 1, 26). Jessica has broken away—her very name being a reference to the strap or 'jess' that normally kept a falcon safe on its master's arm. Even if she was "fledged" and ready to leave home and get married (III, 1, 24) this was no way to have done it. She is described as thief who "slandered her love" (IV, 2, 15).

The following exchange between Lorenzo and Jessica takes the depiction of the couple as immoral to its highest pitch. It is also another Shakespearean 'puzzle' in that immediately following this conversation describing their unsavory characters the couple are seemingly rewarded with Shylock's 'special deed of gift'.

LORENZO

The moon shines bright: in such a night as this,
When the sweet wind did gently kiss the trees
And they did make no noise, in such a night
Troilus methinks mounted the Troyan walls
And sigh'd his soul toward the Grecian tents,
Where Cressid lay that night.

JESSICA

In such a night
Did Thisbe fearfully o'ertrip the dew
And saw the lion's shadow ere himself
And ran dismay'd away.

LORENZO

In such a night
Stood Dido with a willow in her hand
Upon the wild sea banks and waft her love
To come again to Carthage.

JESSICA

In such a night
Medea gather'd the enchanted herbs
That did renew old AEson.

LORENZO

In such a night
Did Jessica steal from the wealthy Jew
And with an unthrift love did run from Venice
As far as Belmont.

JESSICA

In such a night
Did young Lorenzo swear he loved her well,
Stealing her soul with many vows of faith
And ne'er a true one.

LORENZO

In such a night
Did pretty Jessica, like a little shrew,
Slander her love

(V, 1, 1-20)

Therefore, one of the incoherent aspects of the conventional understanding of the play is that Jessica and Lorenzo seems to be rewarded for their immoral behavior at its conclusion. We also know that Shylock stated that he intended to take "revenge". As he put it: "the villainy you teach me I will execute and it shall go hard but I will better the instruction" (III, 1, 59-68). In other words, the playwright has indicated that Shylock intended to gain revenge upon his wicked Christian 'instructors'. But what was the 'bettering the instruction' that Shylock claimed he was going to do?

Viewing the play as a counterattack against the satire in the Gospels makes these seemingly illogical elements coherent. From such a perspective, Shylock did not consent to the Gentile's judgment. After all, he merely said that he was "content" with it, not that he would obey the dictum. In fact he was 'content' because he knew that the judgment gave him a chance to accomplish just what he said he would, that is to 'better the instruction" of Christianity. Under this scenario the original "deed of gift" was not signed but rather a different one, described in the final scene as a "*special* deed of gift", which merely left Jessica and Lorenzo all of his possessions at death. But what did Shylock actually leave to his immoral daughter and her Christian husband? If he did not convert to Christianity, then he had no possessions — other than his (unexercised) entitlement to the pound of Anthony's flesh.

One of the key themes of the play is that there is much talk of food, and Lorenzo has constantly been expecting to eat. However, as time goes on, dinner is continually failing to appear.

> We two will leave you, but at dinner time
> I pray you have in mind where we must eat.

(I, 1, 70)

> We'll we will leave you two until dinner time.

(I, 1, 105)

> Nay we will slink away at dinner time.

(III, 11, 1)

> Whiter thou goest?
> Marry sir to bid my old master the Jew to sup tonight
> With my new master the Christians

(II, 4, 15)

> Even in the lovely garnish of a boy

(II, 4, 45)

The conventional interpretation of the play does not provide any resolution to Lorenzo's hunger and at the play's conclusion he is famished. He should have eaten at five in the evening but has been up all night and it is now "almost morning". At this point in the play, the playwright deliberately takes the reader into a context concerning the sacrament of Communion. Lorenzo tells Jessica:

> Look how the floor of heaven
> Is thick inlaid with patines of bright gold:
> There's not the smallest orb which thou behold'st
> But in his motion like an angel sings,
> Still quiring to the young-eyed cherubins;

(V, 1, 59-62)

These "patines" are the plates off which the Eucharist is served. Lorenzo's words can be compared to the Te Deum, which is generally sung after Mass on certain important occasions:

> To thee all Angels cry aloud :
> the Heavens, and all the Powers therein.
> To thee Cherubim and Seraphim :
> continually do cry,

Portia then delivers something to the staving Lorenzo that he calls "manna". What sort of food was this manna? It was a 'special deed' to Antonio's pound of flesh.

PORTIA

> How now, Lorenzo!
> My clerk hath some good comforts too for you.

NERISSA

> Ay, and I'll give them him without a fee.
> There do I give to you and Jessica,
> From the rich Jew, a special deed of gift,
> After his death, of all he dies possess'd of.

LORENZO

> Fair ladies, you drop manna in the way
> Of starved people.

PORTIA

It is almost morning,
And yet I am sure you are not satisfied

(V, 1, 288)

The Hebrew word "manna' refers to the food that came down from heaven in the Book of Exodus. Seeing the substance the Israelites responded 'manna?' meaning — what is this? So Lorenzo and Jessica also call their inheritance "manna", as they do not know it is the flesh of Antonio. Their confusion reverses that of the Jews at the 'Last Supper'.

Jesus also referred to 'manna', of course. He referred to it as the food of his body. It is not hard to see that Shylock has "bettered the instruction" of those who created Christianity, by presenting the Gentiles with nothing but human flesh.

The imagery concerning the 'pound of flesh' in *The Merchant of Venice* comes from Ser Giovanni's collection of Italian stories *Il Pecorone* (*The Big Sheep*) that was published in 1558 in Italian. The concept of a pound of flesh also appeared in Alexander Silvayn's *The Orator* (translated into English in 1596). When he first mentions this forfeit, Shylock says that it is "an equal pound of your fair flesh to be cut off…in what part of your body pleaseth me". (II, 2,149-150)

In the play, the word 'bond' is repeated numerous times. This agreement is a "merry bond" (I, 3,169); Shylock insists, "I will have my bond" (III, 3, 4-17); and Portia asks whether Antonio "confess the bond" (IV, 1, 176-8). But why does Portia require that the piece of flesh is to be cut out of Antonio's breast, rather than taking off his left hand? One answer, of course, is that it is logical to the storyline, but another is that the author has created a Hebrew pun. The Hebrew word for 'bond' is '*oZeH*' and the Hebrew word for 'breast' is '*aZeH*'. Thus, the inheritance that Shylock left was the 'bond' that he predicted he would have when he said: "I will have my bond". Also, in Hebrew the same word 'DaMiM' means both 'money' and 'blood'; which explains

Portia's view that at the expiration of the bond, Shylock is entitled to take neither money nor blood from Anthony, but only flesh.[91]

Shylock's name is also part of the playwright's satirical system. It is a play on *Shiloh* (Gen. 49.10), a Hebrew word meaning 'the Messiah'. The play reverses the Gospels' satire whereby Jews unwittingly eat the flesh of the Jewish Messiah, and causes that fate to fall instead upon Gentiles and Jews who convert to Christianity. The author has used her understanding that the sacrament of communion is a cannibal feast to create a parody that will be visible to those that know the real nature of Christianity.

Bassanio, Portia and Anthony are left in a more complex and conflicted situation. Portia, masquerading as 'Balthazar', demanded that Bassanio give up the wedding ring that symbolized his love and commitment to Portia. Under Anthony's prodding, Bassanio agreed to yield the ring to 'Balthazar'. When Portia (as a woman) confronts her husband about his faux pas, Antonio steps forward to pledge himself again as security for Bassanio's faithfulness.

ANTONIO

I once did lend my body for his wealth;
Which, but for him that had your husband's ring,
Had quite miscarried: I dare be bound again,
My soul upon the forfeit, that your lord
Will never more break faith advisedly.

PORTIA

Then you shall be his surety. Give him this
And bid him keep it better than the other.

ANTONIO

Here, Lord Bassanio; swear to keep this ring.

---

[91] Florence Amit, *Three Caskets of Interpretation* (Google Play edition, 2012), pp. 68–70.

But Antonio's soul is forfeit at the moment he makes the pledge, because Bassanio must still love Antonio as much as he did before, and Portia has cleverly staged a wedding ceremony between Antonio and Bassanio.

Bassanio's love for Antonio is a 'Shakespearean' riddle in the play: if Antonio represents the Christ, and Bassanio is a crypto-Jew, then why doesn't Bassanio hate Antonio and crave revenge rather than love and fellowship? This is quickly followed by another riddle, as Portia announces:

PORTIA

Antonio, you are welcome;
And I have better news in store for you
Than you expect: unseal this letter soon;
There you shall find three of your argosies
Are richly come to harbour suddenly:
You shall not know by what strange accident
I chanced on this letter.

ANTONIO

I am dumb.

How have Anthony's 'argosies' come safely ashore, and where did Portia get this information? Within the Flavian comic system, one sputters to come up with a solution. Based on Anthony's loss of his soul as well as his pound of flesh, it seems that he is in some way a soulless zombie, or a dead man walking, so it makes sense that he is 'dumb'. How are we to explain Bassanio's love for such an empty shell? Is it possible that privateers captured Antonio's ships, which have richly come to harbor indeed, but now belong to Portia? (Queen Elizabeth was notorious for funding her government with proceeds from pirate raids.) Does Anthony represent the Anglican Church, now safely domesticated, purged of all vitriolic Flavian baggage, and ready at the Queen's service? I will leave it to the reader to decide whether these solutions to Shakespeare's riddles are adequate, or whether the enigmas remain unsolved.

The deeper structure of the play shows that far from being anti-Semitic, *The Merchant of Venice* is completely pro-Jewish. The playwright created an anti-Semitic surface narration that would have appealed to the audiences of Elizabethan England but contained a subtext whose perspective was just the opposite. This is especially clear in Shylock's famous monologue concerning how Gentiles have treated Jews. The speech is the real voice of Emilia Bassano trying to use empathy to elevate humankind to a more 'humane' treatment of one another.

> He hath disgraced me, and hindered me half a million; laughed at my losses, mocked at my gains, scorned my nation, thwarted my bargains, cooled my friends, heated mine enemies; and what's his reason? I am a Jew. Hath not a Jew eyes? hath not a Jew hands, organs, dimensions, senses, affections, passions? fed with the same food, hurt with the same weapons, subject to the same diseases, healed by the same means, warmed and cooled by the same winter and summer, as a Christian is? If you prick us, do we not bleed? if you tickle us, do we not laugh? if you poison us, do we not die? and if you wrong us, shall we not revenge? If we are like you in the rest, we will resemble you in that. If a Jew wrong a Christian, what is his humility? Revenge. If a Christian wrong a Jew, what should his sufferance be by Christian example? Why, revenge. The villany you teach me, I will execute, and it shall go hard but I will better the instruction. (III, 1, 60)

It is difficult not to speculate on Emilia's mental state while she produced such complex literature. Studies of artistic personalities suggest that about half of them suffer from depressive or manic depressive illness. Both Emilia's father and one of her first cousins reportedly suffered from depression. This is notable because blood relatives of those suffering from psychic abnormality are much more likely to suffer from manic-depressive illness, be cyclothymic, or to commit suicide, compared to the general population.

Extreme situations, however, can also produce unusual psychic states, and Emilia's personal situation was difficult. She lived in a pre-Darwinian world where the notion that life had been brought about by some method other than divine intervention was seldom considered. Some of her literature suggests that she was deeply religious: for example, her belief in God is shown in the cryptic dedication to 'Mr. Yahweh' she wrote for her sonnets given below. On the other hand, Hamlet's famous soliloquy shows that she was capable of contemplating a Godless universe. This deep ambiguity, coupled with the understanding of the falseness of Christianity, would have made it difficult for her to doubt that Judaism embodied the truth; yet eventually, she may have experienced earthquakes of uncertainty about that as well.

Not only was Emilia a dark skinned Jewess orphan in a 'fair' world, but since she knew the true nature of the Gospels, she would have experienced that world as literally the triumph of evil over God. Perhaps this is what gave her the extraordinary energy necessary to produce such a body of writing. The early Emilia may have seen herself as religious warrior sent by God to chastise the Gentiles for their wickedness by taking — satirically — 'an eye for an eye' as instructed in the Hebrew Bible; the later Emilia may have seen herself transformed as a vanguard of the Enlightenment and universalism. Such a progression would represent a very special kind of madness, if indeed that is what it was. I would not be surprised if the mind of Emilia Bassano will be the subject of much speculation in the years to come.

DOMITIAN'S TRINITY IN ACTS

During the period when I was analyzing the Shakespearean plays, I found that there was some symbolism in them that was incomprehensible to me. It seemed to have not been based on the typology the Flavians placed into the Gospels, but on a system unknown to me. My curiosity piqued, I began what turned out to be a long journey. To understand this typology required making the chain of discoveries that I will present in the next several chapters.

Domitian, who succeeded Titus as Caesar in 81 CE, was the last of the three Flavian Caesars and, like many of the Caesars before him, he enjoyed making representations of his divinity. Even today the statues and inscriptions he created portraying him as a god litter the landscape of Asia Minor. Domitian's desire to be seen as a god existed even in his private life. Suetonius recorded that Domitian demanded to be addressed as 'Lord God' by those that approached him.

The New Testament works of Acts, Paul's letters and the book of Revelation were among Domitian's efforts to see himself depicted as a god. These works were designed to map onto Suetonius's history of Domitian's life using typological parallels, in the same way that the Gospels were mapped onto Josephus's history of Titus's military campaign. Many scholars believe that the Gospel of John was created after the synoptic Gospels. I concur with this judgment, and will show that this gospel was written, or at least heavily redacted, during the reign of Domitian.

The section of the typology that Domitian controlled is difficult to understand because it was intended to transcend Titus's typology. In the same way that Titus had morphed his typology onto the Jewish messianic prophecies to show that he was the Christ that the scripture predicted, Domitian built his typology on top of his brother's. In other words, by winning a petty literary game of 'Christ typology one-upmanship' Domitian intended to show posterity that it was he, not his dead brother, who was the final 'Christ' whom Christians have unknowingly worshipped.

Surprises are always possible for those who try to make themselves immortal gods, of course, and Domitian suffered a complete reversal of both his role as Caesar and the literary legacy he tried to create. Domitian was assassinated in 96 CE, at age 45, and the Senate passed *Damnatio Memoriae* against him, ending his aspiration to become a divus like his father and brother before him.

Domitian's assassination may be related to his executions of his secretary Epaphroditus and the consul Titus Flavius Clemens, and the exile of Flavia Domitilla. These characters were all notable for their possible affiliation with early Christianity. An Epaphroditus was mentioned in Phillipians (2:25, 4:18) as a companion of the apostle Paul, and Josephus's "Antiquities of the Jews" was also dedicated to an Epaphroditus, if indeed these were all the same person. And, as shown in *Caesar's Messiah*, Titus Flavius Clemens was identified in early Church literature as the first Roman pope after Peter himself, as well as the author of the Epistle of Clement, and the protagonist of the Pseudo-Clementine Recognitions and Homilies. (However, this Titus Flavius Clemens is not to be confused with the theologian Titus Flavius Clemens also known as Clement of Alexandria, mentioned below.)

Domitian's reign ended in a palace coup. According to Suetonius, the conspiracy was headed by Domitian's chamberlain Parthenius (an associate of Epaphroditus) and by a steward of Flavia Domitilla, the wife of the executed consul. Domitian's irrationality was increasingly seen as the real problem, and perhaps cooler (more bureaucratic) minds prevailed. Ultimately, a provincial military operative by Trajan emerged, apparently with the backing of the powerful Piso family, and Christianity was sent in yet another direction.

Trajan's victory will be the topic of the third volume in the *Caesar's Messiah* trilogy, which is now being prepared under the working title: *Spiritual Bazaar Wars; and: A Jewess Strikes Back*. This third volume will be forthcoming soon, and anyone who follows me to the end of this journey will be rewarded with buried golden treasure. Or at any rate, I will be providing a map.

Meanwhile, Domitian's reign started smoothly enough. After gaining the throne, he began to add onto the Gospels that his brother Titus created. Domitian either expanded or introduced the bizarre character of the 'Holy Spirit', thereby creating the trinity: the zany Christian concept of a 'godhead' somehow shared by three individuals.

Although the 'Holy Spirit' is mentioned many times in the three synoptic Gospels and also in the Old Testament, it is typically referred to as an aspect of divinity that descends and fills a righteous person with godliness at important moments. As Margaret Barker explained in *The Great Angel: A Study of Israel's Second God*,[92] this view may have stemmed from the two ancient gods visible in the 'J' and 'E' sources of the Torah; that is, Yahweh and El respectively. Yahweh was seen as being the more accessible of the two, and more involved in human affairs, while El was more fatherly and remote. Thus, Yahweh was associated with the 'Holy Spirit' that would descend upon the Messiah. There was no Hebrew concept of a 'Holy Spirit' that was a third distinct entity within the godhead.

The dualist concept of deity was consistent with the views of the Roman imperial cult, and it was consistent with the initial formulation of Flavian Christianity. Vespasian ('God the father')

---

[92] Margaret Barker, *The Great Angel: A Study of Israel's Second God* (Louisville, Ky.: Westminster/John Knox Press, 1992).

and Titus ('son of God') presumably did not see any need to include Domitian in the system of typology in the Synoptic Gospels, because he had not fought with them on the Judean battlefield. To correct this slight to his 'divinity', Domitian promoted the 'Holy Spirit' to become a fully co-equal partnership with the Father and the Son in his contributions to the New Testament.

A clearly Trinitarian formulation only occurs in the synoptic Gospels in Matthew 28:19, "Therefore go and make disciples of all nations, baptizing them in the name of the Father and of the Son and of the Holy Spirit", which many scholars believe was a late interpolation. In a few other passages in the synoptic Gospels, Jesus refers to the 'Holy Spirit' as a distinct entity from the 'Son of Man', but the use of this latter term is arguably enigmatic. The view of the 'Holy Spirit' as an equal member of the Trinity becomes clearer in the Gospel of John, and is fully developed in Revelation and the epistles of Paul. It is interesting to note that the 'Spirit' (that is, Pneuma) was also a technical term of the Imperial Cult that was used to describe the spirit of the emperor that existed within his statues. [93] One interesting example of Domitian's typology is the 'doubting Thomas' story, which requires that the reader already possesses many facts necessary to understand the story's subtle linkages to the history of the Roman legions. First, one must recognize that 'Gemini' is a Greek word — like 'Didymos' — for twin, which is also the meaning of the Hebrew name 'Thomas'. Moreover, the reader must also be aware that the Legion XIV 'Gemina' did not back Vespasian in his effort to seize the throne, and thus it became an actual historical basis for the concept of a "doubting Thomas". Following Vespasian's ascension, the legion was renamed as 'XIV Flavia Firma', in order to obliterate the memory of their disloyalty. In other words, though the 'doubting twin' was called by a different name, it was still the same Legion.

---

[93] Paul Corby Finney and EBSCOhost, *The Invisible God the Earliest Christians on Art.* (New York: Oxford University Press, Incorporated, 1997), p. 73.

This same Legion was used in Domitian's campaign against the Moesians. Thus, John's Gospel story can be read as an allegory in which Legion XIV, the "Doubting Thomas", is testing Domitian's mettle as the living Flavian god, and this time he wins their acceptance.

> Now Thomas, called the Twin (Didymos), one of the twelve, was not with them when Jesus came. The other disciples therefore said to him, "We have seen the Lord." So he said to them, "Unless I see in His hands the imprint of the nails, and put my finger into the print of the nails, and put my hand into His side, I will not believe." And after eight days His disciples were again inside, and Thomas with them. Jesus came, the doors being shut, and stood in the midst, and said, "Peace to you!" Then He said to Thomas, "Reach your finger here, and look at My hands; and reach your hand [here,] and put [it] into My side. Do not be unbelieving, but believing." And Thomas answered and said to Him, "My Lord and my God!" Jesus said to him, "Thomas, because you have seen Me, you have believed. Blessed [are] those who have not seen and [yet] have believed." (John 20: 25-29)

The Greek word describing the 'imprint' was 'tupos', meaning 'type'; that is, a person or thing prefiguring the future. The typology is quite oblique and a reader must be reading the Gospel story looking for connections to Domitian and Vespasian to recognize it. However, if this analysis is correct, Domitian must have been the one who added the story of 'doubting Thomas' to the Gospels, as his military victory seems to be its focus. Thus, by tracing the typology, it is possible to see the sequence of the writing of the four Gospels. In other words: the synoptics were created first under Vespasian and Titus, while Domitian added the Gospel of John during his reign.

Only those who had already grasped the Jesus/Titus typology can understand Domitian's typology concerning the number three. Domitian built his typology upon his brother's for a reason. He was concerned with his legacy relative to his more famous brother, and thus the purpose for his typology was to communicate to those individuals who already understood Titus's. He did not wish Titus to be the only Flavian leaving a message to posterity about his 'Christian' divinity.

An example of Domitian's trinity typology is a puzzle concerning the number three. To create the puzzle, the author used blocks of text from Josephus, Acts, and the Gospel of John, which were linked by rare triangle numbers. These numbers are: the 153 large fish in John 21:11, the 120 people in the congregation in Acts 1:15, and the 276 people on Paul's ship in Acts 27:38. (The number of the beast in Revelation 13:17-18 is also a triangle number, 666. I will say more about that later.) The nth triangle number may be defined as the number of dots composing an equilateral triangle with n dots on a side, including the dots filling the interior of the triangle on a triangular grid.

E.W. Bullinger (*Number in Scripture*, fourth edition, 1921) identified seven three-digit numbers mentioned in the New Testament, while neglecting the 276 people of Acts 27:38. Thus, I believe there are a total of eight three-digit numbers mentioned in the New Testament. The other four three-digit numbers are: two hundred (John 6:7, John 21:8), four hundred (Acts 7:6), four hundred thirty (Galatians 3:17) and "seventy times seven" (Matt. 18:22). The fact that four of the eight triple-digit numbers in the New Testament are triangle numbers is unlikely to have been coincidental, as there are only 31 such numbers between 100 and 999.

The fact that the typology uses so many texts is unfortunate in that it requires the reader to read quite a bit of material, but necessary as all of the texts are involved in the solution. Three linked texts are to be expected, in a sense, in creating a puzzle about the number three.

The first of the three texts is in the Gospel of John, as the disciples gathered and went fishing:

> They went out and immediately **got into the boat, and that night** they caught nothing. [4] But when the morning had now come, **Jesus stood on the shore**; yet **the disciples did not know that it was Jesus.** [5] Then Jesus said to them, "Children, have you any food?" They answered Him, "No." [6] And He said to them, "Cast the net on the right side of the boat, and you will find [some."] So they cast, and now they were not able to draw it in because of the multitude of fish. [7] Therefore that disciple whom Jesus loved said to Peter, "It is the Lord!" Now when **Simon Peter heard that it was the Lord, he put on [his] outer garment (for he had**

removed it), and plunged into the sea. [8] **But the other disciples came in the little boat** (for **they were not far from land,** but about two hundred cubits), dragging the net with fish. [9] Then, **as soon as they had come to land, they saw a fire of coals** there, and fish laid on it, and bread. [10] Jesus said to them, "Bring some of the fish which you have just caught." [11] Simon Peter went up and dragged the net to land, full of large fish, **one hundred and fifty-three;** and although there were so many, the net was not broken. [12] Jesus said to them, **"Come [and] eat breakfast."** Yet none of the disciples dared ask Him, "Who are You?" — **knowing that it was the Lord.** [13] Jesus then came and **took the bread and gave it to them,** and likewise the fish. [14] **This [is] now the third time Jesus showed Himself to His disciples after He was raised from the dead.** [15] So when they had eaten breakfast, Jesus said to Simon Peter, "Simon, [son] of Jonah, do you love Me more than these?" He said to Him, "Yes, Lord; You know that I love You." He said to him, "Feed My lambs." ... [18] "Most assuredly, I say to you, when you were younger, you girded yourself and walked where you wished; but when you are old, you will stretch out your hands, and **another will bind you** and **carry [you] where you do not wish**. (John 21:3-15,18)

In *Caesar's Messiah,* I showed that the 'fish' were actually Jewish rebels, and that the catching of men as 'fish' completed the cycle in the Gospels that begins with Jesus predicting that his followers would be fishing for men. However, scholars have wondered why the author of John 21 chooses 153 as the number of the fish the disciples caught. One suggestion has been that the author based his story on an earlier one concerning Pythagoras, the Greek mathematician, that is oddly parallel to the fishing story in John 21.

There are a number of extant versions Pythagoras's fishing story, but they all tell roughly the same story. Pythagoras comes across a group of fishermen drawing up their net. He tells the fishermen that he could predict the exact number of fish they would catch, which they, of course, thought was impossible. The fishermen said that if he predicted correctly, they would do anything Pythagoras asked. They counted the fish in their net and discovered that Pythagoras had been accurate in his estimate. Pythagoras then

ordered the fishermen to return the fish to the sea but paid them
the price of the fish and left.

Plutarch, who lived during the Flavian era, commented upon the
story and claimed that it showed Pythagoras's belief that humans
had descended from fish and that eating fish was the equivalent of
cannibalism for humans. In his book *Symposiacs*, Plutarch
described the fish that Pythagoras set free as prisoners, and
referred to them as his own kinsfolk.

Plutarch wrote that Pythagoras had been influenced by the Greek
philosopher Anaximander, who claimed "that men were first
produced in fishes, and, when they were grown up and able to help
themselves, were thrown out, and so lived upon the land.
Therefore, as the fire devours its parents, that is, the matter out of
which it was first kindled, so Anaximander, asserting that fish
were our common parents, condemns our feeding on them"
(Plutarch, *Symposiacs*, Book viii, question viii). Thus, perhaps one
of the inspirations for the Flavian metaphor in the Gospels' story
concerning 'fishing for men' was Pythagoras's belief that fish
were the ancestors to humans.

But the 153 fishes caught in John 21 were linked to Pythagoras in
a more direct way. Pythagoras had discovered that the ratio of
265:153 represents a good approximation of the square root of
three. The ratio is physically represented by a shape known as the
Vesica Piscis, a term that literally means the "bladder of a fish".
The figure is formed by the intersection of two circular surfaces of
the same radius, placed with the center of each circle lying on the
circumference of the other. The ratio of the width of this figure to
its height represents the square root of three. The Vesica Piscis has
been used since antiquity to create the fish shape that represents
Christianity.

The ratio 265/153 is not an exact solution, because the square root
of 3 is an irrational number. Perhaps this was one of the reasons
that Domitian decided to create the 265/153 fish puzzle, as the
ratio shows the trinity — the number 3 — in a way that can only
be represented numerically as an infinite series.

THE VESICA PISCIS

Until now there has been no real explanation as to why the Vesica Piscis was chosen to represent Christianity. It is known that the earliest literary reference to the fish symbol of Christianity came from the recommendation of the early church theologian Titus Flavius Clemens (150 — 215 CE), who is better known as Clement of Alexandria. Titus instructed Christians to engrave their seals with the symbol of a fish (Pedagogues, III, xi). Many readers of *Caesar's Messiah* will automatically suspect that the symbols of someone named Titus Flavius Clemens had some meaning to the Flavian family. As shown below, the fish symbol created by the Vesica Piscis represented the trinity that created Christianity — the three Flavian Caesars.

Titus Flavius Clemens — the first author to claim the fish symbol for Christianity. Notice his blonde hair — Flavian means 'blonde'. Notice also the X shaped crucifix on his vestment. This would have been the shape of the original crucifix of Christianity. It symbolized the Tenth Legion, which was camped on the Mount of Olives during the siege of Jerusalem and captured and crucified Eleazar, the real Christ.

Moving along to the next text in the puzzle, in Acts 1 (containing the triangle number 120), a 'Mathias' is chosen over a 'Justus' and is 'numbered' with the 'eleven' — the number of apostles after Judas had killed himself. Notice that the author repeats the concept that Mathias was 'numbered'. The story began as Peter told the disciples that Judas needed to be replaced:

> And in those days Peter stood up in the midst of the disciples (altogether the number of names was about a **hundred and twenty**), and said, "Men [and] brethren, this Scripture had to be fulfilled, which the Holy Spirit spoke before by the mouth of David concerning Judas, who became a guide to those who arrested Jesus; "for **he was numbered with us** and obtained a part in this ministry" (Acts 1: 15-17).

Two candidates were identified, and one was chosen.

> ...Joseph called Barsabas, who was surnamed **Justus,** and **Matthias**. And they prayed and said, "You, O Lord, who know the hearts of all, show which of these two You have chosen "to take part in this ministry and apostleship from which Judas by transgression fell, that he might go to his own place." And they cast their lots, and the lot fell on **Matthias.** And he was **numbered with the eleven apostles** (Acts 1: 23-26).

There is a connection between a passage in Josephus's short autobiography and this passage. At the beginning of his autobiography, Josephus described how his family members often took the name Matthias. It should be noted that by claiming Mathias as his family name Josephus was trying to graft himself onto the Jews royal family the Maccabees, which were descended from Matthias Maccabeus.

> This Simon Psellus had nine sons, one of whom was **Matthias**...This **Matthias** had a son called **Matthias** Curtus, and that in the first year of the government of Hyrcanus: his son's name was Joseph, born in the ninth year of the reign of Alexandra; his son **Matthias** was born in the tenth year of the reign of Archclaus; as was I born to **Matthias** in the first year of the reign of Caius Caesar. Now, my father **Matthias** was not only eminent on account of his nobility, but had a higher commendation on account of his righteousness..., I was myself brought up with my brother, whose name was **Matthias**... (Josephus, Life 1.3-2.8)

In his autobiography, Josephus also described his competitor, an evil historian named 'Justus'. This 'Justus' wrote a history that contradicted Josephus's.

> I have a mind to say a few things to **Justus,** who hath himself written a history concerning these affairs, as also to others who profess to write history, but have little regard to truth, and are not afraid, either out of ill-will or good-will to some persons, to relate falsehoods (Josephus, Life 65.336).

As in the passage in Acts, 'Mathias' (Josephus's full name was Joseph bar Mathias) was chosen while Justus was not. One obvious typological point that the two stories create is that Josephus's history was the one 'chosen' by the Flavians, while Justus's disappeared. However, another parallel between Josephus's Life and the Acts of the Apostles is so obvious as to have been noticed by other scholars: that is, the parallel shipwrecks of Paul and Josephus.[94] Josephus describes his shipwreck in a passage which follows soon after the description of his family members named Mathias.

> But when I was in the twenty-sixth year of my age, it happened that I took a **voyage to Rome**, and this on the occasion which I shall now describe. At the time when **Felix** was procurator of Judea there were **certain priests** of my acquaintance, and very excellent persons they were, whom on a small and trifling occasion he had **put into bonds, and sent to Rome to plead their cause before Caesar**. These I was desirous to procure deliverance for, and that especially because I was informed that they were not unmindful of **piety towards God**, even under their afflictions, but supported themselves with figs and nuts. Accordingly I came to Rome, though it were through a great number of hazards by sea; for as **our ship was drowned in the Adriatic Sea**, we that were in it, being about six hundred in number, **swam for our lives all the night**; when, **upon the first appearance of the day, and upon our sight of a ship of Cyrene,** I and some others, **eighty in all, by God's providence**, prevented the rest, and were taken up into the other ship. And when I had

---

[94] Robert Gnuse, 'Vita Apologetica: The Lives of Josephus and Paul in Apologetic Historiography', *Journal for the Study of the Pseudepigrapha*, 13 (2002), 151–169.

thus escaped, and was come to Dieearchia, which the Italians call
Puteoli (Josephus, Life 3.13-16).

Acts describes Paul's shipwreck in great detail and it is easy to see
that its shipwreck story was somehow dependent to Josephus's in
that some of the parallel concepts occur in the same sequence —
i.e. Felix, priests being imprisoned and sent to Caesar for
judgment, the ship sinks or runs aground in the Adriatic Sea, the
heroes (Josephus or Paul) act with courage and provide leadership,
all passengers presumably survive, and then on to Puteoli. Thus,
by way of the common link with Josephus's Life, the passage in
Acts 27 describing the shipwreck and containing the triangle
number 276 is paired with the passage in Acts 1 containing the
triangle number 120. (Of course, Acts 1 and Acts 27 are also
paired simply because they both contain rare triangle numbers.)

However, the shipwreck story in Acts also contains many parallels
to the 'coming ashore' story in John 21 featuring the triangle
number 153. Below is the shipwreck story in Acts with its
parallels to John 21 as well as Josephus's Life highlighted.

> Acts 24:1 Now after five days Ananias...gave evidence to the
> governor against Paul. Tertullus began saying: "Seeing that
> through you we enjoy great peace, and prosperity is being brought
> to this nation by your foresight, "we accept [it] always and in all
> places, most noble **Felix...**

> Acts 27:1 And when it was decided that we should sail to Italy,
> **they delivered Paul and some other prisoners** to [one] named
> Julius, a centurion of the Augustan Regiment.... ˙ **the centurion
> found an Alexandrian ship sailing to Italy, and he put us on
> board.** ⁷ ...we ... sailed slowly many days... ¹⁸ And because we
> were exceedingly tempest-tossed, the next [day] they lightened
> the ship. ¹⁹ **On the third [day] we threw the ship's tackle
> overboard with our own hands**. ... ²¹ But after long abstinence
> from food, then Paul stood in the midst of them and said, "Men,
> you should have listened to me, and not have sailed from Crete
> and incurred this disaster and loss. ²² "And now I urge you to take
> heart, for there will be no loss of life among you, but only of the
> ship. ²³ "**For there stood by me this night an angel of the God
> to whom I belong and whom I serve,** ²⁴ "saying, 'Do not be
> afraid, Paul; **you must be brought before Caesar;** and indeed

God has granted you all those who sail with you.' ... **[30]** And as the sailors were seeking to escape from the ship... **[31]** Paul said to the centurion and the soldiers, "Unless these men stay in the ship, **you cannot be saved.**" ... **[33]** And as day was about to dawn, **Paul implored [them] all to take food,** saying, "Today is the fourteenth day **you have waited and continued without food, and eaten nothing....** **[36]** Then they were all encouraged, and also took food themselves. **[37]** And in all we were **two hundred and seventy-six persons on the ship.** **[38]** So **when they had eaten enough,** they lightened the ship and **threw out the wheat into the sea.** **[39] When it was day, they did not recognize the land;** but they observed a bay with a beach, onto which they planned to run the ship if possible... **[42]** And the **soldiers' plan was to kill the prisoners, lest any of them should swim away and escape.** **[43] But the centurion, wanting to save Paul,** kept them from [their] purpose, and commanded that **those who could swim should jump** [overboard] first and get to land, **[44]** and the rest, **some on boards and some on things from the ship.** And so it was that they all escaped safely to land.

Acts 28:1 Now when they had escaped, they then found out that the island was called Malta. **[2]** And the natives showed us unusual kindness; **for they kindled a fire** and made us all welcome... **[3]** But when Paul had gathered a bundle of sticks and laid [them] on the fire, **a viper came out because of the heat, and fastened on his hand.** **[4] So when the natives saw the creature hanging from his hand, they said to one another,** "No doubt this man is a murderer... But ... **they changed their minds and said that he was a god.** **[7]** In that region there was an estate of the leading citizen of the island, whose name was Publius, who received us and entertained us courteously **for three days.** ... **[11] After three months** we sailed in an **Alexandrian ship whose figurehead was the Twin Brothers,** which had wintered at the island. **[12]** And landing at Syracuse, we stayed **three days.** **[13]** From there we circled round and reached Rhegium. And after one day the south wind blew; and the next day we came to **Puteoli...** And so we went toward Rome. **[15]** And from there, when the brethren heard about us, they came to meet us as far as Appii Forum and **Three Inns.** ... And it came to pass **after three days** that Paul called the leaders of the Jews together. So when they had come together, he said to them: "Men [and] brethren... **I was delivered as a prisoner from Jerusalem into the hands of the Romans,...** for the hope of Israel **I am bound with this chain."**

I will go through the linkages between the 'coming ashore' stories in John 21 and Acts 27 & 28 in a general sense. Notice that while there is not a perfect sequence of parallels, the broad outline of the 'coming ashore' story of John 21 is definitely repeated in the 'coming ashore' story in Acts 27 & 28. Further, an informed reader should be looking for such parallels in that the typology of the Gospels is often formed into parallel cycles, and thus it is not surprising that the end of Acts should be compared to John 21 — the end of the Gospels.

In both stories a group spends a night on a boat. They do not eat food and are hungry. They are told to eat. From the sea they fail to recognize something. They were close to shore. Eventually some swim to shore but others come ashore in another way. There is a fire when they get to shore. They believe someone is a god that they first do not. The number three is mentioned in both stories. Finally, Paul mirrors Jesus's predictions for Simon: like Simon, Paul is brought to Rome in chains. The most important parallel is, of course, that each tale contains a triangle number, which indicates that the stories be compared.

Understanding that the two 'coming ashore' stories with triangle numbers were typologically linked allows the meaning of the critical passage from Acts 27 below to be understood.

> And the soldiers' plan was to kill the prisoners, lest any of them should swim away and escape. But the centurion, wanting to save Paul, kept them from [their] purpose, and commanded that those who could swim should jump [overboard] first and get to land, and the rest, some on boards and some on [parts] of the ship. And so it was that they all escaped safely to land. (Acts 27:42-44)

The typology is both ingenious and amusing. The passage is typologically repeating the conclusion of John 21 so as to document yet another 'divine cycle' whereby another a 'Christ' is identified on the beach at a 'coming ashore' conclusion. In this cycle, however, it is not Titus but the third god of the Flavian trinity that is being identified as the Christ — Domitian.

The key typological point is that the prisoners that were mentioned at the conclusion of Paul's shipwreck story above are the eleven disciples that were 'numbered' with Mathias at the beginning of Acts in the passage with the triangle number 120. These eleven disciples include the group that 'came ashore' in John 21, the passage with the triangle number 153. The triangle number 276 in Acts helps us to see that the prisoners are related to the disciples in the passages that were linked by the triangle numbers 153 and 120.

The premise that the prisoners on Paul's boat were the eleven disciples mentioned in Acts 1 is also in a sense obvious as the disciples were constantly being arrested, and when last seen they had just been released from prison. They were told that they must refrain from preaching the Gospel, but they immediately began doing exactly that. However, the primary path to this understanding is through the logic of the typology.

Once a reader recognizes that the 'prisoners' in Paul's shipwreck story were (typologically) the disciples, he or she still needs to recall a passage from Josephus's shipwreck story to understand how the puzzle yields the Vesica Piscis ratio of 153/265. This passage describes the number of 'swimmers' who were with Josephus and were taken onboard another ship.

> **and upon our sight of a ship of Cyrene**, I and some others, **eighty in all, by God's providence**, prevented the rest, and were taken up into the other ship (Josephus, Life 3.15).

The fact that there were eighty men with Josephus created a typological link between Josephus and the centurion in Paul's story. Though originally a centurion commanded 100 soldiers, the century (centuria) had shrunk to a group of eighty men at the time Acts was written. Also, just as Julius the centurion in Acts was determined to save Paul the priest and his fellow prisoners, so also Josephus was determined to save the priests who were sailing with him at the start of his voyage.

So we arrive at the solution of our puzzle: while 'Mathias' (that is, a type of Josephus) was 'numbered with the eleven' in the '120' story, we find the Centurion (that is, another type of Josephus) ordered the prisoners to swim to shore in the '276' story, thus 'subtracting' the 11 prisoners from the 276 on the boat thereby leaving 265 still on the water. This creates the other half of the Vesica Piscis ratio 265/153.

This solution neatly ties together the references to 'Mathias' and the 'eleven' from Acts 1:15-26, the references to prisoners, the centurion and '276' in Acts 27, and the reference to 153 'fish' in John 21. Furthermore, without the information relating to Josephus from his autobiography, and the realization that 'Mathias' and 'Julius the centurion' are both types of Josephus, the puzzle cannot truly be 'solved': there is no other justification for subtracting the eleven from the 276.

The description in the Acts shipwreck story mentions an **"Alexandrian ship whose figurehead was the Twin Brothers"**. Alexandria, of course, is a city associated with the Flavians because of their friendship and family ties with the wealthy Alexanders who ruled there. The "Twin Brothers" were Castor and Pollux, the sons of Zeus. When Castor was killed, Pollux asked Zeus to permit his twin brother to share his own immortality and to keep them together. Zeus consented and they were transformed into the constellation Gemini. With the emphatic references to the number three in these passages from John and Acts, we must recognize that the reference to the "Twin Brothers" should also bring to mind the 'trinity' composed of Zeus and his sons. The three, taken together, are obvious types for Vespasian, Titus and Domitian — two brothers who were sons of a god with one of them needing to share in his brother's immortality.

Another interesting typological connection links Paul's experience with a viper to Moses's parallel experience in Exodus. Considering Titus's typological connections to both Jesus and Moses, the point is to show that the events that led to the first covenant with god were repeated in the creation of the 'final covenant' with Domitian's Christianity.

The connections between the burning bush — serpent — hand stories are too obvious to require an explanation. Below are the texts.

But when Paul had gathered a bundle of sticks and laid [them] **on the fire, a viper came out because of the heat, and fastened on his hand.** However, they were expecting that he would swell up or suddenly fall down dead. But after they had looked for a long time and saw no harm come to him, **they changed their minds and said that he was a god.** (Acts 28: 3-4)

There the angel of the Lord appeared to him in flames of **fire within a bush**...So the LORD said to him, "What [is] that in your hand?" He said, "A rod."   And He said, "Cast it on the ground." So he cast it on the ground, and **it became a serpent;** and Moses fled from it. Then the LORD said to Moses, "**Reach out your hand and take [it] by the tail"** (Exodus 3, 4: 1-4)

In the same was as the Jesus of the Gospels foresees Titus, so Paul's parallel experience of being first overlooked and then discovered to be a god is meant to suggest the third god of the Flavian trinity, Domitian. This oblique typological connection to Domitian's divinity is an example par excellence of the building block style of Roman typology. While no one who did not understand Titus's typology could ever see it, no one familiar with it would miss it.

To digress, understanding Domitian's Trinity typology allows many heretofore-incomprehensible parts of the Shakespearian literature to become coherent. For example, the trio of clown like characters in The Tempest -Stephano, Caliban and Trinculo, were created as a send up of the Flavian trinity.

In the trio 'Stephano' — the word means 'crown' — is Vespasian, 'Caliban' — the name is an anagram of cannibal — is Titus and reverses his claim to have caused the Jews to cannibalize their messiah, and 'Trinculo' is Domitian — the name is a pun upon Domitian's claim of a Flavian trinity.

Caliban is said to have been born of a "devil and" from a "vile race". He is also disfigured -playing off of the pruning humor Titus enjoyed so much. Caliban was "taught language" by Prospero, the Jewish hero who is reclaiming his title that was stolen by a false brother. Caliban learned language from Prospero just as Titus learned the typological language from the Hebrew bible to use it in the Gospels. Caliban worships Stefano as a god just as Titus had his father deified.

At 2,2, Trinculo enters and discovering Caliban and Trinculo hiding by lying on top of one another. He states "here is neither bush nor shrub" 2,2 9 indicating that Titus and Domitian were not part of the real messianic branch. He refers to them as an "ancient fish" and when he sees that the "beast" has four legs he calls it a 'Moon calf'; obviously mocking the 'beast' humor in Revelation. Later, Stephano mentions that Trinculo "like to lose his hair and prove a bald jerkin" referring to Domitian's concern over his baldness.

At the play's conclusion Caliban renounces the Flavians divinity stating:

> "I'll be wise hereafter,
> And seek for grace. What a thrice-doubled ass
> Was I to take this drunkard for a god,
> And worship this dull fool."   (5,1,300-305)

While the Vesica Piscis forms the shape of a fish, it also represents another image of Christian iconography: the eye of God positioned inside a triangle. Thus, Paul's dialogue at the end of Acts where he describes an eye that cannot see may be a subtle reference to putting out the Jews' 'eye of God' which is often represented by an eye inside of a triangle.

All-seeing eye in a Catholic church coming out of a triangle in the sun.

[26] saying, 'Go to this people and say: "Hearing you will hear, and shall not understand; And seeing you will see, and not perceive;

[27] For the hearts of this people have grown dull. Their ears are hard of hearing, And their eyes they have closed, Lest they should see with [their] eyes and hear with [their] ears, Lest they should understand with [their] hearts and turn, So that I should heal them." '

[28] "Therefore let it be known to you that the salvation of God has been sent to the Gentiles, and they will hear it! (Acts 28:26-28)

If this is so, it might explain why the eye in the triangle became — like the trinity — an image often used to represent Christianity. Perhaps the Flavians might have claimed that the' eye of god' of the Jews had been put out, and the eye of god now belonged to their family cult.

REVELATION AND DOMITIAN'S IMPERIAL CULT

The second century church historian Irenaeus believed that the Book of Revelation was written during Domitian's reign. Irenaeus claimed to have received first hand information from those who had seen John, the author of Revelation, "face to face". He recorded that:

> We will not, however, incur the risk of pronouncing positively as to the name of Antichrist; for if it were necessary that his name should be distinctly revealed in this present time, it would have been announced by him who beheld the apocalyptic vision. For that was seen no very long time since, but almost in our day, towards the end of Domitian's reign (Irenaeus, *Against Heresies*, 5, 30, 3).

Like the Gospels and the Epistles, the book of Revelation appears as if it has a surface-level interpretation. However, to a much greater extent than the rest of the New Testament, it is far from obvious what that surface level interpretation should be. Of course, there is obviously a great deal of prophetic imagery and stained-glass talk about God and His greatness, and the book is chock-full of ambiguous allusions to the Old Testament prophets. And, very importantly, Jesus's second coming and the ultimate arrival of the Kingdom of Heaven are deferred for at least a thousand years, if not more. However, aside from that, the general impression is of a deep mystery within an enigma, or perhaps someone's acid trip. Into this void, many mischievous interpretations have stepped, including the notorious views of the modern-day Christian Zionists and Dispensationalists. My intent is to give an alternative interpretation of the text that puts it into its true context as a part of the Flavian Christian canon. Interested readers are invited to make their own comparison between the power of my interpretation, in contrast to whatever other interpretation suits their fancy, and see which one does a better job of resolving the many puzzles and enigmas comprising John's 'Revelation'.

It has been widely recognized that the Christian organization described in Revelation to which letters are sent has many similarities with the *Commune Asiae,* the Roman bureaucracy that administered to Domitian's Imperial Cult in Asia. For example, there seems to have been a special importance attached to a group of seven representative cities in Asia for the Commune, a parallel to the 'Seven Churches' described in Revelation. The city of Magnesia inscribed on its coins the title "Seventh (city) of Asia," referring to the order of precedence among the cities as observed in the *Commune Asiae*[95], the bureaucracy that oversaw the imperial cult in the eastern provinces. There is also a reference to the Commune in Acts 19:31, where, incredibly, members of that organization, the "Asiarches" or "chief officers of Asia," were mentioned as friends of Paul.

One issue that this analysis resolves is that of the 'letters' to the seven churches. Since there was no postal service for the use of private individuals during the first century, it has been something of a mystery how Christians were able to send letters to distant churches. If the Christian congregations described in Revelation and by Paul actually sent letters to one another they would have needed to have maintained a private messenger-service for their remote outposts, something that was known to have been within the capacity only of the empire's great trading corporations and the imperial government, who both employed professional mail carriers called the *tabellari*. Training and maintaining such individuals would have been costly, and it has been unclear how a fledging religion that promoted poverty would have been able to afford a mail service. If first century Christianity was under the

---

[95] The Letters to the Seven Churches of Asia, W. M. Ramsay, 1904#

direction of the Commune Asiae, however, the mystery disappears.

Though Domitian has not received any scrutiny to determine if he was the 'god' of Revelation who mailed letters to churches in Asia, he is an obvious candidate. Even a cursory glance indicates that he possessed many of the attributes of the god addressed within the work. The most obvious parallel is the fact that his historians maintained that he claimed both titles of Lord God and Christ. Both Suetonius and Josephus flatly proclaimed that the Flavian Caesars held the mantle of the 'Christ' foreseen by Judaism's prophecies.

For clarification, I present the following list of the characteristics shared by the two 'Gods' below. In the list, Revelation's characteristics of the 'Lord God' are given first, followed by the citation of Suetonius' parallel descriptions of Domitian.

While some of the connections are simply historical facts that the author expected his readers to be familiar with, and others are trivial or comic parallels, some parallels so complex that they indicate a deliberate linkage in and of themselves. Examples of these complex parallels are the 'raised a 'day's wages by a third and increased grain and decreased wine' parallel (Revelation 6:6 and Suetonius, Domitian, 7) and the 'gave a prophetess chance to repent then cast her on a bed of suffering and executed her lovers' parallel found in Revelation 2:20 and Suetonius, Domitian, 8.

As is always the case, however, when attempting to determine if some dependency exists between two works of literature, the parallels must be judged as a collection. And when judged this way, the parallels leave little doubt as to the identity of the 'Lord God' of Revelation. Moreover, the author of Revelation wrote his work for those who understand the typology presented earlier in the New Testament. In other words: the New Testament was designed to be read in its extant sequence, and the authors use the 'secret knowledge' the reader has developed by decoding the prior text as building blocks to be used by the reader in understanding the further text.

- Rode a white horse (Suetonius, Domitian, 2).
- Inner circle were winged creatures with multiple eyes (Suetonius, Domitian, 3).
- Outer circle wore crowns (Suetonius, Domitian, 4).
- Congregation wore white (Suetonius, Domitian, 12).
- Both were called the 'Lord God' (Suetonius, Domitian, 13).
- The 'Lord God' was an archer (Suetonius, Domitian, 19).
- Throne room was encircled with a rainbow and was next to a sea (Suetonius, Domitian, 5&6).
- Raised a 'day's wages' of soldiers by a third at the point he increased grain and decreased wine (Revelation 6, 6 and Suetonius, Domitian, 7).
- Gave a prophetess chance to repent then cast her on a bed of suffering and executed her and her lovers (Suetonius, Domitian, 8).
- Attacked sexual immorality (Suetonius, Domitian, 8).
- Opposed "those who claim they are Jews but are not" (Suetonius, Domitian, 12).
- Was the first and the last — the alpha and the omega — Domitian maintained that he was both the first of the Flavian Caesars and the last (Suetonius, Domitian 13).
- Was the 'morning star' (Suetonius, Domitian, 16).
- Had feet of bronze (Suetonius, Domitian, 18).
- Battled beast with two horns (Suetonius, Domitian, 19).

Among the historical parallels between the 'Lord God' of Revelation and Domitian were the following:

- Was a 'living god'
- Had the power to execute subjects
- Had a Church in Ephesus that was the first in order of importance (Domitian built his personal Temple there).
- Had a group of churches in Asia Minor.
- Father was a God.
- The 'Lord God' of Revelation and Domitian were both the 'Christ' (Suetonius, Vespasian 4).
- Was part of a trinity of gods that shared a 'godhead' — Domitian was one of the three Flavian Caesars, two of whom had already been deified by the Senate, and like them, he possessed the imperial 'pneuma' or divine spirit.

- Finally, — the obvious is always overlooked — the 'lord god' Domitian possessed a mail system capable of sending letters to the seven cities named in Revelation.

Such a collection of parallels would be suspicious under any circumstances, but in light of the analysis in *Caesar's Messiah* showing that the Gospels were written to proclaim the divinity of Titus, there can be no mistaking that they were deliberate or that they were designed to establish Domitian as the 'Christ' of Revelation. The fact that the Pauline material and Revelation was created to link to Domitian is, in a way, to be expected. Domitian's vanity and obsession with his divinity were well known.

Once readers recognize the obvious parallels between Domitian and Revelation's 'Lord God' they are then able to see that the seven overt 'seals' of Revelation were linked to the seven hidden seals in Paul's letters. In fact, these parallel seven seals occur in the same sequence in both works — mirroring the sequential typologically linked events between Jesus and Titus.

The 'seven seal' linkages were also typologically connected to the histories of Suetonius. As shown below, this complicated three-way linkage between the two sets of seven seals and Suetonius's history must be understood to 'open' the seven seals, and to learn that the name of the Christ is Domitian.

I will present the analysis of the 'three book' typology that opens the seven seals only after presenting a basic explanation of Revelation. This basic understanding is necessary to 'open' the seven seals.

I have embedded this analysis within the text of Revelation, which is presented in its entirety. Hopefully this will not only make the analysis easier to understand, but allow a reader to see the overall coherency it creates for a heretofore somewhat incomprehensible work.

REVELATION 1: PROLOGUE

[1] The revelation of Jesus Christ, which God gave him to show his servants what must soon take place.

The Gospels' character John was reused in Revelation as the individual having a vision of God's throne room because he was the disciple who survived the end of the Jewish war.. Revelation's narrator, 'John' — like the Gospels' John — is a fictional character based upon the John who was described in Josephus as a leader of the Jewish rebellion.

The comedy of Revelation is based upon the premise that this 'John' believes that Domitian is a God and therefore sees the things inside his throne room as spiritual items rather than the objects from reality, thus extending the delusion 'John' experienced at the empty tomb in the Gospels.

He made it known by sending his angel to his servant John, [2] who testifies to everything he saw—that is, the word of God and the testimony of Jesus Christ.

[3] Blessed is the one who reads the words of this prophecy, and blessed are those who hear it and take to heart what is written in it, because the time is near.

GREETINGS AND DOXOLOGY

[4] John, To the seven churches in the province of Asia: Grace and peace to you from him who is, and who was, and who is to come, and from the seven spirits before his throne, [5] and from Jesus Christ, who is the faithful witness, the firstborn from the dead, and the ruler of the kings of the earth.

To him who loves us and has freed us from our sins by his blood, [6] and has made us to be a kingdom and priests to serve his God and Father—to him be glory and power for ever and ever! Amen. [7] Look, he is coming with the clouds, and every eye will see him, even those who pierced him; and all the peoples of the earth will mourn because of him. So shall it be! Amen.

[8] "I am the Alpha and the Omega," says the Lord God, "who is, and who was, and who is to come, the Almighty."

The description of God used throughout Revelation as the "the Alpha and the Omega" — the first and the last — simply represents Domitian's claim that he was both the first Flavian Caesar and the last. Domitian was the first Flavian to be referred to as Caesar by the troops loyal to the family during the time between Otha's execution and his father's arrival in Rome to officially take the title, leading to his claim to be the first Flavian Caesar, as explained by Suetonius:

> It was only after the victory that Domitian ventured forth and after being hailed as Caesar, he assumed the office of city praetor with consular powers, but only in name, turning over all the judicial business to his next colleague. But he exercised all the tyranny of his high position so lawlessly, that it was even then apparent what sort of a man he was going to be. Not to mention all details, after making free with the wives of many men, he went so far as to marry Domitia Longina, who was the wife of Aelius Lamia, and in a single day he assigned more than twenty positions in the city and abroad, which led Vespasian to say more than once that he was surprised that he did not appoint the emperor's successor with the rest. (Suetonius, Domitian 1)

Suetonius repeats the important 'Alpha and the Omega' concept later in his history of Domitian.

> On his accession Domitian boasted to the Senate of having himself conferred the imperial power on Vespasian and Titus — it had now merely returned to him. (Domitian 13)

Moreover, notice that the "Lord God" not only "was" and "is" but "is to come". This is an important point; Domitian has constructed Revelation to indicate that he will "come" in the future. This prophecy was intended to have both a literal and comic fulfillment. Note that all of the statements by god in Revelation are from Domitian.

ONE LIKE A SON OF MAN

The "seven churches' of Asia Minor named in Revelation were all key cities of the Imperial Cult administered by the Roman bureaucracy called the 'Commune Asiae'. As not all cities in Asia Minor were part of the Imperial Cult and this fact, on its face, suggests some connection between the Cult and the seven churches in Revelation.

> [9] I, John, your brother and companion in the suffering and kingdom and patient endurance that are ours in Jesus, was on the island of Patmos because of the word of God and the testimony of Jesus.
>
> [10] On the Lord's Day I was in the Spirit, and I heard behind me a loud voice like a trumpet,
>
> [11] which said: "Write on a scroll what you see and send it to the seven churches: to Ephesus, Smyrna, Pergamum, Thyatira, Sardis, Philadelphia and Laodicea."

As the passage continues below, 'John' sees "someone 'like a son of man'", an overt homage to the messianic prophecies of the prophet Daniel. The great image in Nebuchadnezzar's dream is also recalled, although that figure had feet which were fatally flawed by being made "partly of iron and partly of clay" (Daniel 2:32-34), while the figure in Revelation is composed of stronger stuff, with feet of bronze. However, the imagery also describes Domitian. Suetonius pointed out that Domitian had 'hammer toes', thus Domitian was also a god with 'feet like bronze'. The double-edged sword that comes out of the figure's mouth represents the emperor's words, which can cut 'two' ways. In other words: like the Gospels, the words in the Pauline material and Revelation have two meanings.

> [12] I turned around to see the voice that was speaking to me. And when I turned I saw seven golden lampstands,
>
> [13] and among the lampstands was someone "like a son of man," dressed in a robe reaching down to his feet and with a golden sash around his chest.

[14] His head and hair were white like wool, as white as snow, and his eyes were like blazing fire. [15] His feet were like bronze glowing in a furnace, and his voice was like the sound of rushing waters.

In the religious symbolism of the Roman Imperial Cult, a star represented the heavenly existence of the divine Caesar. This concept also appears in the language of the Roman court poets, where the Emperor on earth had a star in heaven that was his heavenly counterpart. An imperial family as a whole could also be represented as a star. For example, Horace (*Odes*, i, 12) speaks of the Julian star shining like the moon amid dimmer fires.

When Domitian built the Temple of the Flavian family in 95 CE, his court poet Statius described him as placing the stars of the Flavians into a new heaven (*Silvae*, v, I, 240f). Statius's poem bears a striking resemblance to the 'star' imagery in Revelation: in both works the new Temple on earth corresponds to a new heaven framed to contain new stars. I show below that the metaphorical description of 'Stars' representing the god in Revelation and *Silvae* is also used to reveal the true identity of the 'morning star' at the conclusion of Revelation.

In the following line the seven stars represent the seven stars of the imperial cult. These are the five deified Caesars before Domitian — Julius, Augustus, Claudius, Vespasian and Titus, Domitian himself of course, and the 'morning star' who is the final Christ and whose secret identity is the 'revelation' of Revelation.

[16] In his right hand he held seven stars, and out of his mouth came a sharp double-edged sword. His face was like the sun shining in all its brilliance.

[17] When I saw him, I fell at his feet as though dead. Then he placed his right hand on me and said: "Do not be afraid. I am the First and the Last.

[18] I am the Living One; I was dead, and behold I am alive for ever and ever! And I hold the keys of death and Hades."

The individual in the following passage holding seven churches is Domitian, who indeed held the 'seven churches' in his hand. In other words, he was the 'god' — and ruler — of the churches of the Commune Asiae. The identity of the 'seven angels' will be presented below.

> [19] Write, therefore, what you have seen, what is now and what will take place later.
>
> [20] The mystery of the seven stars that you saw in my right hand and of the seven golden lampstands is this: The seven stars are the angels of the seven churches, and the seven lampstands are the seven churches.

Within the 'seven churches' of Revelation, Ephesus is addressed first because it was the city in which Domitian had built his official 'church'. The temple for Domitian was dedicated in Ephesus in A.D. 89 or 90. It was a great honor for a city to obtain the Emperor's official temple and from that time on Ephesus boasted that it was the "temple keeper" (*neokoros*) for the living Caesar.

The passage below describes how Ephesus struggled for the honor of having Domitian build his official temple in the city; or in other words, how it "endured hardships for my name".

REVELATION 2: TO THE CHURCH IN EPHESUS

> [1] To the angel of the church in Ephesus write: These are the words of him who holds the seven stars in his right hand and walks among the seven golden lampstands:
>
> [2] I know your deeds, your hard work and your perseverance. I know that you cannot tolerate wicked men, that you have tested those who claim to be apostles but are not, and have found them false.
>
> [3] You have persevered and have endured hardships for my name, and have not grown weary.

The next passage seems to comment upon Ephesus's past status within the Imperial Cult. In 29 BC, the first temple to the deified

Julius Caesar was erected by the city. Coins found at Ephesus proudly state that the city was "First of all the greatest", and "The first and greatest metropolis of Asia." [96]

In the passage, Domitian — who of course actually had the power to "remove a church" — cautions the city to "do the things you did at first" — the slavish worship of the divine Caesar — or he will take their church away. It seems possible that the passage indicates that the 'Christians' in Ephesus were refusing to worship Domitian exactly as he wanted, and that this was the basis for the threat to "remove the lampstand".

[4] Yet I hold this against you: You have forsaken your first love.

[5] Remember the height from which you have fallen! Repent and do the things you did at first.

[6] If you do not repent, I will come to you and remove your lampstand from its place.

In the next passage 'God' — Domitian — states that he hates the "Nicolaitans", a cult that has defied identification. 'Nicolaitans' is compound word. 'Nikos' is normally defined as "a conquest; but it can also mean the conquered and by implication, "dominance over the defeated." "Laos" means "people or laymen."

As the word "Nicolaitans" is used in Revelation, it might refer to the cult that Titus — the victor of the war symbolically represented in the Gospels — established to rule over the Jews he had conquered. In Revelation there are a number of villains; the 'Nicolaitans', the 'Synagogue of Satan — who claim to be Jews but are liars', the '666 beast' (who is identified below as Titus) and those who worship him. I believe that the terms refer to Titus and his cult of Christianity that Domitian wished to replace with his own. Or, some of these references might be to surviving

[96] Dale Bergmann, 'Paul's Missionary Journey'
<http://www.welcometohosanna.com/PAULS_MISSIONARY_JOURNEYS/3mission_1.html> [accessed 16 March 2014].

congregations of radical and rebellious Messianic Jews who never adopted any form of Roman 'Christianity'.

Suetonius recorded that Domitian disparaged Titus: Domitian "often slighted Titus's memory by the use of ambiguous terms in...edicts". (Suetonius, Domitian, 2) It is possible that Revelation was the "edict' Suetonius was referring to, with its "ambiguous terms".

> [6] But you have this in your favor: You hate the practices of the Nicolaitans, which I also hate.

> [7] He who has an ear, let him hear what the Spirit says to the churches.

The next line describes the "tree of life" that is in the "paradise of God". This tree of life is mentioned in the letter to Ephesus because, as shown below, the paradise of God — Domitian's Temple — is in Ephesus and the "tree of life" is a real thing that is to bear real gifts to the individual that decodes Revelation.

> To him who overcomes, I will give the right to eat from the tree of life, which is in the paradise of God.

TO THE CHURCH IN SMYRNA

Domitian refers to a 'synagogue of Satan' made up of those who 'those who say they are Jews and are not'. While 'Jewishness' to the Flavians was in the eye of the beholder, perhaps this is referring to the administrators of Titus's Christ cult in Smyrna. These are the ones that the Lord God of Revelation must overcome.

> [8] To the angel of the church in Smyrna write: These are the words of him who is the First and the Last, who died and came to life again.

> [9] I know your afflictions and your poverty—yet you are rich! I know the slander of those who say they are Jews and are not, but are a synagogue of Satan.

[10] Do not be afraid of what you are about to suffer. I tell you, the devil will put some of you in prison to test you, and you will suffer persecution for ten days. Be faithful, even to the point of death, and I will give you the crown of life.

[11] He who has an ear, let him hear what the Spirit says to the churches. He who overcomes will not be hurt at all by the second death.

TO THE CHURCH IN PERGAMUM

Pergamum was another city of the Imperial Cult. It was another 'neokoros' or temple guardian for the religion. Notice that the individual who addresses the 'seven cities' does so in the manner that was only possible during this era for a Caesar or high ranking Roman authority. He informs others of what pleases him and how they can serve him. He also threatens their execution if they displease him.

[12] To the angel of the church in Pergamum write: These are the words of him who has the sharp, double-edged sword.

[13] I know where you live—where Satan has his throne. Yet you remain true to my name. You did not renounce your faith in me, even in the days of Antipas, my faithful witness, who was put to death in your city—where Satan lives.

[14] Nevertheless, I have a few things against you: You have people there who hold to the teaching of Balaam, who taught Balak to entice the Israelites to sin by eating food sacrificed to idols and by committing sexual immorality.

[15] Likewise you also have those who hold to the teaching of the Nicolaitans.

[16] Repent therefore! Otherwise, I will soon come to you and will fight against them with the sword of my mouth.

The following line mentions a 'new name' that for some reason cannot be disclosed. This is the first of a number of mysterious nondisclosures made in Revelation. The concept of a "new name" is important as it shows the general rational for the work. Why would a "new name" be necessary for those who had read the story of Jesus in the Gospels? The answer is that there is "new name" because there is a new Christ.

> [17] He who has an ear, let him hear what the Spirit says to the churches. To him who overcomes, I will give some of the hidden manna. I will also give him a white stone with a new name written on it, known only to him who receives it.

The missive to the church in Thyatira contains a direct link to Suetonius' biography of Domitian — the woman described below as "Jezebel". The passage has been problematic for Christianity in that 'Jesus' is stating that he will execute not only the prophetess and her lovers, but her children as well. And while such action was normative for Caesar's, it was out of character for the Christian notion of God's son.

TO THE CHURCH IN THYATIRA

Thyatira was a city well known to the Flavians. An inscription from the era cites that Vespasian rebuilt its roads. As far as is known, Thyatira did not have a temple to an emperor in the first century, but it was a city of the Imperial Cult, and worship of Caesar Augustus was practiced before 2 B.C.

> [18] To the angel of the church in Thyatira write: These are the words of the Son of God, whose eyes are like blazing fire and whose feet are like burnished bronze.

> [19] I know your deeds, your love and faith, your service and perseverance, and that you are now doing more than you did at first.

> [20] Nevertheless, I have this against you: You tolerate that woman Jezebel, who calls herself a prophetess. By her teaching she misleads my servants into sexual immorality and the eating of food sacrificed to idols.

> [21] I have given her time to repent of her immorality, but she is unwilling.

[22] So I will cast her on a bed of suffering, and I will make those who commit adultery with her suffer intensely, unless they repent of her ways.

[23] I will strike her children dead. Then all the churches will know that I am he who searches hearts and minds, and I will repay each of you according to your deeds.

In fact, the 'Jezebel prophecy' above foresees the following event from Domitian's life that Suetonius recorded:

> "and the incest of Vestal Virgins, condoned even by his father and his brother, he punished severely in divers ways, at first by capital punishment, and afterwards in the ancient fashion. For while he allowed the sisters Oculata and also Varronilla free choice of the manner of their death, and banished their paramours, he later ordered that Cornelia, a chief-vestal who had been acquitted once but after a long interval again arraigned and found guilty, be buried alive; and her lovers were beaten to death with rods" (Suetonius, Domitian 8)

In both descriptions, not only is a "prophetess" given a period to repent and then "laid on a bed of misery" and killed, but her lovers are murdered as well. These two episodes are certainly among a very few in literature with a depiction of both the murder of a prophetess and her lovers. No such fate was reported for the Jezebel of the Old Testament, whose husband and sons lived on and ruled for years after her death.

This was the first parallel that I noticed between Revelation and Suetonius' history of Domitian, to begin the process by which I was eventually able to understand Revelation. As shown below, just as Titus had used the historian Flavius Josephus to write a history that showed his divinity, Domitian also used his historian Suetonius to do the same thing. Though the literary relationship between Revelation and Suetonius' history of Domitian is different than the typology between Jesus and Titus, like the Gospels and *Wars of the Jews* they were created as a single and interactive work of literature.

The next passage describes a 'deep secret' of Satan. This 'deep secret' will be revealed below in the section describing the 'mystery' of Rome. Humorously, though the speaker states that he will impose no 'other' burden, he neglects to mention that he intends to maintain the burden already imposed.

> [24] Now I say to the rest of you in Thyatira, to you who do not hold to her teaching and have not learned Satan's so-called deep secrets (I will not impose any other burden on you):
>
> [25] Only hold on to what you have until I come.

The next passage looks forward to the work's conclusion where the 'morning star' is given to those who do the will of God. The 'morning star' is a reference to Venus, who was hailed as the divine ancestor of Julius Caesar and the Julio-Claudian dynasty, and (by extension) a representation of Caesar's ascent to the heavens by means of a comet. As shown below, Domitian usurped the symbol as well, as his 'star' appeared in the heavens in the morning. It is also important to recognize that the phrase plays off of Psalm 2:9 that describes the power given to kings who do not break the 'bonds' of the 'anointed'. I will show the meaning of the phrase from Psalm 2 in the analysis of the 'morning star' at the conclusion of Revelation. The passage also mirrors Titus's claim in the Gospels to have received power from the "Father".

> [26] To him who overcomes and does my will to the end, I will give authority over the nations—
>
> [27] 'He will rule them with an iron scepter; he will dash them to pieces like pottery' — just as I have received authority from my Father.
>
> [28] I will also give him the morning star.
>
> [29] He who has an ear, let him hear what the Spirit says to the churches.

In the letter to the Church of Sardis is the first of the numerous statements in Revelation indicating that those that surrounded the 'Lord God' had to be dressed in white. These depictions are linked to Suetonius' recording that Domitian required that all his servants be dressed in white. White clothing is an ancient symbol of purity in many religious traditions including Judaism. However,

Suetonius claimed that Domitian would not allow anyone else to have their servants so dressed, and that he quoted Homer's line: 'Too many rulers are a dangerous thing', as his reason for the rule (Suetonius, *Domitian*, 12). Thus, as with his having 'seven churches in Asia' and having laid a 'prophetess on a bed of misery', the god in Revelation again shares a parallel with Domitian.

REVELATION 3: TO THE CHURCH IN SARDIS

Sardis was another high-ranking city of the Imperial Cult. They were judged second among eleven Asian cities competing to build a temple to the emperor Tiberius in A.D. 26, although the honor was ultimately awarded to Smyrna (Tacitus, *Annals* 4.55-56).

[1] To the angel of the church in Sardis write: These are the words of him who holds the seven spirits of God and the seven stars. I know your deeds; you have a reputation of being alive, but you are dead.

[2] Wake up! Strengthen what remains and is about to die, for I have not found your deeds complete in the sight of my God.

[3] Remember, therefore, what you have received and heard; obey it, and repent. But if you do not wake up, I will come like a thief, and you will not know at what time I will come to you.

[4] Yet you have a few people in Sardis who have not soiled their clothes. They will walk with me, dressed in white, for they are worthy.

[5] He who overcomes will, like them, be dressed in white. I will never blot out his name from the book of life, but will acknowledge his name before my Father and his angels.

[6] He who has an ear, let him hear what the Spirit says to the churches.

TO THE CHURCH IN PHILADELPHIA

Philadelphia also enjoyed a longstanding relationship with the Imperial Cult. A cult devoted to Caesar Augustus was established here in 27-26 B.C. It was also a special city to the Flavians, as it had renamed itself *Philadelphia Flavia* during the reign of Vespasian (A.D. 69-79).

> [7]To the angel of the church in Philadelphia write: These are the words of him who is holy and true, who holds the key of David. What he opens no one can shut, and what he shuts no one can open.
>
> [8] I know your deeds. See, I have placed before you an open door that no one can shut. I know that you have little strength, yet you have kept my word and have not denied my name.

The following passage states the real purpose of Revelation, which was to create a document that would replace Titus' Christ cult with that of Domitian's. In other words, the 'synagogue of Satan that claims to be Jews though they are not' — obviously indicating Titus's 'Christianity' as well as any remaining rebellious (non-Romanized) Jews — will be forced to "*fall down at your feet* (the Titus cult members will fall down at the feet of the new Christ) *and acknowledge that I have loved you*". The sentence means that Domitian will acknowledge that he loved those that worshipped him rather than his brother.

> [9] I will make those who are of the synagogue of Satan, who claim to be Jews though they are not, but are liars—I will make them come and fall down at your feet and acknowledge that I have loved you.

The next lines repeat the theme mentioned above of the 'test' of the "whole earth" that will occur when someone discovers the "new name" of the Christ. It is likely that the passage is addressed to the one who learns the true name of the Christ by opening the seven seals. If so, I would like to refuse Domitian's offer of becoming a pillar in his temple.

> [10] Since you have kept my command to endure patiently, I will also keep you from the hour of trial that is going to come upon the whole world to test those who live on the earth.
>
> [11] I am coming soon. Hold on to what you have, so that no one will take your crown.

[12] Him who overcomes I will make a pillar in the temple of my God. Never again will he leave it. I will write on him the name of my God and the name of the city of my God, the new Jerusalem, which is coming down out of heaven from my God; and I will also write on him my new name.

[13] He who has an ear, let him hear what the Spirit says to the churches.

TO THE CHURCH IN LAODICEA

The relationship between the Imperial Cult and the city of Laodicea was longstanding. As Craig Koester tells us:

In A.D. 23 Laodicea competed with other Asian cities for the honor of building a provincial temple to the emperor Tiberius. Although the temple was built at Smyrna, Laodicea remained supportive of imperial claims. A statue dedicated to Titus in A.D. 79 identifies him as "son of god," since he was the son of the deified emperor Vespasian. Some of the gladiatorial competitions held at Laodicea were sponsored by the high priest of the imperial cult in Asia. An inscription from the second century A.D. refers to Zeus and the Augustan gods (i.e., the deified emperors).[97]

In his address to the church in Laodicea, the individual who speaks as god talks of having a father who also was a god with a throne. While these images may seem trivial, Domitian was, of course, among the very few that could actually claim these attributes.

[14] To the angel of the church in Laodicea write: These are the words of the Amen, the faithful and true witness, the ruler of God's creation.

[15] I know your deeds, that you are neither cold nor hot. I wish you were either one or the other!

---

[97] Craig Koester, 'Laodicea: Imperial Cult'
<http://www2.luthersem.edu/ckoester/Revelation/Laodicea/Imperial%20cult. htm> [accessed 16 March 2014].

[16] So, because you are lukewarm—neither hot nor cold—I am about to spit you out of my mouth.

[17] You say, 'I am rich; I have acquired wealth and do not need a thing.' But you do not realize that you are wretched, pitiful, poor, blind and naked.

[18] I counsel you to buy from me gold refined in the fire, so you can become rich; and white clothes to wear, so you can cover your shameful nakedness; and salve to put on your eyes, so you can see. [19] Those whom I love I rebuke and discipline. So be earnest, and repent.

[20] Here I am! I stand at the door and knock. If anyone hears my voice and opens the door, I will come in and eat with him, and he with me.

[21] To him who overcomes, I will give the right to sit with me on my throne, just as I overcame and sat down with my Father on his throne.

[22] He who has an ear, let him hear what the Spirit says to the churches.

REVELATION 4

The following section focuses upon John's vision of a throne room. What John describes is a true vision of the real throne room of the 'lord god' Domitian. As described above, much of the imagery in Revelation can be interpreted as a mockery describing the hallucinations of 'John' the Jewish leader who was depicted as the Apostle John in the Gospels. 'John' was used by Domitian simply because he was the character whose survival was predicted in John 21, and thus it was logical for him to describe the 'heaven' of the new Christ.

In Revelation the character 'John' sees real objects and events in Domitian's court, but since he understands that Domitian is God he sees these things as metaphysical events occurring in heaven. A number of details help to create the mocking symbolism.

First, notice below that the throne of God below is "encircled with a rainbow". This 'rainbow' represents the many colored chariots that 'encircled' Domitian's court. Suetonius gives a description of the colorful chariots at Domitian's court. "He added two factions of drivers in the Circus, with gold and purple as their colors, to the four former ones." (Suetonius, Domitian, 7) We are left to imagine the colors used by the various other teams. Suetonius recorded that a "hundred races a day" took place (Suetonius, Domitian, 4), thus encircling Domitian with a perpetual 'rainbow'.

The 'sea of glass' John sees is the artificial lake Domitian had built next to the Flavian temple for games. (Suetonius, Domitian, 7)

Moreover, God is referred to as the 'Lord God'. Suetonius recorded that 'Lord God' was Domitian's official title: "'Lord God' became his regular title both in writing and conversation." (Suetonius, Domitian, 13)

Revelation is building a pattern to enable readers who understand the Jesus/Titus typology to recognize that another individual is being 'typed' as the Christ. In other words, that 'John' is actually envisioning Suetonius' description of the 'lord god' Domitian's court. While some of the parallels are vague, the deliberate linkage between the 'lord god' of Revelation and the 'lord god' Domitian can be confirmed by comparing the totality of their shared attributes.

THE THRONE IN HEAVEN

[1] After this I looked, and there before me was a door standing open in heaven. And the voice I had first heard speaking to me like a trumpet said, "Come up here, and I will show you what must take place after this."

[2] At once I was in the Spirit, and there before me was a throne in heaven with someone sitting on it.

[3] And the one who sat there had the appearance of jasper and carnelian. A rainbow, resembling an emerald, encircled the throne. Surrounding the throne were twenty-four other thrones,

and seated on them were twenty-four elders. They were dressed in white and had crowns of gold on their heads.

[5] From the throne came flashes of lightning, rumblings and peals of thunder. Before the throne, seven lamps were blazing. These are the seven spirits of God.

[6] Also before the throne there was what looked like a sea of glass, clear as crystal…

As noted above, the crowned individuals John sees that surround the 'Lord God' of Revelation are simply the gaudily dressed Priests who administered to Domitian and wore crowns.

He presided at the competitions in half-boots clad in a purple toga in the Greek fashion, and wearing upon his head a golden crown with figures of Jupiter, Juno, and Minerva, while by his side sat the priest of Jupiter and the college of the Flaviales, similarly dressed, except that their crowns bore his image as well. (Suetonius, Domitian, 4)

The college of the Flaviales Suetonius mentioned was the 'Sodales Titiales' (Titus's priests), which had around twenty-four members. The Sodales of Augustus, appointed in 14 CE by the Senate for the cult of the deified Augustus, had at first 21 members and later 28. This was the college depicted as the "twenty four elders" above in Revelation.

The 'four living creatures' with multiple eyes and wings that form the inner circle around the god who sits on the throne, symbolically (and comically) represent the flies that were Domitian's closest 'companions'. As Suetonius wrote: "At the beginning of his reign he used to spend hours in seclusion every day, doing nothing but catch flies and stab them with a keenly-sharpened stylus. Consequently, when someone once asked whether anyone was in there with Caesar, Vibius Crispus made the witty reply: 'Not even a fly.'" (Suetonius, Domitian, 3) The parallel verses in Revelation follow:

…In the center, around the throne, were four living creatures, and they were covered with eyes, in front and in back.

[7] The first living creature was like a lion, the second was like an ox, the third had a face like a man, the fourth was like a flying eagle.

[8] Each of the four living creatures had six wings and was covered with eyes all around, even under his wings. Day and night they never stop saying: "Holy, holy, holy is the Lord God Almighty, who was, and is, and is to come."

[9] Whenever the living creatures give glory, honor and thanks to him who sits on the throne and who lives for ever and ever,

[10] the twenty-four elders fall down before him who sits on the throne, and worship him who lives for ever and ever. They lay their crowns before the throne and say:

[11] "You are worthy, our Lord and God, to receive glory and honor and power, for you created all things, and by your will they were created and have their being."

The next passage is a description of God holding a scroll that for some reason — like the "unknown name" above — cannot be revealed to the reader. Perhaps the two-sided scroll was to indicate Revelation and the Pauline material written on one side and Suetonius's history of Domitian on the other. Domitian is described as the "Root of David" because the Flavians had seized this metaphor for themselves in the Gospels with their 'pruning' theme that 'grafted' them onto the Jews' Messianic linage. Domitian is able to 'open' the scroll — to understand the meaning of the seven seals — of course, because he had created it. In other words, he knows how to open the seals and reveal the meaning of the 'two sided' scroll. The passage also describes the central problem of Revelation — how can the reader open (that is, understand) the scroll and the seven seals?

REVELATION 5: THE SCROLL AND THE LAMB

[1] Then I saw in the right hand of him who sat on the throne a scroll with writing on both sides and sealed with seven seals.

[2] And I saw a mighty angel proclaiming in a loud voice, "Who is worthy to break the seals and open the scroll?"

³ But no one in heaven or on earth or under the earth could open the scroll or even look inside it.

⁴ I wept and wept because no one was found who was worthy to open the scroll or look inside.

⁵ Then one of the elders said to me, "Do not weep! See, the Lion of the tribe of Judah, the Root of David, has triumphed. He is able to open the scroll and its seven seals."

John is able to 'see' the Lamb at this point because the Lamb 'comes' from the scroll. He is, of course, Jesus, the literary character described in the Gospels. Domitian approves of the 'Lamb' because Jesus made the Jews serve 'God' — the Flavian Caesar. The notion that the Lamb is the one who opens the seven seals simply reflects the fact that one must first understand the typological nature of Jesus Christ to 'open' the seven seals. Moreover notice that within Christian symbolism the "slain lamb" can only be Jesus and therefore the statement to him: *"You have made them to be a kingdom and priests to serve our God"*, is a blasphemous confession of how the Flavian emperors have manipulated the Christians.

⁶ Then I saw a Lamb, looking as if it had been slain, standing in the center of the throne, encircled by the four living creatures and the elders. He had seven horns and seven eyes, which are the seven spirits of God sent out into all the earth.

⁷ He came and took the scroll from the right hand of him who sat on the throne.

⁸ And when he had taken it, the four living creatures and the twenty-four elders fell down before the Lamb. Each one had a harp and they were holding golden bowls full of incense, which are the prayers of the saints.

⁹ And they sang a new song: "You are worthy to take the scroll and to open its seals, because you were slain, and with your blood you purchased men for God from every tribe and language and people and nation.

¹⁰ You have made them to be a kingdom and priests to serve our God, and they will reign on the earth."

[11] Then I looked and heard the voice of many angels, numbering thousands upon thousands, and ten thousand times ten thousand. They encircled the throne and the living creatures and the elders.

[12] In a loud voice they sang: "Worthy is the Lamb, who was slain, to receive power and wealth and wisdom and strength and honor and glory and praise!"

[13] Then I heard every creature in heaven and on earth and under the earth and on the sea, and all that is in them, singing: "To him who sits on the throne and to the Lamb be praise and honor and glory and power, for ever and ever!"

[14] The four living creatures said, "Amen," and the elders fell down and worshiped.

REVELATION 6: THE SEVEN SEALS

The 'first rider' below is akin to Domitian, who both Suetonius and Josephus recorded rode a white horse (Suetonius, Domitian, 2), and was also skilled as a bowman (Suetonius, Domitian, 19), and, of course, wore a crown. I am not going to open the 'seven seals' at this point, as that analysis will be presented below. Meanwhile, it is only necessary to know that Revelation's 'seven seals' are opened by reading them intertextually with the seven seals hidden in Paul's letters and that the message they give is, predictably enough, that Domitian is the 'Lord God', and also that he has a secret name — Archippus.

[1] I watched as the Lamb opened the first of the seven seals. Then I heard one of the four living creatures say in a voice like thunder, "Come!"

[2] I looked, and there before me was a white horse! Its rider held a bow, and he was given a crown, and he rode out as a conqueror bent on conquest.

[3] When the Lamb opened the second seal, I heard the second living creature say, "Come!"

[4] Then another horse came out, a fiery red one. Its rider was given power to take peace from the earth and to make men slay each other. To him was given a large sword.

The next passage is among the most important in Revelation as it provides a definitive connection to Domitian. To understand the connection one must bear in mind that 'John' is looking into the throne room of a god when he has his vision. The following parallel makes the identity of the god whose throne room John is looking into completely transparent.

> [5] When the Lamb opened the third seal, I heard the third living creature say, "Come!" I looked, and there before me was a black horse! Its rider was holding a pair of scales in his hand.
>
> [6] Then I heard what sounded like a voice among the four living creatures, saying, "A quart of wheat for a day's wages, and three quarts of barley for a day's wages, and do not damage the oil and the wine!"

The above passage from Revelation symbolically represents the following event from Suetonius in which he recorded that Domitian increased the production of grain and decreased the production of wine. In the same paragraph the historian also noted that Domitian had increased the pay of soldiers from 9 to 12 gold coins a year.

> Once upon the occasion of a plentiful wine crop, attended with a scarcity of grain, he made an edict forbidding anyone to plant more vines in Italy and ordering that the vineyards in the provinces be cut down.... He increased the pay of the soldiers one fourth, by the addition of three gold pieces each year. (Suetonius, Domitian, 7)

Thus, the point of the above passage from Revelation is that Domitian's soldiers could now buy four portions of grain instead of three with their new wages, but as there would be less wine they needed to 'mind' it. The martial imagery of the passage in Revelation also helps make the connection to Domitian's army become more visible.

> [7] When the Lamb opened the fourth seal, I heard the voice of the fourth living creature say, "Come!"
>
> [8] I looked, and there before me was a pale horse! Its rider was named Death, and Hades was following close behind him. They

were given power over a fourth of the earth to kill by sword, famine and plague, and by the wild beasts of the earth.

Those who 'had been slain' in the passage below (opening the fifth seal) are the souls of the Jews killed in the war with the Romans. As Domitian is now — according to the author of Revelation — their God, they ask him to "avenge our blood". While this notion seems bizarre, it is actually logical: by linking his typology to Titus's, Domitian has become the individual that the Jewish scripture foresaw as the Messiah, and by this method become the god of those Jews killed in the Flavian campaign through Judea. Domitian tells them to be patient. These 'souls' will reappear later and have their 'vengeance'.

Thus, it appears that each of the 'four horsemen' represents an aspect of Domitian. This begins the unfolding of Revelation's storyline, in which the rider on the white horse in Revelation 6:1 below who is addressed as God, will battle and defeat the 'beast' in Revelation 19:20, thereby 'avenging' the 'souls' mentioned below and at Revelation 20:4. Once the rider on the white horse is identified as Domitian and the '666 beast' is identified as Titus, the plot of Revelation begins to become clear. With Revelation, Domitian has extended the storyline of Titus's campaign so as to make Titus the '666 beast', and to make himself emerge as the 'Jesus' at the conclusion.

In Revelation, Titus's successes in Judea are denigrated, not lauded as in the Gospels. Thus, the Jews whom Titus killed (as mentioned below) were not destroyed because they were 'wicked', as they are characterized in the Gospels and by Josephus, but slain because "of the word of God and the testimony they had maintained". Domitian has, thus, washed his hands of the violence Titus had wrought upon the Jews simply because they worshiped their god and not Caesar. In this way Domitian — very much tongue in cheek — sought to present himself to posterity as blameless of the crime, and even foresaw that the Jews might ultimately be avenged.

There is a black side to the tongue in cheek comedy, however. Domitian mentions that even more Jews will be killed. It is certainly possible that the Jewish rebellion was active during Domitian's reign, even though this was not recorded in the extant history. It is hard to believe that the Jewish rebels were completely quelled by the Roman victory in the Jewish War. If this is the case, this ongoing holocaust would represent the Jews 'predicted' to be killed in Revelation.

Moreover, note that the vision that John experienced when he looked into the throne room of the 'lord god' was not of the future, but of the past. What he experienced was a vision of the history of the deified Caesars and their Imperial Cult that led to Christianity. This will become crystal clear in the analysis of the 'five angels' below. The fact that John's vision was of the past makes a number of the heretofore difficult to understand aspects of Revelation virtually self-evident. For example, when seen from this perspective, the description of the beast gathering his armies at 'Armageddon' is obviously a depiction of Titus gathering his legions at Megiddo — Hebrew for Armageddon — before he assaulted Jerusalem.

> [9] When he opened the fifth seal, I saw under the altar the souls of those who had been slain because of the word of God and the testimony they had maintained.
>
> [10] They called out in a loud voice, "How long, Sovereign Lord, holy and true, until you judge the inhabitants of the earth and avenge our blood?"
>
> [11] Then each of them was given a white robe, and they were told to wait a little longer, until the number of their fellow servants and brothers who were to be killed as they had been was completed.
>
> [12] I watched as he opened the sixth seal. There was a great earthquake. The sun turned black like sackcloth made of goat hair, the whole moon turned blood red,
>
> [13] and the stars in the sky fell to earth, as late figs drop from a fig tree when shaken by a strong wind.
>
> [14] The sky receded like a scroll, rolling up, and every mountain and island was removed from its place.

[15] Then the kings of the earth, the princes, the generals, the rich, the mighty, and every slave and every free man hid in caves and among the rocks of the mountains.

[16] They called to the mountains and the rocks, "Fall on us and hide us from the face of him who sits on the throne and from the wrath of the Lamb! [17] For the great day of their wrath has come, and who can stand?"

REVELATION 7: 144,000 SEALED

The following passage describes the opening of the seventh seal. As shown below, this reveals the true name of the Christ, and also envisions the end of Christianity. The critical information necessary to understand the passage is that 'four angels' are the four deified Caesars before Titus.

Titus enters with the seal of the 'living god'. At the point in history the story is describing, the living god was the Flavian Caesar Vespasian, who gave Titus his authority in Judea. Titus 'sealed' the Jews by killing them. These dead Jews will await their vengeance.

[1] After this I saw four angels standing at the four corners of the earth, holding back the four winds of the earth to prevent any wind from blowing on the land or on the sea or on any tree.

[2] Then I saw another angel coming up from the east, having the seal of the living God. He called out in a loud voice to the four angels who had been given power to harm the land and the sea:

[3] "Do not harm the land or the sea or the trees until we put a seal on the foreheads of the servants of our God."

[4] Then I heard the number of those who were sealed: 144,000 from all the tribes of Israel.

[5] From the tribe of Judah 12,000 were sealed, from the tribe of Reuben 12,000, from the tribe of Gad 12,000,

[6] from the tribe of Asher 12,000, from the tribe of Naphtali 12,000, from the tribe of Manasseh 12,000,

[7] from the tribe of Simeon 12,000, from the tribe of Levi 12,000, from the tribe of Issachar 12,000,

[8] from the tribe of Zebulun 12,000, from the tribe of Joseph 12,000, from the tribe of Benjamin 12,000.

Once again, the followers are described as wearing white as this was the color of Domitian's servants, which is therefore given throughout Revelation as the color worn by believers in the 'Lord God'.

THE GREAT MULTITUDE IN WHITE ROBES

[9] After this I looked and there before me was a great multitude that no one could count, from every nation, tribe, people and language, standing before the throne and in front of the Lamb. They were wearing white robes and were holding palm branches in their hands.

[10] And they cried out in a loud voice: "Salvation belongs to our God, who sits on the throne, and to the Lamb."

[11] All the angels were standing around the throne and around the elders and the four living creatures. They fell down on their faces before the throne and worshiped God,

[12] saying: "Amen! Praise and glory and wisdom and thanks and honor and power and strength be to our God for ever and ever. Amen!"

[13] Then one of the elders asked me, "These in white robes—who are they, and where did they come from?"

[14] I answered, "Sir, you know." And he said, "These are they who have come out of the great tribulation; they have washed their robes and made them white in the blood of the Lamb.

[15] Therefore, "they are before the throne of God and serve him day and night in his temple; and he who sits on the throne will spread his tent over them.

[16] Never again will they hunger; never again will they thirst. The sun will not beat upon them, nor any scorching heat.

[17] For the Lamb at the center of the throne will be their shepherd; he will lead them to springs of living water. And God will wipe away every tear from their eyes."

REVELATION 8

The insight that clarifies the symbolism in Revelation most clearly is that the first five angels who blow trumpets below are representations of the Caesars that Suetonius recorded as having been deified. To recognize the identity of the five 'angels' it is necessary to know that the Senate had not made all of the Caesars before Domitian's reign gods. Suetonius recorded that the only Caesars to whom the title 'divus' was bestowed were Julius, Augustus, Claudius, Vespasian and Titus. The first five 'angels' given below are described in the order of the reigns of the divine Caesars they represent, and each possesses a defining characteristic of that particular 'divus'. Though, as readers can judge for themselves, the symbolism is transparent, it has been overlooked heretofore by scholars.

The first' angel' is Julius Caesar, who had his most famous battle campaigns "on the earth". The second is Augustus, who had his most famous victory over Marc Anthony on the sea, and destroyed Alexandria, a seaside port. The third angel is Claudius, who was poisoned, which is why the name of his star is "wormwood", well known as a poison. (The author of the Shakespearean literature understood Revelation's typological level as evidenced by her character Hamlet muttering 'wormwood' over and over again in Claudius's presence.) The fourth angel who "*blew his trumpet, and a third of the sun was struck, and a third of the moon*" represents Vespasian, who had the pairing of solar and lunar eclipses occur during his consulship. Notice how the author has used the fact that the eclipses occurred during Vespasian's 'third' consulship to create the absurd 'miraculous' typological connection to Revelation wherein a 'third' of the planets were darkened.

For the eclipse of both sun and moon within 15 days of each other has occurred even in our time, in the year of the third consulship of the Vespasian. — (Pliny the Elder, *Natural History*, II. X. 57)

The fifth angel is Titus who led the 'grasshoppers' against Jerusalem. Titus was only to kill those who did not have the 'seal of God on their foreheads' — in other words the Jews who would not worship Caesar.

Following this logic, the sixth angel can only be Domitian — the 'living god' of Revelation's present time. A number of Roman legions were stationed near the Euphrates, so the statement: "release the four angels who are bound at the great river Euphrates, so the four angels were released, who had been held ready for the hour" seems to refer to Domitian's use of the legions in his only significant military campaign, the one against the Sarmatians.

The seventh angel is the character from the Gospels — 'Jesus', who was 'owned' by the six Caesars of the Imperial Cult.

The list of 'angels' makes the relationship between Revelation and the Commune Asiae clear. Not only did that organization hold these individuals as 'divine', but it had headquarters in each of the seven cities that Revelation addresses. An interesting conjecture is that Revelation was read to the hoi polloi (who would not have understood it) and cognoscenti (who would have) upon the opening of Domitian's official Temple at Ephesus.

Knowing that the list of 'angels' is depicting the deified Caesars makes it possible to begin to unwind the complex identifications of the various characters that are mentioned in Revelation. Like the Gospels, Revelation is a puzzle whose solution produces the identities of the characters depicted in it as 'angels', beasts', 'the lamb', 'the morning star' etc.

Notice below that, once again, instead of simply telling the reader what the thunder said, there is only silence. The interpretive framework presented here explains this systematic hiding of information. Also of note is the temple setting of the passage, an appropriate setting for the 'angels' of the Imperial Cult.

The passage begins a symbolic description of the history that led to the Flavians' creation of Christianity. The long preamble to the opening of the seventh seal is simply a vanity moment for Domitian. With it he is stating that all of the history of the Imperial Cult led to the moment when the world would learn that he was the final Christ.

[1] When the Lamb opened the seventh seal, there was silence in heaven for about half an hour.

[2] Then I saw the seven angels who stand before God, and seven trumpets were given to them.

[3] And another angel came and stood at the altar with a golden censer; and he was given much incense to mingle with the prayers of all the saints upon the golden altar before the throne;

[4] and the smoke of the incense rose with the prayers of the saints from the hand of the angel before God.

[5] Then the angel took the censer and filled it with fire from the altar and threw it on the earth; and there were peals of thunder, voices, flashes of lightning, and an earthquake.

[6] Now the seven angels who had the seven trumpets made ready to blow them.

[7] The first angel blew his trumpet, and there followed hail and fire, mixed with blood, which fell on the earth; and a third of the earth was burnt up, and a third of the trees were burnt up, and all green grass was burnt up.

[8] The second angel blew his trumpet, and something like a great mountain, burning with fire, was thrown into the sea;

[9] and a third of the sea became blood, a third of the living creatures in the sea died, and a third of the ships were destroyed.

[10] The third angel blew his trumpet, and a great star fell from heaven, blazing like a torch, and it fell on a third of the rivers and on the fountains of water.

[11] The name of the star is Wormwood. A third of the waters became wormwood, and many men died of the water, because it was made bitter.

¹² The fourth angel blew his trumpet, and a third of the sun was struck, and a third of the moon, and a third of the stars, so that a third of their light was darkened; a third of the day was kept from shining, and likewise a third of the night.

¹³ Then I looked, and I heard an eagle crying with a loud voice, as it flew in midheaven, "Woe, woe, woe to those who dwell on the earth, at the blasts of the other trumpets which the three angels are about to blow!"

REVELATION 9

The fifth 'angel' — Titus — is given the key to the "bottomless pit", the place from where a 'beast' will be unleashed.

¹ And the fifth angel blew his trumpet, and I saw a star fallen from heaven to earth, and he was given the key of the shaft of the bottomless pit;

² he opened the shaft of the bottomless pit, and from the shaft rose smoke like the smoke of a great furnace, and the sun and the air were darkened with the smoke from the shaft.

³ Then from the smoke came locusts on the earth, and they were given power like the power of scorpions of the earth;

⁴ they were told not to harm the grass of the earth or any green growth or any tree, but only those of mankind who have not the seal of God upon their foreheads;

The five-month period of the torture in the next line obviously represents the five months of Titus's siege of Jerusalem.

⁵ they were allowed to torture them for five months, but not to kill them, and their torture was like the torture of a scorpion, when it stings a man.

⁶ And in those days men will seek death and will not find it; they will long to die, and death will fly from them.

⁷ In appearance the locusts were like horses arrayed for battle; on their heads were what looked like crowns of gold; their faces were like human faces,

[8] their hair like women's hair, and their teeth like lions' teeth;

[9] they had scales like iron breastplates, and the noise of their wings was like the noise of many chariots with horses rushing into battle.

[10] They have tails like scorpions, and stings, and their power of hurting men for five months lies in their tails.

[11] They have as king over them the angel of the bottomless pit; his name in Hebrew is Abad'don, and in Greek he is called Apol'lyon.

The "first woe" — the destruction of the Jews in the war "has passed". "Two woes" are still to come however; the first of the two 'woes' would be Domitian's military victory recorded below. The second will be the trial for the "whole world" that will occur when Revelation is decoded and Domitian is shown to be the Christ.

Titus is followed by his brother Domitian, who "released angels bound at the great river Euphrates" — Roman Legions — in his campaign against the Moesians.

[12] The first woe has passed; behold, two woes are still to come.

[13] Then the sixth angel blew his trumpet, and I heard a voice from the for horns of the golden altar before God,

[14] saying to the sixth angel who had the trumpet, "Release the four angels who are bound at the great river Euphrates."

[15] So the four angels were released, who had been held ready for the hour, the day, the month, and the year, to kill a third of mankind.

[16] The number of the troops of cavalry was twice ten thousand times ten thousand; I heard their number.

[17] And this was how I saw the horses in my vision: the riders wore breastplates the color of fire and of sapphire and of sulphur, and the heads of the horses were like lions' heads, and fire and smoke and sulphur issued from their mouths.

¹⁸ By these three plagues a third of mankind was killed, by the fire and smoke and sulphur issuing from their mouths.

¹⁹ For the power of the horses is in their mouths and in their tails; their tails are like serpents, with heads, and by means of them they wound.

²⁰ The rest of mankind, who were not killed by these plagues, did not repent of the works of their hands nor give up worshiping demons and idols of gold and silver and bronze and stone and wood, which cannot either see or hear or walk;

²¹ nor did they repent of their murders or their sorceries or their immorality or their thefts.

REVELATION 10

Having depicted the six gods of the imperial cult during Domitian's reign, Revelation then moves on to its great 'mystery'; this is the identity of the seventh god. It is important to recognize the transition the author makes when he comes to the 'seventh angel'. To this point he has been describing the achievements of the deified Caesars but here he changes his direction and describes something that he does not reveal. John is told to not write what he has been told but to "Seal up what the seven thunders have said, and do not write it down."

As shown below, John's secret is simply the new name of the final Christ. In other words, the "great mystery" of Revelation is simply to reveal which of the Caesars was not only a god of the imperial cult, but was also the final 'Christ' of Christianity. While the 'secret name' of the 'Jesus' at the end of the Gospels was Titus Flavius — with Revelation, Domitian created a new ending and a new secret name of Jesus.

¹ Then I saw another mighty angel coming down from heaven, wrapped in a cloud, with a rainbow over his head, and his face was like the sun, and his legs like pillars of fire.

² He had a little scroll open in his hand. And he set his right foot on the sea, and his left foot on the land,

³ and called out with a loud voice, like a lion roaring; when he called out, the seven thunders sounded.

⁴ And when the seven thunders had sounded, I was about to write, but I heard a voice from heaven saying, "Seal up what the seven thunders have said, and do not write it down."

⁵ And the angel whom I saw standing on sea and land lifted up his right hand to heaven

⁶ and swore by him who lives for ever and ever, who created heaven and what is in it, the earth and what is in it, and the sea and what is in it, that there should be no more delay,

⁷ but that in the days of the trumpet call to be sounded by the seventh angel, the mystery of God, as he announced to his servants the prophets, should be fulfilled.

⁸ Then the voice which I had heard from heaven spoke to me again, saying, "Go, take the scroll which is open in the hand of the angel who is standing on the sea and on the land."

The seventh 'angel' tells John to eat the little scroll and that it will taste like "honey in his mouth" but will turn sour thereafter. This may refer to the black comedy of Paul's letter to Philemon shown below.

⁹ So I went to the angel and told him to give me the little scroll; and he said to me, "Take it and eat; it will be bitter to your stomach, but sweet as honey in your mouth."

¹⁰ And I took the little scroll from the hand of the angel and ate it; it was sweet as honey in my mouth, but when I had eaten it my stomach was made bitter.

¹¹ And I was told, "You must again prophesy about many peoples and nations and tongues and kings."

REVELATION 11

The two witnesses who "stand before" — in other words came before the "living god" — Domitian — and tormented those who lived on earth were Vespasian and Titus. They were 'olive trees' because they had seized the messianic 'branch' from the Jews with the Gospels and then 'grafted' themselves onto it.

¹ Then I was given a measuring rod like a staff, and I was told: "Rise and measure the temple of God and the altar and those who worship there,

² but do not measure the court outside the temple; leave that out, for it is given over to the nations, and they will trample over the holy city for forty-two months.

³ And I will grant my two witnesses power to prophesy for one thousand two hundred and sixty days, clothed in sackcloth."

⁴ These are the two olive trees and the two lampstands which stand before the Lord of the earth.

⁵ And if any one would harm them, fire pours out from their mouth and consumes their foes; if any one would harm them, thus he is doomed to be killed.

⁶ They have power to shut the sky, that no rain may fall during the days of their prophesying, and they have power over the waters to turn them into blood, and to smite the earth with every plague, as often as they desire.

The following lines are a witty description of the legacy Domitian sought. When the 'testimony' of the "two olive trees" is finished — when the Gospels and Revelation are decoded — the 'beast' – will 'attack' Vespasian and Titus. In other words, Revelation is anticipating that when the Gospels and Revelation are decoded and revealed, the status of Vespasian and Titus as 'god the father' and 'Jesus Christ' will be usurped by that of the 'Morning Star'.

⁷ And when they have finished their testimony, the beast that ascends from the bottomless pit will make war upon them and conquer them and kill them,

⁸ and their dead bodies will lie in the street of the great city which is allegorically called Sodom and Egypt, where their Lord was crucified.

[9] For three days and a half men from the peoples and tribes and tongues and nations gaze at their dead bodies and refuse to let them be placed in a tomb,

[10] and those who dwell on the earth will rejoice over them and make merry and exchange presents, because these two prophets had been a torment to those who dwell on the earth.

[11] But after the three and a half days a breath of life from God entered them, and they stood up on their feet, and great fear fell on those who saw them.

In spite of the damage done to their reputation when posterity learns that they invented Christianity, Domitian maintains that the two 'prophets' will be admitted to heaven. This was to be expected because the 'heaven' was where the 'stars' of the gods of the Imperial Cult were placed, and Titus and Vespasian had already been deified. In trying to understand Revelation's imagery, it must be remembered that though it is designed to build up Domitian, the literature also reflects the general mindset of the imperial cult and promotes the immortal legacy of all of it members.

[12] Then they heard a loud voice from heaven saying to them, "Come up hither!" And in the sight of their foes they went up to heaven in a cloud.

[13] And at that hour there was a great earthquake, and a tenth of the city fell; seven thousand people were killed in the earthquake, and the rest were terrified and gave glory to the God of heaven.

[14] he second woe has passed; behold, the third woe is soon to come.

[15] Then the seventh angel blew his trumpet, and there were loud voices in heaven, saying, "The kingdom of the world has become the kingdom of our Lord and of his Christ, and he shall reign for ever and ever."

[16] And the twenty-four elders who sit on their thrones before God fell on their faces and worshiped God,

[17] saying, "We give thanks to thee, Lord God Almighty, who art and who wast, that thou hast taken thy great power and begun to reign.

[18] The nations raged, but thy wrath came, and the time for the dead to be judged, for rewarding thy servants, the prophets and saints, and those who fear thy name, both small and great, and for destroying the destroyers of the earth."

On the Arch of Titus there is a relief that some believe depicts the Ark of the Covenant being brought to Rome. If this was, in fact, the case, then it is no surprise to have the Ark mentioned below as being in Domitian's throne room. Though there is no concrete evidence, it is interesting to speculate on the historicity of the passage, though it could certainly be simply symbolically representing the Flavians' capturing the Jews' religion.

[19] Then God's temple in heaven was opened, and the ark of his covenant was seen within his temple; and there were flashes of lightning, voices, peals of thunder, an earthquake, and heavy hail.

REVELATION 12

Revelation now begins a symbolic description of the Flavians' seizing of the messianic branch — the title of the Christ — from the Jews. First, Nero, the 'dragon', fights with a woman representing Judaism, and is hurled out of 'heaven' — which depicts the messianic Jews throwing Nero's image out of their Temple and beginning the war. Nero then attempts to destroy the woman's children — the messianic lineage; after which Nero then hands his authority over to Vespasian.

[1] And a great portent appeared in heaven, a woman clothed with the sun, with the moon under her feet, and on her head a crown of twelve stars;

[2] she was with child and she cried out in her pangs of birth, in anguish for delivery.

[3] And another portent appeared in heaven; behold, a great red dragon, with seven heads and ten horns, and seven diadems upon his heads.

[4] His tail swept down a third of the stars of heaven, and cast them to the earth. And the dragon stood before the woman who was about to bear a child, that he might devour her child when she brought it forth;

[5] she brought forth a male child, one who is to rule all the nations with a rod of iron, but her child was caught up to God and to his throne,

[6] and the woman fled into the wilderness, where she has a place prepared by God, in which to be nourished for one thousand two hundred and sixty days.

[7] Now war arose in heaven, Michael and his angels fighting against the dragon; and the dragon and his angels fought,

[8] but they were defeated and there was no longer any place for them in heaven.

[9] And the great dragon was thrown down, that ancient serpent, who is called the Devil and Satan, the deceiver of the whole world—he was thrown down to the earth, and his angels were thrown down with him.

[10] And I heard a loud voice in heaven, saying, "Now the salvation and the power and the kingdom of our God and the authority of his Christ have come, for the accuser of our brethren has been thrown down, who accuses them day and night before our God.

[11] And they have conquered him by the blood of the Lamb and by the word of their testimony, for they loved not their lives even unto death.

[12] Rejoice then, O heaven and you that dwell therein! But woe to you, O earth and sea, for the devil has come down to you in great wrath, because he knows that his time is short!"

[13] And when the dragon saw that he had been thrown down to the earth, he pursued the woman who had borne the male child.

[14] But the woman was given the two wings of the great eagle that she might fly from the serpent into the wilderness, to the place where she is to be nourished for a time, and times, and half a time.

¹⁵ The serpent poured water like a river out of his mouth after the woman, to sweep her away with the flood.

¹⁶ But the earth came to the help of the woman, and the earth opened its mouth and swallowed the river which the dragon had poured from his mouth.

¹⁷ Then the dragon was angry with the woman, and went off to make war on the rest of her offspring, on those who keep the commandments of God and bear testimony to Jesus. And he stood on the sand of the sea.

REVELATION 13

Vespasian is the first of the Caesars to be called a beast, and this starts a lineage of 'Caesar beasts' whose identity can be ascertained. The 'mortal wound' the beast experiences is the wound Vespasian received during the Galilean campaign.

¹ And I saw a beast rising out of the sea, with ten horns and seven heads, with ten diadems upon its horns and a blasphemous name upon its heads.

² And the beast that I saw was like a leopard, its feet were like a bear's, and its mouth was like a lion's mouth. And to it the dragon gave his power and his throne and great authority.

³ One of its heads seemed to have a mortal wound, but its mortal wound was healed, and the whole earth followed the beast with wonder.

The next passage describes Nero as a 'dragon' that insisted upon being worshiped as a god and had given his "authority" to Vespasian.

⁴ Men worshiped the dragon, for he had given his authority to the beast, and they worshiped the beast, saying, "Who is like the beast, and who can fight against it?"

As the war lasted seven years, the beast from the sea –Vespasian — had authority for 42 months, or one half the time or 'week' of the seven year war. Vespasian returned to Rome before the siege of Jerusalem in 70 CE, and the war did not conclude until the destruction of Masada in 73 CE.

> ⁵ And the beast was given a mouth uttering haughty and blasphemous words, and it was allowed to exercise authority for forty-two months;
>
> ⁶ it opened its mouth to utter blasphemies against God, blaspheming his name and his dwelling, that is, those who dwell in heaven.
>
> ⁷ Also it was allowed to make war on the saints and to conquer them. And authority was given it over every tribe and people and tongue and nation,
>
> ⁸ and all who dwell on earth will worship it, every one whose name has not been written before the foundation of the world in the book of life of the Lamb that was slain.
>
> ⁹ If any one has an ear, let him hear:
>
> ¹⁰ If any one is to be taken captive, to captivity he goes; if any one slays with the sword, with the sword must he be slain. Here is a call for the endurance and faith of the saints.

The beast from the earth is Titus, who marched into Judea to force the Jews to worship Caesar. When Vespasian left Judea, he gave Titus "all the authority of the first beast". As noted above, Suetonius recorded that Domitian had slighted Titus's memory in "edicts", in other words Domitian had referred to him as the 'two horned beast' in Revelation. Suetonius also recorded that Domitian had Titus deified, and this makes the identity of Titus as a 'beast' in Revelation almost automatic, in that so few can be seen as having been 'slighted in edicts' and also made a god. The passage again makes note of Vespasian's wound that he received on the Judean battlefield.

> ¹¹ Then I saw another beast which rose out of the earth; it had two horns like a lamb and it spoke like a dragon.
>
> ¹² It exercises all the authority of the first beast in its presence, and makes the earth and its inhabitants worship the first beast, whose mortal wound was healed.

[13] It works great signs, even making fire come down from heaven to earth in the sight of men;

[14] and by the signs which it is allowed to work in the presence of the beast, it deceives those who dwell on earth, bidding them make an image for the beast which was wounded by the sword and yet lived;

The well-known '666' — the number of the beast — is simply a clever way of identifying Titus.

[15] and it was allowed to give breath to the image of the beast so that the image of the beast should even speak, and to cause those who would not worship the image of the beast to be slain.

[16] Also it causes all, both small and great, both rich and poor, both free and slave, to be marked on the right hand or the forehead,

[17] so that no one can buy or sell unless he has the mark, that is, the name of the beast or the number of its name. [18] This calls for wisdom: let him who has understanding reckon the number of the beast, for it is a human number; its number is six hundred and sixty-six

Notice above that one must possess 'wisdom' to understand how '666' is the number of the beast. This wisdom is the knowledge of a complex intertextual puzzle, which I did not include in *Caesar's Messiah*. The puzzle involves 'counting', and identifies Titus as the Jesus who interacts with the disciples in John 21. This puzzle must be solved first to create the wisdom necessary to understand the phrase: *"that no one can buy or sell unless he has the mark, that is, the name of the beast."*

The puzzle begins in Matthew 17, where Jesus is asked to pay the temple tax. Jesus then asks Peter if "kings of the earth" take tribute from their children, or from strangers, implying that the 'children of God' do not need to pay tax to their 'father'. He then instructs Peter to nevertheless 'cast a hook' and take a gold coin out of the 'fish' he will catch, and use it to pay the tax.

As "fish" represent men in the Gospels, it is not hard to see that Matthew 17 links to the passage in Josephus's *Wars of the Jews*

(5, 13, 548-561) describing Jews who hid gold coins in their bellies and then were slit open after they were captured trying to escape Jerusalem. Thus, Matt. 17 is actually (like the rest of the Gospels) a prophetic satire concerning an event from the Flavian campaign.

The concept of 'fishing for men' creates a typological link between Matt. 17 and John 21 (the conclusion of the Gospels), while the concept of the 'Temple Tax' links these passages to Josephus' description of Masada (the conclusion of the war). Titus states that the Temple Tax must now be paid to him by Jews, "where so ever they were" (Josephus, *Jewish Wars* 7, 6, 218) and then goes on immediately to attack Masada. At Masada, 960 rebels try to hold off the Romans. All are killed except seven, who, as is shown in *Caesar's Messiah*, are the replacement for the Maccabean dynasty. The seven represent Titus's 'children'.

So the question is this: How did the Jews at Masada pay the 960 units of tax demanded by Titus?

The answer is by the 153 fish in John 21. The seven "Christians' who survived do not need to pay the tax because, as Jesus said, the 'children of the King' do not need to pay the tax. As these seven now worship Titus they are his 'children'. The paragraph stating that Titus demanded the tax is the same one in which Josephus noted that Titus did not found any city in Judea but he did "assign a place" for 800 of his soldiers noted above, so those 800 'children' did not need to pay any tax either, and the Jews thereby only owe him 153 units of tax (960 minus 800 minus 7). This is then covered by the catching of the 153 'fish' — that is 153 Jews with coins in their bellies — in John 21. "Titus gave order that all Judea should be exposed to sale as he reserved the country for himself. He assigned a place for 800 men only who he had dismissed from his army." (*Wars of the Jews* 7, 6, 216-218).

Thus, the oblique puzzle shows that Titus took control over all those who would 'buy or sell' and only those with his 'mark' — the insignia of the Roman soldier — were given ownership. Revelation links to the puzzle by stating that the beast will not let anyone 'buy or sell' without the 'mark of the Beast'.

I would also note that the passage by Josephus is significant in that by "reserving the country for himself", Titus transferred ownership of Israel from the Jews to the Romans. This transfer of the ownership of Judea on Passover 73 CE was the completion of the forty years cycle begun by the sacrifice of the Passover Lamb of the New Covenant — Jesus — on Passover 33 CE.

Further, the actual 'mark' of the beast was likely the 'X' of the tenth Legion that was stationed on the Mount of Olives during the war. The 'T' shaped cross is a later Christian symbol, while to the Flavians the 'X' was the shape of a crucifix. This image is clearer in the Greek as the first letter for Christ (*Chi*) is 'X'-shaped, as in the Chi Rho Cross or St. Andrews cross. For example, see the crosses on Titus Flavius Clement's vestments shown above.

While this analysis explains what Revelation meant by "the mark of the beast", the explanation of the triangle number '666' is much simpler. Titus's name in Greek — 'Teitan' — equals '666' when its letters are added up, using the system common in that era of identifying particular Greek letters with specific numbers.

Irenaeus was perhaps the first church historian to try and determine the "number of the beast", and, perhaps without knowing it, got it right. He wrote:

> Teitan too, the first syllable being written with the two Greek vowels ε and ι, among all the names which are found among us, is rather worthy of credit. For it has in itself the predicted number, and is composed of six letters, each syllable containing three letters; and [the word itself] is ancient, and removed from ordinary use; for among our kings we find none bearing this name Titan, nor have any of the idols which are worshipped in public among the Greeks and barbarians this appellation. Among many persons, too, this name is accounted divine, so that even the sun is termed "Titan" by those who do now possess [the rule]. This word, too, contains a certain outward appearance of vengeance, and of one inflicting merited punishment because he (the Antichrist) pretends that he vindicates the oppressed. And besides this, it is an ancient name, one worthy of credit, of royal dignity, and still further, a name belonging to a tyrant. Inasmuch, then, as this name "Titan" has so much to recommend it, there is a strong degree of probability, that from among the many names

suggested, we infer, that perchance he who is to come shall be called "Titan." (Irenaeus, *Against Heresies* 5,30,3)

T	E	I	T	A	N	TOTAL
300	5	10	300	1	50	666

Because he seems to have not understood the typology of Revelation, Irenaeus thought that the beast named 'Teitan' was coming, when in fact he had already come. Many Christians have shared in his confusion. This analysis also explains the how term 'antichrist' is used in Revelation. 'Anti' or "Αντί" in Greek, can mean "the opposite of" but can also mean "in place of". Titus was the 'antichrist' — stood in the place of — the next 'Christ' Domitian.

REVELATION 14

The author now repeats the image of the 144,000 who were 'pure' and 'offered as first fruits'. Within the sequence of events Revelation is depicting, these are certainly to be understood as the Jews that Titus, the 'beast', killed.

[1] Then I looked, and lo, on Mount Zion stood the Lamb, and with him a hundred and forty-four thousand who had his name and his Father's name written on their foreheads.

[2] And I heard a voice from heaven like the sound of many waters and like the sound of loud thunder; the voice I heard was like the sound of harpers playing on their harps,

Below a "new song" is sung to Domitian the new Christ.

[3] and they sing a new song before the throne and before the four living creatures and before the elders. No one could learn that song except the hundred and forty-four thousand who had been redeemed from the earth.

⁴ It is these who have not defiled themselves with women, for they are chaste; it is these who follow the Lamb wherever he goes; these have been redeemed from mankind as first fruits for God and the Lamb,

⁵ and in their mouth no lie was found, for they are spotless.

⁶ Then I saw another angel flying in midheaven, with an eternal gospel to proclaim to those who dwell on earth, to every nation and tribe and tongue and people;

⁷ and he said with a loud voice, "Fear God and give him glory, for the hour of his judgment has come; and worship him who made heaven and earth, the sea and the fountains of water."

⁸ Another angel, a second, followed, saying, "Fallen, fallen is Babylon the great, she who made all nations drink the wine of her impure passion."

During the war, Titus killed thousands of Jews. In the first part of Revelation's next chapter, Domitian absolves himself of any blame in their deaths. That infamy he leaves to his brother, who he refers to as the 'Destroyer'. The chapter then moves on to a discussion of three angels. The 'wrath of God' that the third angel brings is directed towards those who have the 'mark of the beast'. This seems to indicate that Domitian stamped out the bureaucracy that administers Titus's Jesus cult. This coup was apparently the basis for the traditions of Domitian's persecutions of 'Christians'. The traditions reflect the fact that Domitian exterminated those family members that held that Titus, not Domitian, was 'Jesus'.

Suetonius recorded that Domitian executed his "extremely stupid cousin" Flavius Clemens, who was recorded as the Christian Pope that succeeded Simon in the Acts of Nereus and Achilleus. It is likely that the reason Suetonius recorded Clemens as 'stupid' is that he was killed for resisting Domitian's attempt to replace Titus as the Christ.

⁹ And another angel, a third, followed them, saying with a loud voice, "If any one worships the beast and its image, and receives a mark on his forehead or on his hand,

[10] he also shall drink the wine of God's wrath, poured unmixed into the cup of his anger, and he shall be tormented with fire and sulphur in the presence of the holy angels and in the presence of the Lamb.

[11] And the smoke of their torment goes up for ever and ever; and they have no rest, day or night, these worshipers of the beast and its image, and whoever receives the mark of its name."

The next passage completes the description of Titus's destruction of Jerusalem. The passage is easy to understand in that the Gospels identify Titus as Daniel's envisioned 'son of man' who came on *"a white cloud, and seated on the cloud one like a son of man"*.

[12] Here is a call for the endurance of the saints, those who keep the commandments of God and the faith of Jesus.

[13] And I heard a voice from heaven saying, "Write this: Blessed are the dead who die in the Lord henceforth." "Blessed indeed," says the Spirit, "that they may rest from their labors, for their deeds follow them!"

[14] Then I looked, and lo, a white cloud, and seated on the cloud one like a son of man, with a golden crown on his head, and a sharp sickle in his hand.

[15] And another angel came out of the temple, calling with a loud voice to him who sat upon the cloud, "Put in your sickle, and reap, for the hour to reap has come, for the harvest of the earth is fully ripe."

[16] So he who sat upon the cloud swung his sickle on the earth, and the earth was reaped.

[17] And another angel came out of the temple in heaven, and he too had a sharp sickle.

[18] Then another angel came out from the altar, the angel who has power over fire, and he called with a loud voice to him who had the sharp sickle, "Put in your sickle, and gather the clusters of the vine of the earth, for its grapes are ripe."

The image from the Gospels' 'wine press', or Gethsemane, adds to the clarity of Revelation's picture of the destruction of Jerusalem.

[19] So the angel swung his sickle on the earth and gathered the vintage of the earth, and threw it into the great wine press of the wrath of God;

[20] and the wine press was trodden outside the city, and blood flowed from the wine press, as high as a horse's bridle, for one thousand six hundred stadia.

REVELATION 15

The next chapter returns to Domitian's throne room. One interesting speculation is that John — as with his description of the rainbow above — was actually describing something real in the passage; a pageant put on in Domitian's court honoring the deified Caesars.

[1] Then I saw another portent in heaven, great and wonderful, seven angels with seven plagues, which are the last, for with them the wrath of God is ended.

[2] And I saw what appeared to be a sea of glass mingled with fire, and those who had conquered the beast and its image and the number of its name, standing beside the sea of glass with harps of God in their hands.

[3] And they sing the song of Moses, the servant of God, and the song of the Lamb, saying, "Great and wonderful are thy deeds, O Lord God the Almighty! Just and true are thy ways, O King of the ages!

[4] Who shall not fear and glorify thy name, O Lord? For thou alone art holy. All nations shall come and worship thee, for thy judgments have been revealed."

[5] After this I looked, and the temple of the tent of witness in heaven was opened,

[6] and out of the temple came the seven angels with the seven plagues, robed in pure bright linen, and their breasts girded with golden girdles.

[7] And one of the four living creatures gave the seven angels seven golden bowls full of the wrath of God who lives for ever and ever;

[8] and the temple was filled with smoke from the glory of God and from his power, and no one could enter the temple until the seven plagues of the seven angels were ended.

REVELATION 16

[1] Then I heard a loud voice from the temple telling the seven angels, "Go and pour out on the earth the seven bowls of the wrath of God."

[2] So the first angel went and poured his bowl on the earth, and foul and evil sores came upon the men who bore the mark of the beast and worshiped its image.

[3] The second angel poured his bowl into the sea, and it became like the blood of a dead man, and every living thing died that was in the sea.

[4] The third angel poured his bowl into the rivers and the fountains of water, and they became blood.

[5] And I heard the angel of water say, "Just art thou in these thy judgments, thou who art and wast, O Holy One.

[6] For men have shed the blood of saints and prophets, and thou hast given them blood to drink. It is their due!"

[7] And I heard the altar cry, "Yea, Lord God the Almighty, true and just are thy judgments!"

[8] The fourth angel poured his bowl on the sun, and it was allowed to scorch men with fire;

[9] men were scorched by the fierce heat, and they cursed the name of God who had power over these plagues, and they did not repent and give him glory.

[10] The fifth angel poured his bowl on the throne of the beast, and its kingdom was in darkness; men gnawed their tongues in anguish

[11] and cursed the God of heaven for their pain and sores, and did not repent of their deeds.

[12] The sixth angel poured his bowl on the great river Euphra'tes, and its water was dried up, to prepare the way for the kings from the east.

The three foul spirits who came out of the mouth of the false prophet — Jesus Christ — were the 'trinity' of the three Flavian gods of Christianity.

[13] And I saw, issuing from the mouth of the dragon and from the mouth of the beast and from the mouth of the false prophet, three foul spirits like frogs;

[14] for they are demonic spirits, performing signs, who go abroad to the kings of the whole world, to assemble them for battle on the great day of God the Almighty.

The famous passage below concerning 'Armageddon' simply depicts Titus's gathering of his armies together at Caesarea, from whence he went on to Jerusalem to crush the rebellion of the real messianic movement. Caesarea is directly below Mount Geddon, the word in Hebrew for Armageddon. It is not a prediction of some coming event. In the passage, the angel says "It is done" — echoing Jesus's final words when he was on the cross — to indicate that Titus has replaced the Jews' Messiah with himself. This theme repeats itself later in Revelations when Domitian then adds on to the story so that he and not Titus will be the 'last' Jesus. At that point a second "it is done" will be recorded indicating Domitian's replacement of Titus as the Christ.

The reference to the nakedness of the 'thief' refers to the typology in the Gospels and *Wars of the Jews* where the escape of the naked young man in Mark 15 foresees Titus's 'naked escape' from the Garden of Gethsemane. Titus is again denigrated as being 'naked' and he is also now 'shamefully exposed' as the thief who stole the Jews' religion.

The storyline of Revelation is understandable — it is divided into sections in which Titus's conquest of the Jews and creation of

Christianity is described and then added onto with the arrival of the 'god on the white horse'. Domitian created a literary fantasy in the same manner that his brother did with the Gospels to 'document' a 'history' whereby he, not Titus, became the 'Jesus' who is 'coming'.

[15] ("Lo, I am coming like a thief! Blessed is he who is awake, keeping his garments that he may not go naked and be seen exposed!")

[16] And they assembled them at the place which is called in Hebrew Armageddon.

[17] The seventh angel poured his bowl into the air, and a loud voice came out of the temple, from the throne, saying, "It is done!"

[18] And there were flashes of lightning, voices, peals of thunder, and a great earthquake such as had never been since men were on the earth, so great was that earthquake.

[19] The great city was split into three parts, and the cities of the nations fell, and God remembered great Babylon, to make her drain the cup of the fury of his wrath.

[20] And every island fled away, and no mountains were to be found;

[21] and great hailstones, heavy as a hundred-weight, dropped on men from heaven, till men cursed God for the plague of the hail, so fearful was that plague.

REVELATION 17

[1] Then one of the seven angels who had the seven bowls came and said to me, "Come, I will show you the judgment of the great harlot who is seated upon many waters,

[2] with whom the kings of the earth have committed fornication, and with the wine of whose fornication the dwellers on earth have become drunk."

³ And he carried me away in the Spirit into a wilderness, and I saw a woman sitting on a scarlet beast which was full of blasphemous names, and it had seven heads and ten horns.

⁴ The woman was arrayed in purple and scarlet, and bedecked with gold and jewels and pearls, holding in her hand a golden cup full of abominations and the impurities of her fornication;

At this point, the storyline of Revelation goes past what is 'foreseen' in the Gospels or recorded by Josephus, and looks into the future. In effect, the author is speaking directly to those in the future who are able to decode Revelation. The following chapters describe the 'mystery' of Rome and what will befall the city for casting a "magic spell" by which "all nations were led astray." Domitian is envisioning the anger at the Caesars for creating a false religion but is also explaining exactly why they did it — to promote commerce.

The disclosure concerning the 'mystery' links back to the preface where God describes a 'mystery' of Satan who has a synagogue of people claiming to be Jews but are not. The two 'mysteries' are one and the same. Rome's great mystery is Christianity; a religion that — as Revelation playfully 'reveals' — was a 'synagogue' ruled by Romans who were claiming to be Jews but were not. As legacy was a main goal of the literature, Domitian would of course use Revelation to try and frame how posterity would view him.

⁵ and on her forehead was written a name of mystery: "Babylon the great, mother of harlots and of earth's abominations."

⁶ And I saw the woman, drunk with the blood of the saints and the blood of the martyrs of Jesus. When I saw her I marveled greatly.

⁷ But the angel said to me, "Why marvel? I will tell you the mystery of the woman, and of the beast with seven heads and ten horns that carries her.

The following passage describes a beast that was, is not and is to come, and will ascend from a pit. This reveals a puzzle that will be discussed in my next book.

[8] The beast that you saw was, and is not, and is to ascend from the bottomless pit and go to perdition; and the dwellers on earth whose names have not been written in the book of life from the foundation of the world, will marvel to behold the beast, because it was and is not and is to come.

The next passage describes seven Kings; five of whom have fallen — these are the five deified Caesars: Julius, Augustus, Claudius, Vespasian, and Titus. The king that 'is' is Domitian. The 'wisdom' the reader must have is to have already opened the seven seals and to have learned that the seventh seal reveals Domitian's secret name and that ' the master of the four horses' intends to 'return' from the dead.

[9] This calls for a mind with wisdom: the seven heads are seven mountains on which the woman is seated;

[10] they are also seven kings, five of whom have fallen, one is, the other has not yet come, and when he comes he must remain only a little while.

To understand the next line also requires a "mind with wisdom". As in the passage above, the beast is described as "was and is not"; but there is an important difference. Unlike the beast above "that you saw", the beast described below was not "seen" and "belongs" to the seven. This 'beast' is the human Passover Lamb, the character in the Gospels named Jesus Christ, who was not "seen" because he was a fictional character. He belongs to the 'seven' — the Caesars — because he was invented to support the goals of the Imperial Cult. The Gospels' character Jesus Christ will go to perdition once the Gospels are decoded and his fictional nature is revealed.

[11] As for the beast that was and is not, it is an eighth but it belongs to the seven, and it goes to perdition.

The ten kings described in the next passage who have not yet received royal power are simply the future Caesars who will use their great 'mystery' — Christianity — to rule. In other words, the Caesars began using their other name — the Pontiff or Pope of Christianity. If the following passages were written in Domitian's reign and not added by a later Caesar such as Constantine, they represent an extraordinary understanding of the future of Christianity.

> [12] And the ten horns that you saw are ten kings who have not yet received royal power, but they are to receive authority as kings for one hour, together with the beast.

> [13] These are of one mind and give over their power and authority to the beast;

> [14] they will make war on the Lamb, and the Lamb will conquer them, for he is Lord of lords and King of kings, and those with him are called and chosen and faithful."

> [15] And he said to me, "The waters that you saw, where the harlot is seated, are peoples and multitudes and nations and tongues.

> [16] And the ten horns that you saw, they and the beast will hate the harlot; they will make her desolate and naked, and devour her flesh and burn her up with fire,

> [17] for God has put it into their hearts to carry out his purpose by being of one mind and giving over their royal power to the beast, until the words of God shall be fulfilled.

> [18] And the woman that you saw is the great city which has dominion over the kings of the earth."

Though today virtually everyone sees Christianity as a religion, it was actually a system of mind control created by the Caesars to produce ignorant serfs that believed that God had decreed their slavery. From their positions as the 'Pontiff Maximus' — the official title for Caesar's position as head of the pagan college of Roman priests — the Pontiffs of the Roman Catholic Church oversaw the feudal system wherein Christianized serfs gave their work products to the authorities without complaint. Their docility was caused by the fact that they were Christians and therefore believed the Apostle Paul when he wrote: " slaves should be obedient to their masters in everything". (Titus, 2)

The serfs were indeed slaves — the word "serf" can be traced back to the Latin word *servus*, meaning "slave". The group that became serfs did not start out as slaves and were originally called coloni (sing. *colonus*), a Latin word meaning a farmer who farmed his own land. (One interesting etymological point is that the word 'colonized' was first used to depict a coloni changing wild land into farm land.)

Before Constantine the coloni had legal rights, including the ability to sell their land. Around 300 CE the Caesar Diocletian implemented a tax that unified a piece of land with its inhabitants. It thereby became more difficult for coloni to sell their plots.

In 306 CE, upon the death of his father Constantius, Constantine became co-Emperor with his brother-in-law Maxentius. The two were bitter rivals and war soon broke out. Before the battle of the Milvian Bridge in 312 CE, Constantine had his absurd vision in which Christ purportedly instructed him to place a particular sign on the battle standards of his army. This symbol was called the Chi-Rho, which superimposed the first two letters of the Greek word "ΧΡΙΣΤΟΣ" (Christ) in such a way to produce a monogram that invoked the crucifixion of Jesus. The symbol was described by Eusebius as "a long spear, overlaid with gold, which included a bar crossing the spear to form the shape of the Christian cross. On the top of the whole was fixed a wreath of gold and precious stones, and within this the symbol of the Savior's name, two letters indicating the name of Christ by means of the initial letters, the letter X intersection P at the center." Included with the banner were the words: "In hoc signo vinces" (In this sign thou shalt conquer.)

Armed with the 'power of Jesus', Constantine defeated his rival and became sole dictator of the empire. His reign is best remembered for the Edict of Milan in 313, which fully legalized Christianity, and the Council of Nicea, which he chaired in 325, that began the era where Christianity officially and openly began to enjoy the power of the Roman state.

Because of his assistance in making Christianity the state religion, Constantine enjoys a positive historical legacy. What historians have overlooked is that his efforts on behalf of Christianity were just one component of his legal 'reforms', and when one half is juxtaposed to the other an entirely different picture emerges. Constantine used Christianity to make the enslavement of most of the European population acceptable to the victims because it was an act of God!

Constantine's other edicts were the true beginning of medieval serfdom. They officially ended the colonis' ability to sell their land, but bound them to it forever. Another set of edicts forbade the lower classes from changing professions. Constantine thereby froze an unfair society in place. And to prevent any intellectual resistance from the newly created slaves, Constantine also began the process that made Christianity the state religion. Viewed in their true historical context, the specific combination of Constantine's edicts can be seen to serve a sole purpose: to enslave serfs and make their rebellion a sin.

Below is the order of rank that Constantine's edicts created — the Feudal System :

The Pope
The King
Bishops
Nobles
Knights / Vassals
Priests
Freemen
Yeomen
Servants
Serfs

Eventually, the degradation of the coloni's legal status to serf was formalized with the creation of a ceremony known as "bondage". During the ceremony, a serf placed his head in the lord's hands — akin to the ceremony where a vassal placed his hands between those of his overlord. The serf would then swear oaths that bound him to his lord in a feudal contract defining the terms of his slavery.

A 7th century Anglo-Saxon "Oath of Fealty" between a serf and his Lord still exists. It states: "By the Lord before whom this sanctuary is holy, I will be true and faithful, and love all which he loves and shun all which he shuns, according to the laws of God and the order of the world. Nor will I ever with will or action, through word or deed, do anything which is unpleasing to him, on condition that he will hold to me as I shall deserve it, and that he will perform everything as it was in our agreement when I submitted myself to him and chose his will."

For over a thousand years, Christianity was a government enforced system of mind control designed to make rebellion by slaves a sin. Hopefully this information will be useful to help current citizens understand the techniques rulers use to control them.

REVELATION 18

Chapter 18 describes the eventual destruction of Rome, which will suffer because of the 'magic spell' of Christianity it cast to lead "all nations" astray. The author is anticipating the hatred that will be hurled upon Rome if their conspiracy to create Christianity is ever discovered by the hoi polloi. It is difficult to tell whether this is a prophecy, or a warning to the Roman elite. This chapter is interesting in that it depicts a very far-reaching plan for Rome's fictitious Judaism that was beyond the scope of controlling the messianic religion of Judea. The passage also provides the justification for Rome's 'casting the spell' — the advantage to commerce of a pacifistic state religion. In my opinion, the patrician class knew far more about long-range social engineering than it has revealed to history.

[1] After this I saw another angel coming down from heaven, having great authority; and the earth was made bright with his splendor.

[2] And he called out with a mighty voice, "Fallen, fallen is Babylon the great! It has become a dwelling place of demons, a haunt of every foul spirit, a haunt of every foul and hateful bird;

[3] for all nations have drunk the wine of her impure passion, and the kings of the earth have committed fornication with her, and the merchants of the earth have grown rich with the wealth of her wantonness."

[4] Then I heard another voice from heaven saying, "Come out of her, my people, lest you take part in her sins, lest you share in her plagues;

[5] for her sins are heaped high as heaven, and God has remembered her iniquities.

[6] Render to her as she herself has rendered, and repay her double for her deeds; mix a double draught for her in the cup she mixed.

[7] As she glorified herself and played the wanton, so give her a like measure of torment and mourning. Since in her heart she says, 'A queen I sit, I am no widow, mourning I shall never see,'

[8] so shall her plagues come in a single day, pestilence and mourning and famine, and she shall be burned with fire; for mighty is the Lord God who judges her."

[9] And the kings of the earth, who committed fornication and were wanton with her, will weep and wail over her when they see the smoke of her burning;

[10] they will stand far off, in fear of her torment, and say, "Alas! alas! thou great city, thou mighty city, Babylon! In one hour has thy judgment come."

As noted above, the next lines are of interest in that they document the commercial rationale of the Caesars for "casting the spell" of Christianity. I suspect Domitian added them to bolster how he would be seen by posterity.

[11] And the merchants of the earth weep and mourn for her, since no one buys their cargo any more,

[12] cargo of gold, silver, jewels and pearls, fine linen, purple, silk and scarlet, all kinds of scented wood, all articles of ivory, all articles of costly wood, bronze, iron and marble,

[13] cinnamon, spice, incense, myrrh, frankincense, wine, oil, fine flour and wheat, cattle and sheep, horses and chariots, and slaves, that is, human souls.

[14] "The fruit for which thy soul longed has gone from thee, and all thy dainties and thy splendor are lost to thee, never to be found again!"

[15] The merchants of these wares, who gained wealth from her, will stand far off, in fear of her torment, weeping and mourning aloud,

[16] "Alas, alas, for the great city that was clothed in fine linen, in purple and scarlet, bedecked with gold, with jewels, and with pearls!

[17] In one hour all this wealth has been laid waste." And all shipmasters and seafaring men, sailors and all whose trade is on the sea, stood far off

[18] and cried out as they saw the smoke of her burning, "What city was like the great city?"

[19] And they threw dust on their heads, as they wept and mourned, crying out, "Alas, alas, for the great city where all who had ships at sea grew rich by her wealth! In one hour she has been laid waste.

[20] Rejoice over her, O heaven, O saints and apostles and prophets, for God has given judgment for you against her!"

[21] Then a mighty angel took up a stone like a great millstone and threw it into the sea, saying, "So shall Babylon the great city be thrown down with violence, and shall be found no more;

[22] and the sound of harpers and minstrels, of flute players and trumpeters, shall be heard in thee no more; and a craftsman of any craft shall be found in thee no more; and the sound of the millstone shall be heard in thee no more;

[23] and the light of a lamp shall shine in thee no more; and the voice of bridegroom and bride shall be heard in thee no more; for thy merchants were the great men of the earth, and all nations were deceived by thy sorcery.

[24] And in her was found the blood of prophets and of saints, and of all who have been slain on earth."

REVELATION 19

By having provided the rationale for the great prostitute — Rome — casting of the 'magic spell' of Christianity to deceive nations, Domitian the Lord God has exonerated himself for the crime and can now go on to depict the legacy he wishes posterity to receive him with.

[1] After this I heard what seemed to be the loud voice of a great multitude in heaven, crying, "Hallelujah! Salvation and glory and power belong to our God,

[2] for his judgments are true and just; he has judged the great harlot who corrupted the earth with her fornication, and he has avenged on her the blood of his servants."

[3] Once more they cried, "Hallelujah! The smoke from her goes up for ever and ever."

[4] And the twenty-four elders and the four living creatures fell down and worshiped God who is seated on the throne, saying, "Amen. Hallelujah!"

[5] And from the throne came a voice crying, "Praise our God, all you his servants, you who fear him, small and great."

[6] Then I heard what seemed to be the voice of a great multitude, like the sound of many waters and like the sound of mighty thunder peals, crying, "Hallelujah! For the Lord our God the Almighty reigns.

[7] Let us rejoice and exult and give him the glory, for the marriage of the Lamb has come, and his Bride has made herself ready;

[8] it was granted her to be clothed with fine linen, bright and pure"—for the fine linen is the righteous deeds of the saints.

[9] And the angel said to me, "Write this: Blessed are those who are invited to the marriage supper of the Lamb." And he said to me, "These are true words of God."

[10] Then I fell down at his feet to worship him, but he said to me, "You must not do that! I am a fellow servant with you and your brethren who hold the testimony of Jesus. Worship God." For the testimony of Jesus is the spirit of prophecy.

[11] Then I saw heaven opened, and behold, a white horse! He who sat upon it is called Faithful and True, and in righteousness he judges and makes war.

[12] His eyes are like a flame of fire, and on his head are many diadems; and he has a name inscribed which no one knows but himself.

[13] He is clad in a robe dipped in blood, and the name by which he is called is The Word of God.

[14] And the armies of heaven, arrayed in fine linen, white and pure, followed him on white horses.

[15] From his mouth issues a sharp sword with which to smite the nations, and he will rule them with a rod of iron; he will tread the wine press of the fury of the wrath of God the Almighty.

[16] On his robe and on his thigh he has a name inscribed, King of kings and Lord of lords.

[17] Then I saw an angel standing in the sun, and with a loud voice he called to all the birds that fly in midheaven, "Come, gather for the great supper of God,

[18] to eat the flesh of kings, the flesh of captains, the flesh of mighty men, the flesh of horses and their riders, and the flesh of all men, both free and slave, both small and great."

The following passage links back to 16:16 above where the Kings were 'gathered together' by the beast. All of the plot points that have been established earlier in the storyline are being resolved. Within Revelation's fantasy Titus will be punished for destroying Jerusalem and 'casting the spell' by his brother. Domitian — on his usual white horse — captures the beast and hurls him and his false prophet (the Gospels' Jesus) into a burning lake.

[19] And I saw the beast and the kings of the earth with their armies gathered to make war against him who sits upon the horse and against his army.

[20] And the beast was captured, and with it the false prophet who in its presence had worked the signs by which he deceived those who had received the mark of the beast and those who worshiped its image. These two were thrown alive into the lake of fire that burns with sulphur.

[21] And the rest were slain by the sword of him who sits upon the horse, the sword that issues from his mouth; and all the birds were gorged with their flesh.

REVELATION 20

[1] Then I saw an angel coming down from heaven, holding in his hand the key of the bottomless pit and a great chain.

[2] And he seized the dragon, that ancient serpent, who is the Devil and Satan, and bound him for a thousand years,

Notice that the devil will be loosed for a "short time". Domitian is slyly stating that he will be seen by posterity as both Christ and Satan. This will become clear at the end of Revelation.

[3] and threw him into the pit, and shut it and sealed it over him, that he should deceive the nations no more, till the thousand years were ended. After that he must be loosed for a little while.

Domitian now 'avenges the blood' of the souls Titus killed at Jerusalem. Domitian has in effect washed his hands of their blood — the crime belongs to Titus.

[4] Then I saw thrones, and seated on them were those to whom judgment was committed. Also I saw the souls of those who had been beheaded for their testimony to Jesus and for the word of God, and who had not worshiped the beast or its image and had not received its mark on their foreheads or their hands. They came to life, and reigned with Christ a thousand years.

[5] The rest of the dead did not come to life until the thousand years were ended. This is the first resurrection.

> [6] Blessed and holy is he who shares in the first resurrection! Over such the second death has no power, but they shall be priests of God and of Christ, and they shall reign with him a thousand years.

The author envisions that there will be a 'thousand years' time span before the beast is 'seen' — that is before the Gospels are understood. At this point 'Satan' will be 'loosed', and the identity of the Jesus who is the 'morning star' will also be recognized once the beast is 'seen'.

> [7] And when the thousand years are ended, Satan will be loosed from his prison

> [8] and will come out to deceive the nations which are at the four corners of the earth, that is, Gog and Magog, to gather them for battle; their number is like the sand of the sea.

> [9] And they marched up over the broad earth and surrounded the camp of the saints and the beloved city; but fire came down from heaven and consumed them,

Domitian understands and fears the judgment of history that awaits the Flavians for inventing a false religion.

> [10] and the devil who had deceived them was thrown into the lake of fire and sulphur where the beast and the false prophet were, and they will be tormented day and night for ever and ever.

> [11] Then I saw a great white throne and him who sat upon it; from his presence earth and sky fled away, and no place was found for them.

The next passage also looks to the future and describes the eventual 'opening' or understanding of two distinct works of literature. One of them is described as 'books' — in other words, the Gospels. The other is described as 'the book of life', and is the little scroll described in 10:2 referring to Revelation. With the openings — when they are finally understood — of the two works, \the dead — Titus and Domitian — will be judged and each will receive their posthumous rewards.

¹² And I saw the dead, great and small, standing before the throne, and books were opened. Also another book was opened, which is the book of life. And the dead were judged by what was written in the books, by what they had done.

¹³ And the sea gave up the dead in it, Death and Hades gave up the dead in them, and all were judged by what they had done. ¹⁴ Then Death and Hades were thrown into the lake of fire. This is the second death, the lake of fire;

¹⁵ and if any one's name was not found written in the book of life, he was thrown into the lake of fire.

REVELATION 21

Having rewritten the typology of the Gospels with a conclusion more to his liking, Domitian then describes a sunny future in which Jerusalem is restored, better than ever, and happiness reigns. However, he has also prepared a punch line below to ridicule those that believe in such fantasies. He has left us a clue as to his real self.

¹ Then I saw a new heaven and a new earth; for the first heaven and the first earth had passed away, and the sea was no more.

² And I saw the holy city, new Jerusalem, coming down out of heaven from God, prepared as a bride adorned for her husband;

³ and I heard a loud voice from the throne saying, "Behold, the dwelling of God is with men. He will dwell with them, and they shall be his people, and God himself will be with them;

⁴ he will wipe away every tear from their eyes, and death shall be no more, neither shall there be mourning nor crying nor pain any more, for the former things have passed away."

The next lines describe Domitian's new Christianity. This comes to pass with the second "it is done" statement — the first one described Titus's replacement of the Jewish Christ.

⁵ And he who sat upon the throne said, "Behold, I make all things new." Also he said, "Write this, for these words are trustworthy and true."

⁶ And he said to me, "It is done! I am the Alpha and the Omega, the beginning and the end. To the thirsty I will give from the fountain of the water of life without payment.

⁷ He who conquers shall have this heritage, and I will be his God and he shall be my son.

⁸ But as for the cowardly, the faithless, the polluted, as for murderers, fornicators, sorcerers, idolaters, and all liars, their lot shall be in the lake that burns with fire and sulphur, which is the second death."

⁹ Then came one of the seven angels who had the seven bowls full of the seven last plagues, and spoke to me, saying, "Come, I will show you the Bride, the wife of the Lamb."

The following lines are interesting in that they may be linked to the claim by Suetonius that Domitian had learned of his pending murder through an astrologer who told him that "there will be blood on the moon as she enters Aquarius." Suetonius said that the astrologer was able to predict the exact hour of Domitian's murder: the fifth hour, or around 9:30 in the morning.

In the passage in Revelation below, a 'star' appears in the heavens — the New Jerusalem. It is described as "*jasper, clear as crystal*", which can be a description of a rose colored moonstone. A plausible conjecture is that the twelve gemstones represent the twelve signs of the zodiac, and that the entrance of the "moonstone" — the New Jerusalem — somehow corresponded to the astrological event of the moon entering Aquarius; though this is not demonstrable, as the exact astrological methodology of the Romans is no longer known.

¹⁰ And in the Spirit he carried me away to a great, high mountain, and showed me the holy city Jerusalem coming down out of heaven from God,

¹¹ having the glory of God, its radiance like a most rare jewel, like a jasper, clear as crystal.

[12] It had a great, high wall, with twelve gates, and at the gates twelve angels, and on the gates the names of the twelve tribes of the sons of Israel were inscribed;

[13] on the east three gates, on the north three gates, on the south three gates, and on the west three gates.

[14] And the wall of the city had twelve foundations, and on them the twelve names of the twelve apostles of the Lamb.

[15] And he who talked to me had a measuring rod of gold to measure the city and its gates and walls.

[16] The city lies foursquare, its length the same as its breadth; and he measured the city with his rod, twelve thousand stadia; its length and breadth and height are equal.

[17] He also measured its wall, a hundred and forty-four cubits by a man's measure, that is, an angel's.

[18] The wall was built of jasper, while the city was pure gold, clear as glass.

[19] The foundations of the wall of the city were adorned with every jewel; the first was jasper, the second sapphire, the third agate, the fourth emerald,

[20] the fifth onyx, the sixth carnelian, the seventh chrysolite, the eighth beryl, the ninth topaz, the tenth chrysoprase, the eleventh jacinth, the twelfth amethyst.

[21] And the twelve gates were twelve pearls, each of the gates made of a single pearl, and the street of the city was pure gold, transparent as glass.

[22] And I saw no temple in the city, for its temple is the Lord God the Almighty and the Lamb.

[23] And the city has no need of sun or moon to shine upon it, for the glory of God is its light, and its lamp is the Lamb.

[24] By its light shall the nations walk; and the kings of the earth shall bring their glory into it,

[25] and its gates shall never be shut by day—and there shall be no night there;

[26] they shall bring into it the glory and the honor of the nations.

[27] But nothing unclean shall enter it, nor any one who practices abomination or falsehood, but only those who are written in the Lamb's book of life.

REVELATION 22

Revelation 22 opens with a peculiar image of a river that flowed through "the middle of the street of the city" that came from the throne of God.

[1] Then he showed me the river of the water of life, bright as crystal, flowing from the throne of God and of the Lamb

[2] through the middle of the street of the city; also, on either side of the river, the tree of life with its twelve kinds of fruit, yielding its fruit each month; and the leaves of the tree were for the healing of the nations.

[3] There shall no more be anything accursed, but the throne of God and of the Lamb shall be in it, and his servants shall worship him;

[4] they shall see his face, and his name shall be on their foreheads.

[5] And night shall be no more; they need no light of lamp or sun, for the Lord God will be their light, and they shall reign for ever and ever.

[6] And he said to me, "These words are trustworthy and true. And the Lord, the God of the spirits of the prophets, has sent his angel to show his servants what must soon take place.

[7] And behold, I am coming soon." Blessed is he who keeps the words of the prophecy of this book.

[8] I John am he who heard and saw these things. And when I heard and saw them, I fell down to worship at the feet of the angel who showed them to me;

[9] but he said to me, "You must not do that! I am a fellow servant with you and your brethren the prophets, and with those who keep the words of this book. Worship God."

[10] And he said to me, "Do not seal up the words of the prophecy of this book, for the time is near.

[11] Let the evildoer still do evil, and the filthy still be filthy, and the righteous still do right, and the holy still be holy."

[12] "Behold, I am coming soon, bringing my recompense, to repay every one for what he has done.

[13] I am the Alpha and the Omega, the first and the last, the beginning and the end."

[14] Blessed are those who wash their robes, that they may have the right to the tree of life and that they may enter the city by the gates.

[15] Outside are the dogs and sorcerers and fornicators and murderers and idolaters, and every one who loves and practices falsehood.

The next passage concludes the 'prophecy' given in 2:27 above, where the 'god' Domitian described himself as the 'morning star' which will be given to him that "does my will to the end". The expression 'morning star' stems from the Old Testament description of a pagan Babylonian king who challenged the god of the Israelites. It is easy to see that this passage from Isaiah was the basis for much of the imagery in Revelation and the Pauline material:

[12] "How you are fallen from heaven, O morning star, son of the dawn! [How] you are cut down to the ground, You who weakened the nations!

[13] For you have said in your heart: 'I will ascend into heaven, I will exalt my throne above the stars of God; I will also sit on the mount of the congregation On the farthest sides of the north;

[14] I will ascend above the heights of the clouds, I will be like the Most High.'

[15] Yet you shall be brought down to Sheol, To the lowest depths of the Pit.

[16] "Those who see you will gaze at you, [And] consider you, [saying:] '[Is] this the man who made the earth tremble, Who shook kingdoms,

[17] Who made the world as a wilderness And destroyed its cities, [Who] did not open the house of his prisoners?'

[18] "All the kings of the nations, All of them, sleep in glory, Everyone in his own house;

[19] But you are cast out of your grave Like an abominable branch, [Like] the garment of those who are slain, Thrust through with a sword, Who go down to the stones of the pit, Like a corpse trodden underfoot.

[20] You will not be joined with them in burial, Because you have destroyed your land [And] slain your people. The brood of evildoers shall never be named.

[21] Prepare slaughter for his children Because of the iniquity of their fathers, Lest they rise up and possess the land, And fill the face of the world with cities."

[22] "For I will rise up against them," says the LORD of hosts, "And cut off from Babylon the name and remnant, And offspring and posterity..." (Isaiah 14:12-22)

As a result of his egotistical self-deification, the pagan monarch eventually would experience both the collapse of his kingdom and the loss of his life—an ignominious end that is described in vivid terms. "Sheol (hell) from beneath is moved for thee to meet thee at thy coming," the prophet proclaimed to the king. And when the ruler finally descends into the underworld, captives of that hidden realm will taunt him by saying, "Is this the man that made the earth to tremble, that did shake kingdoms?"

It was in this context that Isaiah referred to the king of Babylon as "the morning star" who ended up in the hidden realm. This provides the basis for linking the word 'Lucifer' — a word that means 'morning star' — with 'Satan'. Domitian understood this connotation, and by describing himself as the 'morning star' he has cast himself both as a god and Satan: a wry comment perhaps intended for the cognoscenti of posterity who would see the humor in Domitian's dual characterizations.

> [16] "I Jesus have sent my angel to you with this testimony for the churches. I am the root and the offspring of David, the bright morning star."

The next line refers back to the river of Christianity described above. Christians are encouraged to take the water "without price", but I believe that the Greek implies a double entendre meaning 'in vain' or 'for naught', once again revealing the author's sarcastic intentions.

> [17] The Spirit and the Bride say, "Come." And let him who hears say, "Come." And let him who is thirsty come, let him who desires take the water of life without price.

The next lines are also significant in that they express the rule of the Caesars concerning their literature. Not a word was to be changed by anyone who did not understand the typology. While they themselves added words to those of Caesars that had come before them, they did not permit anyone else to change the words as that could damage their delicate typological meaning.

> [18] I warn every one who hears the words of the prophecy of this book: if any one adds to them, God will add to him the plagues described in this book,

> [19] and if any one takes away from the words of the book of this prophecy, God will take away his share in the tree of life and in the holy city, which are described in this book.

The final lines of Revelation are a prophecy of the "coming" of the Lord. Though these lines have been a focus of Christians hoping for the second coming of Jesus, they will be disappointed when they learn the true identity of this 'divine' individual.

> [20] He who testifies to these things says, "Surely I am coming soon." Amen. Come, Lord Jesus!

[21] The grace of the Lord Jesus be with the saints. Amen. "

As noted above, those that try to become immortal gods can suffer swift reversals. This, of course, is the fate that met Domitian. Though he had planned to be buried as a god, Domitian was murdered in a palace coup, and his body was taken by his nurse, 'Phyllis', and cremated or buried (Suetonius, Domitian, 17; Dio, LXVII, 18). This is a witticism on 'Phyllis', the character in Greek mythology who gave a casket containing the sacrament of Rhea, the mother of the Olympian gods, to her husband Demophon when he went off to the Trojan war. She told him to open it only when he has given up hope of returning to her. That is, she was telling him that the goddess Rhea would protect him from death. But Demophon decided to open the casket out of curiosity. He was horrified by what he saw, and he rode off terrified and caused his horse to stumble, and he fell on his own sword and died. Dio and Suetonius were joking that 'Phyllis' once again failed to get Rhea to create immortality.

Following his assassination the Roman Senate took the rare action of "damnation memoriae" upon Domitian. Damnatio memoriae was a formal "condemnation of memory" that was intended to erase a person from history, and was usually reserved for traitors to the empire. All images and inscriptions of Domitian were to be destroyed or defaced.

THE SEVEN SEALS AND THE PAULINE LETTERS

Only after a reader understands that Suetonius's history of Domitian was typologically linked to Revelation does it become possible to understand the typology in Paul's letters. There is a three way typological linkage between the seven seals of Revelation, the seven seals hidden in Paul's letters, and Suetonius's history of Domitian. This is far more complicated than the basic typologies used in the Gospels and Revelation. While many of the connections are obvious, the author's most subtle points require a form of literary analysis that depends upon a reader seeing a concept that is only visible when comparing three passages to each other.

Josephus recorded that the Flavians captured the Jews' Scripture and kept it inside their palace. Studying it — no doubt helped by captive rebels — they would have decoded the style of Hebraic writing that requires the reader to discover its deepest meaning by comparing related texts to one another. This style evidently impressed them, as they used it throughout the New Testament. Domitian went beyond the two-book typology Titus developed between the Gospels and Josephus, creating an even more complicated three-book style.

Many scholars have believed that Paul's letters were written before the Gospels, because there are numerous instances where Paul had the opportunity to cite an episode from the life of Jesus, but did not. Therefore, these scholars have concluded that Paul had not read the Gospels, as he certainly would have commented upon them if he had. In accordance with a 'multiple drafts' view of the development of the New Testament, it is certainly possible that some of the Pauline material existed before the Gospels were written; or even that a real historical evangelist wrote some of this material. However, in the following analysis I will show that the Pauline epistles were heavily edited and redacted under Domitian. The extant letters do not focus on the Gospels stories because Domitian wished to transcend that typology, not because he was unaware of it.

Paul's literature describes two Jesuses. He sometimes refers to the Jesus Christ of the Gospels, but more often the 'Christ' Paul describes represents the third member of the trinity: Domitian. In a sense this is not surprising, as the Flavian court historians maintained that the Jews' messianic prophecies foresaw all three Flavian Caesars; thus any of them could claim the title of Christ. The book of Acts depicts Saul — who will shortly become 'Paul' — attacking and persecuting followers of 'The Way'. But, considering that Acts is also a biased commentary written by the Romans, how can we be sure who these followers of 'The Way' really were? Perhaps they represented the messianic religion of the rebel Sicarii, but it's also possible that the Pauline letters and Acts were signaling an attack on earlier forms of Flavian Christianity, which Domitian intended to replace with his version. This is a critical insight that makes all of the Pauline literature coherent. What Saul/Paul realized with his epiphany, is that the Flavian Caesar was the Christ.

The typology indicates that Paul was a deluded, castrated, sodomite slave. In fact his nickname 'Paul', which means 'tiny', is a joke upon his castration. A shown below, the grim typology in the Pauline material builds upon the theme begun in the Gospels of deluded Jews who cannot tell Caesar from their own god.

While the typology is complex, the first step in understanding it is so simple that it is odd it has not been taken up before. This is the recognition that the Pauline letters, like Revelation, describe seven 'seals'. Paul's letters and Revelation even used the same Greek word for 'seal' — 'sphragis'.

But to see the full typological meaning that the two sets of 'seven seals' create, a reader must link them to seven passages in Suetonius. This is unfortunately complicated, but once one gets into the rhythm of the 'three book typology' between Paul's letters, Revelation and Suetonius' history of Domitian, its meaning is not too difficult to grasp. Bear in mind that though the Caesars wished their typology to be hidden, they also wished to have their posthumous glory. Alert readers in the future were supposed to be able to understand their typology. Moreover, to make the three-way typology a bit more recognizable, the three streams of linked events occur in the same sequence.

To begin, the first seal of Revelation (Rev 6: 2) describes a rider on a white horse that is 'given a crown'. Suetonius links to this by simply describing Domitian as riding a white horse in the passage where he is first called 'Caesar'. (Domitian 2)

Once the reader recognizes the obvious linkages between the 'first seal' of Revelation and Suetonius's history, however, a subtle connection to the passage that contains the 'first seal' of the Pauline letters, Romans 4:11-13, becomes apparent.

> And he {the Christ} received the sign of circumcision, a **seal** of the righteousness of the faith which he had while still uncircumcised, that he might be the father of all those who believe, though they are uncircumcised, that righteousness might be imputed to them also, For the promise that he would **be the heir of the world** was not to Abraham or to his seed through the law, but through the righteousness of faith.

In the sentence that leads to his 'white horse' paragraph, Suetonius noted that Vespasian had made the comment that since Domitian had made so many appointments during the time he was 'Caesar' — the period after Vitellius was deposed but before Vespasian arrived in Rome to claim the throne, during which Domitian was referred to as Caesar by the Flavian troops — that he was surprised that Domitian had **"not named my heir while he was at it"**.

Vespasian's comment concerning his 'heir' begins Suetonius' subtle typological point. The "succession" that Vespasian referred to included not just the title of Caesar but the one given to the Flavians by Suetonius and the other Roman historians of the era; that of the 'Christ'. And, as shown below, that is linked to Paul's comment on the 'Christ' in Romans 4:11.-13.

Though scholars have focused on trying to determine the meaning of Paul's distinction in Romans 4 between 'faith" and 'works', the real point to Paul's argument is that the 'uncircumcised' can also be 'righteous' and that therefore a non-Jew (an uncircumcised Gentile) can become — as Paul specifically claimed — "heir to the world" (Rom 4:13). In other words, Paul is stating that it was not with Abraham's 'seed' — the Jews — that God established his covenant with, but the righteousness of Abraham's 'faith'.

What Paul is actually saying in the passage that contains his first 'seal' is that a Gentile can replace Abraham's 'seed' and establish a 'covenant' with God and become the Christ. Notice that Paul's point mirrors the position of the Imperial Cult and the Roman historians who saw Caesar as being able to replace a Jew as the Christ. Thus the 'heir to the world' that Paul describes is the same one that Vespasian mentioned when he stated that he was surprised that Domitian had not named his heir.

While the above connections of the 'heir' and the 'first seal' in these passages may seem forced, the connection between the 'seven seals' of Revelation and the seven seals of Paul will become easier to understand as we move through them. What I am asking of the reader at this point is to understand the nature of the relationship. Revelation and the Pauline letters each have seven 'seals' that on their surface do not seem related. However, when each set of 'seals' is juxtaposed to a related passage in Suetonius the three passages produce a meaning about Domitian.

For clarification, the following diagram shows how the 'first seal' of Revelation is bridged to the 'first seal' of the Pauline literature by the concepts they share with the same passage in Suetonius:

- Revelation; first seal, rider on white horse given a crown,
- Suetonius; rider on white horse given a crown, gentile heir to a god
- Paul; first seal, gentile heir to a god.

The opening of Revelation's second seal reveals a 'rider on a red horse' who has the power to make men "kill each other". This is a power a Domitian possessed, of course. In fact, all of the 'four horseman' of Revelation represent different powers of Domitian. This will be especially clear when we analyze the third horseman.

Revelation's 'red horseman' that makes men 'kill each other' links to Suetonius' description of Domitian (Domitian 4) making men from his own troop engage in gladiatorial combat and thereby 'kill each other'.

> He constantly gave grand costly entertainments, both in the amphitheater and in the Circus, where in addition to the usual races between two-horse and four-horse chariots, he also exhibited two battles, one between forces of infantry and the other by horsemen; and he even gave a naval battle in the amphitheater. Besides he gave hunts of wild beasts, gladiatorial shows at night by the light of torches, and not only combats between men but between women as well. He was always present too at the games given by the quaestors, which he revived after they had been abandoned for some time, and invariably granted the people the privilege of calling for two pairs of gladiators from his own school, and brought them in last in all the splendor of the court. During the whole of every gladiatorial show there always stood at his feet a small boy clad in scarlet, with an abnormally small head, with whom he used to talk a great deal, and sometimes seriously. At any rate, he was overheard to ask him if he knew why he had decided at the last appointment day to make Mettius Rufus prefect of Egypt. He often gave sea-fights almost with regular fleets, having dug a pool near the Tiber and surrounded it with seats; and he continued to witness the contests amid heavy rains. (Suetonius, *Domitian* 4)

Suetonius' passage also mentions the color red twice (the boy wearing scarlet, and the name 'Rufus' which means 'red-head'.) The linkage between Suetonius and Revelation is not difficult to see for anyone aware of the larger pattern linking the 'Lord God' of Revelation to Domitian. It is simply the color red and the ability to make men kill themselves. The linkage between the second seal of Revelation and the second seal of the Pauline literature, however, is the most oblique connection in the New Testament.

The second seal of Paul is found at Romans 15: 28: "Therefore, when I have performed this and have **sealed** to them this fruit, I shall go by way of you to Spain."

In Romans 15 Paul states that Christ has appointed him to be a 'minister'. Paul's comment below is a typical proclamation of the imperial cult and a number of the words in it were actually 'technical terms' of the cult.

> I did write to you brethren reminding of the grace that was given to me by God to be a minister ("leitourgos" or minister of the state) of Jesus Christ to the nations administering the sacred service of the Gospel of God. (Romans 15: 15-16)

Paul also claimed in the passage that he has preached the 'Gospel' from Jerusalem to Illyricum but, for some reason, not in the area where Christ was first "named", as this would "build upon another man's foundation."

> [19] in mighty signs and wonders, by the power of the Spirit of God, so that from in a circle from Jerusalem to Illyricum I have fully preached the gospel of Christ.

> [20] And so I have made it my aim to preach the gospel, not where Christ was named, lest I should build on another man's foundation,

> [21] but as it is written: "To whom He was not spoken of, they shall see; And those who have not understood shall understand." (Romans 15: 19-21)

Paul does not mention where Christ was 'named', or who the individual was that had "named" the Christ, or the nature of the "foundation" he does not wish to "build upon". Though scholars have not been able to answer these questions heretofore, it is now possible. Their answers lie in the passage in Suetonius that links to Revelation's second seal.

The passages above from Romans 15 about the appointment of a minster were linked to Domitian's bizarre question about the appointment of a minister to the pin head.

> During the whole of every gladiatorial show there always stood at his feet a small boy clad in scarlet, with an abnormally small head, with whom he used to talk a great deal, and sometimes seriously. At any rate, he was overheard to ask him if he knew

why he had decided at the last appointment day to make Mettius
Rufus prefect of Egypt. (Suetonius, *Domitian* 4)

The first step in the tortuous process is to realize that Domitian's
question to a pin head is a mystery. Why would Suetonius record a
Caesar asking such a difficult question to a pin head?

To unravel the mystery of Domitian's obviously fictional question
requires a number of things. First, a reader must have already
understood that Suetonius history creates typological connections
to the New Testament. The reader must also recall some facts that
Suetonius had already given in his work: that the first individual to
name Vespasian as Caesar was Tiberius Alexander, who was the
prefect of Alexandria, and that he did so on July the first, which
afterwards became the official day of celebration — Accession
Day — for the beginning of the Flavian era.

Suetonius wrote: "Tiberius Alexander, prefect of Egypt, was the
first to order his legions to take the oath for Vespasian on the
Kalends (the first) of July, the day which was afterwards
celebrated as that of his accession."

For Suetonius therefore, July the first was the day that the Flavian
Caesar was, to use Paul's words, 'named the Christ' because the
historian claimed that the Messianic prophecies foresaw the
Flavian Caesar.

A reader must also know that when Paul stated that he preached
the Gospel in a 'circle' — "kuklo" between Jerusalem and
Illyricum, that the Roman Legions from Jerusalem to Illyricum
accepted Vespasian as Caesar (Tacitus, *Book II*).

So there is little question how Suetonius — or any other member
of Domitian's imperial cult — would have understood Paul's
meaning in Romans 15:19-20. They would have understood Paul
as preaching Vespasian's "signs and wonders" outside of the area
where Tiberius Alexander proclaimed the Christ:

> [19] in mighty signs and wonders, by the power of the Spirit of God,
> so that in a circle from Jerusalem to Illyricum I have fully
> preached the gospel of Christ.

20 And so I have made it my aim to preach the gospel, not where
Christ was named, lest I should build on another man's
foundation, (Romans 15:19-20)

When reading the Pauline literature it is important to ask how a
member of Domitian's inner circle who knew the Flavians had
created Christianity would have understood it. This perspective
often produces coherency when other interpretive frameworks do
not. For example, Suetonius would have recognized that Paul
preached between Jerusalem and Illyricum because this was the
'circle' where the Legions had proclaimed Vespasian as Caesar
and therefore 'Christ'. He would have also recognized that Paul's
words indicated that he did not go into Alexandria as this was
where Tiberius Alexander had first 'named' the Christ and he did
want to "build upon another man's foundation".

One last piece of information is needed to answer Domitian's
question to the child with the tiny skull; "why he had decided at
the last appointment day to make Mettius Rufus prefect of
Egypt?" This is the fact that the 'appointment day' for Roman
Prefects was July the first; the same day Tiberius Alexander
proclaimed Vespasian as Caesar and god.

So now all of the pieces are in place to facilitate the solving of the
question: In other words, Domitian had named Rufus Prefect of
Egypt on July first because if he could answer that question even a
pin head would "see" and "understand" the identities of the
unnamed individuals in Romans 15: 21.

> But as it is written, To whom he was not spoken of, they shall see:
> and they that have not heard shall understand. (Romans 15: 21)

The individual that Paul stated "was not spoken of but they shall
see" is the unnamed individual who had first "named the 'Christ'"
on July first. In other words, once a reader understands the correct
context of Paul's statement, he or she will 'see' the individual who
'named the Christ' — Tiberius Alexander.

Notice that the individual who 'named the Christ' did so in an area
other than that between Jerusalem and Illyricum. Tiberius
Alexander is the only individual who can be seen as having made

this claim in an area outside of Paul's cycle; there are no other candidates.

Paul's final statement in the passage can now also be understood: "and those who have not understood shall understand." The pinhead represents the simple minded followers of Jesus that Paul wrote did not "understand" Domitian's real meaning, but with the opening of the seals the pinheads (the Christians) "shall understand". The humor is vicious.

Yet another passage in Romans 15: 26-27 was linked to a power of the 'red horseman' in Revelation — his ability to make "men kill one another". In the passage, Paul states that he is sending contributions to the Jews in Jerusalem (a 'fruit') from the Gentiles in Greece, whose duty it is to minister unto the Jews in "carnal things". To understand the comic point of this statement a reader must first have already understood the story given in Acts 9:36 — 11:12, where the messianic Jews were made to unwittingly 'kill' one another.

Though the vicious meaning of the story in Acts 9 was designed to become apparent once the cannibal typology in the Gospels — where the human Passover Lamb Jesus had made 'unclean' food clean and thus fit for eating — was finally 'revealed', it is thinly veiled by any standard.

In the story, Peter is said to have 'raised' a woman named 'Tabitha' from the dead. 'Tabitha' means 'gazelle' in Aramaic, a point the author underlines by noting the word is translated as 'Dorcas' in Latin. Peter is then — absurdly — visited by a 'god-fearing' Roman centurion named Cornelius, who suddenly departs. Peter says he is very hungry but somehow falls into a trance during which he sees a sheet filled with "all manner" of quadrupeds that descends from the 'heavens', whereby a voice tells him to 'kill' and eat. Peter does not wish to violate the Jewish dietary laws, but 'God' — repeating the blasphemous cannibal theme in the Gospels — tells him that he has 'cleansed' the animals.

The story's typological meaning is that within the sheet that has "all manner" of quadrupeds is Tabitha, the 'human gazelle'. She must be included within the group because as the author wrote it contains "all manner" of quadrupeds. The sheet is lowered by the Roman soldiers who came with Cornelius. The Romans thereby fool the dim-witted Peter into killing and eating other messianic Jews. These individuals are recorded as being with Peter in Acts 11:12, where instead of the "three brothers" described in 11:11 Peter suddenly remembers six men "accompanying" him. Thus, Domitian expanded the cannibal humor of the Gospels. Not only was the 'Christ' to be eaten, but the members of the movement were 'given permission' to 'kill' and eat one another as well.

The third seal of Revelation describes a horseman carrying a set of scales which for some reason caused one of the 'living creatures' that surrounds the 'Lord God' to state: "A quart of wheat for a day's wages and three quarts of barley for a day's wages and do not damage the oil and wine".

> [5] When the Lamb opened the third seal, I heard the third living creature say, "Come!" I looked, and there before me was a black horse! Its rider was holding a pair of scales in his hand.
>
> [6] Then I heard what sounded like a voice among the four living creatures, saying, "A quart of wheat for a day's wages, and three quarts of barley for a day's wages, and do not damage the oil and the wine!" (Revelation 6:5-6)

Though the connections between the above passage from Revelation and the following passage from Suetonius has escaped notice, they are clear. Irrespective of my interpretation, there are simply too many concepts that are in alignment within the passages for their connections to have come about by circumstance

In the paragraph, Suetonius noted that Domitian had increased the pay of soldiers from 9 to 12 gold coins a year (the reader is required to recognize that 3 is to 4 as 9 is to 12), which is why the 'living creature' made the odd response when he saw the rider with a scale. In others words, the 'black horseman' again represents the power of Domitian; whose soldiers could now buy the precise increases in the weights of grain mentioned in Revelation with their new wages.

> Once upon the occasion of a plentiful wine crop, attended with a scarcity of grain, he made an edict forbidding anyone to plant more vines in Italy and ordering that the vineyards in the provinces be cut down, Domitian also raised the legionaries pay from nine to twelve gold pieces a year. (Suetonius, *Domitian*, 7)

These two related passages are linked to the one that describes Paul's third seal:

> If I am not an apostle to others, yet doubtless I am to you. For you are the **seal** of my apostleship in the Lord. (1 Corinthians 9:2)

The linkage between Suetonius' passage and 1 Cor 9 is witty and describes a question and answer session between Domitian and his slave 'Paul'. To see the meaning a reader must first recognize that 1 Cor describes Paul's third seal. Next, the parallel concepts between 1 Cor 9:2, Revelation and Suetonius must be identified. Some are transparent, while others require an act of cognition by the reader.

The key to seeing these concepts is recognizing that Paul's questions in 1 Cor 9 are being answered by Suetonius' statements in his short paragraph. The exchange between Paul and Suetonius continues the real theme of the 'four horsemen'; depicting the various powers of Domitian.

Thus, when Paul asks: "Have we not the power to eat and drink?"

Suetonius replied: "He did away with the distribution of food to the people."

Paul asks: Or only Barnabas and I [who] have no right to refrain from working?

To which Suetonius answered: "he made an edict forbidding anyone to plant more vines in Italy."

Paul asked: Who ever serves as a soldier at his own wage?

To which Suetonius answered. "He increased the pay of the soldiers by one fourth, by the addition of three gold pieces each year."

Paul asked: Who plants a vineyard and does not eat of its fruit?

To which Suetonius answered: "Once upon the occasion of a plentiful wine crop, attended with a scarcity of grain, thinking that the fields were neglected through too much attention to the vineyards, he made an edict forbidding anyone to plant more vines in Italy."

Paul asks: ⁹ For it is written in the law of Moses, "You shall not muzzle an ox while it treads out the grain." Is it oxen God is concerned about? ¹⁰ Or does He say [it] altogether for our sakes? For our sakes, no doubt, [this] is written, that he who plows should plow in hope, and he who threshes in hope should be partaker of his hope.

Suetonius's answers to the above questions are conceptual. The reader must recognize that by his edict to plant more grain Domitian is ensuring that the 'oxen that thresh grain' are not 'muzzled."

At this point Paul's questions switch to the other subject of Suetonius's passage; the rebellion against Domitian by Lucius Antonius and are again 'answered' by Suetonius's description of Domitian's accomplishments.

Paul asked: If we sow spiritual things to you, is it a great thing if we reap your fleshy thing?

To which Suetonius answered: "Domitian learned of this victory through omens before he actually had news of it, for on the very day when the decisive battle was fought, a magnificent eagle enfolded his statue at Rome with its wings, uttering exultant shrieks; and soon afterward the report of Antonius' death became so current, that several went so far as to assert positively that they had seen his head brought to Rome." The head of Lucius Antonius was the "fleshy thing" that Paul's question 'foresees'.

In 1 Cor 9:12 Paul foresees the "Gospel" or "euaggelion" — a technical term of the imperial cult meaning 'good news concerning Caesar; particularly a military victory or birth' — which is typologically describing Domitian's victory over Lucius Antonius. Notice that Paul's statement is incoherent because it has no context, but makes sense when recognized as a comment upon the rebellion by Lucius Antonius and the common soldiers who stopped it.

Thus, Paul asks the 'disciples' — in other words the Roman legionnaires — the following question. To understand the question it is useful to know that the legions were sometimes symbolically described as the 'followers' of Jesus in the Gospels.

> [12] If others in position of authority over you partake, should not we? But we did not use this authority but we bear all things to not hinder giving the "euaggelion" of the Christ. (1 Cor 9:12)

To which Suetonius answered: "The rebellion of Lucius Antonius was checked by troops who remained loyal and were able to disarm the rebels." The soldiers maintained the correct relationship to the 'lord god' — obedience — while those in authority did not. The soldiers thereby brought an "euaggelion" to Domitian.

In the next lines of the passage Paul notes that 'woe' will come to him — he will be laid on burning coals is the most literal translation — if he does not preach the Gospel. Here again the technical meaning of the word "euaggelion" as it was used by the imperial cult makes the meaning clear. If Paul — a self-described slave in chains — does not preach the 'good news of Caesar's victory' he will be killed.

> [13] Do you not know that those who minister the holy things eat [of the things] of the temple, and those who serve at the altar partake of [the offerings of] the altar? [14] Even so the Lord has commanded that those who preach the gospel should live from the gospel. [15] But I have used none of these things, nor have I written these things that it should be done so to me; for it [would be] better for me to die than that anyone should make my boasting void. [16] For if I preach the gospel, I have nothing to boast of, for

necessity is laid upon me; yes, woe is me if I do not preach the gospel!   *17* For if I do this willingly, I have a reward; but if against my will, I have been entrusted with a stewardship.

18 What is my wages then? That when I preach the gospel, I may present the gospel of Christ without charge, that I may not abuse my authority in the gospel.

19 For though I am free from all [men,] I have made myself a slave (bondservant) to all, that I might win the more;

20 and to the Jews I became as a Jew, that I might win Jews; to those [who are] under the law, as under the law, that I might win those [who are] under the law; (1 Cor 9: 13-20)

The above passage — 1 Cor 9: 18-20 — overtly describes Paul's 'cost' — he is free to all men — and the fact that he is a 'slave', also subtly refers to circumcision when Paul states that "I became a Jew". Paul also states that he became 'impotent' 1 Cor 9:22 ("asthenes" Strong's 772), which the result of his 'circumcision'.

However, in another example of the Roman 'building block' style, a reader must have solved a prior 'puzzle' to understand that Paul was not merely circumcised but castrated. The story of Paul's castration is black comedy and is given in Acts 13: 1-9.

Prior to the scene in Acts 13, Saul/Paul had attacked a member of the 'way' — Stephan — who has been preaching for 'Jesus'. In other words, Stephan had been preaching for the Flavian Christ. Following this event Saul shows up in Antioch with a group that includes a 'stepbrother' of Herod. Then the 'Holy Spirit', for some reason, orders Saul 'separated' — the Greek word used can also mean 'severed' — and the group then "placed their hands on him" — the word used for "placed" can also mean 'attack'. Following the event Saul becomes 'Paul' (Greek: Paulos), a word that means 'tiny' (Latin: Paullus). In other words, Paul has been 'severed' — or castrated — by the group led by Herod's 'stepbrother' as revenge for his participation in the attack on a member of the 'Way' — the Caesars' version of Judaism — and Saul thereby became 'Tiny'.

Paul's original name of 'Saul' is also explained by this reasoning. Saul was the Jewish king that had demanded David obtain 'a hundred Gentile foreskins' and the Romans named their character 'Saul' to imply that his 'circumcision' involved — like the one ordered by his Old Testament forerunner — more than a single foreskin. The author of Acts clarifies the relationship by actually mentioning the Old Testament Saul in the passage where 'Saul' becomes 'Tiny' — Acts 13:21. The Old Testament Saul's reign had the space of forty years. This foresees the forty years between the beginning of Paul's 'ministry' at approximately 40 CE and the start of Domitian's reign in 81 CE — a roughly forty year cycle parallel to the one which linked Jesus to Titus.

This analysis enables the real nature of Paul to be understood. Paul begins as 'Saul', a messianic rebel fighting against the 'Way', which is the Flavians' Christ cult, but has an epiphany and is 'converted' to belief in 'Christ Jesus', in other words he understands that Caesar is the Christ. At his epiphany 'God' — Caesar — told Paul that it is hard to fight against 'insect stings' Acts 26:14. Though the passage is usually translated as; "It is hard for you to kick against the goads", the word actually means 'insect sting,' and is probably wordplay on Vespasian's name, which means 'wasp'.

Thus, the Paul depicted in Acts and the Epistles, like Jesus, was not historical but was constructed as a typological character whose ministry described his efforts to convert the messianic movement into accepting the divinity of the Christ Domitian. Like the mentally debased character 'John' in Revelation who looked into Domitian's throne room and saw miraculous events, the fictional character 'Paul' was created as a deluded, chained, castrated slave who was taken from town to town to promote Domitian as the Christ.

The logic of the interpretation that Paul was castrated in Acts 13 1-9 is confirmed in 2 Timothy 3:11 where Paul speaks of the "persecutions and afflictions" he endured at "Antioch, Iconium and Lystra". The "persecutions" at Iconium and Lystra were recorded at Acts 14:19. However, the only event described at Antioch was the 'severing' which transformed Saul into 'Paul' or

'Tiny'. It is not too difficult to see the comic point — the event that 'Tiny' suffered at Antioch was "persecutions and afflictions".

Suetonius subtly commented upon Paul's condition as 'Tiny' in the passage with a clever and vicious encapsulation. He wrote: "Domitian prohibited the castration of males, and the price of the eunuchs that remained in the hands of the slave dealers was officially controlled." In other words, castration was permitted prior to this — and done to Paul. Paul the eunuch's statement in the linked passage that his price was "free to all men" relates to Domitian's control over the price for eunuchs. In the grim humor, Paul is being slurred as both a eunuch and a very inexpensive sodomite slave.

Finally, in 1 Cor 9 Paul describes a racetrack, where racers try to win the prize.

> [24] Do you not know that those who run in a race course all run, but one receives the prize? Run in such a way that you may obtain [it.] [25] And everyone who competes [for the prize] is temperate in all things. (1 Cor 9:24-25)

Suetonius also references the concept of the racers in a racetrack within his linked passage. He wrote:

> He added two factions of chariot drivers in the Circus, with gold and purple as their colors, to the four former ones.

Thus, while, on their surface, Paul's questions in 1 Cor 9 are incoherent, once their correct perspective is recognized their meaning is clear. The character 'Paul' is Domitian's slave, and his questions were constructed for Paul to show Domitian he understood the proper mentality for one of his slaves. This 'proper mentality' would begin, of course, with the understanding that Domitian was the Lord God and Christ.

At the beginning of 1Cor 9 Paul states that he is answering the questions of those that "examined" him. He is referring to the 'examination' of a slave. Paul only replies to his examiners with questions, which all seem to have an obvious answer. However once a reader understands the real perspective of the questions —

that Paul's questions are from his master to a slave — the obvious answers are reversed. This continues the theme shown above in the Gospel of Luke where a number of questions have an unexpected answer that is Flavian humor.

An exercise that enables a reader to understand the actual purpose of Paul's questions in 1 Corinthians 9 is to answer them as a slave in chains would — which, of course, is Paul's literal description of himself. I believe that this exercise was actually what the author intended an 'informed' reader to do. I also believe the author expected such a reader to see the slave's 'correct answers' to the questions as humorous.

Am I not an apostle?
Yes, of Domitian.

Am I not free?
No, you are a slave.

Have I not seen Jesus Christ our Lord?
Yes, the lord god and Christ Domitian.

Are you not my work in the Lord?
Yes, Paul promotes Domitian.

Do we have no right to eat and drink?
No, a slave has no rights.

Do we have no right to take along a believing wife, as [do] also the other apostles, the brothers of the Lord, and Cephas?
No, you are a castrate.

Or [is it] only Barnabas and I [who] have no right to refrain from working?
No slave may refrain from working.

Who ever goes to war at his own expense?
Soldiers, unlike slaves, are paid.

Who plants a vineyard and does not eat of its fruit?
Slaves.

Or who tends a flock and does not drink of the milk of the flock?
Slaves.

Do I say these things as a [mere] man?
No, as a slave.

Or does not the law say the same also? For it is written in the law
of Moses, "You shall not muzzle an ox while it treads out the
grain." Is it oxen God is concerned about?
The God Domitian cares about his oxen while it treads his grain,
not about his slaves.

It is difficult to argue that 1 Cor 9 is not somehow dependent with
Suetonius's passage. It is unlikely that the concepts of access to
food, "forbearing working", "planting a vineyard", harvesting
grain, would be combined with the concept of a "race course" in
two short passages by circumstance. It borders on the impossible
that such parallels would appear in passages that can be logically
seen as linked to a 'third seal', as this is such a rare concept. I
present Suetonius's entire passage below to show its short length.

He made many innovations also in common customs. He did
away with the distribution of food to the people, and revived that
of formal dinners. He added two factions of chariot drivers in the
Circus, with gold and purple as their colors, to the four former
ones. He forbade the appearance of actors on the stage, but
allowed the practice of their art in private houses. He prohibited
the castration of males, and kept down the price of the eunuchs
that remained in the hands of the slave dealers. Once upon the
occasion of a plentiful wine crop, attended with a scarcity of
grain, thinking that the fields were neglected through too much
attention to the vineyards, he made an edict forbidding anyone to
plant more vines in Italy and ordering that the vineyards in the
provinces be cut down, or but half of them at most be left
standing; but he did not persist in carrying out the measure. He
opened some of the most important offices of the court to
freedmen and Roman equites. He prohibited the uniting of two
legions in one camp and the deposit of more than a thousand
sesterces by any one soldier at headquarters because it was clear
that Lucius Antonius had been especially led to attempt a
revolution by the amount of such deposits in the combined winter
quarters of two legions. He increased the pay of the soldiers by

one fourth, by the addition of three gold pieces each year. (Suetonius, *Domitian*, 7)

Returning to Revelation, the fourth seal describes a rider who has the power to sentence people to death, has the power to kill with hunger and has power over wild beasts.

This power of the rider of the fourth seal links to Suetonius' description of Domitian sending someone who spoke ill of him to the arena to be torn apart by dogs. At this point Suetonius also describes a number of other individuals that Domitian sentenced to death. (Suetonius, *Domitian* 10)

One of the death sentences handed out by Domitian that Suetonius described was to a Vestal Virgin for sexual debauchery. As shown below, it was the death sentence that killed with 'hunger'. Suetonius' description was linked to the missive to the church in Thyatira in Revelation that contains a woman who, like the Vestal, is a "prophetess" who is also described below as "Jezebel".

[18] To the angel of the church in Thyatira write: These are the words of the Son of God, whose eyes are like blazing fire and whose feet are like burnished bronze.

[19] I know your deeds, your love and faith, your service and perseverance, and that you are now doing more than you did at first.

[20] Nevertheless, I have this against you: You tolerate that woman Jezebel, who calls herself a prophetess. By her teaching she misleads my servants into sexual immorality and the eating of food sacrificed to idols.

[21] I have given her time to repent of her immorality, but she is unwilling.

[22] So I will cast her on a bed of suffering, and I will make those who commit adultery with her suffer intensely, unless they repent of her ways.

[23] I will strike her children dead. Then all the churches will know that I am he who searches hearts and minds, and I will repay each of you according to your deeds.

The passage is problematic for Christianity in that 'Jesus' is stating that he will execute not only the prophetess and her lovers, but her children as well. While such actions were normative for Caesars, it seems out of character for the Christian notion of God's son. In fact, the 'prophecy' foresees the following event from Suetonius' recording of Domitian's life:

> and the incest of Vestal Virgins, condoned even by his father and his brother, he punished severely in divers ways, at first by capital punishment, and afterwards in the ancient fashion. For while he allowed the sisters Oculata and also Varronilla free choice of the manner of their death, and banished their paramours, he later ordered that Cornelia, a chief-vestal who had been acquitted once but after a long interval again arraigned and found guilty, be buried alive; and her lovers were beaten to death with rods (Suetonius, *Domitian* 8)

In both descriptions, not only is a "prophetess" given a period to repent and then "laid on a bed of misery" and killed, but her lovers are murdered as well. These two episodes are certainly among the very few in literature with a depiction of both the murder of a prophetess and her lovers. The nature of the execution of Vestal Virgins also 'fulfills' the 'killing by hunger' envisioned by rider released by Revelation's fourth seal. As Vestal Virgins were not to be harmed by humans, to execute them — for violating the taboo prohibiting a Vestal having sex — they were sealed in a cave and starved to death.

These passages are then linked to Paul's fourth seal described in 2 Cor 1:22; "who also has **sealed** us and given us the Spirit in our hearts as a guarantee."

In the passage that presents his fourth seal, Paul describes himself as being under a "sentence of death" "in Asia" (2 Cor 9) where his hometown of Tarsus is. The 'death sentence' was not carried out, however, because Paul was "delivered" by God. Paul then describes the nature of his writing. He states that it is something that the recipient of the letter 'knows well' — "epiginosko". The author of 2 Cor underlines the importance of the fact that the nature of Paul's writing is not 'incautious' but 'known well' by repeating the word "epiginosko" three times.

Though overlooked by scholars, there was another writer from Taurus who writings were 'known well' by the 'Christ' and also faced a "death sentence". His fate was a mirror opposite to that 'Paul of Tarsus', however. Even though his writing was 'well known" to 'God', he was not 'delivered'.

Suetonius described the other writer from Tarsus's fate at the point in his history where it links to the fourth seal in Revelation. He wrote: *"Hermogenes of Tarsus died (was executed by the 'Lord God' Domitian) because of some allusions in his "History", and even the slaves who had acted as his copyists were crucified."* (Suetonius, *Domitian* 10)

Within the context of this analysis the nature of the 'allusions' (the Greek word is "figura" — a word meaning "one which contains hints") that displeased Domitian are clear. They were 'hints' concerning the authorship of the Gospels. This typological meaning is confirmed by Suetonius's lead-in sentence to the paragraph describing 'Hermogenes of Tarsus': "An Emperor who does not punish informers encourages them". (*Domitian* 9)

The 'disappearance' of Hermogenes described by Suetonius is then comically referenced by Paul in 2 Timothy 1:15 — "Everyone in the province of Asia (the location of Tarsus) has deserted me, including Phygelus (the word means "the little fugitive") and Hermogenes." The character's name of "Hermogenes" was probably selected because that was the name of the well-known Greek logician, a member of the Socratic school. As the Gospels were written to be perfect in their 'divine logic'– which is what the term 'Logos' refers to in the Gospels — Suetonius named his fictional character that 'informed' — in other words revealed the logic of Domitian's authorship of the Pauline literature — after a logician. The concept that the "copyists were crucified" is grim typology, and may answer a question I have wondered about: what happened to the scribes that actually worked with the Caesars and their intellectuals to write up the various pieces of the New Testament?

The fifth seal of Revelation describes the followers of the Christ being given white robes and is linked to Suetonius' description of Domitian's servants wearing white robes. (*Domitian* 12).

> [9] When he opened the fifth seal, I saw under the altar the souls of those who had been slain because of the word of God and the testimony they had maintained.
>
> [10] They called out in a loud voice, "How long, Sovereign Lord, holy and true, until you judge the inhabitants of the earth and avenge our blood?"
>
> [11] *Then each of them was given a white robe*, and they were told to *wait a little longer, until the number of their fellow servants and brothers who were to be killed as* they had been was completed.

Notice how obviously Suetonius's passage below links to the one above from Revelation with the three parallel concepts: brothers, servant, white robes and coming murder. Moreover notice that Revelation is actually describing the murder of Titus's Christ cult and very likely Titus himself with the phrase about "servants and brothers who were to be killed", which produces its typological meaning when compared to the phase — "Too many rulers are a dangerous thing". This understanding also makes the traditions stating that Domitian killed 'Christians' easy to understand and identifies the 'tribulation' described in Revelation. It was Domitian's purging the family members and officials who oversaw Titus's Christ cult.

Suetonius wrote: "He [Domitian] was vexed that his **brother's** son-in-law had attendants clad in white" — Domitian's own **servants wore white livery** — and quoted Homer: "**Too many rulers are a dangerous thing.**" (Domitian 12)

This typology clarifies the extant Christian history. The first head of Titus's Christ cult was Flavius Clemens (identified as the first Roman Catholic Pope whose feast day is 22 June) whom Domitian murdered during his purge of that cult. Clemens was the son in law of the Roman Catholic saint Flavia Domitilla, who was either Titus's sister or niece. Flavia then in turn helped with the assassination of Domitian; her steward Stephanus is credited with the act.

> Finally he (Domitian) put to death his own cousin Flavius Clemens, suddenly and on a very slight suspicion, almost before the end of his consulship; and yet Flavius was a man of most contemptible laziness and Domitian had besides openly named his sons, who were then very young, as his successors, changing their former names and calling the one Vespasian and the other Domitian. And it was by this deed in particular that he hastened his own destruction. (Suetonius, *Domitian* 15)

> Stephanus, Domitilla's steward, dealt the first blow...the emperor grappled with Stephanus and bore him to the ground, where they struggled for a long time, Domitian trying now to wrest the dagger from his assailant's hands and now to gouge out his eyes with his lacerated fingers. (Suetonius, *Domitian*, 17)

These 'white robed' passages are linked to Paul's fifth seal.

> In Him you also [trusted,] after you heard the word of truth, the gospel of your salvation; in whom also, having believed, you were **sealed** with the Holy Spirit of promise... (Ephesians 1:13)

In the passage Paul talks about Christ "adopting children" which depicts Domitian adopting the children of Clemens above and changing their names to Vespasian and Domitian, thereby eliminating Titus's 'Christians'. The general point is simply to record Domitian's 'adopting' Titus's followers as his own.

Finally, the passage in Revelation depicting the 'white robed' servants who have been 'sealed in the 'Lord' states that they shall rest until a time in the future.

> [13] *Then one of the elders asked me,* "These in white robes—who are they, and where did they come from?"

¹⁴ I answered, "Sir, you know." And he said, "These are they who have come out of the great tribulation; they have washed their robes and made them white in the blood of the Lamb.

¹⁵ *Therefore, "they are before the throne of God and serve him day and night in his temple; and he who sits on the throne will spread his tent over them.*

¹⁶ Never again will they hunger; never again will they thirst. The sun will not beat upon them, nor any scorching heat.

¹⁷ For the Lamb at the center of the throne will be their shepherd; he will lead them to springs of living water. And God will wipe away every tear from their eyes." (Revelation 7: 16-17)

The Pauline passage that contains the 'fifth seal' and links to the 'white robed servants' passages above in Revelation, contains the same unusual concept of the 'adopted of the Lord' 'resting' until the 'coming age'.

¹⁷ that the God of our Lord Jesus Christ, the Father of glory, may give to you the spirit of wisdom and revelation in the knowledge of Him,

¹⁸ the eyes of your understanding being enlightened; that you may know what is the hope of His calling, ***what are the riches of the glory of His inheritance in the saints,***

¹⁹ and what [is] the exceeding greatness of His power toward us who believe, according to the working of His mighty power

²⁰ which He worked in Christ when He raised Him from the dead and seated [Him] at His right hand in the heavenly [places,]

²¹ far above all principality and power and might and dominion, and ***every name that is named, not only in this age but also in that which is to come.*** (Ephesians 1: 17-21)

Revelation's sixth seal describes a strong wind that drops figs from a tree.

[12] I watched as he opened the sixth seal. There was a great earthquake. The sun turned black like sackcloth made of goat hair, the whole moon turned blood red,

[13] and the stars in the sky fell to earth, as late figs drop from a fig tree when shaken by a strong wind.

[14] The sky receded like a scroll, rolling up, and every mountain and island was removed from its place.

[15] Then the kings of the earth, the princes, the generals, the rich, the mighty, and every slave and every free man hid in caves and among the rocks of the mountains.

[16] They called to the mountains and the rocks, "Fall on us and hide us from the face of him who sits on the throne and from the wrath of the Lamb!

[17] For the great day of their wrath has come, and who can stand?"

This is linked to Suetonius's description of a strong wind that blew over a Cyprus tree. While the metaphor is not presented clearly here, as shown below in Suetonius's biography of Vespasian it is clarified and likened to a messianic branch. Thus the 'inscription' at its base would have been concerning the Flavian 'doctrine' of their divinity — a point that becomes clear below.

> The inscription, too, on the base of a triumphal statue of his was torn off in a violent tempest and fell upon a neighboring tomb. The tree which had been overthrown when Vespasian was still a private citizen but had sprung up anew, then on a sudden fell down again. (Suetonius, Domitian 15)

These passages are then linked to Paul's sixth seal, which, keeping in the sequence, is found at Ephesians 4.

> And do not grieve the Holy Spirit of God, by whom you were **sealed** for the day of redemption. Ephesians 4:30

Ephesians 4 is linked to Suetonius' passage by the concept of a wind that tosses 'doctrine' about: "*that we should no longer be children, tossed to and fro and carried about with every wind of doctrine, by the trickery of men, in the cunning craftiness of deceitful plotting,"* Ephesians 4:14

Ephesians 4 also contains one of the more amusing typological connections between Paul and Suetonius.

In the passage that links to the sixth seal of Revelation Suetonius wrote: *"On his accession Domitian boasted to the Senate of having himself conferred the imperial power on Vespasian and Titus — it had now merely returned to him."* (Domitian 13)

This is an extremely important concept. In other words, Domitian claimed that he was not only the last Flavian Caesar, but also the first to "ascend". This is the basis for the 'living god's' claim in Revelation to be the 'alpha and the omega' — the first and the last. Suetonius' passage describing the 'Living God' Domitian's claim to be the first to ascend is linked to Ephesians 4: 9-10.

> [8] Therefore He says: "When He ascended on high, He led a group of captives captive, And gave gifts to men."
>
> [9] Now this, "He ascended"—what does it mean but that He also first descended into the lower parts of the earth?
>
> [10] He who descended is also the One who ascended far above all the heavens, that He might fill all things. (Ephesians 4: 8-10)

Notice in the above Pauline passages the author avoids simply stating that the 'Christ' ascended first. The reader must deduce that he who 'descended first' would logically also the be one that first 'ascended', therefore– like Suetonius' comment on Domitian above — 'Christ' also 'ascended' first.

In the Pauline passages that depict the 'ascension' are descriptions of the 'measurement' of a man. It is this specific vein of comedy that, in my opinion, most clearly reveals the true mindset of the authors of the Pauline material.

Suetonius described seeing a 90-year-old Jew — he is referring to 'Paul' — whose penis is inspected. It is strange that scholars have not investigated to see whether Suetonius' passage below somehow relates to 'Paul' because, irrespective of this analysis, 'Paul" was around same age as the Jew who was 'measured', was brought to Rome for a legal hearing, described himself as naked, met before a procurator in Judea, and was famous for being circumcised.

> I recall being present in my youth when a ninety year old man was stripped before the procurator and a very crowded court, to see whether he was circumcised. (Suetonius, Domitian 12)

By juxtaposing the Pauline passage to Suetonius' statement concerning the 'inspection' of a penis a reader is able to comprehend that Ephesians 4 is not a theological comment, but another description of a penis, the penis of the Christ — Domitian. I have provided a literal translation of the Greek below. In such a translation the 'penis size' humor and the even grimmer underlining comedy is more apparent than in most translations, which tend to try and contort the passage's bizarre language and render it coherent.

Unfortunately, the 'penis of the Christ' is not simply being inspected but is "filling all things" in the following passage. The sarcasm is vicious and it must be remembered that the Flavians wished to degrade the members of the messianic movement to the greatest degree possible.

[7] But to each of us was given grace according to the measure of the gift of the Christ.

[8] Wherefore he says; having ascended up on high he led a group of captives captive and gave gifts to men

[9] Now that he ascended, what was it that he first descended into the lower parts of the plowable land?

[10] He that descended was the same who also ascended above all heavens that he might fill "pleroo" all things;

[11] And he gave some Apostles and some prophets and some evangelists and some Shepherds and teachers,

[12] With a view to perfecting the saints; for a work of service for building up the body of the Christ;

[13] Until all may arrive at the unity of the faith and the knowledge of the Son of Man full grown at the measure of the stature of the fullness of the Christ;

[14] that we should no longer be children, tossed to and fro and carried about with every wind of doctrine, by the trickery of men, in the cunning craftiness of deceitful plotting,

[15] but, speaking the truth in love, may grow up in all things into Him who is the head—Christ —[16] from whom the whole body, joined and knit together by what every joint supplies, according to the effective working by which every part does its share, causes growth of the body for the edifying of itself in love. (Ephesians 4: 7-16)

Notice above that the one who 'descended' gave a 'work of service' — that will cause growth of his body for the edifying of itself in love — to "prophets, evangelists, shepherds and teachers". This may link back to Acts 13, the passage where Saul/Paul is castrated. Paul is at Antioch with a group that contains "certain prophets and teachers". Thus, the grim typology suggests that Paul was with the "group of captives" that was violated by the Christ — Domitian — in Ephesians 4.

It is clear that it was the 'Christ' Domitian, not his brother Titus, that ordered Saul castrated at Antioch as Acts 13:4 states that the "holy spirit" sends the group that laid hands on Paul forth. The Greek words that are interpreted as "Holy Spirit" — 'hagios pneuma' — are always used in the Pauline literature to indicate Domitian — the third component of the trinity.

It is interesting to watch the development of the term 'hagios pneuma' — literally " the terrible spirit" — in the New Testament, as it may mirror Domitian's control over the literature. The term occurs just over twenty times in the Gospels, but over sixty in the Pauline literature. In the Gospels it sometimes clearly represents Domitian — for example Matthew 28:19 — though not to my mind, always. In the Pauline literature Domitian used the term exclusively as a name for himself and the activity of the 'hagios pneuma' becomes more animated — he gives orders and speaks — than in the Gospels.

The odd unification of three individuals as 'god' — the Christian concept of the trinity — is simply another way of expressing the claim of their court historians that the Flavian Caesar was the fulfillment of the Jews' messianic prophecies:

> What did the most to induce the Jews to start this war, was an ambiguous oracle that was also found in their sacred writings, how, about that time, one from their country should become governor of the habitable earth. The Jews took this prediction to belong to themselves in particular, and many of the wise men were thereby deceived in their determination. Now this oracle certainly denoted the government of Vespasian, who was appointed emperor in Judea. (Flavius Josephus, *Jewish War* 6.312-313)

> There had spread over all the Orient an old and established belief, that it was fated for men coming from Judaea to rule the world. This prediction, referring to the emperor of Rome -as afterwards appeared from the event- the people of Judaea took to themselves. (Suetonius, *Life of Vespasian* 4.5)

> The majority [of the Jews] were convinced that the ancient scriptures of their priests alluded to the present as the very time when the Orient would triumph and from Judaea would go forth men destined to rule the world. This mysterious prophecy really referred to Vespasian and Titus, but the common people, true to the selfish ambitions of mankind, thought that this exalted destiny was reserved for them, and not even their calamities opened their eyes to the truth. (Tacitus, *Histories* 5.13)

I want to conclude this chapter with a number of typological linkages between Suetonius and the New Testament to show how completely his literature was developed around its typological linkages to the New Testament. Suetonius claimed that Vespasian had performed several 'Christ-like' miracles immediately after his 'Ascension'. Suetonius recorded that after a "certain divinity" — i.e. the mantle of 'Christ' — was "given him" Vespasian preformed miracles obviously parallel to those of the better-known 'Christ', the character in the Gospels.

Vespasian as yet lacked prestige and a certain divinity, so to speak, since he was an unexpected and still new-made emperor; but these also were given him. A man of the people who was blind, and another who was lame, came to him together as he sat on the tribunal, begging for the help for their disorders which Serapis had promised in a dream; for the god declared that Vespasian would restore the eyes, if he would spit upon them, and give strength to the leg, if he would deign to touch it with his heel. Though he had hardly any faith that this could possibly succeed, and therefore shrank even from making the attempt, he was at last prevailed upon by his friends and tried both things in public before a large crowd; and with success. (Suetonius, *Vespasian* 7)

The 'identification of the Christ' story in Luke was typologically linked to Josephus's passage wherein the Flavians gained the throne and fulfilled Josephus's 'prophecy' that they would become both Caesar and Christ.

"Who do the crowds say that I am?" So they answered and said, "John the Baptist, but some [say] Elijah; and others [say] that one of the old prophets has risen again." He said to them, "But who do you say that I am?" Peter answered and said, "The Christ of God." Luke 9:18-20

(In Matthew: "the son of the living God".) Luke's passage was linked to the following one in Josephus which described Vespasian becoming the Christ during his stay in Alexandria in November 69 CE.

. . . he (Vespasian) had not arrived at the government without Divine Providence, but a righteous kind of fate had brought the empire under his power. (Josephus, *Jewish War*, 4, 10, 622)

The fact that by becoming emperor Vespasian was also turning into the "Christ of God" was placed in another part of the text.

. . . what did the most to induce the Jews to start this war was an ambiguous oracle that was also found in their sacred writings, how, "about that time, one from their country should become governor of the habitable earth." The Jews took this prediction to belong to themselves in particular, and many of the wise men were thereby deceived in their determination. Now this oracle certainly denoted the dynasty of Vespasian, who was appointed emperor in Judea. (Josephus, *Jewish War* 6, 5, 312-313)

Mark's version of the 'Christ identification' story is different than Luke's in that it is preceded by an odd tale about Jesus using spit to restore sight to a blind man. This miracle has puzzled scholars in that Jesus's powers seemed to have failed him on his first try and he had to lay hands on the man a second time to get him to see clearly.

> So He took the blind man by the hand and led him out of the town. And when He had spit on his eyes and put His hands on him, He asked him if he saw anything.

> And he looked up and said, "I see men like trees, walking."

> Then He put His hands on his eyes again and made him look up. And he was restored and saw everyone clearly.

> Then He sent him away to his house, saying, "Neither go into the town, nor tell anyone in the town."

> Now Jesus and His disciples went out to the towns of Caesarea Philippi; and on the road He asked His disciples, saying to them, "Who do men say that I am?"

> So they answered, "John the Baptist; but some [say,] Elijah; and others, one of the prophets."

> He said to them, "But who do you say that I am?" Peter answered and said to Him, "You are the Christ." (Mark 8: 22-26)

Josephus's history of Vespasian becoming Caesar and Christ does not have any typological linkage to the story of the 'spit miracle' in Mark. However, Josephus does link Vespasian's ascension to the throne to the Exodus story in the Old Testament. (The passages are found at Josephus *Wars* 4, 10 lines 610 — 615 and Exodus 14) His typology is to be expected as Josephus claimed that the Romans were replacing the Jews in God's favor. Notice in the passage below the subtle typology Josephus creates between his description of the harbor Vespasian will leave from to journey to Rome and story of the Israelites leaving Egypt.

First, Josephus links his description of the harbor of Alexandria to
Exodus by describing it as walled in on the right hand and on the
left. As always is the case in the Flavians typological genre notice
that the parallel concepts occur in the same sequence.

> And thus is Egypt walled about on every side. The haven also of
> Alexandria is not entered by the mariners without difficulty, even
> in times of peace; for the passage inward is narrow, and full of
> rocks that lie under the water, which oblige the mariners to turn
> from a straight direction: its left side is blocked up by works made
> by men's hands on both sides; on its right side lies the island
> called Pharus,

…which is linked to this passage in Exodus

> [22] So the children of Israel went into the midst of the sea on the
> dry [ground,] and the waters [were] a wall to them on their right
> hand and on their left.

Once a reader recognizes that Josephus is mapping his story onto
Exodus 14, spotting the connections becomes easy as they occur
in the same sequence. Then Josephus depicts a fiery pillar:

> which is situated just before the entrance, and supports a very
> great tower, that affords the sight of a fire

…which is linked to this passage in Exodus

> Now it came to pass, in the morning watch, that the LORD
> looked down upon the army of the Egyptians through the pillar of
> fire.

Then Josephus describes the destructive power of the sea breaking
through the "walls' just as happened to the Egyptians;

> when the sea dashes itself, and its waves are broken against those
> boundaries, the navigation becomes very troublesome, and the
> entrance through so narrow a passage is rendered dangerous;

…which is linked to this passage in Exodus

> Then the waters returned and covered the chariots, the horsemen, [and] all the army of Pharaoh that came into the sea after them. Not so much as one of them remained.

Finally, Josephus describes the safety of the passage "once you got into it."

> yet it (the passage through the dangerous water) is the haven itself when you are got into it, a very safe one

...which is linked to this passage in Exodus

> But the children of Israel had walked on dry [land] in the midst of the sea, and the waters [were] a wall to them on their right hand and on their left. (Josephus *Wars* 4, 10 lines 610 — 615 and Exodus 14)

Josephus's Exodus typology is important in that it shows that fictional typology linking the Flavian Caesar to Exodus was being produced in the Flavian court. This suggests that the other story that used this genre — the Gospels — emerged from the same location.

Moreover, Domitian's court historian, Suetonius, also created a transparent parallel to Mark's 'spit miracle', in his account Vespasian's stay in Alexandria during which he was 'identified as the Christ' by Josephus. My conjecture is that Suetonius's passage was based on a passage in an early edition of Josephus, which some later editor removed as it was deemed too obvious. This was wise editing because, as readers may judge for themselves, if Suetonius's passage was placed in Josephus's account of Vespasian's Alexandria visit the overall sequence of Josephus's linkages to the Gospel story would have been too vivid. However, it is also possible that Suetonius intended to provide typological evidence that he knew and understood the Christian gospels.

First, Suetonius mentions Josephus and then his prophecy that the Flavian Caesar will become the Christ: "one of his high-born prisoners, Josephus by name, as he was being put in chains, declared most confidently that he would soon be released by the same man, who would then, however, be emperor." "There had spread over all the Orient an old and established belief, that it was fated at that time for men coming from Judaea to rule the world. This prediction, referring to the emperor of Rome, as afterwards appeared from the event, the people of Judaea took to themselves;" (Suetonius, *Vespasian*)

Next, Suetonius provides the 'secret' basis for the image the blind man that Jesus cured first saw — "trees like men walking". The passage shows that — far from having blurred vision — the man saw the truth; the Flavian Christs were 'messianic trees'.

> On the suburban estate of the Flavii an old oak tree, which was sacred to Mars, on each of the three occasions when Vespasia was delivered suddenly put forth a branch from its trunk, obvious indications of the destiny of each child. The first was slender and quickly withered, and so too the girl that was born died within the year; the second was very strong and long and portended great success, but the third was the image of a tree. Therefore their father Sabinius announced to his mother that a grandson had been born to her would be a Caesar. (Suetonius, *Vespasian*)

…which is linked to this passage in Mark:

> And he looked up and said, "I see men like trees, walking." (Mark 8: 24)

Suetonius next shows he understands the Gospels precisely as he describes Vespasian as lacking a "certain divinity as a new made emperor", which of course relates to its parallel in the Gospels of the "new made" god Jesus Christ :

> Vespasian as yet lacked prestige and a certain divinity, so to speak, since he was an unexpected and still new-made emperor; but these also were given him. (Suetonius, *Vespasian*)

Suetonius then comes to the typological event that Jesus's 'spit miracle' foresaw, which was Vespasian's performance of the same miracle.

> A man of the people who was blind, and another who was lame, came to him together as he sat on the tribunal, begging for the help for their disorders which Serapis had promised in a dream;

> for the god declared that Vespasian would restore the eyes, if he would spit upon them, and give strength to the leg, if he would deign to touch it with his heel. Though he had hardly any faith that this could possibly succeed, and therefore shrank even from making the attempt, (Suetonius, *Vespasian*)

...which was linked to Mark 8: 24-25.

> So He took the blind man by the hand and led him out of the town. And when He had spit on his eyes and put His hands on him, He asked him if he saw anything. He was at last prevailed upon by his friends and tried both things in public before a large crowd; and with success. Then He put His hands on his eyes again and made him look up. And he was restored and saw everyone clearly. (Mark 8: 24-25)

Finally, I would like to show how the `prophecies' given in 2 Thessalonians 2:1-12 provide a clear dating of Paul's letters. Paul predicts that a `son of destruction' will enter the temple and claim to be God at the same time that the Christ `comes'. Some have naturally wondered if Paul was `predicting' Titus's sacrifice at the temple of Jerusalem that Josephus described at *Wars* 6,6,1.

Logic and knowledge of the history can be answer this question. Paul claims that Christ was a human Passover lamb of a new covenant (1 Cor 5, 7 and 2 Cor 3, 6.) It is not possible that the Passover of a new covenant accidentally started at exactly the same point in the forty-year cycle that the Passover of the `old covenant' ended. These two concepts could only have been created through back calculation following the end of the Roman/Jewish war at Passover 73 CE.

In other words, the old covenant of Moses had a forty-year period between the Passover and Jews taking possession of Israel. The Gospels obviously reuse these concepts to establish their New Covenant — the exact forty-year period between the human Passover, and the Flavians taking possession of Israel.

The authors of the Gospels could have only created their concepts of a human Passover lamb of a New Covenant with a forty-year cycle by backward calculation from the fall of Masada at Passover

73 CE. And Jesus's prediction of the coming of a 'son of Man' at the time of the temple's destruction were also developed after the war as part of the new covenant story.

1&2 Corinthians and 2 Thessalonians describe a human Passover lamb of a New Covenant and the coming of the Christ at the time the 'son of destruction' violates the temple. These concepts could not have been developed independently and are based upon the New Covenant story found in the Gospels. Therefore the New Covenant concepts found in 1&2 Corinthians and 2 Thessalonians provide a dating of their authorship to sometime after the war.

THE ASS-HEADED CHRIST

It is well known that early Christians were often accused of worshiping an ass; Tacitus, Minucius Felix, and Tertullian all recorded this fact (Tac., I, v, 3, 4; Tert. *Ad nationes*, I, 14; Minucius, *Octavius*, ix). For example, Tertullian claimed that an "apostate Jew" "one day appeared in the streets of Carthage carrying a figure robed in a toga, with the ears and hoofs of an ass, and that this monstrosity was labeled: *Deus Christianorum Onocoetes*" (the God of the Christians begotten of an ass).

Other representations of the 'ass-headed Christ" have been discovered including a terra-cotta fragment found in 1881 near Naples, which has been dated to the first century and shows a figure with the head of an ass wearing a toga and seated on a chair with a roll in his hand, instructing a number of baboon-headed pupils. There is also an ancient gem with the carving of an ass-headed teacher of two human pupils who is dressed in the 'pallium', the form of cloak peculiar to sacred personages in early Christian art. Another ancient Syrian terra-cotta fragment also represents Jesus; book in hand, with the ears of an ass.

What lies in back of this ass-head imagery is a deeply hidden level of typological symbolism in the Gospels that indicates that the Jewish 'Christ' was an 'ass' that had been beheaded. I did not include it in the first edition of *Caesar's Messiah* as it is so complex and obscene that I felt it would make the simpler Jesus/Titus typology — which is grim enough — more difficult to accept.

Recognizing the Gospels' symbolism concerning the 'ass' begins with understanding the typological meaning of the phrase "there they made him a supper" (John 12:2).

In brief, the typological meaning of the phrase is established by its linkage to Josephus' description of a 'human Passover Lamb that was a son of Mary' (Josephus, *Jewish Wars* 6, 201-219). Both Josephus and the Gospels' stories of the 'human Passover Lamb' contain the concepts of Lazarus, Mary, eating, and a 'fine portion' that was not taken away. This linkage builds upon the foundation established by the positioning of the 'human Passover Lambs' relative to the overall sequential typological mapping that exists between Jesus' ministry and Titus campaign.

Further, as I also show in *Caesar's Messiah*, when Jesus 'raised' Lazarus from the dead, he did not restore Lazarus to life, but merely 'raised' his decomposing body from the ground.

These facts enable the typological meaning of the Gospels' story that next describes Eleazar after he is 'raised' from the dead — the 'anointing party' where Jesus and his followers are described as 'reclining' and preparing 'supper' and 'anointing' — to become clear. When the author uses the pronoun 'his' to define whose head is covered with perfume is it not necessarily Jesus'. In fact, the passage links back — logically enough — to the Gospels' last mention of a scent — the smell emanating from Lazarus's corpse; and the author used the ambivalence inherent in pronouns to mask his real meaning.

Thus, it is the head of Lazarus that is covered with perfume in Mark 14:3. It was done to mask its odor. This is also why 'his' feet were 'perfumed' in the version of the story given in John 12; 1-9, and why the feet were 'saved' for the day of the burial. The dark humor behind this mentioning of Lazarus's body parts is that to "make a meal" of any large animal it must first be butchered, and this is the activity that occurred during the 'anointing party' where 'they made him a supper'. The supper being prepared was the "last Supper' in the Gospels, which would eat the 'bread' of Eleazar's body.

Following this logic, in Mark 14: 5 after the anointing of a 'head', Judas complains that 'it' could have been "sold for more than 300 denarii". In the typological level of the story he is not referring to the perfume but to the head of Lazarus. The basis for the price he is asking is found in 2 Kings 6:25, where the price of an 'ass's head' is said to be 80 shekels. As a shekel was worth four denarii, the head would have fetched was 320 denarii had it been sold.

I won't go into the typological linkage between Josephus' cannibal Mary and 2 Kings 6: 25 at this point, but only note that it should be obvious to anyone who has read *Caesar's Messiah* as the story is about a mother who cannibalizes her son during a siege of Jerusalem. The use of the word 'denarii' also builds on the "ass' imagery in that the word — 'den arius' — literally means "ten asses". I show the linkage between the '300 denarii' in the Gospels and Titus's campaign below.

The theme describing Lazarus's 'body parts' continues in John 12:12-19 as, following the 'anointing party' Jesus is said to have previously found (the past tense) a 'young ass' to sit upon. Notice that in John 12:1 Lazarus is said to be 'reclining' — the only way the dead can posture — hence he was easy to be 'sat' upon. I must note that there is an unfortunate sexual 'innuendo' behind the image as the Romans sought to humiliate the Jewish Christ in the most extreme (and to them comic) manner possible.

The Gospel author's narration immediately following Lazarus's butchering and being 'sat upon' by Jesus is a masterpiece of sarcasm and double meaning.

"At first his disciples did not understand all this. Only after Jesus was glorified did they realize that these things had been written about him and they had done these things to him." John 12:16

The meaning of John 12:16 is that only after Titus has been recognized as the 'Jesus' of John 21 — the Jesus that lived forever and whose followers 'fished for men' — will the 'things' that had been written about him and done to 'him' — that is, in this story to Lazarus — be comprehended. Notice how the passage becomes coherent with the shift in context.

Moving through the typology, the 'anointing party' described in the Gospels obviously 'foresees' the 'anointing party' described by Josephus which is easily determined by both the parallel contexts — the events are perhaps the only two 'anointing parties' in literature — and the relative positioning of the parallel events in the 'ministries' of Jesus and Titus.

"John emptied the Temple's vessels of the sacred wine and oil and distributed it amongst the multitude who used them in drinking and anointing themselves." Josephus *Wars* 5, 13, 565

However, the typological relationship between the Gospels and the next event Josephus describes — concerning a 'son of Lazarus' and the 'hauling of bodies through the Jerusalem's gates' — is much more difficult to determine and can only be understood once the typological meaning of the stories of Jesus's 'triumphal entrance' on an ass in the synoptics is understood.

A reader must first recognize that the stories in Matthew, Mark and Luke occur following the 'triumphal entrance' in John, which took place four days before the Passover. This is necessary because, as shown below, it establishes Lazarus as an 'ass that has been sat on before' and therefore distinct from the asses Jesus asks to be brought to him in Mark and Luke, which he stipulates can not have previously been 'sat on'.

What the author is actually doing is providing just enough details to make it logically clear that four 'asses' were brought to Jesus — Lazarus and the 'donkey' that are described in Matthew, and the two colts described in Mark and Luke. The image that the author is working to create is a spoof of the prophecy in Jeremiah 9:9, which, if read literally, seems to indicate that the king of the Jews rode three asses simultaneously.

> See your King comes to you,
> Righteous and having salvation,
> Gentle and riding on a donkey,
> On a colt, the foal of a donkey.

(Zech. 9: 9)

To digress, it should be noted that the literary technique the author is using occurs throughout the Gospels. The Romans loved to hide their meanings 'in plain sight', so to speak. Thus, the literal meaning of the words is often used to convey the typological linkage, as in 'fishing for men', or 'eat of my flesh'. In this vein the synoptics' story of Jesus's 'triumphal entrance' is a literal 'fulfillment' of Zechariah 9:9 and shows that the Jewish 'king' did indeed 'ride' on three Asses.

To see the typological point they make, a reader must pay close attention to every detail of the three versions of the story in the synoptics. The 'young ass' in Matthew is said to be at Bethany — the place where Lazarus was last seen 'reclining' — and is not described as being 'tied', while the colts in Mark and Luke are both described as tied and having never having been sat upon before. Further, Mark's colt is said to have been brought to Jesus immediately, while the one in Luke is not.

Thus, the logical reading of the stories indicate that the 'young ass' in Matthew must be Lazarus who has been depicted as an 'ass' in the earlier story in John. He must be the 'young ass' described at Bethany because not only was he last described there, but he was not 'bound' as the asses in Mark and Luke were as he has already been 'loosed'. (Note that the same word that describes the untying of the asses in Mark and Luke was used to describe the 'loosening' of Lazarus from his burial clothes in the prior story in John.) And as he has been 'sat on' in the earlier story in John, he cannot be either of the asses described in Mark and Luke who have never been sat on before.

Moving through the typological storyline, the 'need' that Jesus tells his disciples in the synoptics' 'triumphal entrance' story that he has for 'asses', is actually to transport the Passover meal — the butchered 'ass' Lazarus — to Jerusalem. And once he has his 'quartet' of 'asses', he places Lazarus' body onto the team of three mules. Jesus can now 'fulfill' the prophecy in Jeremiah because he has assembled three donkeys and the 'King of the Jews' — the 'ass' Lazarus. The 'triumphal entry' that the Gospels actually describe is that of three mules carrying the butchered body of the king of the Jews, while he is being sat upon by the Romanized Christ, Jesus.

Once this image is understood, the Gospels' 'triumphal entrance' typological linkage to a passage in Josephus becomes visible. Jesus's 'triumphal entrance' is linked to *Wars* 5, 13, 567-568, a story that — mirroring the Gospels — follows the description of an 'anointing party'. Josephus describes a character he names 'Manneus, son of Lazarus' who is obviously related to the Gospels' 'Lazarus'. This character is responsible for hauling the dead bodies of the 'poor' through the gates of Jerusalem and for paying the public stipend for the work. Between the 14th of Nisan (Passover) and the first of Tamuz (75 days) he tells Titus that he has hauled 115,880 bodies of the 'poor' through the gates, or 1545 per day.

Thus, when Judas states two days from Passover in Mark 14:5 that the 'more than 300 denarii' could have been given to the 'poor', the author is making a hidden, comical, point. As '300 denarii' literally translates as '3000 asses', the money is just enough to cover the cost for the more than three thousand 'asses' being taken through the gates in the two days prior to Passover in Josephus.

The Gospels' transformation of the Jewish Christ into an 'ass' was also documented by Josephus in another story. In fact, Josephus wrote his longest exposition concerning the Gospels' typology entirely about its ass-head imagery. This revelation is found in *Against Apion*, Book 2, chapters 7, 8, & 9. The three chapters are another masterpiece of sarcasm, and use a thinly veiled typological symbolism to document the Roman achievement of having placed an 'ass head' — the Roman Christ — in the Jewish Temple.

In the three chapters Josephus rails against another historian — Apion — because Josephus states that Apion had falsely claimed that the Jews placed an ass's head in their temple that was discovered by Antiochus Epiphanies when he sacked Jerusalem. Everything that Josephus claimed in his passages about Apion is true, of course. In other words, the Jews certainly did not place an ass head in their Temple. In fact, all of the claims that Josephus states Apion made are ludicrous and were never made.

What Josephus is doing with the chapters is claiming that Apion was a false historian because he wrote the exact opposite of the truth. In other words, while Apion's claims are all false, they are a mirror image of the truth. It was not the Jews, but the Romans who placed an ass head in the Jews' Temple. With this simple sleight of hand Josephus is able to inform posterity of the way in which the Romans had placed a false god — the ass head — in the Jew's Temple.

AGAINST APION, BOOK 2

...for Apion hath the impudence to pretend that 'the Jews placed an ass's head in their holy place;' and he affirms that this was discovered when Antiochus Epiphanies spoiled our temple, and found that ass's head there made of gold, and worth a great deal of money.

Josephus notes correctly that the Jews would never place an ass head in their temple as this would violate their laws.

Apion ought to have had a regard to these facts, unless he had himself had either an ass's heart or a dog's impudence; of such a dog I mean as they worship; for he had no other external reason for the lies he tells of us. As for us Jews, we ascribe no honor or power to asses, as do the Egyptians to crocodiles and asps, when they esteem such as are seized upon by the former, or bitten by the latter, to be happy persons, and persons worthy of God.

Josephus notes that the Romans beat their asses with 'stripes', like the flogging of Jesus in the Gospels.

Asses are the same with us which they are with other wise men, viz. creatures that bear the burdens that we lay upon them; but if they come to our thrashing-floors and eat our corn, or do not perform what we impose upon them, we beat them with a great many stripes, because it is their business to minister to us in our husbandry affairs.

Josephus next states that, *"Apion of ours was either perfectly unskillful in the composition of such fallacious discourses, or however, when he begun [somewhat better], he was not able to persevere in what he had undertaken, since he hath no manner of success in those reproaches he casts upon us."* The point of this sarcasm will become clear shortly.

Josephus then states that Apion became "other men's prophet" with his claim that the Jews kept a man in the Temple to be eaten "at the same time each year". This man, whose body is somehow able to feed 'thousands', is an obvious spoof of the character in the Gospels that told his followers to eat of his flesh. The 'prophecy' that Apion is making is clear enough. I would also note that the 'Grecian fable' Josephus refers to as being added to below is Aesop's 'The Ass Carrying the Image', which describes an ass who thought he had become a god.

> (Apion's history) adds another Grecian fable, in order to reproach us. In reply to which, it would be enough to say, that they who presume to speak about Divine worship ought not to be ignorant of this plain truth, that it is a degree of less impurity to pass through temples, than to forge wicked calumnies of its priests. Now such men as he are more zealous to justify a sacrilegious king, than to write what is just and what is true about us, and about our temple; for when they are desirous of gratifying Antiochus, and of concealing that perfidiousness and sacrilege which he was guilty of, with regard to our nation, when he wanted money, they endeavor to disgrace us, and tell lies even relating to futurities. Apion becomes other men's prophet upon this occasion, and says that "Antiochus found in our temple a bed, and a man lying upon it, with a small table before him, full of dainties, from the [fishes of the] sea, and the fowls of the dry land; that this man was amazed at these dainties thus set before him; that he immediately adored the king, upon his coming in, as hoping that he would afford him all possible assistance; that he fell down upon his knees, and stretched out to him his right hand, and begged to be released; and that when the king bid him sit down, and tell him who he was, and why he dwelt there, and what was the meaning of those various sorts of food that were set before him the man made a lamentable complaint, and with sighs, and tears in his eyes, gave him this account of the distress he was in; and said that he was a Greek and that as he went over this province, in order to get his living, he was seized upon by foreigners, on a sudden, and brought to this temple, and shut up therein, and was seen by nobody, but was fattened by these curious provisions thus set before him; and that truly at the first

such unexpected advantages seemed to him matter of great joy; that after a while, they brought a suspicion [to] him, and at length astonishment, what their meaning should be; that at last he inquired of the servants that came to him and was by them informed that it was in order to the fulfilling a law of the Jews, which they must not tell him, that he was thus fed; and that they did the same at a set time every year: that they used to catch a Greek foreigner, and fat him thus up every year, and then lead him to a certain wood, and kill him, and sacrifice with their accustomed solemnities, and taste of his entrails, and take an oath upon this sacrificing a Greek, that they would ever be at enmity with the Greeks; and that then they threw the remaining parts of the miserable wretch into a certain pit."

The last line is important and links to the 'pruning' of the Messiah typology in the Gospels. Moreover, as shown below, by placing the man's 'body parts' in a pit, this enables a character named 'Zabidus' to steal the 'Ass head' which he will then place in the Temple at the end of the final story. Obviously, these 'body parts' were a 'foreseeing' of the 'anointing party' in the Gospels, described above.

The above passage is a caricature of the Roman cannibalized Christ described in Josephus. To camouflage the description until the Gospels typology was uncovered it describe the individual as a 'Greek' not a Jew, but this is transparent. The 'same time every year' the man is to be eaten is, of course, a 'type' for the human Passover lamb and the "certain wood" where he is killed 'foresees' (notice that the story is a typological prophecy of what the Gospels claim will occur) the cross of crucifixion. The "law" that they "must not tell him" is the "law" that will be established by Titus with the Gospels' and Josephus' typology.

Josephus claims that Apion went on to write that:

" the man said there were but a few days to come ere he was to be slain, and implored of Antiochus that, out of the reverence he bore to the Grecian gods, he would disappoint the snares the Jews laid for his blood, and would deliver him from the miseries with which he was encompassed." Now this is such a most tragical fable as is full of nothing but cruelty and impudence; yet does it not excuse Antiochus of his sacrilegious attempt, as those who write it in his vindication are willing to suppose; for he could not presume beforehand that he should meet with any such thing in coming to the temple, but must have found it unexpectedly. He was therefore still an impious person, that was given to unlawful pleasures, and had no regard to God in his actions. But [as for Apion], he hath done whatever his extravagant love of lying hath dictated to him, as it is most easy to discover by a consideration of his writings; for the difference of our laws is known not to regard the Grecians only, but they are principally opposite to the Egyptians, and to some other nations also for while it so falls out that men of all countries come sometimes and sojourn among us, how comes it about that we take an oath, and conspire only against the Grecians, and that by the effusion of their blood also? Or how is it possible that all the Jews should get together to these sacrifices, and the entrails of one man should be sufficient for so many thousands to taste of them, as Apion pretends?

The meaning of the above passage is clear and is a comic description of the feeding of thousands, 'miraculously' accomplished by Jesus in the Gospels. It is another example of the strange lack of attention by New Testament scholars to the overt relationships between the Gospels and Josephus. As Jesus had flatly stated that his flesh was to be eaten and 'somehow' fed thousands, the possibility that the passage is a spoof of Jesus should be explored irrespective of the analysis in *Caesar's Messiah*.

The next passage is witty and describes exactly what the Romans did with the Jews' Messiah. They brought him back to Rome, figuratively, where they used him to remove the 'demons' of the Jews. The passage repeats the theme found in Antiquities 8, 2, 46-49, where, following the war, the 'pruned' Messiah Eleazar was used to 'exorcize' the 'demonic' hatred of the Jewish rebels.

Or why did not the king carry this man, whosoever he was, and whatsoever was his name, (which is not set down in Apion's book,) with great pomp back into his own country? when he might thereby have been esteemed a religious person himself, and a mighty lover of the Greeks, and might thereby have procured himself great assistance from all men against that hatred the Jews bore to him.

The next passage in the story is one of the clearest descriptions the Romans left us of the real nature of the Gospels and for whom they were intended. The hatred is palpable.

> But I leave this matter; for the proper way of confuting fools is not to use bare words, but to appeal to the things themselves that make against them.

This statement, of course, applies to not only the Gospels but to the "words" that Josephus is writing. The 'bare words' of *Against Apion* and the Gospels are not their real meaning, but are simply the method by which the Romans 'appealed' to the 'things' that showed the fools that they were in error. Josephus's point is that the Jews believed that their God was more powerful than Caesar, and looked into their Scripture for 'divine patterns' that would show them when their Messiah would come. The Gospels and works of Josephus were thus created to 'confute' these 'fools'.

As he did with the Testimonium Flaviaium and the two tales that follow it, Josephus unified the three tales concerning the 'ass head' in *Against Apion* into a conceptual whole. In his final part of the three-piece set he describes a 'star' that walks the earth — a play on the Jew's 'Star' prophecy of the Messiah that the Flavians claimed foresaw themselves. This 'star' is using a certain "wooden instrument in three rows" (representing the three crucifixes at Golgotha) in order to keep the Jews "quiet" and at a "distance", so that he might break into the Temple and steal the ass head, which was left behind in the pit by the cannibalized 'Jesus' in the prior story. This story precisely recalls the descriptions of Jesus's followers during the crucifixion of Jesus and the two robbers.

In other words, just as the fictitious ass-head story in the Gospels leads to the fictitious history of Josephus whereby Titus replaced the Jews' god, the prior story leads to the character named 'Zabidus' leaving behind an ass-head in the Jewish Temple. I need to point out the craftsmanship by the authors in that the three 'ass-head' stories compressed the entire Gospel/Josephus topological 'histories' into a tiny literary space.

The passage is witty, but to understand it requires knowing that 'Zabidus' is actually a pun on 'Sabazius', the original Roman name for the Jews' God. Thus 'Zabidus' is also a type for Titus who named himself the Jewish god 'Christ' and used a 'certain wooden instrument' — the cross. Josephus comments on the fictional aspect of the Gospels' character Jesus with the comment: "But still it seems that while Zabidus took his journey over the country, where were so many ten thousands of people, nobody met him."

> What then can we say of Apion, but that he examined nothing that concerned these things, while still he uttered incredible words about them? but it is a great shame for a grammarian not to be able to write true history. Now if he knew the purity of our temple, he hath entirely omitted to take notice of it; but he forges a story about the seizing of a Grecian, about ineffable food, and the most delicious preparation of dainties; and pretends that strangers could go into a place whereinto the noblest men among the Jews are not allowed to enter, unless they be priests. This, therefore, is the utmost degree of impiety, and a voluntary lie, in order to the delusion of those who will not examine into the truth of matters; whereas such unspeakable mischiefs as are above related have been occasioned by such calumnies that are raised upon us.

> Nay, this miracle or piety derides us further, and adds the following pretended facts to his former fable; for he says that this man related how, "while the Jews were once in a long war with the Idumeans, there came a man out of one of the cities of the Idumeans, who there had worshipped Apollo. This man, whose name is said to have been Zabidus, came to the Jews, and promised that he would deliver Apollo, the god of Dora, into their hands, and that he would come to our temple, if they would all come up with him, and bring the whole multitude of the Jews with them; that Zabidus made him a certain wooden instrument, and put it round about him, and set three rows of lamps therein, and walked after such a manner, that he appeared to those that stood a great way off him to be a kind of star, walking upon the earth; that the Jews were terribly affrighted at so surprising an appearance, and stood very quiet at a distance; and that Zabidus, while they continued so very quiet, went into the holy house, and carried off that golden head of an ass, (for so facetiously does he write,) and then went his way back again to Dora in great haste." And say you

so, sir! as I may reply; then does Apion load the ass, that is, himself, and lays on him a burden of fooleries and lies; for he writes of places that have no being, and not knowing the cities he speaks of, he changes their situation; for Idumea borders upon our country, and is near to Gaza, in which there is no such city as Dora; although there be, it is true, a city named Dora in Phoenicia, near Mount Carmel, but it is four days' journey from Idumea. Now, then, why does this man accuse us, because we have not gods in common with other nations, if our fathers were so easily prevailed upon to have Apollo come to them, and thought they saw him walking upon the earth, and the stars with him? for certainly those who have so many festivals, wherein they light lamps, must yet, at this rate, have never seen a candlestick!

But still it seems that while Zabidus took his journey over the country, where were so many ten thousands of people, nobody met him. He also, it seems, even in a time of war, found the walls of Jerusalem destitute of guards. I omit the rest.

Now the doors of the holy house were seventy cubits high, and twenty cubits broad; they were all plated over with gold, and almost of solid gold itself, and there were no fewer than twenty men required to shut them every day; nor was it lawful ever to leave them open, though it seems this lamp-bearer of ours opened them easily, or thought he opened them, as he thought he had the ass's head in his hand.

Josephus then concludes his spoof on Titus's placing the Ass's head in the Jews' Temple by writing:

Whether, therefore, he returned it (the ass head) to us again, or whether Apion took it, and brought it into the temple again, that Antiochus might find it, and afford a handle for a second fable of Apion's, is uncertain.

In other words, Josephus sets up the future of the 'ass head' to again appear in the Temple within a 'second fable' — the Gospels.

THE SERVANT'S COMMENTARY

To end the dark journey of the ass head in the Temple on a positive note: some time after Christianity began to be promoted in Rome someone, likely a servant, came to understand the symbolism concerning the 'pruned Christ' with the 'ass head'. Perhaps the servant had overheard patricians joking about how they had given the Jews an 'ass's head' to worship, or perhaps the owner simply told the individual the truth so as to keep him or her from succumbing to the false religion intended for slaves.

Whatever these facts are, someone decided to record the secret they had learned. It is just a crude scratching on a wall in the servant's quarters of the palace of the Caesars on Palatine hill, but it is a treasure almost beyond words. It is one of the few depictions of Jesus's crucifixion ever made by someone who knew the truth.

The Greek text inscribed here reads as follows:

Galilee font   ALEXAMENOSSEBETEQEON

Unicode   Α Λ Ε Ξ Α Μ Ε Ν Ο Σ Σ Ε Β Ε Τ Ε Θ Ε Ο Ν

Transliterated   ALEXAMENOSSEBETETHEON

This is translated as: "Alexamenos, worship God."

THE SCOPE OF ROMAN PLANNING: RABBINICAL JUDAISM

It is strange that while the differences between Christianity and Rabbinical Judaism are well known, their similarities are not. Few are aware that both religions purport to have been organized in Palestine during the first century and that each religion claims its original leadership stemmed from the house of David. Fewer still know that both religions superseded and replaced the militaristic form of Judaism, which though it had been widespread before the war against the Romans, disappeared at the very time the two new religions were developing their first congregations.

One reason that these facts are not well known is that, until now, they have not been seen as having much significance. Few historians have seen the coincidence that the new forms of Judaism came into existence at the same time as suspicious, or requiring an explanation.

In *Caesar's Messiah,* however, I presented evidence indicating that Christianity had been invented by a group of intellectuals working for the Flavians, the family that had crushed the revolt of the messianic movement that Christianity and Rabbinical Judaism replaced. This new understanding regarding Christianity may lead to a different opinion of the origins of Rabbinical Judaism as well.

As the story is told by Cliff Carrington:

There are many Jewish legends about the founding of their post-temple religion. These are found in the Talmud and Haggadah. With minor variations the story goes like this:

 During the siege of Jerusalem in the summer of 70 CE a Jewish priest, the deputy head of the Sanhedrin, a Pharisee named Johanan (Jochanan) ben Zakkai defected to the Romans. It is written that he communicated to the Roman camp, via arrow-mail, that he was a 'Friend of Vespasian' and wished to come over. The Romans gave him a promise of safe-conduct, if he could get out of the strife-torn city.

Rabbi Johanan devised a scheme, with the assistance of a relative who was in charge of a gate, to be carried out of Jerusalem in a coffin. This deception was needed because none but the dead were allowed out of the city. His disciples, with permission, carried their master out to the cemetery and placed the coffin in a burial cave. Later, at night, Rabbi ben Zakkai got out of the coffin and made his way to the Roman camp, where he was welcomed.

The Rabbi then has an interview with Vespasian (Sic), the commander of the siege. During the interview Rabbi ben Zakkai gives Vespasian a prophecy, very similar to Josephus', that he would soon become emperor (Sic). He was taken into the camp to await the outcome of the war. Then Vespasian becomes emperor, fulfilling ben Zakkai's prophecy. After the destruction of Jerusalem and the Temple the Rabbi was rewarded.

Vespasian allotted Rabbi Johanan ben Zakkai and his disciples, who had also defected or somehow survived the destruction, a place of refuge in the coastal town of Jamnia. This little town was on the main highway along the Mediterranean sea, the Via Maris. There, under Roman protection, and perhaps guidance, the rabbis founded an academy for the study of the Jewish Scriptures, which gained the name The Vineyard. This name either came from the fact that the academy was actually set up in an old vineyard, or because the students sat in rows like planted grape-vines. Either way, the members of this academy were the roots of modern Judaism. [98]

---

[98] Cliff Carrington, 'Gophna to Galilee: The Bridge Between Jewish and Christian Beginnings' <http://carrington-arts.com/cliff/Gophna2.htm> [accessed 16 March 2014].

After learning that the Flavians had invented Christianity, I became curious as to why they provided the Rabbis with a land grant to establish Rabbinical Judaism.It seemed logical to me that as the Flavians had created one of the two religions that had replaced the militaristic form of Judaism, they also created the other.

I began an analysis of the literature of Rabbinical Judaism to determine if it contained clues, like those within the Christian canon, indicating that the Flavians had created that religion. This study led to the following conclusions:

1. Rabbinical Judaism was, like Christianity, a religion created by the Flavians.

2. Many of the original 'Rabbis' of the religion were not Jews, but Roman 'converts' or proselytes to Judaism, who were under the employment of the Flavians.

3. Much of the canon of the religion was not created for a theological purpose, but to mind-shape Judaism's religious warriors into docile students obsessed with legal minutia.

4. Exactly as they had done with the Gospels, the Flavians constructed a satirical message within the religion's canon to notify posterity that they had created Rabbinical Judaism and that the 'God' the Jews worshiped was the Flavian Caesar.

5. Rome was successful in both destroying the real Judaism, which was the xenophobic religion of the Maccabees, and, incredibly, in hiding this fact from history.

An obvious question is: why would the Flavians have found it necessary to create two new versions of Judaism? To answer this question we must look to the political situation the Flavians faced in Judea following their war with the messianic Jewish rebel forces.

The Flavians' war with the Jews was part of the broader and longer conflict between Judaism and Hellenism. Judaism was based upon monotheism and faith, and was simply incompatible with Hellenism, the Greek culture that promoted polytheism and rationalism.

Hellenism spread into Judea following the area's conquest by Alexander the Great in 333 B.C.E.. The people of Israel, in spite of their historic resistance to outside influences, began to assimilate certain traits of their ruling class. Many Semites found it desirable, if not necessary, to speak Greek. Wealthy Jews sought a Greek education for their young men. Gymnasia introduced Jewish students to Greek myths, sports, music and arts. However, there was a backlash to Hellenism's engulfing of Jewish culture. In 167 B.C.E. the Maccabees, a family of religiously zealous Jews, led a revolution against the Seleucids, the Greek descendants of a General in Alexander's army that had come to rule the region. The Maccabees sought to not only repel the Seleucids, but to restore the religion that they believed was mandated by God for his holy land. They required all of the inhabitants of the cities they conquered to convert to Judaism. Males either permitted themselves to be circumcised or were slain. After a twenty-year struggle, the Maccabees eventually prevailed. To quote 1 Maccabees: "the yoke of the Gentiles was removed from Israel" (13:41).

Though the Maccabees ruled Israel for over a hundred years, their kingdom was never secure. The Seleucid threat to the region was replaced by a greater one, Rome. Roman expansionism and Hellenistic culture constantly threatened to engulf the Judaic nation that the family had established. In 65 B.C.E. a civil war broke out between two Maccabean rivals for the throne. It was at this time that the family of Herod appeared on the scene. The Herods were not Jewish, but of Greek and Arab descent, and thoroughly Hellenized. The father of Herod, the wily Antipater, managed to become an advisor to Hyrcanus, one of the Maccabees vying for power. Through him Antipater helped bring about a Roman intervention to the civil war. When Pompey sent a Roman army into Israel, it marked the beginning of the end of the Maccabean religious state. For the next thirty years, (65-37 B.C.E.) Israel suffered through one war after another. In 40 B.C.E. the last Maccabean ruler, Mattathias Antigonus, seized control of the country. By this time, however, the Herodian family had become firmly established as Rome's surrogate in the region and, with Roman support, defeated Mattathias' army and gained control of Judea. After capturing Jerusalem, Herod executed all of the Maccabean Sanhedrin with the exception of Pollio and Sameas, two Pharisees who had instructed the people to open the gates to Herod's army.

Though the Flavians were later able to put down the revolt of 70 CE, they still faced a potential threat to their financial interests in the region. Josephus recorded that what had 'most elevated' the Jews to rebel against Rome was their belief that God would send to Israel a Messiah. Following the war many Jews continued to hope for the coming of a 'son of David'. Though they had crushed their revolt, the families had not destroyed the messianic religion of the Jewish rebels. The families needed to find a way to prevent the zealots' belief that God would send them a warrior Messiah from inspiring future uprisings.

Caesar's Messiah presented one of the methods the families concocted to head off any future revolts. They created Christianity as a replacement messianic religion whose 'Son of David' was, absurdly, not a warrior but a tax-paying pacifist. Though their new version of Judaism would succeed beyond their highest hopes, it was not useful in controlling those Jews who would not accept the new religion. Those Jews would always be vulnerable to the messianic prophesies that had inspired the revolt. To end this threat, Judaism itself would need to be transformed, and to do that required controlling its leadership and theology.

Following their seizing of the throne, the Flavians took control over the centers of learning throughout the empire. They made appointments to the chairs and payments of the salaries to the instructors in philosophical schools in Rome, Athens and Alexandria.[99] Viewed from this perspective, the academy that produced Rabbinical Judaism was simply another Flavian educational center. It produced thousands of 'rabbis', a word that

---

[99] Carrington.

is often translated as 'teacher' but actually means 'master' and stems from the Hebrew word 'rab' meaning 'great'. These 'rabbis' would have, presumably, taught the theology that they learned at the Flavian academy.

A passage from *Wars of the Jews* may describe the actual beginnings of the academy. Josephus recorded that a group of priests defected to Titus during the siege of Jerusalem and were given Roman protection and temporarily housed in Gophna. Titus promised the priests to respect their customs and that following the war he would return their property. This was most likely the group of priests, possibly including the founder of Rabbinical Judaism, Johanan ben Zakkai and his disciples, who were finally settled at Jamnia by the Flavians.

> "Some also there were who, watching a proper opportunity when they might quietly get away, fled to the Romans, of whom were the high priests Joseph and Jesus, and of the sons of high priests three, whose father was Ishmael, who was beheaded in Cyrene, and four sons of Matthias, as also one son of the other Matthias, who ran away after his father's death, and whose father was slain by Simon the son of Gioras, with three of his sons, as I have already related; many also of the other nobility went over to the Romans, together with the high priests.

> "Now Caesar [Titus] not only received these men very kindly in other respects, but, knowing they would not willingly live after the customs of other nations, he sent them to Gophna, and desired them to remain there for the present, and told them, that when he was gotten clear of this war, he would restore each of them to their possessions again; so they cheerfully retired to that small city which was allotted them, without fear of any danger." (Jewish War, 6. 2. 2.)

Why did Titus protect these priests? The Flavians would not have given favors to Jews cheaply at this point in history. They had just completed a costly war with Judaism and were looking to make certain that the religion did not erupt against the Roman Empire again. Therefore, why did the Flavians create a compound for the study of Judaism and the production of rabbis? Like the authors of the Gospels, the rabbis at Jamnia created a new form of Judaism. Their canon had a completely different theological and political perspective than that found in the Dead Sea Scrolls, which contained references to the Messiah and to the struggle with the Romans. The rabbis' canon was purged of references to revolutionary activity to such an extent that, for example, it no longer even included a mention of the Maccabean victory that the Jewish holiday of Hanukkah was based upon. This new Jewish canon was completely removed from the messianic and military struggle that dominated the focus of whoever had produced the Dead Sea Scrolls. The focus of the new rabbinical literature was almost entirely upon the study of the minutia of Judaic law.

The academy's location within Galilee was moved from time to time, first to Usha at the time of the Bar Kochba revolt, and then to Bet Shearim, Tiberius, Caesarea and finally Lydda at the end of the fourth century. The academy would have needed to obtain an imperial land grant for each new location, showing the longstanding approval the Roman emperor had for the work of the rabbis.[100]

Rabbinical literature records many of the individuals who assisted in this multi-generational endeavor, including some women. Gamaliel II, Nasi, of the House of David, eventually took over from Zakkai as head of the academy. He was recognized as Patriarch by the emperor, an endorsement that indicated the emperor's approval of the work of the academy. During his era the academy's scholars were recorded as having advised Rome on the content of their teaching. The Talmud contains a story regarding four rabbis, including Gamaliel II, who travel to Rome about the year 95CE to confer with a 'Min', that is the non-Jew, to discuss theology. Gamaliel II was the great-great-grandson of Hillel, whose name is still proverbial in Judaism today.

Gamaliel II's grandfather was the Gamaliel, who was the 'doctor of the law' that was an instructor to Paul and the Apostles, as described in Acts 5:34 and Acts 22:3. The fact that the grandfather of one of the founders of Rabbinical Judaism was also a teacher of the apostles has struck scholars as notable heretofore, but with no

---

[100] Carrington.

clear meaning. However, again with the insights gained through *Caesar's Messiah*, a sinister picture emerges. In Acts, Gamaliel describes the death of Judas the Galilean, the founder of the Sicarii movement.

> Judas the Galilean arose in the days of the Census and led many people astray. He perished and all of them scattered. (Acts 5:37)

Such a statement by Gamaliel II's grandfather concerning Judas the Galilean's leading people "astray" suggests that the effort to transform Judaism was multi-generational; perhaps beginning with the creation of the Herodian Sanhedrin that Gamaliel presided over. Judas the Galilean was the individual who Josephus recorded as being a founder of the messianic movement or "innovation" that rebelled from Rome. Both Gamaliel's association with Paul and his perspective on Judas the Galilean suggest that he, like Paul, was directly linked to Rome.

Many of the rabbis involved with the establishment of Rabbinical Judaism possessed known connections to Rome. The 'friends of the emperor' Rabbi Johanan ben Zakkai and Gamaliel II presided over the first setting of the canon of the Hebrew Scriptures. Rabbi Meir, a Roman who purportedly converted to Judaism on a trip to Judea, organized the Mishnah, and Judah Ha-Nasi, the confidant of the Antonine emperors, began the organization of the central work of Rabbinical Judaism, the Talmud.

There are two 'Talmuds', one called the 'Babylonian Talmud' and the other the 'Jerusalem Talmud', because one was edited in Iraq and the other in Palestine. Each 'Talmud' preserves the 'Halachah' (the legal traditions purportedly inherited by the rabbis following the destruction of the temple), the so-called 'Oral Law', and the Mishnah. Later scholars and redactors added a great number of commentaries to this literature.

We have, unfortunately, only the descriptions recorded in this single body of literature to learn the truth regarding the process that established Rabbinical Judaism following Rome's crushing of the messianic rebellion. There is no Jewish voice that speaks to history, other than those that came from the academies established by the Flavians.

The history that we have been given indicates that the rabbis made a number of changes to Judaism following the rebellion. The first 'Rabbis' caused Jews to abandon Israel, the Temple, Holy War and their Messiah. To replace Israel, Jews were given the Roman Commonwealth, for the Temple the Rabbinical Academy, for Holy War the endless interpretation of Scripture, and for the Messiah, the Rabbi. What they were given is the religion we know today as Rabbinical Judaism. Though this religion has been always seen as a legitimate form of Judaism, it was not the religion of the Jews who brought about the rebellion.

Rabbinical literature records four different but related versions of how the academy that produced the new Judaism was created following the destruction of the Temple in 70 CE. Each of the two versions of *Abot de Rabbi Nathan* ("The Fathers according to Rabbi Nathan") is distinct, while another version is told in the Babylonian Talmud and yet another is found in *Lamentations Rabbah*.

Scholars have experienced severe problems in dating rabbinic material. It is not known exactly when the extant editions of the rabbinic works were created, when the stories that they contain were originally written, or by whom. Further, it is apparent that over the centuries redactors had made numerous changes and additions to the original stories, making it even more difficult to determine the original author's meaning. Such is the case with the tales concerting Zakkai's escape. Nevertheless, the four variations all tell a similar version of the story.

In the summer of 70 CE, during the Roman siege of Jerusalem, a Jewish priest and Pharisee named Johanna (Jochanan) ben Zakkai, the deputy head of the Sanhedrin, defected to the Romans. One version of the story states that he communicated to the Roman camp by shooting an arrow with a message attached to it that stated he was a 'Friend of the Roman General Vespasian' and wished to defect. The Romans somehow communicated back to him a promise of a safe-conduct, but he needed to find a way out of the encircled city.

Rabbi Johanna, with the assistance of a relative who was in charge of a gate, devised a scheme for him to be placed in a coffin and taken out of Jerusalem. His disciples carried their master's coffin out to the city's cemetery and placed it in a burial cave. That night Rabbi ben Zakkai left the coffin and made his way to the Roman camp, where he was taken to Vespasian.

The Rabbi then had an interview with the Roman general. During this meeting Zakkai is described in the rabbinic sources as applying Judaism's 'Star Prophecy', the most precious prophecy of the Jewish people at that time, to Vespasian, stating that the Roman commander would soon become the ruler of the world. Three days after Zakkai's amazing prophecy a messenger came from Rome and stated that Nero had died and Vespasian was to be made emperor.

Vespasian then rewarded Zakkai and his disciples, who had also managed to escape, and gave them a land grant to establish an academy for the study and promotion of Judaism in the coastal town of Jamnia, a town on the Via Maris, the main Roman highway along the Mediterranean Sea.

There are a number of problems with the various stories describing Zakkai's escape, perhaps the least of which being that Vespasian was not present during the siege of Jerusalem; the commander there was his son Titus. Further, when Rabbi Johanna ben Zakkai purportedly escaped from the siege in the summer of 70 CE and 'foresaw' that Vespasian would become the ruler of the world he was already emperor. The most fundamental problem with the legend, however, is that Zakkai, the deputy head of the governing body that presided over Jewish law, chose to apply Judaism's 'Star Prophecy' to a non-Jew.

The application of the Star Prophecy to a non-Jew would be suspect at any time as it would have been in complete violation of Jewish Law and tradition. To have such an act presented in the Jewish canon as the very foundation of modern Judaism demands an explanation. Why would a Jewish scholar create an obviously fictitious tale glorifying the head of the family that had destroyed Jerusalem and razed the Temple? And why would later rabbinic scholars have allowed this tale to remain in their canon, presented as the origin of their religion? Scholars have taken the position that these inconsistencies can never be resolved because of the lack of reliable source material from this era.

The discoveries presented in *Caesar's Messiah,* however, provide us with the means to understand the complex story that describes Zakkai's defection to the Romans. That work showed that the Roman intellectuals who produced the Gospels created them as inter-textual typological literature. They created typological relationships between the Gospels and different texts, particularly Josephus' *Wars of the Jews,* to produce meanings beyond that which is conveyed in the surface narration. To create these relationships they employed elements that are used throughout Hebraic literature to create types, which are parallel concepts, locations and sequences.

Understanding the typological relationship that exists between the Gospels and the histories of Josephus provides the real meaning of the story of Zakkai's escape and subsequent meeting with Vespasian. This is because that story shares parallels with a tale in Flavius Josephus's *Wars of the Jews* regarding the future Roman emperor.

In the story, Josephus, who claimed to have been commander of the Jewish revolutionary forces of Galilee, took refuge with several companions in a cave following the collapse of the defenses of Jotapata. Rather than surrender to the Romans, Josephus entered into a suicide pact with his compatriots. After he and another rebel had dispatched all of the others, however, Josephus blithely decided that they should surrender to the Romans rather than take their own lives. Brought before Vespasian, Josephus proceeded to apply the 'Star Prophesy' to the Roman General. When this came to pass, so to speak, and Vespasian became Emperor, he rewarded Josephus by adopting him into the Flavian family and permitting him to live within the Flavian court at Rome. Josephus' meeting with Vespasian shares numerous parallels with the descriptions in Rabbinical literature of Zakkai's escape. Both events take place during Roman sieges where a Jewish priest escapes in a manner that figuratively brings him back from the dead, is captured by the Romans and taken to Vespasian to whom he, improbably, applies the 'Star Prophecy'. Vespasian then rewards the priest when his prediction comes to pass.

Such parallels are, in and of themselves, unusual enough to raise the question of whether or not the two stories were deliberately linked. It is not merely that the stories share the same plot and circumstances, but these are the only tales that apply the Judaic messianic prophesies to a non- Jew.

Moreover, Josephus' application of the 'Star Prophecy' to Vespasian is the moment when Messianic Judaism was converted into the Caesar cult of Christianity. At that moment, Caesar became the 'Messiah' of Judaism. Below is the passage from *Wars of the Jews* describing Josephus' escape and subsequent interview with Vespasian. Notice that, like Jesus, Josephus was in the cave for three days and was discovered by a woman.

> AND now the Romans searched for Josephus...among the dead; but...he was assisted by a certain supernatural providence; for he withdrew himself from the enemy when he was in the midst of them, and leaped into a certain deep pit...Thus he concealed himself two days; but on the third day, when they had taken a woman who had been with them, he was discovered. Whereupon Vespasian sent immediately and zealously two tribunes...and ordered them to give Josephus their right hands as a security for his life, and to exhort him to come up. Josephus...was not unacquainted with the prophecies contained in the sacred books, as being a priest himself, and just then was he in an ecstasy; he put up a secret prayer to God, and said, "Since it pleaseth thee, who hast created the Jewish nation, to depress the same, and since all their good fortune is gone over to the Romans, and since thou hast made choice of this soul of mine to foretell what is to come to pass hereafter, I willingly give them my hands, and am content to live. And I protest openly that I do not go over to the Romans as a deserter of the Jews, but as a minister from thee." But when those Jews who had fled with him understood that he yielded to those that invited him to come up, they came about him in a body,

and cried out, " O Josephus! art thou still fond of life? ...Thou hast therefore had a false reputation for manhood...we ought to take care that the glory of our forefathers may not be tarnished. We will lend thee our right hand and a sword; and if thou wilt die willingly, thou wilt die as general of the Jews; but if unwillingly, thou wilt die as a traitor to them." As soon as they said this, they began to thrust their swords at him, Upon this Josephus was afraid of their attacking him...trusting himself to the providence of God, he put his life into hazard [in the manner following]: "And now," said he, "since it is resolved among you that you will die, come on, let us commit our mutual deaths to determination by lot...He who had the first lot laid his neck bare to him that had the next, as supposing that the general would die among them immediately; for they thought death, if Josephus might but die with them, was sweeter than life; yet was he with another left to the last, whether we must say it happened so by chance, or whether by the providence of God. And as he was very desirous neither to be condemned by the lot, nor, if he had been left to the last, to imbrue his right hand in the blood of his countrymen, he persuaded him to trust his fidelity to him, and to live as well as himself.

Thus Josephus escaped in the war with the Romans...and was led to Vespasian...Vespasian gave strict orders that he should be kept with great caution, as though he would in a very little time send him to Nero. (War of the Jews, 3,8,1-8)

The following part of the story contains its most important message. To understand its real meaning requires knowing that Josephus was one of the group that created the Gospels to act as a 'type' of the story of Titus' campaign. Understanding the typological relationship between Jesus' ministry and Titus' campaign reveals that the following passage establishes Vespasian as "God the father", and his son Titus as the "Son of God" that the New Testament predicts will destroy Jerusalem. This moment is the beginning of Christianity as we know it.

When Josephus heard him give those orders, he said that he had somewhat in his mind that he would willingly say to himself alone. When therefore they were all ordered to withdraw, excepting Titus and two of their friends, he said, "Thou, O Vespasian, thinkest no more than that thou hast taken Josephus himself captive; but I come to thee as a messenger of greater tidings; for had not I been sent by God to thee, I knew what was the law of the Jews in this case? and how it becomes generals to die. Dost thou send me to Nero? For why? Are Nero's successors till they come to thee still alive? Thou, O Vespasian, art Caesar and emperor, thou, and this thy son. Bind me now still faster, and keep me for thyself, for thou, O Caesar, are not only lord over me, but over the land and the sea." When he had said this, Vespasian supposed that Josephus said this as a cunning trick, in order to his own preservation; but in a little time he was convinced, and believed what he said to be true, God himself erecting his expectations, so as to think of obtaining the empire, and by other signs fore-showing his advancement...Yet did he not set Josephus at liberty from his hands, but bestowed on him suits of clothes, and other precious gifts; he treated him also in a very obliging manner, and continued so to do. (*War of the Jews*, 3,8,9)

For clarification, the following chart outlines the relationship between the parallel escape stories. The first seven parallels have puzzled scholars. With the discovery of the eighth parallel, however, the meaning of the others becomes clear.

1. Both take place during a Roman siege
2. Both involve the defection of a Jewish priest to the Romans
3. In each the priest figuratively returns from the dead
4. Both involve a waiting period of three day
5. In each the priest is taken to Vespasian
6. In each the priest applies the 'Star Prophecy' to Vespasian
7. In each Vespasian rewards the priest
8. Both stories are the beginning of a religion

In my opinion, the parallels between Zakkai and Josephus' escape stories were deliberately created. Such parallel tales could not, by chance, also have been the beginnings of the two religions that superseded messianic Judaism. This is self-evident. The story of Zakkai's escape from Jerusalem was deliberately based upon the depiction of Josephus' escape from Jotapata so as to establish that the founding of Christianity had been a prophetical 'type' of the founding of Rabbinical Judaism. In other words, the story of Zakkai's escape is based on the same typological system the Flavians used to inform posterity that Christianity was a Flavian religion. By linking the story of Zakkai's meeting with Vespasian to that system, the author of the Talmudic tale deliberately identified Rabbinical Judaism as another Flavian religion.

In fact, the entire passage in the Talmud containing Zakkai's surrender to Vespasian is a symbolic landscape that was designed to notify posterity that Caesar was the 'God' that Rabbinical Judaism has worshiped. To explain how the passage achieves this requires a detailed explanation. Therefore, the version of the story found in Gittin 55-57 in the *Babylonian Talmud* is presented below, interspersed with the analysis.

The reader will note that the passage is made up of a series of distinct satires, and that each of these satires seems, on its surface, unfocused and incoherent. However, when these seemingly unrelated and incoherent tales are viewed as a unified satire regarding how and why the Flavians created Rabbinical Judaism; they suddenly come to life and make perfect sense.

The first satire describes a 'Kamza' and a 'Bar Kamza'. Though each of the satires is a distinct story, as a group they create a chronologically accurate depiction of the war between the Romans and the Jews. Thus, the first satire describes the refusal of the Jews to sacrifice to the Roman Emperor, the act of defiance that precipitated the war.

The tale contains a pertinent witticism. The central characters' names are 'Kamza' and 'Bar Kamza', meaning literally 'locust' and 'son of the locust'. The story describes a 'son of the locust' who has his identity mistaken for someone named 'locust'. The confusion regarding the identity of a 'son' caused by different individuals having similar names is a central comic theme within the Gospels, and is repeated here. Further, the son who had his identity mistaken in the Gospels — Titus — was like 'Kamza' in that he had a father named for an insect — Vespasian — whose name means 'wasp'. The satire also clearly states that the Romans attempted to buy their way into the Jew's religious graces before the war began, a fact also shown in *Caesar's Messiah.*

The destruction of Jerusalem came through a Kamza and a Bar Kamza, in this way. A certain man had a friend named Kamza and an enemy named Bar Kamza. He once made a party and said to his servant go and bring Kamza. The man went and brought Bar Kamza. When the man who gave the party found him there he said, See, you tell tales about me; what are you doing here? Get out. Said the other: Since I am here, let me stay and I will pay you for what I eat and drink. He said: I won't. Then let me give you half the cost of the party. No said the other. Then let me pay for the whole party. He still said: No, and he took him by the hand and put him out. Said the other, Since the Rabbis were sitting there and did not stop him, this shows that they agreed with him. I will go and inform them to the Government. He went and said to the Emperor, the Jews are rebelling against you. He said, How can I tell? He said to him: Send them an offering and see whether they will offer it on the altar. So he sent with him a fine calf. While on the way he made a blemish on its upper lip, or as some say on the white of its eye, in a place that we Jews count it a blemish but they do not. The Rabbis were inclined to offer it in order not to offend the Government. Said R. Zechariah b. Abkulas to them: People will say that blemished animals are offered on the altar. They then proposed to kill Bar Kamza so that he would not go and inform against them, but R. Zechariah b. Abkulas said to them. Is one who makes a blemish on consecrated animals to be put to death? R. Johanan thereupon remarked: Through the scrupulousness of R. Zechariah b. Abkulas our House has been destroyed, our Temple burnt and we ourselves exiled from our land. (Gittin 55-56)

The story then presents another satire, this time regarding the Emperor Nero. In it Nero is said to have converted to Judaism and that 'Rabbi Meir' was descended from him. Rabbi Meir was, next to Zakkai, the most important figure in the creation of Rabbinical Judaism. He was Zakkai's student and subsequent head of the Academy. He was also the individual who organized the Mishna, the work that was used as the foundation for the Talmud. This is the first of four descriptions in the story of either a member of the patrician class that either converted or is considering converting to Judaism, or of a Jew who is described as a member of the Roman nobility. In the context of the story this repetition of this theme makes the point that the original leaders of Rabbinical Judaism were either Romans posing as Jews, or Jews who were on Rome's payroll. As we continue, we will go into this subject in depth.

Notice that Nero is afraid that the blame for the destruction of the temple and Jerusalem will fall upon him and not the individuals who actually performed the acts, the Flavians. This satirical bit may document a strategy on the part of the Flavians — who indeed saw themselves as "The Holy One"- to hoist the blame for the war onto Nero and his linage, the Julio-Claudians. By doing so the Flavians may have hoped to deflect any impulse toward revenge on the part of the Zealot survivors away from their family. Nero was also set up as a villain of Christianity by the Flavians, both in Revelation and in their 'official' histories of the era.

> He (the Emperor) sent against them Nero the Caesar. As he was coming he shot an arrow towards the east, and it fell in Jerusalem. He then shot one towards the west, and it again fell on Jerusalem. He shot towards all four points of the compass, and each time it fell in Jerusalem. He said to a certain boy: Repeat to me the last verse of Scripture you have learned. He said: And I will lay my vengeance upon Edom by the hand of my people Israel. He said: The Holy one, blessed be He, desires to lay waste his House and to lay the blame on me. So he ran away and became a proselyte, and Rabbi Meir was descended from him. (Gittin 56)

The next satire deals with the onset of the war. Notice that it also describes another connection between the Roman patrician class and the Jews in power. In this case a 'Jew' of great wealth is described as having his 'seat', or origins, in "the nobility of Rome."

> He then sent against them Vespasian the Caesar who came and besieged Jerusalem for three years. There were in it three men of great wealth, Nakdimon b. Gorion, Ben Kalba Shabua and Ben Zizith Hakeseth. Nakdimon b. Gorion was so called because the sun continued to shine for his sake. Ben Kalba Shabua was so called because one would go into his house hungry as a dog and come out full. Ben Zizith Hakeseth was so called because his fringes (zizith) used to trail on cushions (keseth). Others say he derived the name from the fact that his seat (kise) was among the nobility of Rome. (Gittin 56)

The passage next records the onset of the famine that gripped Jerusalem during the Roman siege. It purports that the Rabbis caused the famine by deliberately setting fire to the stores of grain owned by the wealthy Jews, after the "biryoni" — a word describing the Zealots who had taken control of the city — prevented them from making peace with the Romans.

This sabotage of the Zealots by the rabbis is logical given that Herod, who was described by Josephus as a person not wanting Jews around him, had previously purged the Sanhedrin of anyone he suspected of Maccabean leanings and installed 'rabbis' of his liking. In other words, there would have been a number of 'Jewish' leaders in Jerusalem at this time that held an anti-Zealot pro-Herod/Roman perspective. The satire creates a picture of two types of Jews, one group fighting the Romans and another group of wealthy Jews with connections to Rome who fought against the Zealots.

> One of these said to people of Jerusalem, I will keep you in wheat and barley. A second said I will keep them in wine, oil and salt. The third said, I will keep them in wood. The Rabbis consider the offer of wood the most generous, since R. Hisda used to hand all his keys to his servant save that of the wood for R. Hisda used to say. A storehouse of wheat requires sixty stores of wood for fuel. These men were in a position to keep the city for twenty-one years.

> The biryoni were then in the city. The Rabbis said to them: Let us go out and make peace with the Romans. They would not let them, but on the contrary said, Let us go out and fight them. The Rabbis said: You will not succeed. They then rose up and burnt the stores of wheat and barley so that a famine ensued. (Gittin 56)

The following passage is the most important in the story, in that it provides clear proof that the author is aware of the comic framework that exists between the Gospels and the works of Josephus, documented in *Caesar's Messiah*. Specifically, it repeats the central concept of Gospels/Josephus typology — that of a "Mary" who ate her child during the siege of Jerusalem.

In the following passage a 'Martha' — the Aramaic word for 'Mary' — is described as slowly succumbing to the famine that occurred during the siege. When she ventured out to find food "some dung stuck to her foot" and she died.

Martha the daughter of Boethius was one of the richest women in Jerusalem. She sent her manservant out saying. Go and bring me some fine flour. By the time he went it was sold out. He came and told her. There is no fine flour, but there is white flour. She then said to him, Go and bring me some. By the time he went he found the white flour sold out. He came and told her. There is no white flour but there is dark flour. She said to him, Go and bring me some. By the time he went it was sold out. He returned and said to her: There is no dark flour but there is barley flour. She said, Go and bring me some. By the time he went this was also sold out. She had taken off her shoes, but she said. I will go out and see if I can find anything to eat. Some dung stuck to her foot and she died. Rabban Johanan b. Zakkai applied to her this verse:

"The tender and delicate woman among you that would not adventure to set the sole of her foot upon the ground." (Gittin 56)

The Martha in this passage is the sole 'Mary' described in the Talmud. This parallels *"Wars of the Jews"*, which also has only one 'Mary' depicted within it, the 'Mary' who was starving during the same siege. The author of the Talmudic passage links these 'Marys' by stating that Rabbi Zakkai "applied" a passage to Martha from Deuteronomy regarding a "tender and delicate woman."

Zakkai's use of the phase from Deuteronomy links the "Martha" in the Talmud to the typological framework that exists between the 'cannibal Mary' in Wars of the Jews and the 'Mary' in the Gospels because the phrase he 'applies' is only the beginning of the Biblical passage. Following is the complete passage:

The tender and delicate woman among you, that would not adventure to set the sole of her foot upon the ground for delicateness and tenderness, her eye shall be evil toward the husband of her bosom, and toward her son and toward her daughter.

And toward the young one that cometh out from between her feet and toward the children that she shall bear: for she shall eat them for want of all things secretly in the siege, wherewith thine enemy shall distress thee in thy gates. (Deuteronomy 28: 56-57)

Deuteronomy 28 is the only passage within the Bible that describes a woman eating her son, let alone having done so during a siege, and therefore it is implausible that its 'application' by Zakkai to a 'Mary' who, like the 'Mary' who ate her son in *War of the Jews,* was starving during the same siege, could have been accidental.

Only by 'applying' this exact Biblical passage to a woman named 'Martha' could the author of the story in the Talmud have used Josephus' "cannibal Mary" as a 'type', and thereby linked his tale to the typological system between the Gospels and *Wars of the Jews.* No other name or passage would have created this effect. This is why the author concocted the ludicrous story regarding 'Martha' stepping on dung and perishing. This obviously fictitious story enabled its author to cleverly 'apply' the beginning of the needed scriptural phrase without overtly stating the parts of the passage that related to a mother eating her child. The author expected that a reader who knew of the typological system between the Gospels and *Wars of the Jews* would be able to see the 'unwritten' connection. Notice that this implies that the author expected that the typological system between the Gospels and Wars of the Jews to eventually be discovered and provide a method to understand the real meaning of the story of Zakkai's meeting with Vespasian. Also of interest is the fact that since the author is using the typological relationship between the Christian Gospels and *Wars of the Jews,* this would indicate that Rabbinical Judaism 'sprang' from Christianity, not vice versa, a complete reversal of the heretofore historical understanding. A fact that supports the above interpretation of the passage is that the Talmudic story regarding the 'cannibal Mary' also contains the tale of Zakkai's escape and subsequent application of the 'Star Prophecy' to Vespasian, which, as shown above, is a perfect parallel to the tale of Josephus' escape. This combination of parallels would not have occurred by chance.

There is another, more complicated, link between the 'cannibal Marys' in the Talmud and *Wars of the Jews.* 'Mariamme' is the Hebrew analogue for the Aramaic name 'Martha', and can also be translated as 'Mary.' Therefore, the 'Martha, daughter of Boethius' in the Talmud was based upon a real person —

Mariamme, the daughter of Boethius — the second of two of Herod's wives who were named 'Mariamme.'

Why did the author choose — and clearly he did this deliberately — to link his 'Martha' to the wife of Herod who was the daughter of Boethius? Bear in mind that the real 'daughter of Boethius', was not contemporaneous with the events depicted in the story, she had lived nearly a hundred years before the destruction of the temple. I believe the author chose to name his character 'Martha, daughter of Boethius' to identify the true origin of Rabbinical Judaism and to differentiate that religion from the other Flavian invention — Christianity.

To explain the author's point here requires some background information. Though the effort by Rome to control Judaism had its roots as far back as Julius Caesar, Rabbinical Judaism truly began when, following his destruction of the Maccabean Sanhedrin, Herod brought in a priest named 'Boethius' from Egypt to take control of Jewish governance and legal interpretation. It was with the introduction of Boethius that the Sanhedrin was transformed from a Maccabean religious organization into the Romanized bureaucracy that eventually controlled the academy where Rabbinical Judaism originated. The Herodian Sanhedrin was an essential part of what became Rabbinical Judaism and will be discussed at length below. However, the point that the author is making here by naming his 'cannibal Mary' 'the daughter of Boethius' is simply that she was of a different background than Herod's first wife named 'Mariamme', who was a Maccabean. In other words, the author of the Talmudic tale named his 'Mary' Boethius because that family was associated with the founding of the Herodian Sanhedrin, the organization that became Rabbinical Judaism. This identifies Rabbinical Judaism as a separate religion from Christianity, albeit in a complicated manner, because the 'cannibal Mary' who was involved with its origin was a Boethius, and not a Maccabean, as had been the case with Christianity.

Each of the individual tales that make up the Talmud's story of Zakkai's escape is part of the symbolic landscape the author is creating. As noted above, the individual tales are incoherent in and of themselves, but when viewed as a unified satire depicting the

Flavian invention of Rabbinical Judaism, they make perfect sense. This is also the case with all of the 'applications' of phrases of scripture by Zakkai to the various individuals within the passage. In each case the 'application' seems incoherent in and of itself, but when seen as a method of creating a subtext linking the Flavians to the origin of the religion, all of the 'applications' become coherent.

> Some report that she ate a fig left by R. Zadok, and became sick and died. For R. Zadok observed fasts for forty years in order that Jerusalem might not be destroyed, and he became so thin that when he ate anything the food could be seen as it passed through his throat. When he wanted to restore himself, they used to bring him a fig, and he used to suck the juice and throw the rest away. When Martha was about to die, she brought out all of her gold and silver and threw it in the street, saying: What is the good of this to me, thus giving effect to the verse, They shall cast their silver in the streets. (Gittin 56)

Once again the author has chosen to use a passage that is clearly related to the siege of Jerusalem, Ezekiel VII. Moreover, Ezekiel VII describes an ending to the contract between God and Israel.

> Now is the end come upon thee, and I will send mine anger upon thee, and will judge thee according to thy ways, and will recompense upon thee all thine abominations. And mine eye shall not spare thee, neither will I have pity: but I will recompense thy ways upon thee, and thine abominations shall be in the midst of thee: and ye shall know that I am the LORD.

> Thus saith the Lord GOD; An evil, an only evil, behold, is come. An end is come, the end is come: it watcheth for thee; behold, it is come. They will cast their silver into the streets...(Ezekiel 7: 3-6 & 19)

By the 'application' of Ezekiel VII at this precise point the author cleverly set the stage for the passage that immediately follows, in which Zakkai applied the 'Star Prophecy' to Vespasian and thereby 'ended' Israel's covenant with Yahweh and turned Judaism into a Flavian religion.

The application of the passage from Ezekiel is the exact perspective of the Flavians and the Gospels. That is that the Jews were wicked — because they had rebelled from Rome — and the 'Lord' -Titus- came and punished them. At the very least, by the 'application' of this passage from Ezekiel the author is implying that the Flavians were the agents of God's wrath. In the above passage the author also continues to mimic the black comedy regarding cannibalism found in the New Testament. The passage that described the 'tender and delicate woman' refers to her children as "fruit'.

> You shall eat the fruits of your own body, the flesh of your sons and your daughters, whom the Lord has given you, in the siege and desperate straits in which your enemy shall distress you. (Deuteronomy 28: 53)

Thus, the 'fig' that she and Zadok ate was in fact, her child. As Martha ate the 'fig' after Zadok had sucked out all of its 'juice', it naturally could not pass through her throat — notice that the author highlighted the image of the juice passing through Zadok's throat — and she choked to death. The viciousness of this strain of comedy indicates that not only was the author of the passage not Jewish, but he (or she) had a passionate hatred of them.

Note that the Talmudic depiction of Jerusalem's destruction is also 'Roman' in its coldness and utter lack of any compassion for the plight of the Jews and the destruction of their sacred city. Compare that attitude with that of the author of the following Dead Sea Scroll, which describes a similar event.

> ...all our misdeeds and it is not within our power; for we did not obey...Judah, that all these things should befall us, by evil...his covenant.

> Woe to us...has become burned by fire and overthrow...our destruction, and there is nothing pleasing in it, in...his holy courts have become...Jerusalem, city of [the sanctuary, has been handed over] to wild animals, and there is no...and he avenues...all her fine buildings are desolate...there are no pilgrims in them, all the cities of Judah...our inheritance has become like the desert, no...we no longer hear rejoicing and [there is none] who seeks

God...no one to heal our wounds. All our enemies...our offenses our sins.

Woe to us, for the wrath of God has come upon...that we should congregate with the dead...like an unloved wife Israel neglected her babies and my dear people have become cruel...her young men are desolate, the children of...fleeing from winter when their hands are weak...Ash heaps are now the home of the house of [Israel]...they ask for water but there is no attendant...those who were worth their weight in gold...there is nothing to delight those who drew their strength from scarlet clothing...nor fine gold, their garments bearing jewelry...no longer do my hands tough purple stuff...has risen...the sensitive women of Zion with them…

How lonely she sits the city once full of people...the princess of all of the nations is as desolate as an abandoned woman, and all her daughters are likewise abandoned...like a woman abandoned and miserable, whose husband has left her. All her fine buildings and walls are like a barren woman, all her streets are like a woman confined...like a woman whose life is bitter and all of her daughter[s?] are like those in mourning for their husbands...like those bereft of thief only children...Jerusalem keeps on weeping...tears on her cheek for her children.. (DSS 4Q179)

The Talmudic story then goes on to describe the events that led up to Zakkai's escape and meeting with Vespasian.

Abba Sikra the head of the biryoni in Jerusalem was the son of the sister of Rabban Johanan b. Zakkai. The latter came to him saying, Come and visit me privately. When he came he said to him, How long are you going to carry on in this way and kill all the people with starvation? He replied: What can I do? If I say a word to them, they will kill me. He said: Devise some plan for me to escape. Perhaps I shall be able to save a little. He said to him: Pretend to be ill, and let everyone come and inquire about you. Bring something evil smelling and put it by you so that they will say that you are dead. Let then your disciples get under your bed, but no others, so that they shall not notice that you are still light, since they know that a living being is lighter than a corpse. He did so, and R. Eliezer went under the beir (coffin) from one side and R. Joshua from the other. When they reached the door, some men wanted to put a lance through the beir. He said to them: Shall the Romans say, They have pierced their Master? They wanted to give it a push. He said to them. Shall they say that they pushed their master? They opened the Gate for him and they got out. (Gittin 56)

The following passage describes the meeting where Zakkai indicates that Vespasian is to be the 'God' of the Jews. Though Zakkai uses the word "king", the scriptural passages he applies to Vespasian each pertain not to the coming of a 'king', but of God. We would note that in a number of the versions of this story Zakkai addresses Vespasian with the expression — Peace to you, O King, peace to you O King — in Latin. A Latin-speaking Rabbi being another of the links between Rome and the founders of Rabbinical Judaism.

> When he reached the Romans he said, Peace to you, O King, peace to you O King. He (Vespasian) said: Your life is forfeit on two counts, one because I am not a king and you call me king, and again if I am a King, why did you not come to me before now? He replied: As for your saying that you are not a king, in truth you are a king, since if you were not a king Jerusalem would not be delivered into your hand, as it written, And Lebanon shall fall by a mighty one. Mighty one is an epithet applied only to a king, as it is written, And their mighty one shall be of themselves etc: and Lebanon refers to the sanctuary as it says, This goodly mountain and Lebanon. (Gittin 56)

The author is again making a point by the use of the beginning of a Biblical passage that he expects an informed reader to know *en toto*. When Zakkai states — And their mighty one shall be of themselves etc: — he is referring to Jeremiah 30: 21. Below is the complete passage.

> And their mighty one shall be of themselves and their governor shall proceed from the midst of them; and I shall cause him to draw near, and he shall approach unto me; for who is this that engaged his heart to approach unto me? Saith the Lord.

> And ye shall be my people, and I will be your God. (Jeremiah 30: 21-22)

As in the fanciful story above regarding the 'delicate woman' the author has searched through the Scripture to find just the right phrase to communicate his real point. Here the passage from Jeremiah indicates that "their governor shall proceed from the midst of them' and "shall approach unto me", can certainly be seen as a description of Zakkai's coming to Vespasian, who is known to have seen himself as "God" and, therefore, can logically be seen as the 'Lord' who "will be your God". In other words, Caesar has replaced Yahweh. The author of the Talmudic story actually assists the reader in seeing the implication of the part of the passage he does not quote by including the expression "etc" at the conclusion of the sentence.

This interpretation is especially plausible in light of the fact that a major goal for the Romans in their war with the Jews was to establish Caesar as the god of the Jews. In fact, at this point in history what other incentive would have been sufficient to induce the Flavians to establish a Judaic academy in Judea? Further, within *Caesar's Messiah* the Flavians are shown to have 'applied' Judaic Scripture to themselves to prove that they were 'Gods', the same technique that Zakkai used in the conversation with Vespasian. Since the Flavians set themselves up as the 'God' and the 'Son of God' of Christianity without its faithful knowing it, it is hardly surprising that they achieved the same thing with Rabbinical Judaism, a religion that they are known to have controlled from its beginning.

The Talmudic tale then continues with a description of the meeting between Vespasian and Zakkai. The following passage contains perhaps the most telling 'application' of Scripture to Vespasian – *"God turneth wise men backward and maketh their knowledge foolish."*

> As for your question, why if you are a king I did not come until now, the answer is that the biryoni among us did not let me. He said to him: If there is a jar of honey round which a serpent is wound, would they not break the jar to get rid of the serpent? He could give no answer. R. Joseph, or as some say R. Akiba, applied to him the verse, God turneth wise men backward and maketh their knowledge foolish. He ought to have said to him: We take a pair of tongs and grip the snake and kill it, and leave the jar intact. (Gittin 56)

The phrase "God turneth wise men backward and maketh their knowledge foolish" comes from Isaiah 44, the passage in which God reiterates his 'chosen people' contract with Israel. For Zakkai to apply it to Vespasian simply underlines the meaning of his previous applications from the Bible. That is to say, Vespasian is to be the 'God' of the Jews.

Whether or not one accepts the interpretation of the passage given here, there is something wrong; something illogical, with the founder of Rabbinical Judaism "applying" a precise litany of Scriptures to Vespasian that on its face indicates he sees Vespasian is 'God'. Again, this is clearly suspicious historically as the only religion that the Flavians would have permitted in Judea at this time was one that worshiped them, and Zakkai's circumstances indicate that he needed something to bargain with.

By applying Isaiah 44 to Vespasian, Zakkai is reversing the passage's original meaning, which was that the God of Israel was stronger than other gods. Within the context of Zakkai's usage it is Vespasian who is the stronger God, which was, of course, the Flavian perspective. By defeating Yahweh's chosen people, Vespasian had proven that Caesar was the greater 'God'.

Zakkai's application of the phase *"That frustrateth the tokens of the liars, and maketh diviners mad; that turneth wise men backward, and maketh their knowledge foolish;* indicates the ability of 'God', that is Vespasian, to turn the wisdom and knowledge of 'wise men' against themselves. In other words, by recording that Zakkai believed Vespasian was 'God', the Flavian Caesars were able to have Rabbinical Judaism worship them without its followers knowing it, exactly as they had done to the converts to Christianity.

The use of Isaiah 44 in this context seems to be a comment upon Maccabean Judaism. Notice below that the worship of 'half burned' and 'roasted' meat is condemned as a form of idolatry. These concepts link the passage to the fate of the real Messiah presented in *Caesar's Messiah,* who was roasted and half eaten by his mother. The phrase also states that it would be an 'abomination' to 'fall down' before the 'stock of a tree' and worship a false god, which is transfigured by the Talmud into a reference to the worship of Christians of their crucified Messiah

[5]Yet now hear, O Jacob my servant; and Israel, whom I have chosen:

[6] Thus saith the LORD the King of Israel, and his redeemer the LORD of hosts; I am the first, and I am the last; and beside me there is no God...

[8] Fear ye not, neither be afraid: have not I told thee from that time, and have declared it? ye are even my witnesses. Is there a God beside me? yea, there is no God; I know not any.

[9] They that make a graven image are all of them vanity; and their delectable things shall not profit; and they are their own witnesses; they see not, nor know; that they may be ashamed.

[10] Who hath formed a god, or molten a graven image that is profitable for nothing?

[11] Behold, all his fellows shall be ashamed: and the workmen, they are of men: let them all be gathered together, let them stand up; yet they shall fear, and they shall be ashamed together.

[12] The smith with the tongs both worketh in the coals, and fashioneth it with hammers, and worketh it with the strength of his arms: yea, he is hungry, and his strength faileth: he drinketh no water, and is faint.

[13] The carpenter stretcheth out his rule; he marketh it out with a line; he fitteth it with planes, and he marketh it out with the compass, and maketh it after the figure of a man, according to the beauty of a man; that it may remain in the house.

[14] He heweth him down cedars, and taketh the cypress and the oak, which he strengtheneth for himself among the trees of the forest: he planteth an ash, and the rain doth nourish it.

[15] Then shall it be for a man to burn: for he will take thereof, and warm himself; yea, he kindleth it, and baketh bread; yea, he maketh a god, and worshippeth it; he maketh it a graven image, and falleth down thereto.

¹⁶ He burneth half of it in the fire; with part thereof he eateth flesh; he roasteth roast, and is satisfied: yea, he warmeth himself, and saith, Aha, I am warm, I have seen the fire:

¹⁷ And the residue thereof he maketh a god, even his graven image: he falleth down unto it, and worshippeth it, and prayeth unto it, and saith, Deliver me; for thou art my god.

¹⁸ They have not known nor understood: for he hath shut their eyes, that they cannot see; and their hearts, that they cannot understand.

¹⁹ And none considereth in his heart, neither is there knowledge nor understanding to say, I have burned part of it in the fire; yea, also I have baked bread upon the coals thereof; I have roasted flesh, and eaten it: and shall I make the residue thereof an abomination? shall I fall down to the stock of a tree?

²⁰ He feedeth on ashes: a deceived heart hath turned him aside, that he cannot deliver his soul, nor say, Is there not a lie in my right hand?

²¹ Remember these, O Jacob and Israel; for thou art my servant: I have formed thee; thou art my servant: O Israel, thou shalt not be forgotten of me...

²³ Sing, O ye heavens; for the LORD hath done it: shout, ye lower parts of the earth: break forth into singing, ye mountains, O forest, and every tree therein: for the LORD hath redeemed Jacob, and glorified himself in Israel.

²⁴ Thus saith the LORD, thy redeemer, and he that formed thee from the womb, I am the LORD that maketh all things; that stretcheth forth the heavens alone; that spreadeth abroad the earth by myself;

²⁵ That frustrateth the tokens of the liars, and maketh diviners mad; that turneth wise men backward, and maketh their knowledge foolish; (Isaiah 44: 5-25)

Finally, there is another comic point created by linking this particular passage from Isaiah to the dialogue regarding the "honey pot" that is surrounded by a "serpent." By claiming that

Vespasian will "turn wise men backward", Zakkai is indicating the purpose of the new Flavian religion of Rabbinical Judaism, which was to use the "honey pot" of their religion to control the masses. Within the context of the conversation the "serpent" is clear enough; it refers to the messianic zealots who controlled the city. The "honey pot", therefore, is Judaism itself, and is being referred to here as such because the Flavians recognized that the messianic religion could be used for control over the *hoi polloi.* The Messiah and Judaism were not to be 'broken', but rather were a 'honey pot' to be preserved as used by the imperial family to control its subjects.

The next passage in the Talmudic story is fascinating for two reasons: first, because the scriptural 'application' by Zakkai seems to indicate that the Romans paid him a bribe for his labors; and also because the same bizarre tale concerning the healing of Vespasian's foot was recorded in one ancient version of Josephus' parallel interview with Vespasian.

> At this point a messenger came to him from Rome saying, Up, for the Emperor is dead, and the nobles of Rome have decided to make you head of the State. He had just finished putting on one boot. When he tried to put on the other he could not. He tried to take off the first but it would not come off. He said: What is the meaning of this" R. Johanan said to him: Do not worry: the good news has done it, as it says, Good tidings make the bone fat. What is the remedy? Let someone whom you dislike come and pass before you, as it is written, A broken spirit driest up the bones. He did so, and the boot went on. He said to him: Seeing that you are so wise, why did you not come to me till now? He said: Have I not told you? He retorted: I too have told you.

The passage in the Bible that pertains to a "broken spirit" drying the bone is Proverbs 17:22. Below is the passage and the one that follows it.

> A merry heart does good, like medicine, but a broken spirit dries the bones. A wicked man accepts a bribe behind the back to pervert the ways of justice. (Proverbs 17:22 & 23)

The passage may also provide a glimpse into how the Flavians controlled Rabbinical Judaism. By stating that they will make the "Wise Men"'s knowledge foolish the author seems to be communicating the idea that Rome did not create an entire new group of Jewish priests, but rather simply establish a group of leaders under Roman control (the Patriarchs) who 'made foolish' those Jewish priests that already existed.

> He said: I am going, and will send someone to take my place. You can however—, make a request of me and I will grant it. He said to him: Give me Jabneh and its Wise Men, and the family chain of Rabban Gamaliel, and physicians to heal R.*Zadok*. R. Joseph, or some say R. Akiba, applied to him the verse, God turneth wise men backward and maketh their knowledge foolish. He ought to have said to him: Let them [the Jews] off this time. He however, thought that so much he would not grant, and so even a little would not be saved. (Gittin 56)

The next part of the Talmudic tale contains the story's most interesting literary device. In it "Zadok" is brought back from the dead by reversing the process that led to Martha's starvation above. Whereas Martha went from looking from flour to coarse meal, "Zadok" goes from the coarse meal to flour. The comic point is that to recover from starvation, you must reverse the process that caused it. Once again the 'reversal motif' is in play here. The author is hereby also providing a clue to the condition that actually killed Martha — starvation. This in turn helps to illuminate the meaning of the 'delicate lady' passage: that is to say, because she was starving Martha ate her child.

> How did physicians heal R. Zadok? The first day they let him drink water in which bran had been soaked: on the next day water in which there had been coarse meal: on the next day water in which there had been flour, so that his stomach expanded little by little. (Gittin 56)

The next part of the passage, keeping with the chronology of events during the war, describes Titus' assault upon Jerusalem. A number of elements in the passage confirm the premise that the story was designed to document the divinity of the Flavians. First, Titus asks the question — Where is their God, the rock in whom they trusted? This phrase comes from Deuteronomy 32: 37, and is a statement spoken by God.

> He will say: Where are their gods, the rock in which they sought refuge?
> Who ate the fat of their sacrifices, and drank the wine of their drink offering/ Let them rise and help you, and be your refuge. Now see that I, even I, am He, and there is no God besides Me; I kill and I make alive. (Deuteronomy 32:37-39)

Titus then proceeds to desecrate the house of Yahweh and thereby prove himself the greater 'God'. Of note is the statement that Titus "thought that he had slain himself". The Hebrew word used in the statement for 'himself' is a euphemism for God, which completely clarifies both the passage and the entire story. Further, the expression that is translated below as "mighty in self-restraint" literally means "mighty and hard", which in this context is certainly a joke regarding Titus' sexual prowess.

> Vespasian sent Titus who said, Where is their God, the rock in whom they trusted? This was the wicked Titus who blasphemed and insulted heaven. What did he do? He took a harlot by the hand and entered the Holy of Holies and spread out a scroll of the Law and committed a sin on it. He then took a sword and slashed the curtain. Miraculously blood spurted out, and he thought that he had slain himself, as it says, Thine adversaries have roared in the midst of thine assembly, they have set up their ensigns for signs. Abba Hanan said: Who is a mighty one like thee unto thee O Jah? Who is like thee mighty in self-restraint, that Thou didst hear the blaspheming and insults of that wicked man and kept silent? In the school of R. Ishmael it was taught: Who is like thee among the gods (elim)? Who is like thee among the dumb ones (illemin). Titus further took the curtain and shaped it like a basket and brought all the vessels of the Sanctuary and put them in it, and then put them on board ship to go and triumph with them in his city, as it says, And withal I saw the wicked buried and they that come to the grave and they that had done right went away from the holy place and were forgotten in the city. Read not keburim [buried] but kebuzim collected: read not veyishtakehu [and were not forgotten} but veyishtabehu [and triumphed] Some say that keburim [can be rescued], because even things that were buried were disclosed to them. (Gittin 56)

No Jewish author would apply the words of God to a Roman about to desecrate the Holy of Holies, let alone from a passage that proclaimed the speaker to have "no Gods besides me". Given the known desire of the Flavians to become the Gods of the Jews, what other interpretation is even possible here than that the author is proclaiming the divinity of the Flavians?

The concluding satire contains the most concrete description of the Flavians effort to control Rabbinical Judaism. It describes an "Onkelos" who raises Titus, Balaam and Jesus from the dead with help from a "necromancer". In the version of the passage that we give below, Onkelos is described, flatly, as the nephew of the emperor Titus. In another version it states that Onkelos was the son of Kolomikos who was the son of Titus' sister, in other words, Titus' grand nephew. This description is important in that it depicts a genealogy known to historians. Titus did have a sister who had a son named Clemens, corrupted above as "Kolomikos".

In *Caesar's Messiah,* "Clemens", the son of Titus' sister, Flavia Domitilla, was shown to have been Pope Clemens the First, the Pope who, according to Jerome, was ordained by Peter himself. Because Clemens was recorded as having been a Pope, the fact that his son "Onkelos" was a convert to Judaism is very notable.

Onkelos was not merely a Jewish proselyte but the composer of the Targum, a key part of the foundation literature of Rabbinical Judaism. In fact, the official Targum to the Pentateuch is designated by the name "Onkelos" as homage to its author — Titus's nephew. His labors are referred to in Megillah 3a as follows:

> Rab Jeremiya, according to others Rab Hiya bar Abba says: "According to the statement by Rab Eliezer and Rab Josua, Onkelos the proselyte has said, that is, has orally formulated the Targum of the Torah."

It is hard to imagine that both of the versions of Judaism to have emerged at this time would have circumstantially had traditions stating that members of the Flavian family were its leaders. A more solid explanation is simply that the traditions reflect the insertion of Flavians into positions of power in these religions for the purpose of controlling them.

The story describing Onkelos is also interesting in that it links Titus and Jesus to Balaam. Balaam is a complex figure in the Old Testament, who refuses to curse Israel though his neighbors beg him to do so. God communicated to Balaam the promise of the Messiah, the "Star". This was the prophecy that to quote Josephus, "did most elevate" the zealots who waged war against the Roman Empire.

> He hath said, which heard the words of God, and knew the knowledge of the most High, which saw the vision of the Almighty, falling into a trance, but having his eyes open:
>
> I shall see him, but not now: I shall behold him, but not nigh: there shall come a Star out of Jacob, and a Sceptre shall rise out of Israel, and shall smite the corners of Moab, and destroy all the children of Sheth.
>
> And Edom shall be a possession, Seir also shall be a possession for his enemies; and Israel shall do valiantly. (Numbers 24:16-18)

This was the prophecy that Josephus and Zakkai 'applied' to Vespasian and thereby reversed its meaning from envisioning a Jewish Messiah to a Roman one. In the satire a Biblical passage is once again reversed. In the original version God's statement "Thou shalt not seek their peace nor their prosperity' is a curse upon the enemies of Israel, in the satire the statement becomes a curse against Israel.

> [1] He that is wounded in the stones, or hath his privy member cut off, shall not enter into the congregation of the LORD.
>
> [2] A bastard shall not enter into the congregation of the LORD; even to his tenth generation shall he not enter into the congregation of the LORD.
>
> [3] An Ammonite or Moabite shall not enter into the congregation of the LORD; even to their tenth generation shall they not enter into the congregation of the LORD for ever:

[4] Because they met you not with bread and with water in the way, when ye came forth out of Egypt; and because they hired against thee Balaam the son of Beor of Pethor of Mesopotamia, to curse thee.

[5] Nevertheless the LORD thy God would not hearken unto Balaam; but the LORD thy God turned the curse into a blessing unto thee, because the LORD thy God loved thee.

[6] Thou shalt not seek their peace nor their prosperity all thy days for ever. (Deuteronomy 23: 1-7)

Onkelos, son of Kalonymus, was the nephew of the emperor, Titus. Onkelos was thinking about becoming a ger, a convert to Judaism. So he went and, with the aid of a necromancer, raised his uncle Titus from the dead and asked him, "Who is held in the highest regardin the Other World?" Titus answered, "Israel." "What then," Onkelos asked, "would you say about my joining them?" Said Titus: 'Their observances are so numerous that it is impossible to endure them. Instead, go and attack the Jews in your world, and you will become master over them, as it is written, 'Her adversaries are now masters' (Lamentations 1:5); whoever harasses Israel becomes a master of men."Next Onkelos went and, with the aid of a necromancer, raised Balaam from the dead. He also asked him, "Who is held in the highest regard in the Other World?" Balaam answered, "Israel." "What then," Onkelos asked, "do you say about my joining them?" Balaam said: 'Thou shalt not seek their peace nor their prosperity all thy days forever." — Deuteronomy 23:7 (Gittin 56-57)

Then Onkelos went and, with the aid of a necromancer, raised Jesus from the dead. He asked him, "Who is held in the highest regard in the Other World?" Jesus said, "Israel." "What do you say about my joining them?" Jesus said, "Seek their welfare, seek not their harm. Whoever touches them touches the apple of God's eye. Observe the differences in behavior between the sinners in Israel and the prophets among the nations of the world." (Gittin 57)

The story ends with another short passage regarding "Bar Kamza", the son of the insect, whose shunning by the rabbis led to the war between the Romans and the Jews. The passage begins with:

> It has been taught: Note from the incident how serious a thing it is
> to put a man to shame, for God espoused the cause of Bar Kamza
> and destroyed His house and burnt his temple. (Gittin 57)

This statement is an amazing declaration. Not only does it confirm
the premise that the 'son of the Locust', "Bar Kazma" is a satire of
Titus, the 'son of the wasp', as it was obviously Titus' cause that
God "espoused" by destroying the temple, but it discloses the real
reason for the war — the vanity of the Caesars. The entire
holocaust of the war and the creation of Christianity and
Rabbinical Judaism were brought about simply because of "how
serious a thing it is to put a man to shame". When the man put to
shame is a megalomaniac with unlimited power it can be very
serious indeed. The passage goes on to note Titus's assault on
Jerusalem.

> Onkelos son of Kolomikos was the son of Titus' sister. He had a
> mind to convert himself to Judaism. He went and raised Titus by
> magical arts, and he asked him: Who is the most repute in the
> other world? He replied: Israel. What then, he said, about joining
> them? He said: Their observances are burdensome and you will
> not be able to carry them out. Go and attack them in that world
> and you will be at the top, as it is written, Her adversaries have
> become her head etc.: whoever harasses Israel becomes head.
> (Gittim 56)

These stories seemed to have been placed into the Jews' canon by
the Roman administrators of Rabbinical Judaism to document the
creation of the religion by the Flavians.

CONCLUSION

Finally, in her plays *The Merry Wives of Windsor* and *As You Like It*, Emilia Bassano documented her view of the murder of Christopher Marlowe, as well as her love for him. As discussed above, Marlowe's play *The Jew of Malta* opens with his character Barabas counting his vast wealth, and explaining the value of private secrets in accumulating such estates:

> And thus methinks should men of judgment frame
> Their means of traffic from the vulgar trade,
> And, as their wealth increaseth, so inclose
> Infinite riches in a little room.

(I, 1)

Realizing that the details of Marlowe's execution had been falsely described in the Coroner's Report, Emelia built on Marlowe's verse in order to record the truth for posterity. Here is her statement, which is a model of brevity and discretion, and yet speaks volumes:

> When a man's verses cannot be understood, nor a man's good wit be seconded by the forward child, understanding, it strikes a man more dead than a great reckoning in a little room" (*As You Like It*, III, 3).

She echoed the expression *'le recknynge'* or 'the reckoning', given in the Coroner's Inquest as the cause of Marlowe's death, adding that the event occurred in "a little room" so that no one could mistake that she was referring to the poet who so tellingly used that phrase in *Jew of Malta*. Furthermore, she was also playing with Marlowe's double entendre, and referring to his 'reckoning' that Christianity had been invented by Gentile nobles so that they could rule over the masses. And, in the genius of a triple entendre, she hinted at the deeper meaning of the word 'reckoning' — understanding — to create a more honest description as to why she believed Marlowe was murdered: that is, he was killed because of what he had understood.

Emilia wanted to record the fact that his verse should be 'understood' and his wit 'seconded'. With the Shakespearean literature she would make certain that Marlowe would not die 'a second death' because she would 'understand' and 'second' his work. It is interesting to consider that the Shakespearean literature began as Emilia's homage to Marlowe.

The surface meaning of this passage is also, ironically, expressing deep sadness about readers who are too dense to understand "a man's verses", or to laugh at his "good wit". For such readers, Marlowe remains as a dead man; and so also, 'Shakespeare' depends on those of us who are alive, to understand what she is trying to tell us.

Emilia also placed her testimony in *The Merry Wives of Windsor*. As the play begins, Shallow and Slender are discussing turning Falstaff's abuse of them into a 'Star Chamber' matter. The Star Chamber was the institution that dealt with matters of heresy and was the English equivalent of the Holy Roman Inquisition. As I will show, this should be read as an allegory of Christopher Marlowe's situation: at the time of his murder Marlowe was also under investigation by the Star Chamber for the crime of 'heresy', and it was responsible for his murder.

[Enter SHALLOW, SLENDER, and SIR HUGH EVANS]

SHALLOW

Sir Hugh, persuade me not; I will make a Star-
chamber matter of it: if he were twenty Sir John
Falstaffs, he shall not abuse Robert Shallow, esquire.

SLENDER

In the county of Gloucester, justice of peace
and 'Coram.'

(I, 1)

Shallow describes himself as 'Custalourum' and Rato-lorum, words that are based upon 'Custos Rotulorum', the keeper of the Judicial archives. This is a reference to not only the keeping of the records of the crimes of Titus and his religion against the Jews, but to the 'legal archive' concerning Marlowe that Shallow is about to create in the passage:

SHALLOW

Ay, cousin Slender, and 'Custalourum.

SLENDER

Ay, and 'Rato-lorum' too; and a gentleman born, master parson; who writes himself 'Armigero,' in any bill, warrant, quittance, or obligation, 'Armigero.'

SHALLOW

Ay, that I do; and have done any time these
three hundred years.

SLENDER

All his successors gone before him hath done't; and all his ancestors that come after him may: they may give the dozen white luces in their coat.

SHALLOW

It is an old coat.

SIR HUGH EVANS

The dozen white louses do become an old coat well; it agrees well, passant; it is a familiar beast to man, and signifies love.

SHALLOW

The luce is the fresh fish; the salt fish is an old coat.

SLENDER

I may quarter, coz.

SHALLOW

You may, by marrying.

SIR HUGH EVANS

It is marring indeed, if he quarter it.

SHALLOW

Not a whit.

Slender seemingly confuses 'successor' with 'ancestor' but is simply referring to Falstaff as both Titus and the character in the play, which would have been Emilia's position concerning the Christian nobility. In her eyes, they were the heirs to Titus and, like Falstaff, an iteration of his evil. They have both fresh and old fish on their coats because the 'fishers of men' — that is 'Christian cannibals' — have been at it since the start of the religion and are still at it as the play begins.

The playwright repeats the possibility of taking the matter of Falstaff's abuse to the 'council' or 'Privy Council', an arm of the Star Chamber. Evans points out that the Council wants only to hear 'the fear of 'Got' — God — not a riot. This was, of course, the position of the Christian state. They wanted their subjects to 'fear Got' and thereby accept the 'divine right' of the nobility. They certainly did not want 'a riot', which would have occurred if Marlowe's 'book against scripture' had been made public. Though the playwright's meaning here is veiled, it will become clear shortly.

SIR HUGH EVANS

Yes, py'r lady; if he has a quarter of your coat, there is but three skirts for yourself, in my simple conjectures: but that is all one. If Sir John Falstaff have committed disparagements unto you, I am of the church, and will be glad to do my benevolence to make atonements and compromises between you.

SHALLOW

The council shall bear it; it is a riot.

SIR HUGH EVANS

It is not meet the council hear a riot; there is no fear of Got in a riot: the council, look you, shall desire to hear the fear of Got, and not to hear a riot; take your vizaments in that.

SHALLOW

Ha! o' my life, if I were young again, the sword should end it.

SIR HUGH EVANS

It is petter that friends is the sword, and end it: and there is also another device in my prain, which peradventure prings goot discretions with it: there is Anne Page, which is daughter to Master Thomas Page, which is pretty virginity.

SLENDER

Mistress Anne Page? She has brown hair, and speaks small like a woman.

SIR HUGH EVANS

It is that fery person for all the orld, as just as you will desire; and seven hundred pounds of moneys, and gold and silver, is her grandsire upon his death's-bed—Got deliver to a joyful resurrections! —give, when she is able to overtake seventeen years old: it were a goot motion if we leave our pribbles and prabbles, and desire a marriage between Master Abraham and Mistress Anne Page.

SLENDER

Did her grandsire leave her seven hundred pound?

SIR HUGH EVANS

Ay, and her father is make her a petter penny.

SLENDER

I know the young gentlewoman; she has good gifts.

SIR HUGH EVANS

Seven hundred pounds and possibilities is goot gifts.

SHALLOW

Well, let us see honest Master Page. Is Falstaff there?

SIR HUGH EVANS

Shall I tell you a lie? I do despise a liar as I do despise
one that is false, or as I despise one that is not true. The
knight, Sir John, is there; and, I beseech you, be ruled by
your well-willers. I will peat the door for Master Page.

[Knocks]

What, hoa! Got pless your house here!

PAGE

[Within]

Who's there?

[Enter PAGE]

SIR HUGH EVANS

Here is Got's plessing, and your friend, and
Justice Shallow; and here young Master Slender,
that peradventures shall tell you another tale, if matters
grow to your likings.

PAGE

I am glad to see your worships well. I thank you for my
venison, Master Shallow.

SHALLOW

Master Page, I am glad to see you: much good do it your good heart! I wished your venison better; it was ill killed. How doth good Mistress Page?—and I thank you always with my heart, la! with my heart.

PAGE

Sir, I thank you.

SHALLOW

Sir, I thank you; by yea and no, I do.

PAGE

I am glad to see you, good Master Slender.

The following lines are among the most important and poignant in all the Shakespearean plays and are a description of the fate of Christopher Marlowe. Slender asks about Page's 'fallow greyhound' that was 'outrun on Cotsall'. The word 'Cotsall' here is a reference to the 'Cotsall games' that took place on the seventh Sunday following Easter, usually on May 30 or 31. The playwright is using symbolism here to describe Marlowe's fate. Marlowe was 'fallow' — had yellowish brown hair — and was 'outrun' — caught and murdered — on the 'Cotsall', that is May 30. He 'could not be judged' because a public trial would expose the information the Star Chamber was trying to conceal — Marlowe's understanding of the satire in the New Testament.

The lines regarding 'confessing' and 'fault' are, I suspect, regarding Marlowe's refusal to confess to the Star Chamber who he was working with, and the 'fault' Emilia felt over Marlowe's fate. The playwright helps the reader understand that the play, and therefore this key passage, is regarding Marlowe by including both a number of references to his plays in *The Merry Wifes of Windsor* and by the creation of another, more obvious, homage to him shown below.

Notice that, within this interpretation, Marlowe is described as 'good and fair', this description links to sonnet 105 that states that until the 'fair boy' that 'fair, kind and true' have never 'kept seat in one'. This supports the premise that Marlowe was Emilia's inspiration for Shakespeare: the 'fair boy' of the sonnets.

> SLENDER
>
> How does your fallow greyhound, sir? I heard say he was outrun on Cotsall.

> PAGE
>
> It could not be judged, sir.

> SLENDER
>
> You'll not confess, you'll not confess.

> SHALLOW
>
> That he will not. 'Tis your fault, 'tis your fault; 'tis a good dog.

> PAGE
>
> A cur, sir.

> SHALLOW
>
> Sir, he's a good dog, and a fair dog: can there be more said? he is good and fair.

(I, 1, 82)

Falstaff enters with his men. Shallow accuses him of breaking into his 'lodge', symbolically indicating Jerusalem, and again states he will take the matter to the Council. Falstaff replies that the information would be better held "in counsel", that is in private, because the Council will laugh at him if he tries to make tell them the truth of Christianity. The playwright makes certain the reader understands that the play is in a 'Marlovian' context: the very next line following the discussion mentions Mephistopheles, the Devil's name from Marlowe's play *Doctor Faustus*. As I interpret the passage, therefore, it is suggesting that Marlowe tried to inform the Star Chamber and the English nobility of the truth of the origins of Christianity but was laughed at and executed. This is

why Emilia continued with the 'in counsel' representation of
Flavian Christianity through the Shakespearean satires.

SHALLOW

Knight, you have beaten my men, killed my deer,
and broke open my lodge.

FALSTAFF

But not kissed your keeper's daughter?

SHALLOW

Tut, a pin! this shall be answered.

FALSTAFF

I will answer it straight; I have done all this. That is now
answered.

SHALLOW

The council shall know this.

FALSTAFF

'Twere better for you if it were known in counsel: you'll
be laughed at.

(I,1,111)

SIR HUGH EVANS

Pauca verba, Sir John; goot worts.

FALSTAFF

Good worts! good cabbage. Slender, I broke your head:
what matter have you against me?

SLENDER

Marry, sir, I have matter in my head against you; and
against your cony-catching rascals, Bardolph, Nym, and
Pistol.

BARDOLPH

You Banbury cheese!

SLENDER

Ay, it is no matter.

PISTOL

How now, Mephostophilus!

(I, 1, 121)

The following passage from the play confirms its subtext is about Marlowe's murder and is perhaps the saddest and most personal in all of the plays. First, for clarification, here is the beginning of Marlowe's poem "From a Passionate Shepard to his Love":

> COME live with me and be my Love,
> And we will all the pleasures prove
> That hills and valleys, dale and field,
> And all the craggy mountains yield.
>
> There will we sit upon the rocks
> And see the shepherds feed their flocks,
> By shallow rivers, to whose falls
> Melodious birds sing madrigals.
>
> There will I make thee beds of roses
> And a thousand fragrant posies,
> A cap of flowers and a kirtle
> Embroider'd all with leaves of myrtle.

Marlowe's poem was the basis for the following passage in *The Merry Wives of Windsor*:

> Sir Hugh Sings:
>
> To shallow rivers, to whose falls
> Melodious birds sings madrigals;
> There will we make our peds of roses,
> And a thousand fragrant posies.

> To shallow—
> Mercy on me! I have a great dispositions to cry.

(III, 1)

After stating that the song makes the character feel like crying, Emilia then creates her own verse to the poem by inserting a phrase from the beginning of Psalm 137. In doing so she changes the theme from a description of the false Jesus — the Shepard — to that of Hebrew vengeance.

> Melodious birds sing madrigals —
> When as I sat in Pabylon —
> And a thousand vagram posies.
> To shallow —

By inserting the beginning of Psalm 137 into Marlowe's poem, Emilia brought into play the fiercest piece of Hebrew revenge literature in the Bible. The Psalm graphically describes her desires to destroy the Gentiles — the 'Children of Edom' — who had killed Marlowe. The passage is important in that it also conveys the intensity of emotion Emilia held for Marlowe: the very mention of his poem bringing her character to tears. The Psalm is given below.

By the rivers of Babylon, there we sat down, yea, we wept, when we remembered Zion. We hanged our harps upon the willows in the midst thereof. For there they that carried us away captive required of us a song; and they that wasted us required of us mirth, saying, Sing us one of the songs of Zion. How shall we sing the LORD's song in a strange land?

If I forget thee, O Jerusalem, let my right hand forget her cunning. If I do not remember thee, let my tongue cleave to the roof of my mouth; if I prefer not Jerusalem above my chief joy. Remember, O LORD, the children of Edom in the day of Jerusalem; who said, Rase it, rase it, even to the foundation thereof. O daughter of Babylon, who art to be destroyed; happy shall he be, that rewardeth thee as thou hast served us. Happy shall he be, that taketh and dasheth thy little ones against the stones.

The premise that Emilia and Marlowe had been lovers is supported by another passage from *As You Like It* that uses the same technique as above — the blending in of quotes from Marlowe's work with Shakespeare's verse. In that play a lovesick woman describes Marlowe as a 'dead shepherd' and states he had a "saw of might", in other words that she found his insights to be powerful. She then quotes perhaps Marlowe's most famous line about love, from the poem of the same name: *"Who ever loved that loved not at first sight?",* which, in the context that it occurs — a statement by a lovesick woman — is almost certainly a comment on the actual relationship between 'Kit' Marlowe and Emilia.

> Dead shepherd, now I find thy saw of might:
> "Who ever loved that loved not at first sight?"

> *(III, 5, 82-83)*

EPILOGUE

As I walk the streets of New York I pass by Hassidic Jews, unmistakable in their dark suits, hats and beards. They are also identifiable by their spirit, which seems hermetically sealed. They take no notice of me and gaze into another world. They are the descendants of the religious warriors that rebelled from Rome and were punished by having their future poisoned. A determined group, they learned how to fight back, though they seem as unaware of how the scars effect them today as they are of me as we walk past each other.

later I walked by Christians leaving church services. The Caesars wanted their comic Judaism to become widespread so that when the meaning of the New Testament was discovered, their legacy would be vast and immortal. They believed that the pain that Christians would experience when they learned the truth would contribute to their legacy.

As I mentioned in *Caesar's Messiah*, after I made my discoveries I did not publish them for a number of years because I knew they would cause pain. But in the end I made them public because every human has the right to the truth, even a painful one.

Without the truth we cannot make use of our intelligence. This was one of the reasons that the Caesars developed their religions. They did not wish their subjects to think clearly, as this might lead them to question why a small group ruled over millions. I hope that those who experienced any pain from my work will understand my reason for publishing it. I wanted to the crimes the oligarchs had committed against us, and are committing against us, to become visible.

The Caesars will not have the legacy they wanted. The blunder in their calculation was to have believed that posterity would care about individuals who only cared about themselves. This error reverses their typology. Their literature does not show them as gods, but as fools whose vanity caused them to lose the chance for true immortality.

Real legacy is given to those who have given real benefit. Had the Caesars thought more clearly they would not have replaced technological progress with Christianity and the Dark Ages.

I had dedicated *Caesar's Messiah* to the 'star-crossed lovers' Kit and Emilia, I wish to place my dedication of this work to my wife, Elisa, here, next to my analysis of Emilia's relationship with Marlowe.

I would hope that my dedication might serve as an example of how we can bend the typology of hatred into something worthwhile. No matter how clever, literature that stems from hatred will one day not be worth a single strand of my wife's hair.

For Elisa
At true knowledge's heart is love,
And knowledge of love is through your heart.

J.E.A.

BIBLIOGRAPHY

Ancient primary sources are called out so frequently in this volume that we chose to use MLA in-line style references for these items, which can be readily located in libraries, or online, in various editions & translations. *Caesar's Messiah* is also referenced in MLA style. This bibliography lists the modern secondary sources used.

'A Conversation on the Caesar's Messiah Thesis', *Freethought Nation* <http://freethoughtnation.com/a-conversation-on-the-caesars-messiah-thesis/> [accessed 17 March 2014]

Amit, Florence, *Three Caskets of Interpretation* (Google Play edition, 2012)

Anderson, Mark, 'Shakespeare's Good Book', *Valley Advocate* (Massachusetts, 10 March 1994) <http://www.shakespeare-oxford.com/?p=2160> [accessed 9 March 2014]

Barker, Margaret, *The Great Angel: A Study of Israel's Second God* (Louisville, Ky.: Westminster/John Knox Press, 1992)

'Bassano', *Jewish Encyclopedia*, 1906 <http://www.jewishencyclopedia.com/articles/2642-bassano> [accessed 14 March 2014]

Bauer, Bruno, *Christ and the Caesars: The Origin of Christianity from Romanized Greek Culture* (A. Davidonis, 1998)

Bell, Albert A., 'Josephus the Satirist? A Clue to the Original Form of the "Testimonium Flavianum"', *The Jewish Quarterly Review*, 67 (1976), 16 <http://dx.doi.org/10.2307/1454525>

Bergmann, Dale, 'Paul's Missionary Journey'
<http://www.welcometohosanna.com/PAULS_MISSIONARY_J
OURNEYS/3mission_1.html> [accessed 16 March 2014]

Bettenson, Henry Scowcroft, *Documents of the Christian Church*
(Oxford University Press, H. Milford, 1943)

Bevington, D, 'A.L. Rowse's Dark Lady', in *Aemilia Lanyer:
Gender, Genre, and the Canon*, by Marshall Grossman
(University Press of Kentucky, 1998)

Bloom, Harold, *Shakespeare: The Invention of the Human* (New
York: Riverhead Books, 1998)

Bowers, Fredson, *Elizabethan Revenge Tragedy 1587-1642.
[1940].* (Princeton University Press, 1971)

Burkert, Walter, *Ancient Mystery Cults* (Harvard University Press,
1987)

Carotta, Francesco, *Jesus Was Caesar: On the Julian Origin of
Christianity : An Investigative Report* (Soesterberg: Aspekt,
2005)

————, 'The Gospels as Diegetic Transposition', 2007
<http://carotta.de/subseite/texte/articula/Escorial_en.pdf>
[accessed 16 March 2014]

Carrier, Richard, *Proving History: Bayes's Theorem and the Quest
for the Historical Jesus* (Amherst, N.Y.: Prometheus Books, 2012)

Carrington, Cliff, 'Gophna to Galilee: The Bridge Between Jewish
and Christian Beginnings' <http://carrington-
arts.com/cliff/Gophna2.htm> [accessed 16 March 2014]

'Carringtons Classical & Christian Library' <http://carrington-
arts.com/cliff/cccl.html> [accessed 26 February 2014]

'CATHOLIC ENCYCLOPEDIA: Saint Petronilla'
<http://www.newadvent.org/cathen/11781b.htm> [accessed 26
February 2014]

Courtney, Gary, *ET TU, JUDAS? Then Fall Jesus!* (iUniverse, 2004)

Duffin, Ross W., *Shakespeare's Songbook* (W. W. Norton & Company, 2004)

Ehrman, Bart D, *Did Jesus Exist?: The Historical Argument for Jesus of Nazareth* (New York: HarperOne, an imprint of HarperCollinsPublishers, 2013)

Einhorn, Lena, 'Jesus and the "Egyptian Prophet"', 2012 <http://lenaeinhorn.se/wp-content/uploads/2012/11/Jesus-and-the-Egyptian-Prophet-12.11.25.pdf> [accessed 15 March 2014]

Einhorn, Lena, and Rodney Bradbury, *The Jesus Mystery: Astonishing Clues to the True Identities of Jesus and Paul* (Guilford, Conn.: Lyons Press, 2007)

Eisenman, Robert H, *James, the Brother of Jesus: The Key to Unlocking the Secrets of Early Christianity and the Dead Sea Scrolls* (New York: Penguin Books, 1998)

———, *The New Testament Code: The Cup of the Lord, the Damascus Covenant, and the Blood of Christ* (London; New York: Watkins Pub. ; Distributed in the USA by Sterling Pub. Co., 2006)

Ellis, R, *Jesus, King of Edessa* (Cheshire; Kempton, Ill.: Edfu Books ; Adventures Unlimited, 2012)

———, *King Jesus: From Kam (Egypt) to Camelot* (Cheshire; Kempton, Ill.: Edfu Books ; Adventures Unlimited, 2008)

Farey, Peter, 'Marlowe's Sudden and Fearful End', 2011 <http://www2.prestel.co.uk/rey/sudden.htm> [accessed 11 March 2014]

Finn, S. M., 'Antonio: The Other Jew in The Merchant of Venice', *Literator*, 10 (1989) <http://www.literator.org.za/index.php/literator/article/view/819/0> [accessed 28 February 2014]

Finney, Paul Corby, and EBSCOhost, *The Invisible God the Earliest Christians on Art.* (New York: Oxford University Press, Incorporated, 1997)

Forsythe, Gary, *Time in Roman Religion: One Thousand Years of Religious History* (Routledge, 2012)

Frazer, Robert, *The Silent Shakespeare* (W. J. Campbell, 1915)

Gnuse, Robert, 'Vita Apologetica: The Lives of Josephus and Paul in Apologetic Historiography', *Journal for the Study of the Pseudepigrapha*, 13 (2002), 151–169

Goldstein, Gary, 'Shakespeare's Little Hebrew', *Elizabethan Review*, 7 (1999), 70–77

Gould, Andrew, 'Robert Eisenman's "New Testament Code"' <http://roberteisenman.com/articles/ntc_review-gould.pdf> [accessed 14 March 2014]

Greenstreet, James, 'A Hitherto Unknown Noble Writer of Elizabethan Comedies', *The Genealogist*, 7 (1891)

Grillo, Ernesto, *Shakespeare and Italy* (The University Press, 1949)

Grossman, Marshall, ed., *Aemilia Lanyer: Gender, Genre, and the Canon* (University Press of Kentucky, 1998)

Grove, George, *Grove's Dictionary of Music and Musicians* (T. Presser Col, 1918)

Gurr, Andrew, *Playgoing in Shakespeare's London* (Cambridge: Cambridge University Press, 1987)

Harrison, Barbara E., *The Bassanos: Italian Musicians at the English Court, 1531-1664*, 1991

Hitchcock, Susan Tyler, and John L. Esposito, *Geography of Religion: Where God Lives, Where Pilgrims Walk* (National Geographic, 2004)

Hotson, Leslie, *The Death of Christopher Marlowe* (Nonesuch Press, 1925)

Hudson, John, *The Dark Lady The Woman Who Wrote Shakespeare's Plays.* (Amberley Pub Plc, 2014)

Hughes, Stephanie, 'New Light on the Dark Lady', *Shakespeare Oxford Newsletter*, 36 (2000), 1, 8–15

Huller, Stephan, *The Real Messiah: The Throne of St. Mark and the True Origins of Christianity*, Reprint edition (Watkins Publishing, 2012)

Hunt, John, 'A Thing of Nothing: The Catastrophic Body in Hamlet', *Shakespeare Quarterly*, 39 (1988), 27

James Greenstreet, 'Testimonies against the Accepted Authorship of Shakespear's Plays', *The Genealogist*, 8 (1892)

Jones, Eldred D., and Fourah Bay College, *Othello's Countrymen: The African in English Renaissance Drama* (Published on behalf of Fourah Bay College, the University College of Sierra Leone [by] Oxford University Press, 1965)

Kathman, David, 'Oxford's Bible' <http://shakespeareauthorship.com/ox5.html> [accessed 9 March 2014]

Knight, G. Wilson, *Principles of Shakespearean Production* (London: Faber & Faber, Ltd., 1936)

Kocher, Paul H., *Christopher Marlowe* (New York: Russell and Russell, 1962)

Koester, Craig, 'Laodicea: Imperial Cult' <http://www2.luthersem.edu/ckoester/Revelation/Laodicea/Imperial%20cult.htm> [accessed 16 March 2014]

Lanyer, Aemilia, *The Poems of Aemilia Lanyer: Salve Deus Rex Judaeorum*, ed. by Susanne Woods (Oxford University Press, 1993)

Lanyer, Aemilia, and A. L Rowse, *The Poems of Shakespeare's Dark Lady = Salve Deus Rex Judaeorum* (New York: C.N. Potter : Distributed by Crown Publishers, 1979)

Lasocki, David, and Roger Prior, *The Bassanos: Venetian Musicians and Instrument Makers in England, 1531-1665* (Aldershot, England; Brookfield, Vt., USA: Scolar Press ; Ashgate Pub. Co., 1995)

Lefranc, Abel, *Sous Le Masque de 'William Shakespeare'*, 2 vols. (Payot & cie, 1919)

Levin, Richard, 'On Fluellen's Figures, Christ Figures, and James Figures', *PMLA*, 89 (1974), 302

MacDonald, Dennis R., *The Homeric Epics and the Gospel of Mark* (Yale University Press, 2000)

Marx, Steven, *Shakespeare and the Bible* ([Oxford]: Oxford University Press, 2000)

McBride, Kari Boyd, 'Biography of Aemilia Lanyer' <http://nzr.mvnu.edu/faculty/trearick/english/rearick/readings/authors/specific/lanyer.htm> [accessed 11 March 2014]

Meyers, William, '« Shakespeare, Shylock, and the Jews Commentary Magazine', *Commentary*, April 1996 <http://www.commentarymagazine.com/article/shakespeare-shylock-and-the-jews/> [accessed 25 February 2014]

Michell, John, *Who Wrote Shakespeare?* (New York, N.Y.: Thames and Hudson, 1996)

Moss, Candida R, *The Myth of Persecution: How Early Christians Invented a Story of Martyrdom* (New York, NY: HarperOne, 2013)

Ogawa, Yasuhiro, 'Grinning Death's-Head: Hamlet and the Vision of the Grotesque', *eNotes* <http://www.enotes.com/topics/hamlet/critical-essays/grinning-

deaths-head-hamlet-and-vision-grotesque> [accessed 13 March 2014]

Oliver Lodge, 'Shakespeare and the Death of Marlowe', *Times Literary Supplement*, 1925

Overtherainbow, 'Get Real News: Shakespeare as Jewish Literature', *Get Real News*, 2008 <http://getrealnews.blogspot.com/2008/06/shakespeare-as-jewish-literature.html> [accessed 16 March 2014]

Pandit, Lalita, 'Language and the Textual Unconscious: Shakespeare, Ovid and Saxo Grammaticus', in *Criticism and Lacan: essays and dialogue on language, structure, and the unconscious*, ed. by Patrick Colm Hogan and Lalita Pandit (Athens: University of Georgia Press, 1990)

Parenti, Michael, *The Assassination of Julius Caesar: A People's History of Ancient Rome* (New York: New Press, 2003)

Patterson, Annabel M., *Censorship and Interpretation: The Conditions of Writing and Reading in Early Modern England* (Univ of Wisconsin Press, 1984)

Van Pelt, Deborah, '"I Stand for Sovereignty": Reading Portia in Shakespeare's The Merchant of Venice', 2009 <http://scholarcommons.usf.edu/etd/65>

'Philo Judaeus', *Jewish Encyclopedia*, 1906 <http://www.jewishencyclopedia.com/articles/12116-philo-judaeus> [accessed 16 March 2014]

Pinciss, G. M., 'Bartholomew Fair and Jonsonian Tolerance', *Studies in English Literature, 1500-1900*, 35 (1995), 345

Price, Diana, *Shakespeare's Unorthodox Biography: New Evidence of an Authorship Problem* (Westport, Conn.: Greenwood Press, 2001)

Prior, Roger, 'Jewish Musicians at the Tudor Court', *The Musical Quarterly*, 69 (1983), 253–265

————, 'More (Moor? Moro?) Light on the Dark Lady',
Financial Times (London), 10 October 1987, p. 17

Rabkin, Norman, *Shakespeare and the Problem of Meaning*
(University of Chicago Press, 1981)

Reuchlin, Abelard, and Hevel V Reek, *The True Authorship of the
New Testament* (Kent, WA: Abelard Reuchlin Foundation, 1979)

'Review — Atwill's Caesar's Messiah: The Roman Conspiracy to
Invent Jesus by Robert M. Price'
<http://www.robertmprice.mindvendor.com/rev_atwill.htm>
[accessed 26 February 2014]

Roger Stritmatter, 'Shakespeare's Censored Personality',
Shakespeare Oxford Fellowship
<http://www.shakespeareoxfordfellowship.org/shakespeares-
censored-personality-by-roger-stritmatter/> [accessed 9 March
2014]

Schnell, Lisa Jane, 'Breaking "the Rule of Cortezia: Aemilia
Lanyer's Dedications to Salve Deus Rex Judaeorum', *Journal of
Medieval and Early Modern Studies*, 27 (1997), 77–101

Scoufos, Alice-Lyle, *Shakespeare's Typological Satire: A Study of
the Falstaff-Oldcastle Problem* (Athens: Ohio University Press,
1979)

Shaheen, Naseeb, *Biblical References in Shakespeare's Plays*
(University of Delaware, 2011)

Shakespeare as Jewish Literature
<http://www.youtube.com/watch?v=sU4ExIB62Gw> [accessed
15 March 2014]

Shapiro, James, *Shakespeare and the Jews* (Columbia University
Press, 1996)

Sohmer, Steve, 'Another Time: The Venetian Calendar in
Shakespeare's Plays', *Shakespeare Yearbook*, X (1999), 141–161

————, *Shakespeare's Mystery Play: The Opening of the Globe Theatre 1599* (Manchester, U.K.; New York; New York: Manchester University Press ; Distributed in the USA by St. Martin's Press, 1999)

Stone, Alan, 'Redeeming Shylock', *Boston Review*, May 2005 <http://new.bostonreview.net/BR30.2/stone.php> [accessed 28 February 2014]

Terrel, Erin, 'Leave Not a Rack Behind: Shakespeare's Voice Through the Character of Prospero', *Yahoo Contributor Network* <http://voices.yahoo.com/leave-not-rack-behind-shakespeares-voice-through-333642.html> [accessed 9 March 2014]

Titherley, Arthur Walsh, *Shakespeare's Identity: William Stanley, 6th Earl of Derby* (Warren, 1952)

Trobisch, David, *The First Edition of the New Testament* (Oxford University Press, 2000)

Underwood, Anne, 'Was the Bard a Woman?', *Newsweek*, 2004 <http://www.newsweek.com/was-bard-woman-128759> [accessed 10 March 2014]

'Vridar » How Literary Imitation Works: Are Differences More Important than Similarities?' <http://vridar.org/2013/05/15/how-literary-imitation-works-are-differences-more-important-than-similarities/> [accessed 26 February 2014]

Weinstock, Stefan, *Divus Julius* (Oxford; New York: Clarendon Press, 1971)

Whalen, Richard, 'The Queen's Worm', *Shakespeare Oxford Newsletter*, Summer 1998 <http://www.shakespeare-oxford.com/?p=59> [accessed 9 March 2014]

Williams, Robin, *Sweet Swan of Avon: Did a Woman Write Shakespeare?* (Santa Fe, NM: Wilton Circle Press, 2012)

Woods, Susanne, *Lanyer: A Renaissance Woman Poet* (New York; Oxford: Oxford University Press, 1999)

INDEX

15933777R00257

Made in the USA
San Bernardino, CA
11 October 2014